# Research and Innovation in African Higher Education

Damtew Teferra
Editor

# Research and Innovation in African Higher Education

## Trends, Challenges and Prospects

palgrave
macmillan

*Editor*
Damtew Teferra
School of Education
University of KwaZulu-Natal
Durban, South Africa

ISBN 978-3-031-92908-3 ISBN 978-3-031-92909-0 (eBook)
https://doi.org/10.1007/978-3-031-92909-0



Cover illustration: Marina Lohrbach_shutterstock.com

This Palgrave Macmillan imprint is published by the registered company Springer Nature Switzerland AG
The registered company address is: Gewerbestrasse 11, 6330 Cham, Switzerland

# Preface

The higher education landscape in Africa has witnessed massive expansion both in undergraduate and graduate education and also an uptick in research productivity. Over recent decades, the importance of research has grown tremendously across the continent, driven by the realization that Africa's path to sustainable development, innovation, and global competitiveness depends on the advancement of a knowledge economy. Institutions, governments, and stakeholders have recognized the need to build robust research ecosystems capable of producing highly skilled individuals that are able to tackle the complex challenges facing the African continent. However, despite some progress, research and innovation in Africa continue to face an array of challenges and prospects, which are explored in depth throughout this book.

This book, *Research and Innovation in African Higher Education: Trends, Challenges and Prospects*, brings together insights from academics, researchers, and policymakers which are also engaged in advancing research and innovation in the continent. Through its chapters, the book examines a multitude factors that shape research and higher education system in Africa by focusing on a number of issues including funding, internationalization, international partnerships, open science, knowledge production, industry-university partnerships, and research collaboration, among others.

This book marks the second volume in the African Higher Education Book Series, which was launched to systematically generate evidence-based knowledge through a rigorous process of collective academic and professional endeavor. Earlier supported through a grant from a collaborative partnership between European Union and African Union Commissions to advance African higher education, it intends to generate new insights, impact policy formulation and analysis, shape discourses, and generate actionable insights from diverse perspectives.

The historical and economic contexts of African higher education systems have had a significant impact on the development of research in the continent. In recent years, there has been a notable shift in policy and practice as African countries seek to develop the research capabilities of their universities to meet national, continental and international goals. The African Union's Agenda 2063 and the United Nations' Sustainable Development Goals (SDGs) are instrumental frameworks that emphasize the role of research and innovation as cornerstones of development.

*Research and Innovation in African Higher Education: Trends, Challenges and Prospects* is a timely contribution to the meagre literature on African research and innovation—which are key in the advancement of higher education. This book aims to serve as a vital resource for policymakers, university administrators, academics, researchers, and development partners who are working at the forefront of research in Africa by providing a comprehensive analysis of the current state of research on the continent from multiple vantage points. It is worth noting that the insights here are not only relevant to the African context but also contribute to the broader discourse on the role of higher education in advancing societal progress and sustainable development through research and innovation in the Global South as well.

Africa's universities have a crucial role to play in building a prosperous and sustainable future, not only for the continent but for the global community as a whole. They can contribute significantly to the body of knowledge required to achieve economic development and tackle global challenges through strong higher education systems and promoting high-quality research. The book is both a reflection of the progress that has been made and a call to action for continued investment and reform in these areas.

This book has engaged numerous contributors and stakeholders for over two years. The work underwent multiple revisions and blind peer reviews, overseen independently by the editors and the publisher, Palgrave

Macmillan. It is anticipated that the rich and diverse perspectives and wealth of knowledge will contribute significantly to the advancement of policy, practice, and dialogue on research and innovation in Africa.

It is worth noting that several issues explored in this book transcend individual chapters and intersect across multiple themes. As a result, readers may encounter variations in perspectives, interpretations, and even figures, reflecting the diverse sources and methodologies employed by the contributors. This thematic interconnection underscores the complexity and multidimensionality of the subject matter. Rather than offering a uniform narrative, the book intentionally incorporates a diversity of viewpoints to provide a richer and more nuanced exploration of the topics at hand. These differences are not inconsistencies but rather reflections of the varied contexts, scholarly traditions, and data sources that inform the analysis. In so doing, the book aims to stimulate critical analysis, foster dialogue, and offer a more comprehensive understanding of the issues it addresses, by embracing such an approach.

Finally, I extend my sincere gratitude to the authors of the chapters and the respective reviewers, including those who remain anonymous. Their professionalism and dedication have been instrumental in bringing this book to fruition.

Durban, South Africa
January 2025

Prof. Damtew Teferra
General Series Editor, African Higher Education Book Series,
Founding Director, International Network for Higher Education in Africa

# Contents

# Notes on Contributors

**Olu Akanmu** was until recently President and Co-CEO of OPay-Nigeria, one of Nigeria's largest fintech platforms with Unicorn valuation. He has a diverse C-level strategic leadership experience across several industries including healthcare, FMCG, telecommunications, banking, fintech and non-profit industries. He was Executive Director of Retail Banking at First City Monument Bank, Nigeria; Chief Marketing Officer at Airtel, Nigeria; Managing Executive of Retail Banking at former Bank PHB; General Manager of Consumer Marketing; MTN-Nigeria and Client Service Director-Insight Communications (West Africa's largest advertising agency). He was also Chief Operating Officer at Society for Family Health and Population Services International (Nigeria and South Africa) and Marketing Manager at former Glaxo-Nigeria. Olu holds a Bachelor of Pharmacy degree from the University of Ife, a Master in Business Administration from the Lagos State University and a Distinction in the Management Advancement Program of the University of Witwatersrand Business School in South Africa.

**Pearl Akazue** is a distinguished academic with a Bachelors and Master's degree in Biochemistry from the University of Benin in Nigeria, and a PhD in Molecular and Cell Biology of Infectious Diseases from the University of Ghana—where she was awarded the Vice Chancellor's Award for the Most Outstanding Doctoral Dissertation in the Sciences. With over 10 years in academia, she has held various research and teaching positions in institutions such as the University of Benin, Federal

University of Technology, Akure; West African Centre for Cell Biology of Infectious Pathogens; and Oxford Brookes University. Pearl has an extensive knowledge in data analysis and strategic communication.

**Daniel Gelaw Alemneh** is Head of the Digital Curation Unit at the University of North Texas and teaches at the College of Information. For the past 20 years, Daniel has been actively involved in various professional activities including membership on ASIS&T and ICKM Board of Directors. He was a Fulbright Scholar, both at Addis Ababa University in Ethiopia (2019–2020) and at the University of Pretoria in South Africa (2021–2022). He is also a research associate at the Department of Information Science, University of Pretoria and honorary professor in the Faculty of Computing and Informatics, Jimma University in Ethiopia. His research interests include knowledge management, digital curation, open access and scholarly communications.

**Achille Ephrem Assogbadjo,** an agronomist and forester with a PhD from Ghent University in Belgium, is a full Professor at the University of Abomey-Calavi, Benin, and a visiting professor internationally. He has developed several doctoral programs and centers of excellence, secured over 20 research grants, and participates in more than 10 international scientific groups. He is the Permanent Secretary of the Scientific Council of the Faculty of Agronomic Sciences and Coordinator of Doctoral Training in Natural Resources. Achille has authored and co-authored 215 scientific articles, 26 books or chapters, 11 proceedings, and 9 technical reports. He has received 11 international awards for his rigorous work aimed at generating innovative research and technologies for societal benefit.

**Charles Ayo** was until his death in 2023 a Professor of Computing. He was the Vice-Chancellor of Covenant University in Nigeria, between 2012 and 2016, and the Pioneer Vice-Chancellor of Trinity University in Lagos. He held a B.Sc., M.Sc., and PhD in Computer Science. His research interests included mobile computing, internet programming, e-business, e-government, and software engineering. He was a member of the Nigerian Computer Society, the Computer Professionals of Nigeria, a fellow of the Courier and Logistics Management Institute, as well as a fellow of the African Scientific Institute, a member of the Review Committee of the European Conference on e-Government and the editorial board of the *International Journal of Scientific Research in Education* among others. He supervised about 200 postgraduate thesis and had several publications in scholarly journals and conference proceedings. Charles was a Senior Fulbright Research Scholar and an Awardee of the Ford Foundation for Teaching and Innovations.

**Chux Daniels** splits his time at the Graduate School of Technology Management (GSTM), Department of Engineering and Technology Management, University of Pretoria (South Africa) and at the Science Policy Research Unit (SPRU), University of Sussex Business School in UK. He is the Founding Director of the Transformative Innovation Africa Hub (TIAH), the Africa arm of the global Transformative Innovation Policy Consortium (TIPC), based at the Future Africa Campus, University of Pretoria in South Africa. Besides research and teaching Chux is actively involved in policy work and have delivered projects on transformative research and innovation policy for several governments and international organizations including the United Nations, European Commission, and the World Bank. He holds a PhD in Science and Technology Policy Studies from the University of Sussex in UK.

**George Owusu Essegbey** was the Director of Science and Technology Policy Research Institute (STEPRI) of the Council for Scientific and Industrial Research (CSIR) of Ghana. Currently, he is the CEO of the CSIR-Technology Development and Transfer Centre (CSIR-TDTC). He holds a PhD in Development Studies from the University of Cape Coast and did PhD internship at the United Nations University (now UNU-MERIT) in Maastricht, Netherlands. He was a Commonwealth Fellow at the Policy Research in Engineering, Science and Technology (PREST), University of Manchester in UK. Essegbey has served various international organizations including UNESCO, UNCTAD, UNEP, FAO, IFPRI, and the World Bank. He was a member of the UN 10-Member Group appointed by the UN Secretary-General to support the UN Technology Facilitation Mechanism. George was the President of the African Network for Economics of Learning, Innovation and Competence Building Systems (AfricaLics) headquartered in Nairobi, Kenya.

**Angel Y. Ford** is an Assistant Professor at University at Albany's College of Emergency Preparedness, Homeland Security, and Cybersecurity and the director of the Global Epistemic Justice Lab. Angel has worked on several national and international research projects and partnerships and was a Fulbright Scholar to Ethiopia for the 2019–2020 academic year and a Fulbright Specialist to Zanzibar, Tanzania in 2024. Her research interests include global justice in scholarly communication; improving learning environments; student and educator motivations, aspirations, well-being, and persistence; fair and equitable partnerships and collaborations; and the benefits of cross-national and international investigations. Angel is the immediate past president of the International Society for Educational Planning (ISEP).

**James Otieno Jowi** is the Founding Director of the African Network for Internationalization of Education (ANIE) and the current Chair of the ANIE research and partnerships committee. Currently, he is the deputy executive secretary to the East African Kiswahili Commission and has been serving as the principal education officer at the East African Community (EAC) where he has been coordinating education programs and frameworks for the EAC countries. Prior to this, he was teaching Comparative and International Education at the School of Education, Moi University in Kenya. He holds a PhD in Higher Education Policy Studies from the University of Twente, Netherlands and a Masters in Comparative and International Education from the University of Oslo in Norway and a Masters in Linguistics from Moi University, Kenya. He has researched and published extensively on higher education in Africa, especially on its international dimension. James also sits in the boards of several international education organizations and has coordinated several projects on higher education in Africa.

**Gift Masaiti** is an Associate Professor of Economics of Education at the University of Zambia, Zambia where he has served the University in different capacities including Dean in charge of research in the Faculty of Education since 2005. He is currently the academic board member for Eastern and Southern African Management Institute (ESAMI), a Pan-African organization representing 10 countries. He has been involved in consultancy, commissioned and grant-aided research in different organizations both on short- and long-term engagements with European Union, World Bank, USAID, JICA, UNESCO, British Council, UNICEF, World Vision, and Ministries of Education among others. He has published numerous journal articles, book chapters and books mostly in higher education, economics of education, education management, financing higher education and education policy among others. He has supervised and examined both masters and PhD candidates from a number of universities. Gift sits on a number of advisory and editorial boards such as

International Journal of African Higher Education (IJAHE) and Journal of Scholarship of Teaching and Learning in the South (SOTL).

**Jonathan Chuks Mba** is currently International Higher Education and Quality Assurance Consultant and Member of the Council of Laweh University in Ghana. Until 31 December 2021, he had been the director of Research & Programmes and coordinator of Projects at the Association of African Universities (AAU), Accra, Ghana where he worked for 12 years. He successfully managed all of the AAU's flagship multi-country multi-institution projects, worth over US$30 Million. These projects included: European Commission funded Harmonization of African Higher Education Quality Assurance and Accreditation (HAQAA) Initiative; Research Management Project of the Science Granting Council Initiative (SGCI) and Research Infrastructure Project funded by the International Development Research Centre (IDRC); World Bank funded Africa Higher Education Centres of Excellence (ACE) Project; and Swedish International Development Cooperation Agency (Sida) Institutional Support to AAU. Before joining the AAU he had worked at the University of Ghana for 11 years. He has written articles in peer-reviewed journals, and contributed to reports and book chapters. Jonathan has PhD MPhil, and M.A. degrees in Demography and B.Sc. (Hons.) degree in Statistics.

**Bright Nwaru** is a Professor of Epidemiology in Respiratory Diseases and Allergology at the Institute of Medicine, University of Gothenburg in Sweden, where he has worked since 2017. Prior to that, he worked at the University of Edinburgh in UK, combined with a research position at Tampere University, Finland. His research includes various clinical and population investigations into respiratory diseases and allergy, resulting in over 200 original publications in leading respiratory and allergy journals. He is a recipient of over 15 million USD in research grants during the last 10 years. He is an adjunct professor of epidemiology at Tampere University and was an honorary fellow at the University of Edinburgh until 2023. He is an academic editor for Plos One and Scientific Reports, and Associate Editor of Frontiers in Allergy. Bright is the founder of the African Science Frontiers Initiatives (ASFI) and editor-in-chief of ASFI Research Journal.

**Oanda Ibrahim Ogachi** is former Head of the Training, Grants and Fellowships program, and Acting Head of the Publications and Dissemination Program at the Council for the Development of Social Science Research in Africa (CODESRIA), a Pan-African Social Science Research Council headquartered in Dakar, Senegal. As head of the training, grants and fellowships program, Oanda was in charge of various interventions targeting building capacity of doctoral schools and supporting doctoral students across Africa universities. Oanda was instrumental in setting up CODESRIA's college of senior academic mentors for doctoral students. Oanda joined CODESRIA from Kenyatta University in Kenya where he was an associate professor in the Department of Educational Foundations. An academic background in the area of Higher Education and Sociology of Knowledge, he has pursued research interests in a broad range of issues in African higher education and published a number of journal articles and book chapters. Ibrahim has served as managing editor of the *Journal of Higher Education in Africa* (JHEA), besides serving in editorial boards of a number of higher education related journals in Africa.

**Moses Osiru,** with over two decades of experience in agricultural development and higher education, managed the Regional Scholarship and Innovation Fund at the International Centre of Insect Physiology and Ecology, focusing on building sustainable postgraduate education systems, research collaborations, and cultivating public-private partnerships. As Deputy Executive Secretary at RUFORUM, a network of 170 African universities in 40 countries, he supported the establishment of regional PhD programs, including securing over USD 45 million for research. With over 60 publications and active participation in global higher education and research networks, Moses' expertise is well-regarded. Moses holds a PhD and M.Sc. in Agriculture from Makerere University, and his contributions are significantly impacting Eastern, Southern, and Western Africa.

**Abebe Rorissa** is Professor and Director of the School of Information Sciences in the College of Communication and Information at the University of Tennessee in Knoxville. He is a research associate in the Department of Information Science, University of Pretoria in South Africa. Prior to his current position, he worked in four countries as an educator, practitioner, and administrator, including Associate Dean for Faculty Development at the University at Albany, State

University of New York (SUNY). He has consulted for academic institutions, national governments, and international organizations, including the United Nations. His research interests include multimedia information organization and retrieval, scaling of users' information needs/ perceptions, use/acceptance/adoption and impact of information and communication technologies, and data analytics. Abebe is the immediate past president of the Association for Information Science & Technology (ASIS&T).

**Eman Sobh** is an Egyptian pulmonologist and researcher. She is an assistant professor of Chest Diseases at Al-Azhar University in Egypt, and Taibah University in Saudi Arabia. She graduated from Al-Azhar University, Faculty of Medicine for Girls with excellence and honor receiving a Master of Science degree (M.Sc.) and Medical Doctorate degrees (M.D., PhD). She is an editorial board member and reviewer for several international journals. She is a certified trainer for soft skills, scientific publishing, and project management and is engaged in capacity building in science and research. Her research interests include respiratory diseases, smoking cessation, non-communicable diseases, research and development, and capacity building in science and research. Eman is the Director of Science and Communication for African Science Frontiers Initiatives (ASFI) and co-convener of the ASFI science seminar series.

**Tesfaye Semela** received his PhD in Social Science from University of Tűbingen in Germany. Semela is a recipient of the prestigious senior research fellowship award of the Alexander von Humboldt Foundation, Germany (2009–2012) and DAAD's visiting professor at Justus-Liebig University of Giessen (2019–2020). Since 2015, he is a fellow of the Ethiopian Academic of Sciences (EAS). Currently, he is serving as the Director of the Institute of Policy and Development Research (IPDR) and Professor of Sociology of Education and Educational Psychology at Hawassa University, Ethiopia. Tesfaye is Associate Editor of the *International Journal of Educational Development*(Elsevier) and has extensively published in the fields of higher education policy and development, social justice, gender issues in education, youth development and migration-education nexus.

**Frejus Ariel Kpedetin Sodedji** is the associate program officer of TAGDev 2.0 at the National University of Agriculture (UNA) and a researcher at the University of Abomey-Calavi (UAC) in Benin. He holds a PhD in Genetics and Plant Breeding from Felix Houphouët Boigny University, Côte d'Ivoire, and a Master's in Plant Breeding and Seed Systems from Makerere University, Uganda. His research focuses on biofortification, genetics, plant breeding, and sustainable agriculture. He was a Research Fellow at the Korea Institute of Science and Technology and has authored over 20 publications. Frejus has received several scholarships and awards, including a full PhD Scholarship from PASET-RSIF and the SAMSUNG Dream Scholarship Foundation. He actively participates in regional and international research programs and networks.

**Damtew Teferra** is a professor of higher education and founding director of the International Network for Higher Education in Africa, earlier at the Center for International Higher Education, at Boston College in the USA and at the University of KwaZulu-Natal in South Africa, for over a decade now. He is a convener and founder of the Higher Education Forum for Africa, Asia and Latin America (HEFAALA) and is founding editor-in-chief of the Scopus-indexed journal: *International Journal of African Higher Education*. He co-coordinates the Higher Education Cluster of the African Union's Continental Education Strategy for Africa (CESA) 2016–25—a strategy document which he helped develop with other experts invited by the Union. He has published over 150 peer-reviewed articles, book chapters, and other think pieces and 10 books—including *Scientific Communication in African Universities: External Assistance and National Needs* (Routledge, 2003), *African Higher Education: An International Reference Handbook* (Indiana University Press, 2003) and *Funding Higher Education in Sub-Saharan Africa* (Palgrave Macmillan, 2013)—the last two, award winning in the United States and South Africa, respectively. As the General Editor and Coordinator of the African Higher Education Book Series, Damtew had the first jointly edited book *Emerging Dynamics in the Provision of Private Higher Education in Africa* published by Palgrave Macmillan in 2024.

**Flora Ismail Tibazarwa** has over twenty years of leadership experience in national research and innovation (R&I) institutions. She headed a public university scientific department and has been a director for Life Sciences at the national science, technology, and innovation think-tank COSTECH. Flora is passionate about sustainable transformation using innovative green and blue solutions and shares this with other international players as a member of the advisory board of the World Bioeconomy Forum, the International Advisory Committee of the Global Bioeconomy Council, and the Transformative Innovation Africa Hub. Flora is an active player in the design and administration of innovation funds for R&I, evidenced by the work she did at COSTECH and the regional Southern Africa Innovation Support Programme.

**Ayenachew Aseffa Woldegiyorgis** is an assistant professor at Addis Ababa University's Center for Comparative Education and Policy Studies, Ethiopia. He holds a PhD from Boston College, USA, where he also completed a postdoctoral fellowship at the Center for International Higher Education (CIHE), Boston College. His research focuses on higher education partnerships, international higher education, and scientific diaspora engagements. Ayenachew's work explores the dynamics of global academic collaboration and the role of diasporas in knowledge transfer. He is actively engaged in professional services, including serving as the managing editor of the *International Journal of African Higher Education*.

**Abena Asefuaba Yalley** is currently a research fellow in Zukunftskolleg, University of Konstanz in Germany. She holds a PhD in Gender Studies from the University of Ibadan in Nigeria and a Master's degree in Development and International Cooperation from the University of Jyvaskyla in Finland. Her research focuses on post-colonialism and gender in Africa, gender inequalities, violence against women, masculinity, policing domestic violence, African feminism and development, migration, and obstetric violence. Abena particularly investigates how systems of patriarchy are replicated in institutions that seem to promote feminist agenda and how gender norms in Ghana and Nigeria combine to put women in a vulnerable position. Abena has published several peer-reviewed articles in leading international journals.

# List of Figures

# List of Tables

CHAPTER 1

# Research and Innovation in African Higher Education: Setting the Scene

*Damtew Teferra*

Universities, since their origins in medieval Europe, have always been concerned with the transmission, preservation, and interpretation of knowledge, although not primarily with the creation of new knowledge and research orientation, until Von Humboldt's idea of a modern research university became a reality at the University of Berlin established in 1818. This model got subsequently adopted in the United States, combining it with a land-grant model, Japan and others including their colonial entities (Altbach, 2007). Currently, the three missions of a modern-day typical university—teaching, research, and public service—live in constant tension with each other at different levels where institutions are expected to develop their own plans and programs making hard choices in setting priorities and allocating resources (Altbach et al., 2002).

Research currently occupies a central place in advanced economies as an engine of economic growth and job creation, innovation and industrial competitiveness, national security, and advancing the frontiers of human

D. Teferra (✉)
School of Education, University of Kwazulu-Natal, Durban, South Africa
e-mail: teferra@ukzn.ac.za



D. Teferra (ed.), *Research and Innovation in African Higher Education*,
https://doi.org/10.1007/978-3-031-92909-0_1

knowledge. In the contemporary world, academic and research activities, power houses of knowledge production and innovation, provide crucial support for the national innovation system (World Bank, 2002).

Accordingly, governments, universities, industries, non-profit organizations, and others make substantial investments in research and development (R&D). For instance, since 2000, total global R&D expenditures have more than tripled in current dollars, from $676 billion to $2.0 trillion in 2018 (Congressional Research Service, 2020)—a nearly threefold growth. At a national level, some of the major notable endeavors around the world include the Chinese 211 and 985 projects, which are now replaced by World-Class 2.0 project since 2017 (Liu, 2007; Ma, 2007; Li, 2018); the Japanese national endowment fund for research (Kakuchi, 2024), the Korean "Investment Direction for 2025" (Ministry of Science & ICT, 2024) are just some of them.

Economically advanced countries have long occupied the top ladder for research funding (Figure in the Funding chapter in this book). Overall, research expenditure in the European Union and the United States stands at 2% and 3% of GDP (2.82 according to UNESCO-UIS) respectively. In 2018, the global expenditure on research and development stood at 2.27% of GDP (UNESCO-UIS). In the United States, for example, the public expenditure on research is only just over 20% with the majority, nearly 70%, originating from businesses (Pethokoukis, 2020).

As knowledge becomes a key commodity in global marketplace, countries are engaged both in competition—and cooperation—in its production, distribution, management, and use. For instance, the United States and China are now openly tussling over economic and industrial espionage involving research, innovation, and knowledge as a consequence China is "decoupling" of research and technology collaboration with the United States and other Western countries (Sharma, 2022). On the other hand, while the United States and Russia are openly at war with each other—on land and at sea—they, however, continue to cooperate on space. Within the overarching context of globalization today, a combination of technological, economic, political, and cultural changes has led to an acceleration in the pace of international research and collaboration (Gornitzka, 2008 in Woldegiyorgis et al., 2022). The interplay between cooperation and competition in research undertaking could not be starker.

A direct correlation between economic wealth and research funding is evident. Countries with a high percentage of GDP to research and development are found at the top of the development index while those with lower commitment are at the lower end, with consequent implications to economic advancement and global competitiveness. In terms of research expenditure, Latin America and the Caribbean, as a region, do not exhibit considerable differences from Africa. According to UNESCO statistics, it had a 0.7% expenditure of GDP in 2017 with the highest in Brazil at 1.26% of GDP (in 2017) and, in contrast, Mexico at 0.31% (in 2018). Considerable contrast is evident in Asia, where South Asia spent 0.65% of GDP, while East Asia and the Pacific spent 2.51% of GDP in 2018. Evidently, the high figures for East Asia are attributed to, among others, Japan (3.27%) and South Korea (4.81%) in 2018 (UNESCO-UIS). In countries where research is not the exclusive pasture of universities, considerable resources are managed and deployed outside higher learning institutions, including industry and businesses.

Research, especially high-end, is an expensive enterprise involving highly trained experts, expensive equipment, robust infrastructure and facilities, and superb management. Thus, building a strong financial research system is not a one-off effort, but instead requires a sustained and systematic, logistical issues, and policy support. This makes research an unlikely primary candidate for support in the multitude of competing national development imperatives and institutional priorities that countries constantly grapple with (Teferra, 2013).

Likewise, the global research output is also skewed toward these wealthy countries, which have committed considerable resources toward it. According to *Nature Index*, an open database of author affiliations and institutional relationships that tracks contributions to research articles published in 82 high-quality natural-science journals, similar patterns of predominance in research output prevails (as indicated in Fig. 1.1). In the top 50 countries, only South Africa, which stood at 34, appears in the list.

African higher education depends heavily on external resources for research and innovation through bilateral and multilateral arrangements and private organizations such as U.S.-based foundations. The low global research productivity in Africa—which accounts for 13.5% of the global population but less than 1% of global research output (Fonn et al., 2018)—is attributed to a pitiful financial contribution to the sector.

The advent of COVID-19 epidemic in the world has made matters worse. In a recent survey on its effect on higher education research, IAU (2020) reported that 80% of HEIs affirm that the pandemic affected

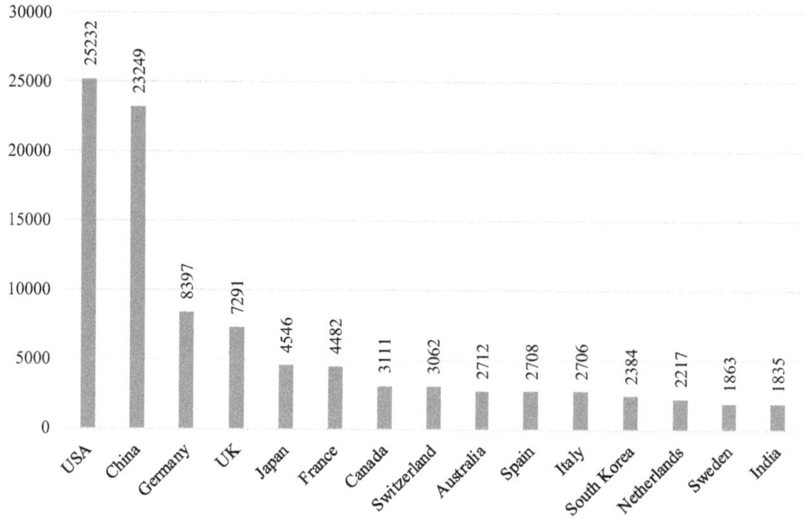


**Fig. 1.1** Global research output from nature index from 1 December 2021 to 30 November 2022 https://l1nq.com/LcnRc

research in their institutions. The most common impact of COVID-19 has been the cancelling of international travel (at 83%) and the cancellation or postponement of scientific conferences (81%). Moreover, it noted that scientific projects were at risk of incompletion in half of the institutions (52%).

That noted, increasingly, there has been a louder call for supporting research, research collaboration, and partnership around the world following the outbreak and impact of COVID-19. The pandemic created an opportunity—and goodwill—for joint research, supervision, and action unprecedented in the past, though many wonder if that momentum and practice continue to be fully capitalized to address the multitude of global challenges. On the other hand, a call for the "loss and damage" fund to support vulnerable countries from the adverse effects of climate change—such as rising sea levels, extreme heat waves, desertification, forest fires, and crop failures—is also anticipated to support research centers geared toward climate change research (Anderson, 2023; Sawahel, 2022).

## The Realm of Doctoral Education in Research and Innovation

One of the major indicators of a sustained research development is the state of graduate studies in a country. Despite the remarkable expansion of the higher education sector in Africa in the last decade, postgraduate studies remain comparatively dwarfed—if not directly affected (Teferra, 2014). Hayward and Ncayiyana (2014) argued that Africa needs to confront the challenges facing graduate studies in the continent. They further noted that no nation advances into the realm of developed economies without a high-quality higher education system, particularly graduate education.

Research and innovation are typically fueled by graduate education in many countries, specially developing ones, and are an avenue for building research competence of potential academics and researchers. The modalities of doctoral graduate education vary considerably with two dominant ones in the play: the typical American model, increasingly popular, with embedded courses/modules and a dissertation and the other European one, "research-based" which is only pursued through a dissertation and a few, often, non-mandatory courses. Though Woldegiyorgis et al. (2020) hold that in recent decades changes in the global environment related to higher education, the labor market, the overarching move to a knowledge economy, the inevitable forces of globalization and internationalization, and other factors have forced doctoral education to open up to change with multiple versions of the dominant ones.

It is clear that the large majority of doctorates are earned in the main research-producing countries in North America, Europe and Japan, but countries like China are rapidly expanding doctoral programs. It is clear that many countries are experiencing major variations between the demand and production of doctorates, in terms of both specific fields and overall numbers. Doctoral-level training, in particular, by fostering research and innovation, plays a unique role in human capacity development, producing the workforce fit for the knowledge- and technology-based approach to solve the multifaceted challenges of this century (Yudkevich et al., 2020).

Graduates of doctoral programs are not only expected to have highly specialized knowledge and skills in their respective fields but also presumed to be tomorrow's leaders (Bernstein et al. 2014 in Woldegiyorgis et al (2020)—not only in research and academe but also in other fields, as more positions demand a doctoral degree. As the main hub of knowledge production, the overall importance of doctoral education for research productivity, human capital development, (under)graduate teaching and supervision, and ultimately socioeconomic development has been well established. Examining policy statements and practices from Europe, the United States, Canada, and Australia, three major common areas regarding doctoral programs are considered by Bernstein et al. (2014): (a) doctoral graduates are expected to have a solid knowledge in their areas of expertise, (b) through original research, doctoral studies should contribute to knowledge, and (c) doctoral-level training must incorporate the development of transferable skills and competencies.

All too often, the talent pipeline in tertiary education is overlooked, with priority going to inputs such as student enrolment numbers or faculty salaries. But, fundamental to the successful outcomes of teaching and research investments—and thus to the efficient delivery of tertiary education—is a high-quality, well-trained academic and researcher. This training of the "trainers" happens in postgraduate education as well as through schemes of staff development. Graduate schools (postgraduate studies)—and policy makers and institutions more generally—often ignore or underinvest in training doctoral candidates—future academic staff—in modern effective pedagogical methods for their fields (Arnhold & Bassett, 2022).

## Contemporary Issues and Perspectives

This book explores and analyzes the state and trajectory of research and innovation in Africa on the account of multiple contributors from Africa and beyond. The book features 12 chapters that identify and discuss a number of major issues surrounding research and innovation in the continent, including funding, internationalization, academic and research collaboration, industry-university partnerships, diaspora, research infrastructure, and research ethics, among others. This section succinctly introduce the chapters in the order in which they appear in the book. Further, some of the topics are also engaged in the final chapter.

### *Funding*

Financing higher education is an expensive enterprise—knowledge creation, knowledge dissemination, and innovation do not come cheap.

High-end expertise, expensive equipment and instruments, extensive infrastructure (such as labs, libraries, and dormitories) and the accompanying requisite logistics (such as information technology) and a complex academic culture, that are key for research and innovation, is costly—without comparison (Teferra, 2013).

Without probably an exception, the primary challenge for research globally, and particularly in Africa, remains funding, with direct and indirect consequences for the advancement of the sector. The massification of the higher education sector in Africa in recent decades has meant that resources had to be rationed in the spreading systems, leaving the research and graduate education space wanting. While the knowledge dissemination aspect of higher education, i.e., teaching, has expanded, the knowledge production capacity, i.e., research, has been considerably constrained.

Gift Masaiti and Damtew Teferra in a dedicated chapter on funding research in Africa in this book, note that it is beset by numerous difficulties, including limited governmental support, heavy reliance on external sources, and the absence of sustainable financial mechanisms. Despite these obstacles, research funding is key for addressing the continent's developmental challenges, fostering innovation, and building local scientific capacity. Without adequate and sustainable funding, researchers find it difficult to develop solutions and advance innovations tailored to Africa's unique needs, thereby contributing to both scientific progress and socioeconomic development.

No doubt, money stands as an immensely critical element for advancing research. But, funding on its own is not a panacea. Musiige and Maassen (2015) remind that Makerere University's research productivity levels remain low despite the university's status as one of Africa's flagship institutions and the relatively high levels of research funding it has received. As discussed in different chapters in this book, a multitude of ingredients thus remain paramount to harness funds at the disposal of institutions.

### *Internationalization*

Internationalization in higher education typically refers to the integration of international perspectives into teaching, research, and institutional collaboration. Altbach (2002) posits that internationalization refers to the specific policies and initiatives of countries and individual academic institutions or systems to deal with global trends. Further, Altbach et al. (2010), expounded that internationalization is a strategy for societies and institutions to respond to the many demands placed upon them by globalization and a way for higher education to prepare individuals for engagement in a globalized world.

The oft-cited definition of internationalization considers it as "the process of integrating an international, intercultural, or global dimension into the purpose, functions or delivery of post-secondary education" (Knight, 2004). Building on the "back" of this definition, Hans de Wit and Fiona Hunter (2015) engaged in a new definition describing it as "the *intentional* process of integrating an international, intercultural, or global dimension into the purpose, functions, and delivery of post-secondary education, in order to enhance the quality of education and research for all students and staff and to make a meaningful contribution to society".

Teferra (2020) however observed that "contemporary ontological manifestations of the terminology have been appreciably misrepresented, if not wholly distorted, in the process creating dissonance between epistemological reality and a paradigmatic trajectory.... Thus, the definition of internationalization, as it stands [as an intentional phenomenon], does not concur with these basic tenets of intentions, rendering it somewhat irrelevant to most of the Global South, and quite a number of instances in the Global North". In light of the challenges of defining the term, the International Association of Universities (IAU, 2015) describes the lack of a clear-cut definition for such an important process as surprising.

That noted, internationalization plays a crucial role in enhancing research capacity by fostering global academic partnerships and exposing researchers to new ideas, methodologies, and technologies. This, in turn, helps attract external funding and resources, which are often critical in regions like Africa, where local research funding is limited.

Moreover, internationalization improves graduate education by providing students access to global networks, joint degree programs, and international mobility opportunities, preparing them for participation in a globalized academic and professional environment. It also enhances the global reputation of African universities, helping them gain recognition in international pecking orders and attracting foreign students and faculty.

However, internationalization also presents challenges for African higher education. One major issue is the unequal power dynamics in partnerships between African and Western institutions, where the latter often dictate research agendas, sidelining local priorities. There is also the risk of brain drain, as talented African academics and students may be drawn abroad by more lucrative opportunities, leaving their home institutions at a disadvantage. Furthermore, African universities face significant infrastructural and financial limitations that can hinder their ability to fully engage in international collaborations.

Despite these challenges, internationalization remains a powerful tool for capacity building and development, with ongoing efforts to address the inequalities and to tailor international partnerships to African needs and contexts.

James Jowi in a chapter "The Significance and Implications of Internationalization on Research and Graduate Education in Africa", in this book, holds that internationalization is transforming Africa's higher education, especially postgraduate training and research landscape. He posits that the developments in internationalization so far recorded and the growing prioritization of research and postgraduate studies should open a new page in Africa's higher education especially in knowledge generation and repositioning of the universities to addressing the growing developmental challenges of the continent. He, however, reminds that despite these contributions of internationalization to the strengthening of African universities and rejuvenating its knowledge system, he reckons that it has also, over the years, had its unintended consequences and downsides.

### *Research Infrastructure*

Effective research infrastructure provides access to cutting-edge tools and technologies, advanced computing systems, and state-of-the-art labs. Well-established research infrastructure facilitates collaboration among institutions, making it easier to work on complex, multidisciplinary projects, instrumental in attracting funding and top talent, which they often tend to be drawn to environments where ample tools and support systems to advance their work exist.

It has been well established that the state of research infrastructure in Africa is typically dismal which, in effect, hampers research output, reduces competitiveness, limits innovation, and triggers brain drain.

Writing on "Conceptualizing research infrastructures to enhance the resilience of science systems in Africa: mapping, management and policy directions" Chux Daniels, Pearl Akazue, George Essegbey, Abena Yalley, Flora Tibazarwa, Jonathan Mba, and Damtew Teferra, in this book, observe that research infrastructures form the foundation for scientific endeavors and innovation that foster research for advancement, socioeconomic progress, and transformation. The second Strategic Objective of the Continental Education Strategy for Africa (CESA 2016–25) that emphasizes the need to "build, rehabilitate, preserve education infrastructure and develop policies that ensure a permanent, healthy and conducive learning environment in all sub-sectors and for all, so as to expand access to quality education" (AUC, 2016, p. 8). Earlier on, in the Second Action Plan of the Joint Africa-EU Strategy (2011–13), research infrastructure was recognized as a priority focus for Africa-EU science and technology cooperation to enhance as part of the overall Africa-EU S&T partnership to advance sustainable development.

The authors sought to address the conceptualization of research infrastructure to enhance the resilience of the science systems in Africa. In so doing, they systematically analyzed the concept of research infrastructure on the basis of practices, impact, policy, and understanding within the continent's science, research, and innovation ecosystems. They also discussed strategies to strengthen the research infrastructure across the ecosystems and proposed a framework for conceptualizing research infrastructure. They note that the role of research infrastructures in scientific and technological advancement are well understood by the key actors in STI fields and beyond though their concept is still an emerging field of study, requiring further research and empirical evidence. That noted research infrastructure is understood as comprising facilities, resources, and relevant service systems to enable research communities to conduct research and innovation.

This study highlighted the challenging nature of identifying and classifying research infrastructures as there appears to be no objective measure. With the growing pace of technological advancement and pursuit of multidisciplinary research, research infrastructures are dynamic and constantly developing which brings additional complexities. Yet, there are opportunities for adaptability, flexibility, and innovation for research infrastructures, especially as new demands for research emerge in various directions, including processes and products.

The authors note that the efforts to promote research infrastructures in Africa and create an enabling environment for their establishment, maintenance, and development have been ongoing at national, sub-regional, and international levels for some years. They caution that initiatives to map them in Africa needs careful conceptualization, planning, and execution to effectively address the key challenges. They, however, acknowledge that it is far from clear how best to formulate, implement, and evaluate policies, strategies, and frameworks on research infrastructures at regional and continental levels to ensure mutually reinforcing and complementary benefits for countries in Africa.

### *African Intellectual Diaspora*

Intellectual Diaspora wields a powerful force in integrating host institutions at the center of the knowledge capital with often marginal home country institutions by transferring new technologies and mediating the knowledge divide, which can be achieved in a number of ways (Teferra, 2010). Of recent, the conversation around the intellectual diaspora has moved from a "deficit" mode, within the framing of a "brain drain" to "gainful" mode within the framing of brain circulation. The discourse of intellectual mobility has moved from typical lamentation to adoration. Accordingly, a growing interest in deploying the intellectual diaspora in research, innovation, networking, curricula development, and graduate supervision is slowly emerging (Teferra, 2021).

The potential of the African intellectual Diaspora, to promote higher learning, research and innovation in the region, can be gauged from the staggering statistics of university professors, researchers, engineers, medical doctors, accountants, and high level technicians around the world (Teferra, 2010). For instance, African immigrants have higher levels of education than the general U.S. population, with 40% having at least a bachelor's degree. This is 30% higher than the U.S. population overall (New American Economy, 2018). Nigerians and South Africans were the most highly educated among the top sending-country nationalities to the United States, with 64% and 58% respectively holding at least a bachelor's degree (Lorenzi & Batalova, 2022).

Drawing on extensive literature, a previous work of the author and personal communications and professional encounters with members of the African academic diaspora in North America, Ayenachew Assefa Woldegiyorgis in "The role of diaspora in research and graduate education in

Africa", in this book, examines the role of the African diaspora to the advancement of research and graduate education in the continent. The chapter analyzes the various mechanisms of deploying high level expertise and experiences among the diaspora in advancing the continent's developments while exploring the enablers and deterrents of engagement of diaspora in higher education.

Woldegiyorgis posits that the rationale for the engagement of the diaspora in advancing research and graduate education in Africa can be explained from two vantage points. First is the state of research and graduate education in the continent that calls for coordinated effort and commitment of resources to capacity building as well as the untapped potential of the African intellectual diaspora and their unique position to make meaningful contribution in the continent's endeavor to improve capacity in research and graduate education.

He posits that engaging the diaspora, as opposed to other expatriates, enjoys more superior benefits. The diaspora trajectory embeds and enhances volunteerism; possesses linguistic and cultural competence that offers unique strength to succeed in their engagements overcoming bureaucracies and institutional red tapes; sense of belongingness and duty; unique understanding, and comparative advantage, of both academic worlds; and the opportunities and aspirations of connecting and engaging with academia at home, at host country, and globally.

It should be noted that while we recognize the immense opportunities and possibilities of deploying the intellectual diaspora, there are also numerous challenges including economic, political, social, cultural, infrastructural, and logistical that hamper it.

## *Centers of Excellence*

Centers of Excellence (CoEs), as specialized institutions or units that focus on high-impact research, innovation, and education in specific areas of expertise, are vital in advancing excellence, innovation, and knowledge transfer in so doing contributing to national and global research in a host of disciplines. CoEs bring together top researchers, resources, and infrastructure in a focused area, fostering breakthroughs and high-quality output. Through the creation of such platforms, which enjoys concentrated expertise, CoEs act as incubators for cutting-edge research and innovation.

CoEs often become magnets for funding from governments, private organizations, and international agencies. They attract not only financial support but also top researchers, faculty, and students, enhancing the institution's academic and research prestige creating a virtuous cycle of talent and funding.

CoEs are becoming increasingly visible in Africa as they serve as catalysts for research, innovation, and development across various sectors. These specialized institutions are tasked with addressing continental challenges and priorities, promoting regional collaboration, and attracting international funding and partnerships, thus contributing to the continent's socioeconomic development and global competitiveness.

Regional, continental and global initiatives are increasingly focusing on identifying potential institutions and universities and selectively support and advance them both on a competitive and non-competitive manner. African flagship institutions have been the main beneficiaries of this emerging trend which is now considered to be one way of consolidating research and enhancing innovation in the continent.

In "Centers of Excellence for Research Development", Frejus Ariel Kpedetin Sodedji, Achille Ephrem Assogbadjo, Moses Osiru, in this book, affirm that research universities can and are actively contributing to changes in Africa and site some prominent examples of innovation from Morrocco, Uganda and South Africa. They observe that hosting such elite research institutions is sustained through highly qualified faculty, robust government and nongovernment funding, highly talented students, and well-equipped facilities and resources, among others.

This chapter analyses ten research networks spanning over 115 CoEs in the continent that were established through collaborations though they typically rely on local expertise while significantly leveraging international partnerships and funding. It affirms that CoEs stimulate and support research-led innovation in Africa and have led to enhanced knowledge generation and dissemination, and extensive internationalization. It is noted that these CoEs vary in their thematic focus, funding levels, operational methods, and verifiable outputs including an estimated 80,000 postgraduates and close to 10,000 publications, among others.

The creation of centers of excellence, the authors' state, builds on concepts around World-Class Research Universities which emerge through either of the three approaches: picking winners, clean-slate and hybrid. The authors' document nearly a dozen major centers of excellence in Africa managed and funded by multiple continental and international players augmented by numerous declarations, agenda, and strategic plans. Following the analysis of this emerging phenomenon, they have discussed issues of strategy, excellence, collaboration, governance, sustainability, regionality, and the impact of COVID.

### *Research and Academic Collaborations*

Academic collaboration has emerged as a powerful driver for advancing knowledge, fostering innovation, and addressing complex global challenges. In recent years, this form of partnership has gained tremendous momentum, as the academic and research communities increasingly recognize that pressing issues—such as climate change, pandemics, and poverty—transcend national borders and cannot be effectively tackled in isolation. Collaborative research efforts across nations, institutions, and disciplines allow for the pooling of diverse expertise, resources, and perspectives, thus enhancing the quality and impact of the research outcomes.

The rise of multi-national, multi-institutional collaborative research reflects a shift toward a more interconnected and cooperative academic landscape. This approach is not only beneficial for advancing scientific and scholarly knowledge but also for building capacity within and between institutions, especially when it involves partnerships between well- and poorly-resourced universities. Such collaborations are expected to contribute to knowledge production, enrich educational opportunities, and support the development of sustainable solutions that are sensitive to local contexts while addressing global needs.

By breaking down artificial boundaries and fostering open exchange, academic collaboration cultivates an environment where ideas and solutions can flourish on a global scale. The resulting partnerships and networks are instrumental in driving forward research that is comprehensive, inclusive, and geared toward addressing some of the most critical issues facing humanity today.

In a chapter "Research and Academic Collaborations in Africa: Imperatives, Potentials and Risks" Damtew Teferra, in this book, discusses research and academic collaboration first by providing a brief introduction to the phenomenon followed by an account on South-South Collaboration before sharply focusing on the African context.

In this context, South-South collaboration is presented not only as an alternative to traditional models but also as a potential pathway for African institutions to assert greater autonomy and foster self-reliant growth. He observes that South-South collaboration—defined as cooperative efforts among institutions across the Global South—remains comparatively underdeveloped despite its potential to drive both regional and global development. Historically overshadowed by North–South partnerships, this form of collaboration is increasingly seen as vital for addressing shared developmental challenges. Recent years have witnessed a surge in interest toward South-South partnerships, reflecting a growing awareness that common issues, such as economic disparities, climate change, and public health crises, may benefit from shared resources and mutual learning between developing regions.

Drawing on a broad perspective that examines the evolution of global academic partnerships, he explores how patterns in collaboration have shifted over time, significantly impacting institutions in the Global South. In particular, he points to Africa's experience under structural adjustment programs and the influence of a contested rate-of-return study, which together cast a long shadow over the continent's higher education systems. These external pressures diverted African institutions from strengthening internal capacities, with lasting implications for both academic and research partnerships.

Today, academic collaboration in Africa remains highly dependent on external funding, largely from Northern institutions and organizations. This reliance, while instrumental, has been criticized for fostering unpredictability, limited contextual relevance, and an imbalance of power that often favors Northern agendas. The chapter highlights various international accords and declarations developed over the years to address these issues, underscoring the entrenched interests in preserving existing structures, even as new players in the collaboration landscape emerge.

The chapter introduces "polygamy" as a metaphor to describe the growing network of global actors engaging with Africa to illustrate the complex dynamics of these partnerships. This concept highlights how African institutions navigate relationships with multiple partners, each with their own agendas and expectations—with great implications for the continent. The chapter also addresses the role of intermediaries—such as NGOs, think tanks, and national institutions—which act as "midwives" in these collaborative efforts. While these entities help facilitate partnerships, they can also serve as gatekeepers, sometimes limiting the agency of African institutions in shaping their own research agendas or effecting the spirit of the partnership to its fullest.

### *University-Industry Partnerships in African Science*

University–industry linkages have been touted by policymakers and academics as vital to advancing research, knowledge transfer, innovation, and technical exchange. These partnerships allow universities to align their research with real-world industrial challenges, driving technological advancements and enhancing societal impact. For industries, such partnerships provide access to cutting-edge research, specialized expertise, and talent pipelines. For universities, it provides the much-needed labs, infrastructure, and resources, as well as insights and opportunities for commercializing their research.

While the potential benefits of this phenomenon have been well recognized—by all parties, i.e., universities, industries, and governments—its implementation has so far been minimal for a number of reasons. Challenges such as intellectual property disputes, cultural differences, and misaligned priorities often require careful management to ensure mutual benefit.

In a chapter in this book, "Industry-University Partnership in African Science: Status, Barriers, and Opportunities", Bright I. Nwaru, Eman Sobh, Olu Akanmu and Charles Ayo, observe the growth of university-industry partnerships in industrialized countries given the crucial role they play in catalyzing innovation and economic and social advancement. Despite a history of interest in mounting university-industry partnerships in Africa, these have been minimal at best and non-existent at its worst.

University-industry collaborations come in different forms. The authors describe some of this phenomenon, including the most common form, where universities conduct research projects, develop strategies, provide training, and support mobility of staff to implement research results on the industry side and academic side. The other form of such partnerships is where universities provide professional consultancy, research management, and expertise to drive and enhance innovations, to provide solutions to identified problems and issues, and to improve the commercialization of products.

They note that the operation of industry-university partnerships is heterogeneous and complex across contexts, and it is this variation that eventually differentiates thriving and poor partnerships and thus signals that different framework of partnerships may be in operation across settings. The authors extensively quote over a dozen generic best practices to create a framework for building an enabling environment for efficient university-industry partnerships. While reckoning lack of such frameworks in the continent, they advise that these practices get adopted for the continent.

Citing a study by the Association of African Universities, they discuss seven areas of barriers that constrain as well as facilitate university-industry partnership in Africa. These barriers span from cultural differences between academia and industry, perceived differences in goals and priorities, the state and nature of African economy and capacity of African universities, among others.

The chapter explores the evolving paradigms of research, innovation, and knowledge production through the frameworks of the triple helix and quadruple helix collaboration models. The triple helix, which emphasizes the interconnectedness of universities, government, and industry, has long been celebrated for fostering innovation ecosystems and driving research and development. However, in recent decades, the quadruple helix has emerged as a more inclusive framework by integrating civil society as a fourth pillar. This addition recognizes the growing importance of public engagement and societal needs in shaping research priorities and innovation strategies.

The authors argue that the traditional triple helix, while effective, often falls short in addressing the multifaceted challenges of contemporary society, such as climate change, deteriorating environment, digital transformation, and social inequality. The inclusion of civil society broadens the scope of collaboration, ensuring that research and development efforts are socially relevant, participatory, and sustainable. Over the past few decades, the quadruple helix model has gained traction, as it better reflects the complexities of modern knowledge terrain and the need for democratized innovation processes. By fostering a balanced partnership among academia, industry, government, and society, this model enables the co-creation of solutions that are not only technologically advanced but also socially impactful.

### *Graduate Education and Knowledge Production*

Oanda Ibrahim Ogachi in a chapter "Graduate Education and Knowledge Production in Africa in the Context of the Knowledge Economies" extensively discusses the nexus between graduate education and knowledge production—one of the key issues African higher education continues to grapple with. Through the lens of political economy, he examines the current state of graduate education in Africa, highlighting the intricate interplay of power, resources, and policy shaping its trajectory. He delves into emerging trends and evolving systems that are impacting the landscape of knowledge production and dissemination across the continent.

The analysis sheds light on how these developments are recalibrating the roles of universities, governments, and external stakeholders in fostering research and innovation. Key areas of focus include the increasing emphasis on public–private partnerships, regional collaborations, and the influence of global funding mechanisms on the autonomy and priorities of African higher education institutions.

Graduate education in Africa is often primarily valued for its role in developing the teaching workforce, with its equally critical functions—research, innovation, knowledge production, and dissemination—frequently relegated to secondary importance. This narrow focus has constrained the broader potential of graduate education as a driver of societal transformation and economic development. Compounding this issue is the persistent scarcity of public funding for graduate-level research and training, which remains negligible across much of the continent.

In terms of knowledge production, despite the rapid growth of digital publishing, the escalating costs of journal article processing fees and subscription charges have placed many of the world's top-ranked journals and dissemination outlets beyond the reach of most academics and graduate students in Africa. These financial barriers are compounded by the fact that funding for academics and graduate students across the continent rarely includes support for publishing and disseminating research findings.

As a result, much of the knowledge generated by African graduate students remains unpublished in high-impact outlets that could provide both the research and the researchers with global visibility. Unable to afford the prohibitive publishing fees demanded by many prestigious journals, these students are often left with no choice but to publish in journals with lower impact factors, limited visibility, and, often, a reputation for lower quality. This situation persists even when the research outputs are of exceptional quality and relevance.

This systemic challenge not only hinders the global recognition of African research but also perpetuates the underrepresentation of African perspectives in critical academic discourses. Addressing this issue requires deliberate investment in funding mechanisms that cover publication costs and the establishment of accessible, high-quality journals within Africa.

Such measures could significantly enhance the visibility, impact, and credibility of knowledge produced by African graduate students, enabling their voices to resonate more effectively within the global academic community.

Despite these significant challenges, promising interventions are emerging. Across Africa, innovative programs are beginning to address the needs of graduate students not only in completing their studies but also in fostering their ability to produce and disseminate cutting-edge knowledge. These initiatives are designed to bridge the gap between education and impactful research, equipping graduates with the resources and platforms necessary to contribute meaningfully to local and global knowledge ecosystems. This evolving landscape, Ogachi notes, signals a growing recognition of the transformative power of graduate education in advancing Africa's research and knowledge production—and consequently its developmental aspirations.

### *The State of Research Integrity*

Integrity and ethics in research are tremendously critical to academia—and society as a whole. Maintaining ethical standards and honesty throughout the research process, truthfulness in data collection, analysis, and reporting, along with fairness in acknowledging contributions and adhering to ethical guidelines for human and animal research are crucial in ensuring the reliability of research results and building trust between researchers, the public, governments, and funding institutions.

Tesfaye Semela in the chapter "Graduate Research in African Universities: The State of Research Integrity", in this book, systematically analyses the state of research integrity and ethics first by providing a background on research capacity, productivity, and expenditure in Africa. Organizing the chapter in multiple sections, he offers conceptual clarity on the principles of research ethics and research integrity as well as theoretical frameworks. He goes on to analyze the state of continental, national, and institutional structures and frameworks that ensure responsible conduct of research and specifically examine it at institutional level with particular reference to graduate research and existing practices related to the state of research integrity, including the serious challenges surrounding contract cheating and emerging technologies.

Semela notes that research ethics committiees in most African states focus on health or medical research giving lesser attention to other areas of research including science and technology, behavioral and social sciences, and humanities and cultural sciences. This trend seems to be replicated at institutional level, where majority of universities give more emphasis to health and medical sciences. He concludes that in general most universities lack a well-organized institutional ethical review boards nor do the host countries provide the necessary legal frameworks complete with the range of disciplinary and multidisciplinary fields in their postgraduate programs.

He notes that graduate research in several countries has been increasingly affected negatively by issues related to research integrity and academic misconduct, particularly in the context of theses and dissertations. Reports from data spanning half a dozen countries reveal widespread incidents of plagiarism, data fabrication, and data falsification, among other serious breaches of research ethics. Such misconduct undermines the quality and credibility of graduate research and, by extension, affects academic reputation and trust in the region's research outputs.

A significant contributor to this issue is the presence of third-party entities—often located beyond university oversight—who offer services that compromise the authenticity of research work. These external influences exploit gaps in institutional vigilance and the lack of widespread inculcation of research ethics, eroding graduate research integrity across the continent.

To counter these challenges, Semela highlights the need to foster a culture that values research integrity, beginning at the undergraduate level. Embedding principles of ethical research conduct early on can set the foundation for more conscientious academic practices. Moreover, integrating research ethics and integrity into the curriculum, particularly within research methodology courses in graduate programs, can help ensure that students are well-versed in the standards and expectations of ethical research. This approach may also involve formal training workshops, access to resources on research integrity, and the implementation of institutional policies that actively discourage misconduct.

Creating such an environment requires support from university leadership and policymakers, who must champion initiatives that prioritize academic honesty and research credibility. These steps are essential to safeguard the quality of academic research and graduate education and to reinforce a research culture that respects integrity, rigor, and ethical accountability.

### *Open Science*

Open science, as a movement toward greater accessibility, collaboration, and transparency in research by making scientific outputs (including publications, data, software, and methodologies) freely available to the global community, has been gaining momentum worldwide. It is anticipated to hold transformative potential, particularly for advancing research and graduate studies in Africa through increased access to research outputs, collaboration and knowledge sharing, research visibility, and impact.

In many African countries, access to scholarly journals and databases remains limited due to high subscription costs. Open science breaks down these barriers by making research publications, data sets, and other scientific resources freely available online. This ensures that African researchers, regardless of their institutional affiliations or financial resources, have access to the latest research, fostering greater participation in global scientific discourse.

Open science holds the key to advancing African research, innovation and graduate education by fostering access, collaboration, and visibility. By embracing open science principles, African researchers and students can overcome resource limitations, contribute to global knowledge, and drive innovation that addresses the continent's unique challenges. For Africa's academic and scientific communities, the future of research lies in openness, inclusivity, and shared progress.

Angel Y. Ford, Daniel Gelaw Alemneh and Abebe Rorissa, in a Chapter "Open science in the African Context", in this book, note what they call a "common misconception" about open science that it is making research outputs open to all as the primary objective. Whereas Open Access (OA), the movement to make research outputs accessible globally, is a large part of open science, they hold that it is only one aspect among others.

The authors observe that in the evolving landscape of open science, both citizen science and indigenous knowledge systems play critical roles in enriching scientific research and advancing graduate education. These contributions are invaluable in addressing global priorities like climate change adaptation, biodiversity preservation, and public health. While these areas are often framed as international or national concerns, the reality is that most impactful decisions occur at the local level. Citizen science initiatives allow community members to actively participate in research processes—gathering data, identifying patterns, and applying local knowledge. Similarly, indigenous knowledge brings deeply rooted, ecosystem-specific insights, which are particularly beneficial in areas like environmental management and health practices, providing practical wisdom built over generations. Integrating these perspectives not only democratizes science but also strengthens research outcomes, aligning them more closely with the needs and insights of local communities.

Despite its potential, open science faces various challenges in achieving comprehensive and effective adoption. The chapter captures key pillars of open science, such as transparency and replicability and introduce their own sets of complexities. Transparency, for instance, requires that all elements of a study—from raw data to analytical methods—be openly accessible, which can be challenging when dealing with sensitive or proprietary information. Further, ensuring that datasets are labeled and organized in a way that is accessible and interpretable across disciplines demands rigorous standards and additional resources. This process involves creating systematic protocols that can accommodate various data structures and cultural perspectives, ensuring that citizen and indigenous knowledge is represented accurately and respectfully.

Moreover, the push for open data access necessitates careful consideration of ethical and cultural sensitivities, especially when indigenous knowledge is involved. Open science frameworks must prioritize data sovereignty, acknowledging that certain forms of knowledge may need to remain protected within indigenous communities or shared under specific terms to prevent misuse or misappropriation. Addressing these nuances requires a thoughtful redesign of scientific protocols and graduate training, incorporating interdisciplinary skills, ethical frameworks, and an appreciation for diverse knowledge systems.

Ultimately, open science can serve as a transformative force in research, innovation and graduate education, equipping future academics and researchers with the tools and sensitivity needed to collaborate effectively across cultural and disciplinary boundaries. The scientific community can foster a more inclusive, responsible, and impactful approach to research, one that resonates with both global and local imperatives, by embracing citizen science and indigenous knowledge.

### *Research and Innovation*

In this last chapter, "Research and Innovation in Advancing Knowledge for African Development" Damtew Teferra, weaves key issues in advancing research, innovation and graduate education in Africa. This particular chapter critically analyzes these multifaceted issues of the knowledge dynamics in Africa by drawing on, among others, a theoretical perspective that drives the imperatives of research and knowledge production.

The chapter which extensively discusses some of the issues noted here, also stresses the need for a differentiated higher education sector and astute leadership in advancing research, innovation and graduate education.

## Conclusion

This book provides an extensive analysis on the challenges, prospects, and trajectories of research and innovation in Africa. It underscores the transformative role that research play in Africa's journey toward sustainable development, innovation, and global competitiveness. While recognizing the hurdles that African institutions face, such as funding constraints, infrastructural inadequacies, and reliance on external partnerships, the book highlights the determination and resilience demonstrated by African scholars, administrators, and policymakers who are shaping a dynamic and impactful educational sector.

The analysis presented emphasizes that research and innovation in Africa operate within a complex global context. Africa's universities are deeply affected by international dynamics, including the flow of knowledge, resources, and collaborations typically spearheaded by the Global North. However, as discussed in the chapters, these interactions, while offering critical support, often reinforces imbalances that constrains the autonomy, agenda, and relevance of African institutions. This highlights the importance of creating a more equitable partnerships, grounded in mutual respect and shared goals, to ensure that Africa's educational priorities align with its own development objectives rather than solely those of external stakeholders.

One of the key themes of this book is the growing call for Africa-centered research agendas that prioritize the continent's unique social, economic, and environmental needs and challenges. By anchoring research in African contexts, universities can produce knowledge that directly contributes to national development, fostering solutions that are both practical and sustainable. In addition, by addressing these local challenges through research, African universities can offer insights that contribute to global understanding in critical areas such as climate change, public health, and food production, among others. The book argues that Africa's specific challenges are often representative of larger global issues, and as such, the continent's research contributions can provide innovative solutions with broader applications.

The book also highlights the importance of nurturing South-South collaboration as an alternative to traditional North–South partnerships. With African and other Global South nations sharing many similar developmental challenges, collaborations within these regions are increasingly seen as effective vehicles for advancing shared research agendas. South-South collaborations offer African universities the opportunity to build research capacity, share resources, and strengthen institutional networks, while also fostering a sense of agency in setting research priorities. In addition, the book advocates for Africa's growing participation in international research networks that are characterized by multidirectional knowledge sharing, as opposed to the historical model of unidirectional knowledge transfer from North to South.

The book further emphasizes the role of policy and governance in fostering an enabling environment for research and innovation. Governmental and institutional policies play a crucial role in establishing frameworks that support academic freedom, research integrity, and institutional autonomy. Throughout the book, contributors advocate for policies that prioritize sustainable investment in higher education, strengthen the capacity of African institutions, and create conditions that empower African universities to pursue contextually relevant research agendas. Effective governance and supportive policies can ensure that African institutions are not only beneficiaries of global research agendas but are also co-creators and innovators in the global academic community.

It is important to reiterate that advancing research and innovation in Africa is not only a continental priority but should be construed as a global imperative. Africa's potential to contribute to global knowledge production is immense, and realizing this potential requires a concerted effort from African institutions, governments, international partners, and the private sector. All stakeholders need to embrace a new paradigm of collaboration that is rooted in equity, respect, and shared vision for a better future. Such partnerships are essential for building robust research ecosystems in Africa, which in turn can produce the knowledge, innovation, and skilled professionals needed to address unique challenges of the continent—and the world.

## References

Altbach, P. G. (2002). Perspectives on international higher education. *Change: the Magazine of Higher Learning, 34*(3), 29–31.

Altbach, P. G. (2007). Doctoral education: present realities and future trends. In James J. F. Forest & Philip G. Altbach (Eds.), *International handbook of higher education* (pp. 65–81). Springer.

Altbach, P. G., Reisberg, L., & Rumbley, L. E. (2010). *Trends in global higher education: Tracking an academic revolution*. Sense Publishers.

Anderson, K. (2023, May 26). *What is the COP27 loss and damage fund?* Leaf. https://acesse.dev/zEIEW. Accessed on November 9, 2024 at 19:37 South African time.

Arnhold, N., & Bassett, R. M. (2022). *Steering tertiary education: Toward resilient systems that deliver for all*. World Bank.

Congressional Research Service. (2020). *Global research and development expenditures: Fact sheet*. https://fas.org/sgp/crs/misc/R44283.pdf

De Wit, H., & Hunter, F. (2015). *Internationalisation of Higher Education*. European Parliament, Directorate-General for Internal Policies.

Hayward, F. M., & Ncayiyana, D. J. (2014). Confronting the challenges of graduate education in Sub-Saharan Africa and prospects for the future. *IJAHE, 2014*, 173–216.

IAU. (2015). *Internationalization of higher education: An evolving landscape, locally and globally*. IAU.

Kakuchi, S. (2024, July 9). *Next-round bids for endowment fund include merged institute*. https://tinyurl.com/apvdkuy2

Li, S. (2018, February 6). *From 985 to World Class 2.0: China's Strategic Move*. https://tinyurl.com/5a4d445b

Lorenzi, J., & Batalova, J. (2022, May 11). *Sub-Saharan African immigrants in the United States*. Migration Policy Institute https://tinyurl.com/33wyt6hp. Accessed on November 6, 2024 at 10:38 SA Time.

Ministry of Science and ICT, Korea. (2024). *Government Boosts Investment in Firsts and Best-in-class R&D*.

Ministry of Science and ICT, Korea. https://tinyurl.com/3dsk53rf. Accessed 17 November 2024.

New American Economy. (2018, January 11). *Immigrants from Africa Boast Higher Education Levels Than Overall U.S. Population*. https://encr.pw/ccIej. Accessed on November 6, 2024 at 10:30 SA Time.

Pethokoukis, J. (2020). *US federal research spending is at a 60-year low. Should we be concerned?* https://l1nq.com/uwilT

Sawahel, W. (2022, November 24). *Academics see research potential of 'loss and damage' fund*. https://encr.pw/t2q02

Sharma, J. (2022, February 17). *More universities become 'world class' to meet China ambitions*. https://tinyurl.com/35xkuy4w

Teferra, D. (2010). Deploying Africa's Intellectual Diaspora: Potentials, Challenges and Strategies. In D. Teferra & H. Greijn (Eds.), *Higher education and globalization: Challenges, threats and opportunities for Africa* (pp. 83–94).

Teferra, D. (2013). Introduction. In D. Teferra (Ed.), *Funding Higher Education in Sub-Saharan Africa* (pp. 1–12). Palgrave MacMillan.

Teferra, D. (2020). The irrelevance of the re-configured definition of internationalisation to the global south: Intention versus coercion. *International Journal of African Higher Education, 7*(2). https://doi.org/10.6017/ijahe.v7i2.12905

Teferra, D. (2021). Editorial: The role of the African intellectual diaspora in advancing higher education. *International Journal of African Higher Education, 8*(2), 1–5.

UNESCO-UIS. (2011). *Financing education in Sub-Saharan Africa meeting the challenges of expansion, equity and quality*. UNESCO.

Woldegiyorgis, A., Rudakov, V., Rozhkova, K., & Melnyk, D. (2020). Trends and practices: The literature concerning doctoral education. In M. Yudkevich, P. Altbach, & H. de Wit (Eds.), *Trends and issues in doctoral education: A global perspective* (pp. 3–32). Sage Publishing.

World Bank. (2002). *Constructing knowledge societies: New challenges for tertiary education*. World Bank.

Yudkevich, M., Altbach, P. G., & de Wit, H. (Eds.) (2020). *Trends and issues in doctoral education*. Sage.

CHAPTER 2

# Funding Research in African Higher Education

*Gift Masaiti and Damtew Teferra*

## Introduction and Context

Financing higher education, especially research, is an expensive enterprise. Knowledge creation, knowledge dissemination, and innovation do not come cheap (Johnstone, 2015; Varghese & Panigrahi, 2023). High-end expertise, expensive equipment and instruments, extensive infrastructure (such as labs, libraries, and dormitories) the accompanying requisite logistics (such as information technology), and a complex academic culture entail that the sector is costly (Johnstone, 2013a, 2013b; Ziderman, 2015). Problems surrounding the financing of higher education institutions are worldwide; however, nowhere in the world is financing research in higher education more problematic than in Africa, especially in Sub-Saharan Africa (Teferra, 2013a, 2013b; World Bank, 2010). As

G. Masaiti (✉)
School of Education, University of Zambia, Lusaka, Zambia
e-mail: gift.masaiti@unza.zm

D. Teferra
University of Kwazulu-Natal, Durban, South Africa
e-mail: teferra@ukzn.ac.za


D. Teferra (ed.), *Research and Innovation in African Higher Education*,
https://doi.org/10.1007/978-3-031-92909-0_2

argued by Mugwagwa et al. (2019), without doubt, African countries' individual and collective ambitions of economic development through research and innovation are in line with trends worldwide. Just like elsewhere in different parts of the world, African countries have been exploring different approaches, institutional reforms, models, and mechanisms towards more efficient and effective funding of research and innovation. Strides are being made to make research and innovations as spring boards to national developments and policy formation.

Despite representing approximately 18% of the global population, currently Africa contributes only about 2% to global knowledge production, a situation that is widely believed to account for its underdevelopment, and about only 1% to 2% of the world's research and innovation outputs (Thondhlana & Garwe, 2021). This underrepresentation is largely driven by the continent's reliance on external funding, particularly from partners in the Global North. African research agendas are frequently shaped by the priorities of these external funders, making them vulnerable to fluctuations in funding and shifting priorities (Varghese, 2023). This dependency has constrained the development of locally driven research initiatives, hindering Africa's ability to address its unique challenges and contribute meaningfully to global knowledge production.

Two of the most insightful studies covering many countries on financing higher education research in Africa is by the World Bank (2010, 2022). These reports demonstrate that the key for success in a globalized world lies increasingly in how effectively a country can assimilate the available knowledge, research, and build comparative advantages in areas with good growth prospects and then use technology to address the most pressing challenges. The World Bank argues that higher-level institutions in Sub-Saharan Africa should be equipped to impart quality education and conduct relevant applied research, which can play a critical role in producing workers with the skills to assimilate technology and make effective decisions that help industry to diversify into a broader range of products. The World Bank through strengthening good-quality and relevant higher education intends to stimulate innovations, among others, in new varieties of crops, new materials, or sources of energy that would facilitate progress toward reducing poverty, achieving food security, and improving health (World Bank, 2022).

UNESCO (2024) notes that higher education in Africa is at an important turning point, shaped by the continent's dynamic youth population and pressing development challenges. The study mentions that with over

400 million young people aged between 15 and 35, Africa boasts the youngest population in the world, offering a unique opportunity to harness this potential for economic growth and innovation. Yet it appears significant barriers persist, including low enrollment rates in tertiary education, inadequate alignment between academic programs and labor market demands, and the underrepresentation of women in academia and leadership roles across African higher education institutions, particularly in Science, Technology, Engineering and Mathematics (STEM) fields.

Further, UNESCO notes that Africa should look to HEIs to address pressing challenges like youth unemployment, economic inequality, and climate change through innovation, research, and development in important fields like health, agriculture, and technology. This study makes a passionate appeal to invest in Africa's research infrastructure to counter visible challenges. The study posts that while enrollment in higher education is on the rise and more than doubled between the years 2000 and 2021 (from 4 to 9%), it is still low compared to the global average of 38%. Additionally, underinvestment within African higher education in research and development limits Africa's capacity for innovation, particularly in critical fields like health, agriculture, and technology. Africa invests only 0.6% of its GDP in research and development, compared to the global average of 1.79% (UNESCO, 2024).

The current state of research funding in African higher education is characterized by limited resources, fragmented funding sources, and inefficiencies in distribution and utilization (Ayuk & Koma, 2019; Le Roux & Breier, 2012; Masaiti & Mboyonga, 2022). The private sector and philanthropic organizations play a critical role in funding research by providing financial support, technical expertise, and opportunities for collaboration (Rohayati et al., 2016; Shaker & Borden, 2020). The chapter highlights several successful initiatives and strategies of research funding in African institutions, which demonstrate the transformative power of strategic research funding in driving innovation and development.

As early as 2004, Sawyerr (2004) asserted that enhancing research capacity and infrastructure in African institutions requires a coordinated effort from governments, institutions, and international partners. This entails investing in human capital development, improving access to research funding, and promoting a culture of research excellence (Plan, 2020). By addressing these challenges and capitalizing on successful funding models, African countries can unlock the full potential of their higher education institutions as catalysts for innovation and development on the continent. As part of a 2007 project to strengthen research management in African universities, funded by the Carnegie Corporation of New York, the Association of Commonwealth Universities (ACU) conducted a benchmarking exercise that highlighted critical funding challenges. While there was an increased interest in research management among academics, institutions faced significant obstacles related to financial resources. The exercise revealed weaknesses in identifying funding sources, negotiating contracts, and effectively utilizing available financial support for technology transfer and dissemination of research results. The 2010 ACU research management survey further emphasized the gap between perceived encouragement for funding research activities and the actual financial resources allocated to support these initiatives. Addressing these funding limitations is essential for improving the efficacy of research management in African higher education (Chipindi, 2023; Manegold, 1998; World Bank, 2002).

Implementing appropriate policies, infrastructure, and incentives is crucial to support research and development (R&D) efforts including the encouragement of private firms to invest in R&D and adopt best practices (World Development Report, 1998/1999; World Bank, 2022). Addressing local constraints and the availability of complementary inputs are crucial for the success of R&D initiatives. Investment in higher education research is a crucial component of development strategies to foster democratic, knowledge-based economies and societies (Varghese & Panigrahi, 2023). Countries which proportionally spend the Gross Domestic Product (GDP) in R&D have made substantial growth in both social and economic developments and innovations. Examples of these countries making huge investments in R&D are shown in Fig. 2.1.

Research and development comprise among others creative work undertaken on a systematic basis to increase the stock of knowledge, and the use of this knowledge to devise new applications which impacts directly on socio-economic development and innovations. Funding plays a critical role in realizing these. African countries might have to pick a leaf from the countries in Fig. 2.1—with considerable contributions to research—in their strides to advancing development.

Research funding plays a crucial role in advancing knowledge and innovation, particularly in the context of higher education institutions across Africa. However, researchers on the continent face significant challenges in securing sustained and sufficient financial support rendering

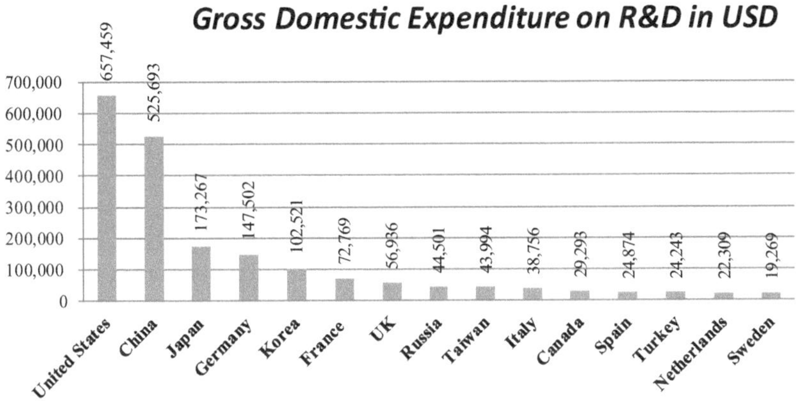


**Fig. 2.1** Gross domestic expenditure on R&D by sector of performance and source of funds (PPP USD, Current prices) (*Source* OECD (2024) stat org website)

them dependent to the shifting whims of external sources. According to Harrison (2021), foreign funding cuts have had a detrimental impact on African research capabilities. For instance, in 2020, when UK Research and Innovation (UKRI) announced budget changes resulting in a US$166 million shortfall in aid-supported programs, many African researchers were directly affected. She noted:

> A number of our researchers were hit, with our young researchers worst impacted, a number simply losing their funding. This reduction in funding disproportionately affected early-career researchers, whose projects were either scaled down or abandoned altogether. (Schendel el at., 2024: 14)

Beyond recurring budget cuts, African researchers are frequently excluded from global funding opportunities entirely. In 2021, this exclusion was starkly highlighted when scientists from Kenya, Nigeria, and Tanzania wrote an open letter to major international funders, drawing attention to the absence of African institutions from the U.S. government's President's Malaria Initiative (PMI) to the non-profit health organization PATH (Wamwayi et al., 2021). These examples illustrate the critical funding gaps and systemic exclusion faced by African researchers, limiting their ability to contribute meaningfully to global research efforts, particularly in areas that directly affect their own regions.

## Conceptual and Theoretical Underpinnings

Nations that increase their scientific research by funding the development of the higher education sector are at the forefront of global competitiveness (Masaiti & Mboyonga, 2022). On the contrary, the narrative on African higher education has disproportionately exhibited a shortage and crisis in faculty and students' access to funding research. Funding challenges in the African higher education sector have been widely reported in different higher education publications and country-profile reports. Some reviews and studies have shown that despite the substantial expansion of higher education in African countries, the sector remains one of the most financially challenged in the world, and proportional investment to research and development is also highly reduced and compromised with implications for each facet of the higher education landscape, mostly research, quality, and excellence (Varghese, 2022).

Further, research plays a significant role in accreditations as well as competitiveness and standing of a university, which eventually allows it to attract top talent in terms of both students and faculty (Teferra, 2013a, 2013b, 2022). Investing in higher education in Africa brings the highest rate of return in the world standing at 21% (African American Institute, 2015 in World Bank, 2019).

Investing in research not only equips students with advanced skills but also fosters innovation that drives economic growth. For countries, this translates into a more competitive workforce, capable of addressing complex challenges and contributing to sustainable development. For individuals, the financial returns from higher education can lead to improved job prospects and higher salaries, ultimately elevating their standard of living. Consequently, prioritizing research funding in higher education is essential for maximizing both societal and personal economic returns, making it a key strategy for enhancing national development (Garrison, 2012; Gillies, 2011).

The pronouncements by multiple global agencies and others are typically underpinned by Human Capital Theory (HCT), which emphasizes the importance of investing in education and research to enhance a nation's productive capacity. HCT rests on the assumption that formal investments in research are crucial for fostering a skilled workforce capable of driving economic growth. Human capital theorists argue that when deliberate or structured investments are made in higher education, the educated population is more likely to be productive, thus leveraging high returns from these research initiatives. By aligning with HCT, global agencies advocate for increased funding and support for higher education research, recognizing that such investments not only benefit individuals but also contribute to the broader economic and social development of countries. This connection reinforces the notion that strategic investments in education and research are essential for unlocking the potential of a nation's human capital, ultimately leading to enhanced productivity and innovation. HCT posits that investments in education, particularly in higher education, significantly enhance the productive capacity of individuals and, by extension, the economy of a country. In the context of African higher education, this theory underscores the critical relationship between funding for research and the development of human capital (Garrison, 2012; Singh et al., 2022; Viaene & Zilcha, 2013).

Investing in research within higher education institutions leads to the cultivation of skilled professionals who contribute to innovation, economic growth, and societal development. The argument is that when governments and private entities allocate substantial financial resources to higher education research, they are not merely funding academic endeavors, but they are also fostering a more knowledgeable workforce capable of driving economic progress. This structured investment is expected to yield high returns, manifesting as increased productivity, improved technological advancement, and enhanced problem-solving capabilities within the labor force.

In Africa, where many countries grapple with challenges such as unemployment, skill mismatches, and economic stagnation, the alignment of research funding with national priorities becomes crucial. When research initiatives are adequately financed, they can address local issues, such as food security, health crises, and infrastructural deficiencies, ultimately creating a direct link between higher education research and economic development. Moreover, funding for research in higher education helps to build and sustain research capacities, leading to the establishment of innovation hubs and research centers that can attract further investment, both domestically and internationally. This creates a positive feedback loop: enhanced research capabilities lead to successful innovations, which in turn attract more funding and support for further research activities (Akuru, 2019; Ayuk & Koma, 2019).

## Significance of Research Funding

Funding is the cornerstone for advancing knowledge, fostering innovation, and ultimately driving socio-economic development across the continent (World Bank, 2010; Ishengoma, 2013, 2021). African universities and research institutions are not mere educational establishments, but they are the pioneers of innovation and the catalysts for progress, tackling some of the most pressing challenges confronting African societies today (Le Roux & Breier, 2012; Wangenge-Ouma & Cloete, 2008; World Bank, 2010). In fields like healthcare, agriculture, and environmental sustainability, African institutions are at the forefront of groundbreaking research that holds the potential to improve lives and transform communities. However, to fulfill their potential and make a genuine impact, these institutions require access to sufficient and sustainable research funding (Uwizeye et al., 2021). Such funding is crucial for attracting and retaining top-tier researchers, equipping them with the necessary resources and infrastructure to conduct cutting-edge research, and ensuring that their work has a tangible social impact (Ayuk & Koma, 2019).

However, insufficient funding constrains institutions' ability to conduct research addressing African societies' multi-faceted and intricate needs (Le Roux & Breier, 2012; Teferra, 2013a, 2013b; World Bank, 2022). It impedes their capacity to invest in state-of-the-art technologies and equipment, collaborate with international partners, and provide vital research support and training. Consequently, their ability to drive meaningful change and progress is severely limited. Therefore, understanding the significance of research funding in African higher education goes beyond recognizing its financial value; it entails acknowledging its role as a catalyst for positive change and progress on the continent. By investing in research, African nations can unlock the full potential of their higher education institutions, empowering them to take the lead in addressing today's challenges and shaping a brighter future for tomorrow (Wangenge-Ouma & Cloete, 2008; World Bank, 2010).

Countries with greater industrial capacity and urbanization, like South Africa and Egypt, are increasingly emphasizing technology, engineering, and environmental science as they seek to address climate change, industrialization, and innovation-driven economic growth. Ethiopia and Zambia, on the other hand, may continue to prioritize agriculture due to the sector's dominant role in their economies, but they are also gradually integrating STEM education and social science to address broader development issues, such as poverty reduction and social equity. Governments, international partners, and private sector actors are increasingly investing in a range of fields to foster innovation and sustainable development. This diversity in research initiatives signals an intention to broaden Africa's research agenda to cover areas that are critical for long-term socio-economic transformation, such as technological adaptation, infrastructure development, and environmental conservation.

Kenya benefits from a strong network of private sector partnerships and international donors, while countries like South Africa relatively allocate substantial amounts to domestic sources. In another contrast, as diversification of funding resources, South Africa, for instance, promotes research excellence through designated chairs and centers, a model that is not uniformly adopted by other nations (McClure et al., 2017; Rohayati et al., 2016). Despite these efforts to diversify research fields, funding remains a critical bottleneck. Many countries face substantial funding gaps between the ambitious research agendas they are setting and the financial resources available to support these initiatives. In South Africa, for example, there is a challenge in balancing efforts to promote equity in access to research opportunities with the need to maintain research excellence, especially as resources are stretched thin. In Nigeria, systemic issues like corruption and mismanagement further exacerbate the already limited financial support for research, preventing efficient use of funds and diminishing research output (McClure et al., 2017; Rohayati et al., 2016).

Most African countries are spending less than one percent of their GDP on R&D. Sub-Saharan Africa on average contributes about 0.4% of its GDP to scientific research. Majority of West African countries spend less than 0.25% of their GDP on R&D while most East and Southern African countries spend 1% or less (Olufadewa, Adesina, & Ayorinde, 2017). Figure 2.2 indicates South Africa leading the continent in research funding at 0.82% followed by Kenya at 0.79% whereas Nigeria and Mozambique only committing 0.22% and 0.34% of GDP respectively—underscoring the need to prioritize investment in R&D.

While the vision of harnessing Africa's intellectual and scientific potential is evident, it is critical to recognize that without significant investment in research infrastructure, clear governance mechanisms, and a concerted effort to reduce funding inefficiencies, this vision may not be fully realized. African countries must not only diversify their research focus but also address systemic challenges that hinder the effective utilization of

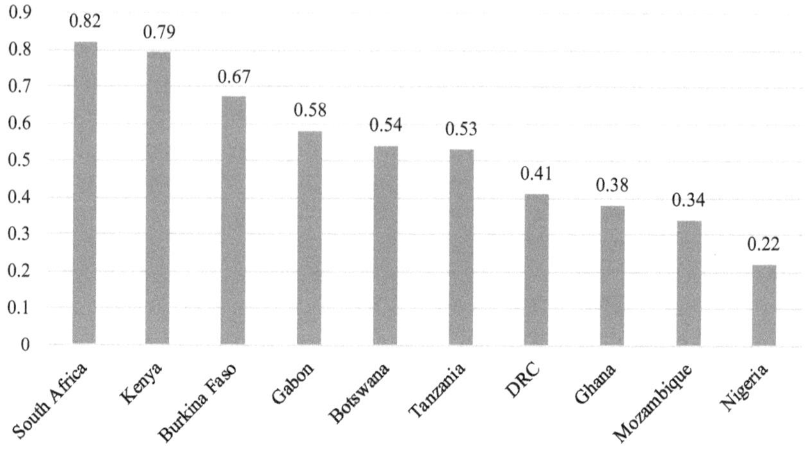


**Fig. 2.2** GDP on R and D in select African countries. World Bank sourced from Olufadewa et al. (2017)

available funding. The issue is not merely a lack of funds but also how existing funds are managed and directed toward achieving sustainable development goals. This complex tapestry of funding mechanisms and obstacles presents a multi-faceted view of the research environment within the continent. The available literature analysis depicts the intricate funding modalities for research in higher education research in African countries, illuminating the blend of government funding, reliance on external donors, and national initiatives that have been implemented to enhance research activities. In the next section, some of the innovative ways of funding research in African Higher Education are discussed.

## Innovative Ways of Research Funding

The economic rationality and realities seem to suggest that in most African countries the public financial support could not keep pace with the increasing social demand for higher education. Most countries and HEIs have adopted two types of market-friendly reforms, namely the privatization of public institutions and promotion of private higher education. The implementation of these reforms involved the introduction of cost-saving strategies, cost-sharing measures, and income generating activities at the institutional level. HEIs are now expected to look for real innovative ways of financing research agendas in the face of declining funding. The following are the possible innovative options already taking foothold.

### *Public–Private Partnerships (PPPs)*

African higher education is increasingly looking for meaningful collaboration with industries. They are beginning to leverage and encourage private sector investment in research by aligning research priorities with industry needs especially in sectors such as energy, agriculture, and, to a large extent, technology. Oanda (2013, 2021) makes a compelling case where University of Nairobi (Kenya) partnered with Google to fund research on local digital solutions and IT innovations. Also, in South Africa, Stellenbosch University worked with the Agricultural Research Council to develop agricultural technologies. This is increasingly becoming an innovative way of financing higher education in Africa as institutions increasingly forming research consortia, where multi-stakeholder partnerships involving universities, businesses, and government agencies to co-fund large-scale research initiatives.

### *Competitive Grants and Crowdfunding*

A new innovative way of financing higher education has manifested itself in crowdfunding platforms which leverage on digital platforms to source small contributions for specific research projects with high societal impact hosted mostly by African Higher education institutions. These manifest themselves in platforms such as Kickstarter and GoFundMe among others—practices of raising money from groups, typically through an online or mobile platform. One good example is the East African Crowdfunding (2016) project. It is generally classified in four distinct models: donations, rewards, lending, and equity based. This study examined the crowdfunding landscape in four East African countries (Kenya, Rwanda, Tanzania, Uganda), and compared it with the crowdfunding ecosystems in South Africa and the United Kingdom. Allied Crowds forecasts crowdfunding to grow by 177% from 2015 to 2016 in East Africa. Kenya was the leader among the four countries ($46.7 m forecast for 2016), followed by Uganda ($30.9 m), Tanzania ($16.0 m), and Rwanda ($9.4 m). This compares with a forecast of $20.6 m to be raised in South Africa for 2016. Some of the funds raised were used to finance research among different universities and higher learning institutions within the Eastern African block and beyond (Allied Crowds, 2016).

Competitive grants from global organizations, foundations, and international donors support research in priority areas in African Higher Education. Some of the best-known examples include the Norwegian and Germany's funding instruments; Mastercard Foundation's support to the African Research Universities Alliance (ARUA); and the UK Research and Innovation (UKRI) for collaborative research programs.

### *Commercialization of Research Outputs and Technology Transfer*

While the phenomenon of research commercialization and technology transfer is quite advanced in the Western World, it is slowly being practiced in the African Universities. In this endeavor, Okuwa and Campbell, (2017) note the commercialization of research outputs in agriculture at the University of Ibadan (Nigeria), to generate funds to support further studies within and outside the discipline. The partnership of Strathmore University (Kenya) with energy companies to commercialize renewable energy innovations is another one. These innovations might involve universities monetizing intellectual property, patents, and innovations through licensing agreements and spin-off companies. So central to technological transfer is Intellectual Property (IP) Revenue based on patenting and licensing university-developed technologies to create revenue streams. Other institutions, like the University of Cape Town run Startup Incubation which support faculty and student startups by providing seed funding and sharing in the profits. These innovative ways of generating research funding should be encouraged across African Higher Education.

### *Endowments, Alumni, and Philanthropy*

There has been increasing funding for higher education research coming from endowments, alumni, and philanthropy. The Kenyan HELB (2023) has funds where successful graduates contribute to the development of research capacity in their former higher education institutions. As a way of attracting research funding, alumni contributions are slowly proving to be one of the innovative ways of financing research in higher education. Another form of financing is increasingly being facilitated by recognizing and incentivizing alumni donors with awards or honorary titles thereby invoking the spirit of philanthropy. Universities like the University of Cape Town in South Africa and Makerere University in Uganda have established endowment funds through contributions from alumni, philanthropists, and corporations to generate ongoing funding for research (Makerere University Endowment Fund, 2023).

### *Innovative Government Support and Tax Incentives*

Some African governments have slowly started gravitating away from historical budget allocations through more "innovative" means of financing research in higher education. Some governments have created dedicated research funds based on innovative financing mechanisms with the focus on taxes and levies. A good example is the South Africa's National Research Foundation (NRF) which provides competitive grants funded by the government and public contributions where researchers and institutions compete. Some other examples include the Kenyan National Research Fund, Ghana's GETFund and Nigeria's Teritiary Education Trust Fund.

As a government mandated research and science development agency, South Africa's National Research Foundation (NRF) funds research, the development of high-end human capacity and critical research infrastructure to promote knowledge production across all disciplinary fields. The NRF intends to create innovative funding instruments, advance research career development, increase public science engagement, and establish leading-edge research platforms. The NRF promotes South African research and innovation interests across the country and internationally, and together with research institutions, businesses, industries, and international partners intends to build bridges between research communities for mutual benefit that contributes to national development (https://www.nrf.ac.za/, 2024).

The Kenyan National Research Fund (NRF), a State Corporation established under the Science Technology and Innovation (ST&I) Act No. 28, Section 32 of 2013 is mandated to facilitate research to advance science, technology, and innovation. The Act stipulates that the Fund will constitute a sum of money amounting to 2% of the country's Gross Domestic Product every year and such other monies designated for the Fund by Parliament, donations, endowment, or grants or gifts designated for the Fund. The grant supports a number of areas: Multidisciplinary Research Grants; Bilateral/Multilateral Research Grants; Strategic Grants;

Support to Scientific Events; Innovation Grants; and Incubation Program Grants. According to the website of the Fund, which has three funding mechanisms that include competitive funding, match grants funding and institutional support funding, it mobilized Ksh 6.1 Billion, funded 539 projects, funded 703 masters students and established 6 partnerships (https://www.nrf.go.ke/#, 2024). That noted the nagging question remains to be the adequacy of the fund and how best to administer it to ensure growth and sustainability.

Ghana's GETFund was established by Act 581 in 2000 with a mission to support the delivery of quality education to nationals from the basic to tertiary level through funding policies aimed at ensuring equitable provision of essential resources for all levels of education by providing, among others, grants for faculty member training and research. The fund is drawn for multiple objectives including an innovative, often an exceptional, support for faculty development and research for private universities (https://en.org/wiki/GhanaEducation_Trust_Fund, 2024).

The Nigerian Tertiary Education Trust Fund (TETFund) was originally established as Education Trust Fund (ETF) by the Act No. 7 of 1993 as amended by Act No. 40 of 1998 (now repealed and replaced with Tertiary Education Trust Fund Act No. 16 of 2011. It is an intervention agency set up to provide supplementary support to all levels of public tertiary institutions with the main objective of using funding alongside project management for the rehabilitation, restoration, and consolidation of tertiary education in Nigeria.

The main source of income available to the Fund is the 2% education tax paid from the assessable profit of companies registered in Nigeria. However, the Tax was reviewed upwards to 2.5% by the Finance Act 2021 and further increased to 3% by the Finance Act 2023, effective September 2023. The funds are disbursed for the general improvement of education in federal and state tertiary education institutions specifically for the provision or maintenance of essential physical infrastructure for teaching and learning; instructional material and equipment; research and publications; academic staff training and development; and any other need which, in the opinion of the Board of Trustees, is critical and essential for the improvement and maintenance of standards in the higher educational institutions. The distribution of funds among the education section has been stipulated in the ratio of 2:1:1 as between Universities, Polytechnics and Colleges of Education (https://tetfund.gov.ng/index.php/mandate-objectives/, 2024). The Nigerian Higher Education annual disbursement

**Table 2.1** Tertiary education trust fund annual disbursement for 2023

| *2023* | | |
|---|---|---|
| | *Universities* | *Allocated Amount* |
| (i) | Physical infrastructure development | 500,000,000.00 |
| (ii) | Zonal intervention (86) | 200,000,000.00 |
| (iii) | Academic staff training & development | 145,000,000.00 |
| (iv) | ICT support | 100,000,000.00 |
| (v) | Library development | 45,000,000.00 |
| (vi) | Conference attendance | 30,000,000.00 |
| (vii) | Institution based research | 40,000,000.00 |
| (viii) | TETFund project maintenance | 50,000,000.00 |
| (ix) | Entrepreneurship centres | 20,732,123.00 |
| (x) | Advocacy and publicity | 4,000,000.00 |
| (xi) | Publication of journal | 10,000,000.00 |
| (xii) | Manuscript development | 10,000,000.00 |
| | Total allocation per university | 1,154,732,123.00 |
| | Total allocation to 86 universities | 99,306,962,578.00 |

*Source* *TETFund Annual Disbursement 2010–2023*

is provided in Table 2.1, which describes the multi-faceted funding profile to boost research financing in universities.

Similarly, the Botswana Innovation Fund was established by the Government of Botswana through Statutory instrument 97, 2017, among others to promote and facilitate collaboration between academics/ scientists, entrepreneurs, public officials, and the citizens whom they serve. Like Ghana, noted above, the fund promotes innovation through technology, product, and business development in the private sector by offering cash grants (https://www.bih.co.bw/fund-guidelines/, 2024).

### *Other Innovative Ways of Financing Research*

Different contributors of the book edited by Teferra (2013a, 2013b) on Funding Higher Education in Africa made different advice and recommendations on how financing for research can be improved in HEIs across Africa. Waweru and Abate (2013) points to the issues related to revenue diversification and prudence in resource utilization. Ronoh et al. (2013) advances entrepreneurship as an alternative model to financing higher education and research agendas. Masaiti (2013) proposes moving to a more inclusive and sustainable model of financing higher education and research based on cost sharing, revenue diversification, and formula funding. At the heart of these publications is innovations based on leveraging research funds, among others, through Diaspora Engagement of African diaspora academics and professionals to provide funding, mentorship, and collaborative opportunities. A good example on this is the African Academy of Sciences (AAS) which engages the diaspora to fund and collaborate on research projects such as the Grand Challenges Africa program which seeks to engage innovators from around the world to solve the multitude of challenges on the African continent and beyond. The Grand Challenges initiatives are united by their focus on fostering innovation, directing research to where it will have the most impact, and serving those most in need across the African continent. The most notable Grand Challenges family includes the Bill and Melinda Gates Foundation, the United States Agency for International Development, and Grand Challenges of Canada, India, Brazil, South Africa, Ethiopia, and Africa, while more are anticipated (https://scienceforafrica.foundation/grand-challenges-africa, 2024).

### *Diaspora Funding*

The African Diaspora Fellowship Program (CADFP) is probably the most prominent initiative that mobilizes African academics overseas to support research and scholarship in African institutions. Funded by a grant from Carnegie Corporation of New York, a total of 748 African Diaspora Fellowships have been granted for scholars to travel to Africa since the program's inception in 2013 (https://www.iie.org/programs/carnegie-african-diaspora-fellowship-program/, 2024).

Funding research through diaspora intervention is a small but growing exercise. Some universities such as the University of Lagos (Nigeria) has benefited from diaspora-funded scholarships and research collaborations.

### *Collaborative Research Consortia*

This involves establishing multi-institutional and cross-border research networks to pool resources and access larger funding opportunities available. This can be seen from associations such as ARUA and Consortium for Advanced Research Training in Africa (CARTA). ARUA connects African universities to conduct joint research in fields like climate change, health, and governance and areas of common interest. CARTA supports collaborative doctoral training and research.

## Notable Initiatives for Research Funding

### *Bilateral Funding*

Mohamedbhai (2020) argues that in sub-Saharan Africa, the Norwegian Agency for Development Cooperation (NORAD) has played a pivotal role in enhancing higher education through initiatives focused on research and graduate collaboration. Notably, the NORAD Programme for Master's Studies (NOMA), which operated between 2004 and 2006, involved 28 higher education institutions across 18 countries in Africa, Asia, and Latin America, collaborating with 12 Norwegian universities (Holmberg et al., 2015). This program aimed to strengthen research capacity and foster academic partnerships that support graduate training in various fields. In addition to NOMA, NORAD has initiated several research programs, such as the Norwegian Programme for Capacity Development in Higher Education and Research for Development (NORHED) and the Norwegian Partnership for Higher Education and Research (NORPART). These initiatives are designed to enhance the quality and relevance of higher education in Africa by promoting collaborative research projects and fostering networks between institutions (Hanada, 2021).

It is also important to highlight the contributions of the Swedish International Development Cooperation Agency (SIDA), which has invested in various educational and research initiatives across sub-Saharan Africa. SIDA's efforts focus on enhancing educational quality, promoting equity, and supporting research that addresses local challenges (Bazine, 2023; Brolin, 2017). Germany's DAAD (German Academic Exchange Service) has similarly established centers of excellence across Africa, aiming to improve research quality and foster collaboration between German and African institutions (Noll & Lentz, 2024). These centers focus on areas such as climate change, health, and sustainable development, facilitating knowledge exchange and capacity building. Together, these initiatives from NORAD, SIDA, and DAAD illustrate an effort by various global partners to support research and higher education in Africa, with the intent to contributing to the continent's development goals.

The African-Asian (AA) University Dialogue for Educational Development is among these collaborations that put research at the center. Launched in 2004 as an international inter-university research initiative, the network comprises 17 African universities in 12 countries and 12 Asian ones across six countries. It is spearheaded by the Center for the Study of International Cooperation in Education at Hiroshima University, Japan. The network aims to foster funding and research collaboration among universities across the two continents as part of the international commitment to "Education for All". It seeks to tackle education challenges and enhance capacity among member universities through joint research and exchange of academic staff and students (Kuroda, 2012; Yoshida 2020).

At the eighth Tokyo International Conference on African Development (TICAD8) held in Tunisia, Japan pledged over 30 billion dollars to support the continent. The fund focuses on alleviating food insecurity, support growth post-COVID-19 pandemic, and finance the development of more robust regional economies. A component of about 1.5 billion USD was committed to financing research capacities on the African higher education terrain and institutions (TICAD 8, 2023).

### *ARUA and Mastercard Foundation*

Continental research collaborations are increasingly becoming common, with African institutions closely working together. For instance, at the culmination of the Dakar Conference in 2015, ARUA (African Research University Alliance), was established as a network of universities of 16 countries to enhance the quality of research in Africa by African researchers. This network of peer African institutions is intended to work together by pooling their own resources, with a view to generating a critical mass that could more effectively support limited but growing numbers of researchers across the countries. Underlying this was the conviction that they could thereby leverage this effectively for additional resources from different partner institution (https://arua.org/about/, 2024).

The ARUA Executive Committee in partnership with Mastercard has approved sixteen (16) Collaborative PhD programs that will begin in January 2026 (https://arua.org/arua, 2024). All the programs are designed to be four-year programs that involve 12 months of common course work to be undertaken at all the participating HEIs, 18 months of immersion in a research project or a period of "research apprenticeship" at another participating institutions and countries. The final 18 months will be spent on students' independent work leading to a thesis under the supervision of a team of both local and international supervisors to enhance quality and sustainability.

### *The Regional Universities Forum for Capacity Building in Agriculture (*RUFORUM*)*

The Regional Universities Forum for Capacity Building in Agriculture (*RUFORUM*). RUFORUM is a network of 129 universities in 38 African countries whose mandate is to strengthen the quality and relevance of postgraduate training and research in African universities. Focused on agriculture, most of its activities are focused and designed to improve the capacity of African universities and research centers, among others seeking research funds to generate knowledge relevant to Africa's development challenges.

### *African Economic Research Consortium (AERC)*

The launch of the African Economic Research Consortium (AERC) goes back to the late 1980s, when a group of Africanists and African scholars recognized the disconnect between economic policy making and economic research in Africa. Over the years, the Consortium has emerged as a premier institution for capacity building in the advancement of research and graduate training in economics. The AERC organizational structure was created to promote research agenda independence and resource management accountability across all member countries.

AERC is supported through bilateral and multilateral arrangements, private foundations, and international organizations. Among the notable benefactors especially in research and training activities are the following: William and Flora Hewlett Foundation; German Academic Exchange Services (DAAD); The Trade and Development Bank of Brazil; The African Export Import Bank; International Development Resource Centre (IDRC); The World Bank; Swedish International Development Cooperation Agency (SIDA); Norwegian Agency for Development Cooperation (NORAD); The Bill & Melinda Gates Foundation; Foreign, Commonwealth and Development Office (FCDO) and African Studies Centre Leiden University (aercafrica.org, 2024).

### *Africa Higher Education Centers of Excellence*

A number of research advancement through the establishment of centers of excellence in Africa have been observed. The Africa Centers of Excellence project (ACEs) is the first large-scale regional program funded by the World Bank to address higher-level skills development needs and innovative research requirements for the continent's priority development sectors (World Bank, 2022). To scale up the impact of existing ACEs and extend the program to more centers, the World Bank, together with the French Development Agency, launched the third phase of the program: "ACE for Development Impact project, ACE-Impact". An extensive discussion is provided on Centers of Excellence in a dedicated chapter in this book.

### *The African Academy of Sciences (AAS)*

The African Academy of Sciences (AAS) has contributed in the advancement of research and innovation on the African continent, particularly through its innovative funding model (Nakweya, 2022). Central to this model is the Grand Challenges Africa program, a flagship initiative that seeks to address pressing health and development challenges through targeted research funding. Through this program, AAS provides financial support to African researchers working on projects that have the potential for significant impact (Nakkazi, 2022). One of the key strengths of the AAS funding initiative is its emphasis on collaboration and partnerships with international organizations, governments, and private sector entities to leverage additional funding for research projects (Nakkazi, 2022; Ngongalah et al., 2019).

Nakweya (2022) reports that the impact of the AAS funding initiative is evident in the significant advancements made in health and development on the continent. The AAS has contributed to improvements in healthcare delivery, disease prevention, and agricultural productivity through its support for research projects (De Villiers & Steyn, 2009). Key actors in AAS's mission include AAS itself, the African Union Commission, AUDA-NEPAD, African governments, universities, research institutions, the private sector, international partners like the European Commission and the Bill and Melinda Gates Foundation, and various multi-stakeholders, and they contribute to research programming, funding, and implementation (African Academy of Sciences, 2023).

### *The South African Medical Research Council (SAMRC)*

The South African Medical Research Council (SAMRC) has developed a funding strategy that serves as a pivotal mechanism for advancing research addressing the health needs of the South African populace (Stats, 2017). Central to this strategy is providing financial support through a diverse array of grants and fellowships, strategically targeting critical health issues including but not limited to HIV/AIDS, tuberculosis, and maternal and child health. A key strength of the SAMRC funding strategy lies in its emphasis on fostering innovation and excellence in research. By providing financial support to researchers, the SAMRC empowers them to explore novel approaches and methodologies, thereby facilitating the generation of cutting-edge research outcomes.

Mathee et al. (2019) adds that moreover, the SAMRC funding strategy is characterized by its adaptability and responsiveness to emerging health challenges. The SAMRC maintains a proactive stance in identifying and addressing new health threats, mobilizing resources to fund research projects that have the potential to yield significant public health benefits. This agility has been instrumental in enabling South African researchers to remain at the forefront of health research, particularly in the face of dynamic and evolving health landscapes. The impact of the SAMRC funding strategy is palpable in the field of health outcomes in South Africa and has contributed in positioning the country as a global leader in health research and innovation (Ngongalah et al., 2019).

### *Science Granting Councils*

The emergence of Science Granting Councils (SGCIs) is increasingly providing some level of relief to the financing of research in African higher education institutions. For the past decade, the SGC Initiative has demonstrated the value of regional collaboration across sub-Saharan Africa. The initiative comprises 17 public science funding agencies and continues to grow and evolve into nationally significant institutions. Regional collaboration has been central to peer learning and collective action, playing a role in the African science landscape. The SGCI is transforming the science, technology, and innovation landscape in Africa by placing governments and the research community at the forefront of science, technology, and innovation research to address their priorities and drive meaningful change. The real question and concern is the continued underfunding to these councils which continuously stifle their capacity to optimally perform. (https://sgciafrica.org/science-granting-councils/ 2024).

## Contextualization of Funding Research

Enhancing research capacity and infrastructure in African higher education institutions is crucial for advancing knowledge, fostering innovation, and driving sustainable development. Africa thus has to be deliberate in unlocking the different potentials in situating research centrally in policy conversations and budget allocations. Uwizeye et al. (2021) note that despite the significant challenges, various strategies can be employed to strengthen research capacity and infrastructure. One key strategy is to improve access to research funding by diversifying funding sources and streamlining administrative processes, which includes engaging with the private sector and philanthropic organizations to secure additional funding and improving grant-writing and fundraising capabilities (Ayuk & Koma, 2019; Wangenge-Ouma & Cloete, 2008). Additionally, enhancing research infrastructure is essential for supporting high-quality research, which involves investing in state-of-the-art laboratories, equipment, and facilities and developing research centers and institutes focused on specific areas to foster collaboration and innovation (Sawyerr, 2004; Whitworth et al., 2008; Varghese and Panigrahi, 2023). Promoting a culture of research excellence and innovation is also vital, which can be achieved by recognizing and rewarding researchers' contributions and creating incentives for interdisciplinary collaboration and partnerships (Wangenge-Ouma & Cloete, 2008) important in mobilizing resources.

The state of research funding in African higher education is currently influenced by various factors that affect the availability, distribution, and utilization of financial resources. One of the principal challenges is the limited availability of government funding for research in many African countries (Masaiti et al., 2021). This insufficiency not only affects the quantity of research conducted but also its quality, as institutions struggle to attract and retain talented researchers and provide them with the necessary resources and infrastructure (Lufungulo et al., 2022; Uwizeye et al., 2021; World Bank, 2010). Private sector and philanthropic funding for research in African higher education institutions is also limited and tends to be directed towards specific projects or initiatives rather than long-term institutional development. Although the private sector in Africa is expanding, its focus often centers on immediate returns on investment rather than long-term research funding. This restricts the availability of sustained funding for research and impedes institutions from conducting research that addresses long-term societal challenges (Ayuk & Koma, 2019; Sawyerr, 2004; Teferra, 2013a, 2013b).

Le Roux and Breier (2012) and Atuahene (2011) note that gaining access to international funding sources can also pose challenges for African institutions due to stringent eligibility criteria and competition from other regions. While various international funding opportunities are available, including grants, scholarships, and collaborative research programs, African institutions often encounter barriers when attempting to access these funds, such as a lack of institutional capacity and limited networking opportunities (Wangenge-Ouma & Cloete, 2008). Dependency on international funding has many more ramifications related to issues of ownership, determining key research agenda without African/ Southern partners, regularly changing development interests (of the North), mismatch of research interests, and fragmentation of research, among others.

An examination of the primary sources of research funding in African higher education institutions reveals a heavy reliance on external donors and limited national government support. The heavy reliance on external financiers or collaborative partners poses significant risks, including the potential for external entities to dictate the strategic research agendas and objectives of African countries and institutions. This dependence undermines the ability of researchers in Africa to independently determine the direction and priorities of their research agendas. Furthermore, external funding often comes with challenges such as asymmetry of information, commonly referred to in economics as the "lemon problem". Donors and financiers typically pursue their own agendas, which may diverge significantly from the priorities and needs of their collaborating partners in Africa.

Masaiti and Mboyonga (2022), in analyzing the intricacies of financing and resourcing international collaboration specifically targeted towards research, observed that in the last 20 years the African higher education landscape has been characterized by increased levels of internationalization in research collaboration and partnerships. The rapid internationalization has also been questioned masking significant discrepancies and system malfunctions in financing and research collaboration in African universities. Evidence seems to suggest that the continent's universities have increased their research output but only contributed around one to two percent of the global knowledge, the lowest in the world (African Union, 2015). Inadequate public funding for research and development has been identified as one of the primary reasons for Africa's poor research productivity.

Finally, money alone is not the panacea to address the challenges of African research. The Makerere experience vividly counters that "the claim that North–South research collaborations increase research productivity" at the institution which has received substantial research funding via North–South research programs over many years. Musiige and Maassen (2015) examined the factors influencing faculty research productivity, including the role of financial rewards. Despite the high levels of research funding Makere received, faculty research productivity still remained low (Ishengoma, 2016). A dedicated chapter in this book extensively discusses partnerships and collaborations.

## Conclusion

Financing research in higher education in Africa is a critical but highly challenging endeavor. Despite significant expansions in higher education, the sector remains financially constrained with limited resources committed to research. The analysis presented in this chapter underscores the critical role of research funding in driving academic and intellectual activities, advancing knowledge, fostering innovation, and contributing to socio-economic development. The current state of research funding in African higher education is characterized by limited resources, fragmented funding sources, and inefficiencies in distribution and utilization. Addressing these challenges necessitates a multi-faceted approach, including increasing government funding for research, fostering private sector engagement, improving access to international funding sources, mounting innovative funding schemes, and promoting efficient and equitable distribution and utilization of research funding. By tackling these challenges, African countries can enhance the research capacity of their higher education institutions and unlock their full potential as drivers of innovation and development.

Even though this chapter has attempted to present innovative ways of soliciting research funding for higher education, and profiled also some of the notable initiatives for research funding, most of the profiled initiatives and innovations are small in magnitude—and might not generate the much-needed wholesale impact on the African Higher

Education terrain. African governments ought to make financing of research as a critical imperative—and a priority. A multi-faceted approach that includes increasing government investment, fostering partnerships with the private sector, and leveraging international collaborations is paramount to advance research. A need for policy reforms that streamline funding processes that enhance regimes for flexibility, accountability, and transparency in the utilization of research funds is paramount.

Sustainable and strategic research funding is crucial for the development and competitiveness of higher education institutions in particular and the continent as a whole. African countries can unlock the full potential of their higher education institutions and contribute to global knowledge and innovation by mitigating the funding challenges and adopting innovative funding initiatives. This is however only possible by strategically and systematically leveraging their own resources—not through continued dependence on external sources, as important as they may be.

It is important to underscore that the heavy reliance on external financiers or international collaborating partners for funding research poses significant risks, including the potential for external entities to dictate the strategic research agendas and objectives of African countries and institutions. Thus, the need to self-sufficiency in advancing research through leveraging one's own resources cannot be overemphasized.

## References

African Economic Research Consortium AERC. (2024, February 8). *Finance and resource mobilization in higher education*. Retrieved on December 11, 2024, from https://aercafrica.org/

African Research Universities Alliance ARUA. (2024, April 14). *Equitable research partnership in Africa*. Retrieved on December 16, 2024, from https://arua.org/arua-and-mastercard-foundation-discuss-equitable-research-partnership/

Akuru, U. B. (2019). Research funding issues in African universities: Penalties and pathways. *Journal of Sustainable Development Studies*, *12*(2).

Ali, M., Mustapha, I., Osman, S., & Hassan, U. (2021). University social responsibility: A review of conceptual evolution and its thematic analysis. *Journal of Cleaner Production, 286*, Article 124931.

AlliedCrowds. (2016). *East Africa crowdfunding landscape study*. Retrieved on October 6, 2024 from https://www.fsdafrica.org/wp-content/uploads/

Arvanitis, R., Mouton, J., & Néron, A. (2022). Funding research in africa: Landscapes of re-institutionalisation. *Science, Technology and Society, 27*(3), 351–367. https://doi.org/10.1177/09717218221078235

Atuahene, F. (2011). Re-thinking the missing mission of higher education: An anatomy of the research challenge of African universities. *Journal of Asian and African Studies, 46*(4), 321–341. https://doi.org/10.1177/0021909611400017

Ayuk, P., & Koma, S. (2019). Funding, access and quality conundrum in South African higher education. *African Journal of Public Affairs, 11*(1), 176–195. https://doi.org/10.10520/EJC-15641a97a6

Balogun, J., Mamuzo, E., Okonofua, F., Balogun, A., & Oyeyemi, A. (2021). Bibliometric profile of the African Academy of Sciences medical and health sciences fellows. *Pan African Medical Journal, 38*(1). https://doi.org/10.11604/pamj.2021.38.60.21004

Bazine, I. (2023). *The role of democracy in the selection of aid recipients: A case study investigating the decision-making process of the Swedish International Development Cooperation Agency (SIDA)* (Masters thesis). Gothenburg University, Retrived on October 6, 2024, from https://hdl.handle.net/2077/77286

Brolin, T. (2017). *Ownership or donorship? Results and ownership in Swedish international development cooperation* (Doctor thesis). Gothenburg University, Retrieved on October 6, 2024, from http://hdl.handle.net/2077/52511

Bruce, L. D. (2016). The Carnegie Corporation Advisory Group on Canadian College Libraries, 1930–35. *Historical Studies in Education/Revue d'histoire De l'éducation, 28*(2). https://doi.org/10.32316/hse/rhe.v28i2.4499.

Ezeh, A. C., Izugbara, C. O., Kabiru, C. W., Fonn, S., Kahn, K., Manderson, L., Undieh, A. S., Omigbodun, A., & Thorogood, M. (2010). Building capacity for public and population health research in Africa: the consortium for advanced research training in Africa (CARTA) model. *Global Health Action, 3*(1). https://doi.org/10.3402/gha.v3i0.5693

Garrison, E. (2012). *States' investment in human capital: Higher education funding EFFORT*. (Graduate Student Theses). Dissertations, & Professional Papers, 1400. https://scholarworks.umt.edu/etd/1400

GETFund. (2024). *Ghana's education trust fund: Its accomplishments*. Retrieved on November 11, 2024, from https://tetfund.gov.ng/index.php/mandate-objectives/

Gillies, D. (2011). State education as high-yield investment: Human capital theory in European policy discourse. *Journal of Pedagogy/pedagogický Casopis, 2*(2), 224–245. https://doi.org/10.2478/v10159-011-0011-3

Gudo, C. (2014). Financing higher education in Kenya: Public-private partnership approach. *International Journal of Educational Policy Research and Review, 1*(1), 1–5.

Hanada, S. (2021). Higher education partnerships between the Global North and Global South: Mutuality, rather than aid. *Journal of Comparative & International Higher Education, 13*(5), 135–144. https://doi.org/10.32674/jcihe.v13i5.3686 | https://ojed.org/jcihe; https://www.google.com/search?q=South+African+Medical+Research+Council+(SAMRC).&rlz

Johnstone, D. B. (2013a). Public universities in an era of continuing austerity: More of the same or profound change. Faculty senate bulletin: A Publication of the State University of New York University Faculty Senate. *Fall/winter, 2013–14*, 11–14.

Johnstone, D. B. (2013b). The politics of higher education: Common misunderstandings about the financing of higher education. *Peking University Education Review, 2013*(2), 36–45.

Johnstone, D. B. (2015). *Financing higher education: World wide perspective and policy Option*, Paper Series No. 6.

Jones, S. R., Torres, V., & Arminio, J. (2021). *Negotiating the complexities of qualitative research in higher education: Essential elements and issues.* Routledge.

KNRF. (2024). *Kenyan national research fund agenda.* Retrieved on September 20, 2024, from https://www.nrf.go.ke/#

Kragelund, P., & Hampwaye, G. (2015). The Confucius Institute at the University of Zambia: A new direction in the internationalisation of African higher education? In *Higher Education and Capacity Building in Africa* (pp. 83–104). Routledge.

Latham, J. M. (2010). Clergy of the Mind: Alvin S. Johnson, William S. Learned, the Carnegie Corporations, and the American Library Association. *The Library Quarterly, 80*(3), 249–265. EJ890546.

Lufungulo, E. S., Mwila, K., & Mambwe, E. (2022). Strategies used to teach online in an EdTech low Resource Environment During COVID-19: A qualitative case study of the University of Zambia. *Proceedings of the International Conference on Open and Innovative Education (ICOIE).* Hong Kong Metropolitan University.

Manegold, D. (1998). World bank-world development report 1998–99, knowledge for development. *German Journal of Agricultural Economics/agrarwirtschaft, 47*(11), 432–432.

Masaiti, G. (2013). 'Students' Perceptions of Financing Public Universities in Zambia: Towards a More Sustainable and Inclusive Policy Strategy'. In D. Teffera *Funding Higher Education in Eastern and Southern Africa: Modalities, Challenges, opportunities and Prospects*, Palgrave Macmillan, 296–326.

Masaiti, G. M., Mwila, K., Kulyambanino, C., & Njobvu, T. (2021). Faculty productivity in Zambian higher education in the face of internationalization: Unpacking research, publication and citation at the University of Zambia.

*Scholarship of Teaching and Learning in the South, 5*(1), 66–86. https://doi.org/10.36615/sotls.v5i1.153

Masaiti, G., & Mboyonga, E. (2022). Financing and resourcing international collaboration in African higher education. *International Journal of African Higher Education, 9*(3), 153–175. https://doi.org/10.6017/ijahe.v9i3.16053

Mathee, A., Naicker, N., & Von Schirnding, Y. (2019). The role of the South African Medical Research Council in reducing lead exposure and preventing lead poisoning in South Africa. *South African Medical Journal, 109*(11b), 25–29.

McClure, K. R., Frierson, L., Hall, A. W., & Ostlund, K. L. (2017). Philanthropic giving by foundations to higher education institutions: A state-level social network analysis. *Philanthropy & Education, 1*(1), 1–28.

Mkandawire, S. B., & Ilon, L. (2018). Higher education systems and institutions, Zambia. In P. Teixeira & J. Shin (Eds.), *Encyclopedia of international higher education systems and institutions*. Springer. https://doi.org/10.1007/978-94-017-9553-1_478-1

Mukhwana, A. M., Kariuki, T., Kay, S., Silva, A. J., & Kirkland, J. (2019). The African academy of sciences research management programme in Africa. *Journal of Research Management and Governance, 2*(1), 31–33.

Mukhwana, E., Kande, A., Nandokha, H., & Too, J. (2020). Financing higher education in Africa: The case of Kenya. *In African Journal of Rural Development, 5*(3), 53–64.

Nakkazi, E. (2022). What is the role of science academies in Africa? *The Lancet Infectious Diseases, 22*(1), 25.

Nakweya, G. (2022). Major research on hold in African Academy of Sciences crisis. *SciDev. net-Governance*. Retrieved on January 7, 2025, from https://www.scidev.net/global/features/major-research-on-hold-in-african-academy-of-sciences-crisis/

Ngongalah, L., Rawlings, N. N., Wepngong, E., Musisi, J., Ngwayu, C., & Mumah, S. (2019). Tackling the research capacity challenge in Africa: An overview of African-led approaches to strengthen research capacity. *bioRxiv*, 518498. https://doi.org/10.1101/518498

Noll, A., & Lentz, C. (2024, April 28). *Early-career funding in German-African academic cooperation: Achievements, challenges, perspectives*. BBAW. https://www.blogs.uni-mainz.de/fb07-ifeas-eng/early-career-funding/

OECD. (2024). *Gross domestic expenditure on R&D by sector of performance and source of funds (PPP USD, Current prices)*. Retrieved on Devember 4, 2024, from stat org website OECD. Stat database, https://stats.oecd.org/Index.aspx?DataSetCode=MSTI_PUB

Okuwa, O. B., Campbell, O. A. (2017). Financing Higher Education in Nigeria. In F. Maringe & E. Ojo (Eds.), *Sustainable Transformation in African Higher*

*Education*. Sense Publishers. https://doi.org/10.1007/978-94-6300-902-7_12

Olufadewa, I. I., Adesina, M. A., & Ayorinde, T. (2017). From Africa to the World: Reimagining Africa's research capacity and culture in the global knowledge economy. *Journal of Global Health, 10*(1), 010321. https://doi.org/10.7189/jogh.10.010321

Ouma-Mugabe, J., & Chaminuka, P. (2020). Africa-Europe science, technology and innovation cooperation: Trends, challenges and opportunities. *The Routledge Handbook of EU-Africa Relations*, 224–232.

Patra, S. K., Muchie, M., & Das, A. K. (2021). Introduction to Special Issue on Science Technology Innovation and Development in Africa. *Journal of Scientometric Research, 10*(3), 352–354.

Plan, A. P. (2020). *South African Medical Research Council (SAMRC)*. Retrieved on November 16, 2024.

Regional Universities Forum for Capacity Building in Agriculture (RUFORUM). (2024). Retrieved on December 10, 2024 https://www.asti.cgiar.org/ruforum

Rochester, M. K. (1999). The carnegie corporation and South Africa: Non-European Library Services. *Libraries & culture*, 27–51.

Rohayati, M. I., Najdi, Y., & Williamson, J. C. (2016). Philanthropic fundraising of higher education institutions: A review of the Malaysian and Australian perspectives. *Sustainability, 8*(6), 541.

Le Roux, P., & Breier, M. (2012). Steering from a distance: Improving access to higher education in South Africa via the funding formula. *One world, many knowledges: Regional experiences and cross-regional links in higher education*, 193–248.

Sawyerr, A. (2004). African universities and the challenge of research capacity development. *Journal of Higher Education in Africa/revue De L'enseignement Supérieur En Afrique, 9*(6), 213–242.

Schendel, R., DeLaquil, T., Rensimer, L., & McCowan, T. (2024). Aid' to higher education in a multiplex world: Exploring the diversity of donor discourses and rationales. *International Journal of Education Development., 111*, Article 103162. https://doi.org/10.1016/j.ijedudev.2024.103162

Shaker, G. G., & Borden, V. M. (2020). Analyzing three decades of philanthropic giving to US higher education (1988–2018). *Philanthropy & Education, 4*(1), 1–42.

Sharma, G., & Dahlstrand, Å. L. (2023). Innovations, informality, and the global south: A thematic analysis of past research and future directions. *Technology in Society, 75*, Article 102359.

Singh, V., Mambwe, D., Korkor, C. M., & Chibale, K. (2022). Innovation experiences from Africa-Led Drug Discovery at the Holistic Drug Discovery and Development (H3D) Centre. *ACS Medicinal Chemistry Letters, 13*(8), 1221–1230.

Stats, S. (2017). South African Medical Research Council (SAMRC); ICF. South Africa Demographic and Health Survey 2016: key indicators. *South African Medical Research Council (SAMRC); ICF. South Africa Demographic and Health Survey 2016: key indicators.*

Styger, A. (2016). Government funding framework for South African Higher Education Institutions. *South African Journal of Higher Education, 29*(2), https://doi.org/10.20853/29-2-470

Teferra, D. (2013). Funding Higher Education in Sub-Saharan Africa *Palgrave Macmillan.*

Teferra, D. (2013b). Funding higher education in Africa: State, trends and perspectives. *Journal of Higher Education in Africa/revue De L'enseignement Supérieur En Afrique, 11*(1–2), 19–51.

Teferra, D., & Altbach, P. G. (2004). African higher education: Challenges for the 21st century. *Higher Education, 47*, 21–50.

UNESCO. (2024, July 17). What you need to know about higher education in Africa, *UNESCO's Proceedings on Forum on Higher Education*, Nairobi, UNESCO Regional Office.

African Union. (2019). *Five-Year Science, Technology and Innovation Plan of Action 2019–2024*. Retrieved on December 10, 2024, from https://tinyurl.com/4wzz482w

Uwizeye, D., Karimi, F., Thiong'o, C., Syonguvi, J., Ochieng, V., Kiroro, F., Gateri, A., Khisa, A. M., & Wao, H. (2021). Factors associated with research productivity in higher education institutions in Africa: A systematic review. *AAS open research, 4.*

Varghese, N. V., & Panigrahi, J. (2023). Innovations in financing of higher education: An overview. In N. Varghese & J. Panigrahi (Eds.), Financing of Higher Education. Springer, Singapore. https://doi.org/10.1007/978-981-19-7391-8_1

Viaene, J.-M., & Zilcha, I. (2013). Public funding of higher education. *Journal of Public Economics, 108*, 78–89.

De Villiers, A., & Steyn, A. (2009). Effect of changes in state funding of higher education on higher education output in South Africa: 1986–2007. *South African Journal of Higher Education, 23*(1), 43–68. https://doi.org/10.10520/EJC37517

Wangenge-Ouma, G., & Cloete, N. (2008). Financing higher education in South Africa: Public funding, non-government revenue and tuition fees. *South African Journal of Higher Education, 22*(4), 906–919.

Whitworth, J. A., Kokwaro, G., Kinyanjui, S., Snewin, V. A., Tanner, M., Walport, M., & Sewankambo, N. (2008). Strengthening capacity for health research in Africa. *The Lancet, 372*(9649), 1590–1593.

Woodland, J. G., Basarab, G. S., Mogwera, K., Winks, S., & Chibale, K. (2023). The 2022 H3D Symposium: Celebrating over a Decade of African-Led Infectious Disease Drug Discovery to Enhance Global Health. *ACS Infectious Diseases, 9*(3), 389–393.

World Bank. (2002). *Constructing knowledge societies: New challenges for tertiary education*. World Bank.

World Bank. (2010). *Financing higher education in Africa*. World Bank. http://hdl.handle.net/10986/2448

World Bank. (2019). *Strengthening higher agricultural education in Africa*. World Bank.

World Bank. (2022). *Education financing watch*, https://thedocs.worldbank.org/en/doc/

Ziderman, A. (Ed.). (2015). Financial Support to Students through Student Loans. *A Special Issue of Higher Education in Europe, 34*(2), 32–46.

CHAPTER 3

# The Significance and Implications of Internationalization on Research and Graduate Education in Africa

*James Otieno Jowi*

## Introduction

Internationalization has become core to higher education globally and is impacting the sector in varied ways leading to several transformations (IAU, 2010). In Africa, internationalization has characterized the developments in the higher education sector since the formative years (Teferra, 2008) and continues to shape and drive some of the main recent transformations (Jowi et al., 2013). Over the past decade, several African universities have begun to prioritize internationalization and are making it part of their strategic agenda. There has been an increase in the number of African universities establishing international offices to coordinate internationalization activities with focus moving beyond student mobility

J. O. Jowi (✉)
African Network for Internationalization of Education (ANIE), Moi University, Eldoret, Kenya
e-mail: jowij@anienetwork.org



D. Teferra (ed.), *Research and Innovation in African Higher Education*,
https://doi.org/10.1007/978-3-031-92909-0_3

to collaborations for research and postgraduate training (Andoh & Salmi, 2019).

The growing role of internationalization as one of the key drivers of change in Africa's higher education has been further fueled by the growth in interconnections, knowledge networks and the central role of research and postgraduate training (Maringe, 2017; Ndofirepi, 2017). Due to their comparatively weaker positions, varying contexts and histories, African universities encounter several vulnerabilities, risks and drawbacks in their engagements with internationalization (Jowi, 2012). In recent years, there have been emerging debates and discourses on how to develop best practices in internationalization especially for more balanced North–South collaborations (Chasi, 2019).

In discussing the impacts of internationalization on research and postgraduate training in Africa, it is important to take cognizance of some of the recent developments and transformations that have taken place in Africa's higher education, some of which are consequences of internationalization. Africa's higher education sector has expanded exponentially in the past couple of years in various ways. This includes the growth in the number and diversity of higher education institutions, the attendant growth in program offering, sharp rise in student enrollments, curricula and policy reforms and new forms of pedagogies among others (Mogaji, 2019; Teferra, 2016). These developments have some positive developments but have also outstretched the institutional capacities of the universities in most African countries.

In Ethiopia, for instance, the number of universities grew from just two in the year 2000 to thirty-six by 2015 with student enrollments growing from 34,589 to over 700,000 over the same period (Nega & Kassaye, 2017). More recent data indicates that Ethiopia currently has 50 universities with over a million students (Tamrat & Fetene, 2022). The situation was similar in a number of other African countries though not in the same proportions. Universities in Kenya grew to over 70 with a student population of over 550,000 in the past ten years (Barasa & Omulando, 2017). As is the case in other African countries, this growth has been mainly due to the growing demand for higher education as a result of Africa's youth boom. Howie (2022) estimated that by 2018, the number of universities in Africa had grown to about 2,000 and with a student population of about 20 million. This growth in enrollment has exacerbated the funding and capacity challenges that have been facing the institutions (Tayo Tene et al., 2021). It has however moved access for higher education in Africa from an average of 5% to about 10% in a span of about ten years (Andoh & Salmi, 2019) making it one of the fastest growing globally.

Private higher education has at the same time flourished in several African countries. This has further expanded access and diversification of the sector. Internationalization has played a role in this growth with a number of international universities setting up branch campuses in Africa. This scenario is more discernible in Rwanda in what Knight (2020) has termed *international program and provider mobility*. While national governments have played a significant role in some of these developments, the regional economic communities have made additional contributions especially in the development of regional policies and frameworks which have facilitated regional harmonization of higher education especially in quality assurance, mobility, mutual recognition of qualifications and capacity building. These efforts have enhanced regional coordination and cooperation in higher education leading to the assertion by Jowi and Mbwette (2017) that internationalization in Africa was beginning to take a regional dimension. Such developments are evident within the East African Community (EAC), Southern African Development Community (SADC) and the Economic Community of West African States (ECOWAS) which have resulted into a number of internationalization activities taking root regionally. In addition to these are developments at the continental level mainly steered by the African Union (AU) in collaboration with other continental agencies and development partners (Woldegiorgis & Scherer, 2019).

Despite these developments, Africa's higher education has continued to encounter several challenges, some of which have already been noted above. The main challenges include inadequate funding, low quality of programs, low capacities for research, inadequate infrastructure, low number of staff with doctoral qualifications and weak governance and management (Shabani et al., 2014), among others. The recent COVID-19 pandemic heralded new challenges and even compounded the existing ones (Kara, 2021; Muftahu, 2020). These challenges are exacerbated by the inadequate institutional capacities and frameworks to enable the universities meaningfully fulfill their mandates and cope with the growing societal demands (Uetela, 2017).

Due to their weak capacities for research and innovation, African universities have faced challenges in responding to the growing developmental and societal challenges. As a result, Africa is still stuck at the margins of the global knowledge society (Jowi & Sehoole, 2016) thus the need for concerted efforts to enhance research and knowledge production in African universities. This underscores the prioritization of research and postgraduate training as a key rationale for internationalization by African universities.

The essence of research and postgraduate training as central in strengthening Africa's higher education and building capacities to respond to the development needs of the continent has been underscored in Continental Education Strategy for Africa (CESA 2016–2025) of the African Union. The African Higher Education Summit held in Dakar, Senegal in 2015, further recognized the essence of research and postgraduate training in Africa, leading to among others, the establishment of the African Research Universities Alliance (ARUA). Over the past few years, ARUA has become a critical platform for collaborations among leading African universities for capacity building in research and postgraduate training.

Despite these efforts research productivity and postgraduate training in Africa still remains dismal and rather fragmented (Van't Land, 2016) thus the need for efforts including by international partners. Due to these efforts, in recent years there has been a growth in research and postgraduate training in several African countries (British Council and German Academic Exchange Service, 2017; Jowi, 2021; Maringe &Ndofirepi, 2017) mainly due to the expansion of local institutional capacities and international collaborations. Internationalization is thus one of the emerging key adaptive strategies that African universities are deploying to strengthening their postgraduate training and research capacities (British Council and German Academic Exchange Service, 2017; Jowi, 2021; Nyerere & Obamba, 2018). Some of the impacts of internationalization activities on research and postgraduate training in Africa are discussed in the next sections.

## Internationalization, Research and Postgraduate Training in Africa

As contextualized in the above section, this paper explores some of the impacts of internationalization on research and postgraduate training in Africa. Internationalization has been recognized as crucial in strengthening research and postgraduate training (Jowi & Sehoole, 2016) in addition to being a driver of some of the transformation in Africa's higher education. Internationalization is thus viewed as one of the ways through which African universities can enhance their research production and postgraduate training. This section therefore explores some of the impacts of internationalization on research and postgraduate training in most African countries.

### *Expansion of Postgraduate Training and Research*

As has been highlighted above, one major challenge facing African universities relates to drawbacks in knowledge production due to deficient research capacities. This has mainly been due to poor infrastructures and inadequate funding to support research and postgraduate training. Despite the growth in access to higher education in several African countries, as discussed earlier, this growth has been mainly at the undergraduate level with limited growth at postgraduate level. In recent years, several African countries have begun to prioritize postgraduate training and research. This is also due to the need for highly skilled human resource for the various sectors of the economy and high level skills to unlock the potentials and new opportunities in these countries (Cloete et al., 2015; Van't Land, 2016). As such opportunities and capacities for postgraduate training have grown in several African countries. Part of the challenge had been the low capacities for postgraduate training, mainly attributed to the low numbers of academic staff with PhD qualifications in most African universities and the high numbers of aging academics (Teferra, 2016). The institutions could thus not cope with the requirements of the expanding higher education sector and other sectors of the economies and the need to establish strong research and postgraduate programs. Recently, it has been noted that the number of staff with PhD qualifications in some of the top African universities stood at a dismal 20% and was even worse in majority of the institutions (Jowi, 2021). This has a significant impact on the quality of graduate training.

The capacity challenges have made it difficult for most of the universities to develop postgraduate programs and train a critical mass of qualified young African scholars. A study that covered six African countries i.e., Ethiopia, Ghana, Kenya, Nigeria, Senegal and South Africa, noted an increase in postgraduate training capacities and growth in research production in all these countries, but noted that it was way far from adequate (British Council and German Academic Exchange Service, 2017) against the national needs. The situation could be worse in some African countries, where institutional capacities are more deficient. As such, internationalization, through academic partnerships and collaborations, has become one of the ways by which African universities are addressing the challenges of postgraduate training and research. African universities now view internationalization as an adaptive strategy to respond to some of their institutional challenges especially those relating to research and developing capacities for postgraduate training (Mulvey, 2021).

It should be noted that African universities are making efforts to prioritize the strengthening of research capacities—which in a way subsumes postgraduate training—as a key rationale for internationalization. There are several examples and illustrations of the internationalization efforts that are playing a key role in supporting research and postgraduate training in African universities. Some of these have been highlighted in other sections of this chapter.

Arising from the recognition of the essence of postgraduate training by governments and the higher education institutions, several universities are developing strategic international partnerships to support their research and training initiatives (Sooryamoorthy & Scherer, 2022). As Andoh and Salmi (2019) observe, in recent years, African universities have responded to deepening their internationalization strategies and policies.

Some African universities such as Ghana, Addis Ababa, Nairobi, Dar es Salaam, Ibadan, among others have prioritized investments on research and postgraduate hinged on international partnerships and collaborations (British Council and German Academic Exchange Service, 2017). The African Network for Internationalization of Education (ANIE) recently launched a network of internationalization practitioners in Africa to enhance the coordination of internationalization activities, develop the capacities of these practitioners for better and strategic outcomes, and coordinate efforts to strengthen postgraduate training and research.

### *International Mobility*

International academic mobility has been one of the main activities of internationalization in Africa and is poised to grow in the coming decades. While opportunities and capacities for postgraduate training and research seem to be growing, academic mobility from Africa and within Africa—an important aspect of internationalization—has been growing. International mobility has characterized Africa's higher education over the years. As from the formative years of Africa's higher education, mobility has been part of the system with pioneer African scholars having attained their trainings out of Africa mainly in Europe and North America. Since then, Africa's place in academic mobility has been growing (Mulvey, 2021; Woldegiorgis et al., 2015). Despite the expansion of the higher education sector in Africa, mobility by African students and academics to other regions of the world has equally continued to grow. By 2020, about 404,000 African students were studying in tertiary institutions outside their countries of origin. This number is expected to increase in the coming years. Arising from this, in recent years Sub-Saharan Africa has had one of the most mobile tertiary students in the world with about 5% of Africa's 20 million students having crossed borders for studies compared to the world average of 2.5% (Oanda et al., 2022). The leading sending countries are however few and include Nigeria, Cameroon, Zimbabwe, Angola, Ghana, Kenya, Democratic Republic of Congo with most of the students heading to France, China, United States, Canada, India and Saudi Arabia. With its youth boom, Africa has become a new target area for international student's recruitment (Mulvey, 2021).

In addition to mobility to other world regions, internationalization in Africa is taking a rather regional dimension (Jowi & Mbwette, 2017). Regionalization is emerging as a new approach for higher education cooperation within some of the African regional economic communities. This is more discernible in the East African Community (EAC) and the Southern African Development Community (SADC) where relevant policies and frameworks to facilitate higher education cooperation and academic mobility have been developed and implemented. The declaration of the EAC as a Common Higher Education Area by the Summit of EAC Heads of State in 2016 was aimed at enhanced collaboration, harmonization, improvement of quality and employability and also comparability of qualifications attained from institutions in the region. The emergence of the regional centers of excellence has been an important development and platform for not only promoting regional mobility but also for strengthening research and postgraduate training in strategic areas for the regions. The regional economic communities—such as the EAC—have undertaken steps to harmonize their higher education systems thus developing regional policies for capacity building, quality assurance frameworks and mutual recognition of qualifications to facilitate mobility of students, staff and other professionals. These developments in regionalization have further led to the emergence of several new regional networks and consortia of universities and other actors to pursue various interests but mainly in research and societal transformation.

In addition to the traditional mobility in pursuit of full degrees abroad, Africa is now witnessing the emerging possibilities of split-site models for postgraduate training and virtual mobility programs that fit the needs of its early career researchers and minimize possibilities of brain drain. In a later section of this paper discussing funding for research and postgraduate training, it will be noted that the various funding arrangements have also contributed to supporting mobility of students and researchers enormously.

### *Curricula and Quality Reforms*

As stated earlier, the quality of postgraduate programs and research has consistently been a challenge. It is thus one of the main rationales for African universities to engage in internationalization. The need by African universities to enhance the quality and relevance of academic programs includes curriculum reforms, development of quality assurance policies and frameworks, capacity building for these and adoption of new learning and curriculum delivery approaches (Tayo Tene et al., 2021). Several internationalization activities have focused on developing new curricula and their reforms with an aim at strengthening the quality of postgraduate training and research.

African universities are developing partnerships and international collaborations aimed at supporting quality of training at postgraduate level including developing new and innovative programs in specialized areas that also support local production of PhDs and research. The emerging efforts and collaborations with international partners to develop centers of excellence in teaching and research are highlights of these developments. Some of these international partnerships are already having positive outcomes especially in curriculum strengthening, supervision and providing access to more academic resources to enhance the quality of their postgraduate training and research in these universities. Some of the regional university networks such as ARUA, RUFORUM, CARTA, are undertaking deliberate efforts to enhance postgraduate training and research and improve the quality of their programs through international collaborations.

### *The Rise of Digitalization*

The effects of the COVID-19 pandemic propelled digitalization and the utilization of ICTs to center stage in many African universities. It is compelling the universities to adopt new ways of teaching, learning and research (Mbiydzenyuy, 2020). It has presented an important turning point for the integration of ICTs and digitalization into the core mandates, programs and activities of the institutions including postgraduate training and research. The effects of the pandemic unveiled the vulnerabilities and poor responses by the institutions to crisis situations partly due to poor ICT infrastructures, ICT capacities and policy environments. As an adaptive strategy to continue with teaching and learning during the closures of the institutions occasioned by the COVID-19 pandemic, most of the higher learning institutions in Africa made efforts to deploy ICTs and digital technologies.

Despite the several challenges it presented to most African universities, it also presented new possibilities especially on the use of ICTs and digital technologies including strengthening research and postgraduate training. It is already creating possibilities for joint supervision, joint research, online and blended trainings and access to vast online resources. It has provided new opportunities for enhancing partnerships and collaborations with higher education institutions in Africa and other world regions thus reducing some of the barriers that had hindered meaningful engagements of African academics to global knowledge networks and platforms (Boshoff et al., 2021).

These developments in digitalization could stem the brain drain that has impacted research capacities in African universities negatively and constrained the efforts in capacity building through various internationalization efforts (Amutuhaire, 2020). It has the potential for possibilities of supervision and learning without the learners necessarily traveling to another country (Jakoet-Salie & Ramalobe, 2022). It is also important in the efforts to develop a critical mass of young African researchers with the competencies and requisite skills for Africa's transformation—with unprecedented opportunities for working together remotely. It could also offer graduate students access to opportunities that were hitherto out of reach such as participation in international conferences and seminars, international academic networks, accessing international knowledge resources and funding opportunities that could support their research and academic careers (Boshoff et al., 2021) thus alleviating some of the barriers that have faced young African researchers and academics in engaging and tapping into several internationalization opportunities and initiatives.

Digitalization and deployment of ICTs could further enable African higher education systems to address the low enrollments and poor quality of postgraduate training programs and even possibly lead to lowering costs of postgraduate training which has been a major barrier to access. This would not only enhance the number of postgraduates produced by African universities but also consolidate a strong foundation for embedding the young African researchers and connecting them to international research networks which could further catapult research and knowledge production in Africa.

There are already several international partners supporting initiatives towards deployment and integration of ICTs and digitalization into teaching and research in African universities. One of these is the EU-supported project on Digitalization and Internationalization for Postgraduate Training and Research in African Universities (DiGIGRAD) that supports several African universities to deploy the opportunities of digitalization and internationalization to strengthen the quality of postgraduate training and research. It is also notable that most of the new funding programs for higher education and research in Africa have focused on support for digitalization and ICTs. This is to enable African universities to take advantage of the stated opportunities of digitalization and ICTs in strengthening their capacities in research and engagements in internationalization. Some of these initiatives are also aimed at responding to some of the emerging challenges of digitalization in several African universities such as academic integrity that could negatively affect the intended outcomes.

### *Growth in Research Production*

As discussed in the introduction, one of the main rationales for African universities to engage in internationalization is to enhance their capacities for research. There is discernible growth in research production from Africa in recent years which is partly attributed to the impacts of these international collaborations (Uetela, 2017). It has been noted that Africa contributes just about 2% of the global research outputs (AAU, 2015), a slight increase from the less than one 1%, a few years ago. This shows that research productivity from Africa is slowly growing and needs even more push. Internationalization could provide some of the possibilities and strategies for turning around this situation especially through funding, joint research between African scholars and others elsewhere and through collaborative research activities (Arvanitis et al., 2022).

The quest for enhancing research production and publications has led to the development and support to academic journals published in Africa with the aim of addressing their challenge the continent. These are aimed at providing opportunities for publications in Africa and also enhancing the visibility of research and knowledge production in the continent. There are also international research projects and Africa-based initiatives to support the development of academic writing skills of emerging African academics to enable them contribute to international journals and also to build Africa-based journals. They are further aimed at strengthening their capacities to compete for international research grants.

### *Funding for Research and Postgraduate Training*

Funding is one of the main challenges facing African universities and also impeding research and postgraduate training in African universities (Maringe & Ojo, 2017; Teferra, 2013). In most African countries, universities cannot execute their mandates and respond to societal expectations due to the persistent funding constraints (Jowi & Sehoole, 2016). Due to the funding challenge and high levels of poverty in most African countries, access, equity and quality have remained perennial challenges of the higher education systems. While some countries are making progress towards diversification of funding sources, funding remains a critical challenge. A number of African countries are setting up loan schemes to support disadvantaged students (Oketch, 2016) though they still remain far from adequate including for postgraduate training. One of the barriers to the expansion of postgraduate training and research has been the perennial funding constraints.

While, national governments have put efforts to support postgraduate training and research, international partners have played a critical role in supporting these two areas due to the deficiencies that still exist. It is evident that there is a growing role of international partners to support research and postgraduate training (Cloete et al., 2015) as demonstrated by the renewed commitment of international partners. According to DAAD, most postgraduate students in African universities drop out or take much longer to complete their studies compared to their counterparts in developed countries, largely due to deficiencies in funding, supervision and support systems for their studies. As a result, in addition to scholarships to support postgraduate training in Germany, the DAAD is offering further scholarships for postgraduate training and research in targeted African universities. Norway also established the Norwegian Partnership Programme for Global Academic Cooperation (NORPART) to support academic cooperation with the Global South through academic cooperation and student mobility that mainly focused on postgraduate training and strengthening research. The Norwegian Programme for Capacity Development in Higher Education and Research for Development (NORHED) is currently running to support similar schemes.

The 5th African Union-European Union forum that was held in 2017 emphasized the need for enhanced investments on research and innovations in African universities through a number of priority areas including research and mobility of African researchers. By 2020, about 35,000 African researchers had benefited from the Erasmus-Plus program with the numbers expected to rise to 105,000 by 2027 (Zygierewicz, 2019). The 6th African Union–European Union Summit held in February 2022 reaffirmed these commitments and announced an Africa-Europe Investment Package to support the implementation of the AU Agenda 2063 including the commitments made in education with a focus on scaling up mobility and employability of students and enhanced access to the digital and data economy. Towards these, the EU has committed €970 million through the Global Gateway Investment Package, whose implementation has commenced, that also has components for learning mobility.

At the forum for China-Africa Cooperation (FOCAC) held in Senegal in November 2021, the Chinese government also committed an ambitious support to capacity building and exchanges focusing on various sectors including investments in digitalization as a response to crisis situations such as the one posed by the COVID-19 pandemic (Ye, 2022). This is in addition to the various infrastructure projects supported by China across several African universities (Zhu & Chikwa, 2021).

There are also developments to further support research and postgraduate training in Africa. In June 2022, under the auspices of the EU, a meeting bringing together high level African and European universities and research centers held in Brussels considered best practices and ways for supporting research collaborations between African and European institutions. Among others, it aimed at addressing the historical imbalances and asymmetries in partnerships and collaborations between Africa and western countries.

The UK-Africa partnerships have in recent years mainly focused on research and strengthening postgraduate training. These efforts are supported through several initiatives by UK's Department of International Development (DFID) such as the one spearheaded by the *Association of Commonwealth Universities* (ACU) and *UK Research and Innovation (UKRI)*. Through these, they collaborate with several networks of African universities with the aim of strengthening research capacities through training and developing supportive environments for research. The UKAid, provides further support within the framework of *Strengthening Research Institutions in Africa* (SRIA) aimed at strengthening regulatory agencies for research in African countries and aligning research funding to national development priorities. The program, with a budget in excess of £19,35 million is coordinated by the African Academy of Sciences, as the main African partner.

In attempts to address brain drain from Africa, the Carnegie Corporation of New York has invested $134.43 million towards the development and retention of the next generation of African academics. The program further aims at connecting Africa's academic diaspora to African higher education institutions mainly to support research, curriculum development and supervision. By 2019, the initiative had provided 2,144 fellowships to African scholars in the diaspora. The program however focuses on just a few African countries including South Africa, Ghana, Uganda and Kenya (Zeleza, 2019). Most of the highlighted partnerships aim at tackling the perennial global inequalities in research by strengthening research production from Africa including enhancing postgraduate training for an Africa-led and Africa-focused research agenda.

In recent years, some African universities are shifting their focus towards developing strategic partnerships to enable them mobilize resources for research and postgraduate training. The members of the ARUA network are a good example of the African universities with this focus. The University of Ghana, for instance, attracted close to $17 million for research and postgraduate training through such initiatives which constituted over thirty percent of the institution's overall budget (Alabi & Mohammed, 2018). Such international collaborations have also gone a long way in supporting joint research and co-supervision especially in areas where the African institutions experience capacity deficits (Jowi, 2021; Sooryamoorthy & Scherer, 2022). The emergence of the African Centers of Excellence such as those supported by the World Bank and the German Academic Exchange Service (DAAD) (extensively discussed in a dedicated chapter in this book) is an example of efforts to develop capacities for research and postgraduate training by supporting strategic research institutions in Africa to advance research and capacity building in disciplines of identified deficits.

### *Impacts of the COVID-19 Pandemic*

As stated in this chapter elsewhere, the COVID-19 pandemic left unprecedented impact on Africa's higher education. It caught most universities unprepared and exposed their limited capacities to respond to such crisis situations. It led to the closure of nearly all the universities bringing to a halt most activities including teaching, research and community engagement activities. Its impact has left long-lasting effects on institutions and further compounded some of their challenges as it also unleashed new ones. Most internationalization activities such as academic mobility including for postgraduate trainings and research were adversely jeopardized during the pandemic. International travel, scholarship opportunities and funding programs that support these initiatives were also suspended during this period. International academic exchange platforms including conferences faced similar consequences. As has been discussed in the earlier sections, some of the developments resulting from the impacts of the pandemic on the higher education sector, such as the opportunities of digitalization, present new possibilities for enhancing internationalization, research and postgraduate training in Africa (Boshoff et al., 2021). The rise in online learning, supportive platforms such as Collaborative Online International Learning (COIL), the effectiveness of virtual collaborations and webinars are examples that are quickly gaining ground in Africa.

## Implications, Challenges and Risks

It is notable from the foregoing that internationalization is transforming Africa's higher education, especially postgraduate training and research landscape in most African countries. The developments so far recorded and the growing prioritization of research and postgraduate training should open a new page in Africa's higher education especially in knowledge generation and repositioning of the universities to play their rightful role not only in addressing the growing developmental challenges of African societies but also Africa's role in the growing knowledge society. However, despite these contributions of internationalization to the strengthening of African universities and rejuvenating its knowledge production and innovation potentials, internationalization has also over the years had its unintended consequences and downsides. These are epitomized by the challenges and risks that internationalization portends to research and postgraduate training in Africa, some of which negate the gains attained by the various efforts.

As noted in the introductory section, Africa is the only world region that consistently views internationalization as presenting some risks to the higher education sector (Jowi, 2012). It is also noted that the threats and risks threaten the capacities of African universities for research and postgraduate training; others relate to the position of knowledge generated from African universities in relation to global knowledge epistemologies and discourses. The risk of brain drain persists but takes new shapes and twists as the international higher education terrain also changes. As such, these programs should ensure that the capacities developed are retained and supported to serve the needs of Africa.

Brain drain comes to center stage as an internationalization activity that in essence weakens the efforts by African universities to build a critical mass of young experts (Jowi, 2012; Moshtari & Safarpour, 2023). These challenges to research, innovation and postgraduate training have been further exacerbated by the unprecedented consequences of the recent COVID-19 pandemic which unveiled the fragilities of Africa's higher education institutions and systems and their inadequate capacities to respond to such crises.

As ascertained, academic rankings and the league tables are other developments that have not worked well for African universities and have even come out as risks to the internationalization and research production efforts in African universities (Kiraka et al., 2020). This has been based on several issues including what is measured by the rankings and their relevance to African universities and the fact that the rankings do not consider contexts and priority focus of universities in different world regions. Some African universities have thus been concentrating their efforts on improving their performance in the rankings, which could turn out to be rather pointless and fruitless efforts which could work to their disadvantage noting the different needs, contexts and realities of their institutions (Teferra, 2021). It has thus been argued that the rankings could be misleading to African universities and drifting them from their key mandates. Further to this has been calls for alternative rankings that could take into consideration the contexts of other universities such as those in Africa (Ndofirepi, 2017).

Some of the efforts of internationalization, as discussed above, are aimed at curriculum transformation, innovations and adoption of new teaching and learning methods. While this could be desirable, it should not lead to unnecessary western influence of the curriculum to the detriment of their relevance to the local context where they should be applied to address ensuing challenges. Since the years just after independence in several African countries, there have been calls for decolonization and Africanization of the curriculum in several African universities to build in locally relevant but quality programs. In recent years, this has escalated especially in South Africa with the Fees Must Fall and a raging quest for decolonization of the university which led to revolts by students and academics. In the same vein, these transformations have to ensure and build in quality into the programs.

Despite the discernible and commendable efforts to support research and postgraduate training in Africa, funding remains a serious challenge. Most potential postgraduate students cannot afford the costs of postgraduate training, thus the low enrollments and high rates of dropouts at this level. Most African governments and institutions have not committed adequate finances towards research and postgraduate training. In addition to the support by international partners, governments need to face the reality and take cognizance of the essence of research and human resource development to the success of their countries. Investments in research and high-quality human resource development has to be a high level imperative.

Funding for research that is accessible to African researchers from international sources have in some cases steered Africa's research agenda to areas where, at times, that are not particularly useful for the continent's needs. In some cases, internationalization projects for research and postgraduate training have mainly responded to the agenda and strategies of the funding western countries and international agencies. This, according to Sehoole and Jowi (2018), has led to research by African universities being focused on the needs of development partners and funding agencies rather than those of African societies and national research agendas.

There have been growing imbalances in partnerships and collaborations including those for research and postgraduate training. African universities thus have very little to do with agenda setting and decision making in these projects. There have been calls to streamline these partnerships and collaborations to advance more equity but those have not borne much result despite the several discussions on these in different fora. As Daniels et al. (2020) observe, it is unimaginable that several decades after independence, African universities are still captives of western knowledge hegemonies including content and method thus relegating contributions and realities from Africa. Some downsides of the impacts of internationalization on curriculum reforms especially those that have promoted the hegemonies and epistemologies of western thoughts have led to calls for reframing these approaches and efforts towards decolonization and Africanization of the curriculum.

Digital transformation holds an enormous potential to enhance research and postgraduate training in African universities. Their requirements, especially infrastructure and human resource capacities, pose new challenges to the already stretched universities. They further require adoption of new and innovative research approaches, methodologies, tools and a supportive research environment. If not well resourced, they could exacerbate the social and economic inequalities, inequities and barriers that face many emerging researchers in using these advancements (Spagnolo et al., 2020: 3).

## Conclusion

This chapter explores some of the impacts of internationalization in supporting research and postgraduate training in African universities. It takes cognizance of the developments being recorded in research and postgraduate training in African universities through these international partnerships and collaborations. The efforts by the various international partners are playing a key role in augmenting the efforts by governments to address a crucial issue that, if successful, would bring a new dimension into Africa's higher education sector.

With Africa's youth boom and the growth noted in the higher education sector in different facets and with the new advancements and opportunities in ICTs and digitalization, it is the opportune time to turn around the research capacities of African universities and to reposition African universities to contribute meaningfully to the global knowledge society and develop solutions to the growing challenges of African societies. It has been noted that to achieve the Sustainable Development Goals (SDGs), the broader Africa Agenda 2063, aspirations of Africa's regional economic communities and those of national governments, there is a crucial and deliberate need to invest in relevant and quality research and human resource development.

The resurgence of academic exchanges and collaborations in Africa could lead to more growth in postgraduate training and research. They also need to take cognizance of and focus on Africa's needs and the perennial risks and challenges that African universities associate with internationalization. The persistent asymmetries and imbalances associated with international partnerships and collaborations need redress for internationalization to be meaningful to African universities. African universities, on the other hand, have to rise up and make meaningful use of these initiatives and opportunities to bring about lasting change especially in expanding capacities for postgraduate training, research and innovations.

The potentials of ICTs and digitalization if used strategically could be a game changer for research and graduate training and for the overall research productivity and development of Africa. It has opened up several opportunities to scale up access, lower costs of postgraduate training, enhance efficiency of supervision, access the postgraduate students to enormous resources for their studies and even open up more possibilities for employment. It offers unprecedented opportunities for African universities to invest in these developments and deploy them for lasting transformations especially for research and postgraduate training. These technologies also create avenues for enhancing collaborations with international partners and even more funding opportunities. In this vein, African universities need to deliberately invest in ICTs and digital technologies to support research, postgraduate training and other key mandates of the institutions. In this, development of viable policies and strategies for postgraduate training and for ICTs and digitization among others would be imperative. These have also brought new challenges to postgraduate students.

While some positive developments have been recorded as discussed in the earlier sections, international partnerships, including research and postgraduate training, have remained unequal over the years and is still founded on colonial legacies and prisms and imbalanced power relations sustaining the superiority of western epistemologies, which have been imposed on and mimicked by African academics. Despite the several debates and engagements on these imbalances, not much seems to be changing with most of the structural barriers also continuing to be strongly embedded. For better outcomes, these need to change to enable African universities and scholars to have their rightful place and make their commensurate contributions.

African governments need to put more efforts in supporting intra-Africa collaborations as a way of strengthening Africa's higher education and as strategy for cross-pollinating the knowledge enterprise in the continent and for sustaining and sharing the capacities developed. African higher education institutions also need to position themselves to take advantage of the opportunities of internationalization in enhancing their graduate training and research productivity. This important area needs more advocacy, policy and strategy development and funding to ensure its realization. It is already clear that the higher education institutions that have deliberately and strategically explored the opportunities of internationalization have made meaningful strides. This is however amid the downsides and negative effects of internationalization on research and graduate training in Africa. There are various possibilities and opportunities, including within the frontiers of internationalization itself that can be deployed to respond to these challenges.

## References

AAU. (2015). *Report of conference of rectors, vice-chancellors and presidents of African universities on internationalization of higher education in Africa*. AAU.

Alabi, G., & Mohammed, I. (2018). *Research and PhD capacities in sub-Saharan Africa* (Ghana report). British Council &German Academic and Exchange Service.

Amutuhaire, T. (2020). African diaspora academics: A proposal for internationalizing higher education and reversing Africa's "brian-drain". In *Multidisciplinary issues surrounding African diasporas* (pp. 27–53). IGI Global.

Andoh, H., & Salmi, J. (2019). The internationalization agenda of African universities in the next decade.

Arvanitis, R., Mouton, J., & Néron, A. (2022). Funding research in Africa: Landscapes of re-institutionalisation. *Science, Technology and Society, 27*(3), 351–367.

Barasa, P. L., & Omulando, C. O. (2017). *Research and PhD capacities in sub-Saharan Africa* (Kenya Report). British Council & .German Academic and Exchange Service British Council & German Academic and Exchange Service.

Boshoff, H., Dhlamini, I., Wiafe, I., Heleta, S., Ayoo, P., & Jowi, J. (2021). *Early career researchers and digitalization: Insights from Ghana, Kenya and South Africa*. NUFFIC.

British Council and German Academic and Exchange Service. (2017). Building PhD capacities in sub-Saharan Africa.

Chasi, S. (2019). *North-South partnerships in public higher education: A selected South African case study* (Doctoral dissertation). University of the Witwatersrand, Faculty of Humanities, School of Education).

Cloete, N., Sheppard, C., & Bailey, T. (2015). South Africa as a PhD hub in Africa. In *Knowledge production and contradictory functions in African higher education* (Vol. 75).

Daniels, C., Byrne, R., Hanlin, R., Pointel, S., & Numi, A. (2020). *Updating the case studies of the political economy of science granting councils in sub-Saharan Africa*. SGCI Publication.

Howie, S. J. (2022). Regional studies in non-western countries, and the case of SACMEQ. *International handbook of comparative large-scale studies in education: Perspectives, methods and findings* (pp. 419–468). Springer International Publishing.

IAU. (2010). *Internationalization of higher education: Global trends, regional perspective* (pp. 159–165). IAU.

Jakoet-Salie, A., & Ramalobe, K. (2022). The digitalization of learning and teaching practices in higher education institutions during the Covid-19 pandemic. *Teaching Public Administration*, 01447394221092275.

Jowi, J. O. (2012). African universities in the global knowledge economy: The good and ugly of internationalization. *Journal of Marketing for Higher Education, 22*(1), 153–165.

Jowi, J. O. (2021). Doctoral training in African universities: Recent trends, developments and issues. *Journal of the British Academy, 9*(1), 159–181.

Jowi, J. O., Knight, J., & Sehoole, C. (2013). Internationalization of African Higher Education. In *Internationalization of African Higher Education* (pp. 11–31). Sense Publishers.

Jowi, J. O., & Mbwette, T. S. A. (2017). The development of new pan-African programs, research centres and networks. In J. Knight & T. E. Woldegiorgis (Eds.), *Regionalization of African higher education: Progress and prospects*. Sense Publishers.

Jowi, J. O., & Sehoole, C. M. (2016). Knowledge and change in the African University: Some prospects and opportunities of internationalization. In M. Cross & Amasa (Eds.), *Knowledge and change in the African university*. Sense Publishers.

Kara, A. (2021). Covid-19 pandemic and possible trends into the future of higher education: A review. *Journal of Education and Educational Development, 8*(1).

Kiraka, R., Maringe, F., Kanyutu, W., & Mogaji, E. (2020). University league tables and ranking systems in Africa: Emerging prospects, challenges and opportunities. In *Understanding the higher education market in Africa* (pp. 199–214).

Knight, J. (2020). The internationalization of higher education scrutinized: International program and provider mobility. *Sociologias, 22*, 176–199.

Maringe, F. (2017). Transforming knowledge production systems in the new African university. In *Knowledge and change in African universities: Volume 2–Re-imagining the terrain* (pp. 1–18).

Maringe, F., & Ndofirepi, E. S. (2017). Sustainable transformation of doctoral training in African universities. In *Sustainable transformation in African higher education* (pp. 53–64). Brill.

Maringe, F., & Ojo, E. (Eds.). (2017). *Sustainable transformation in African higher education: Research, governance, gender, funding, teaching and learning in the African University*. Springer.

Mbiydzenyuy, N. E. (2020). Teaching and learning in resource-limited settings in the face of the COVID-19 pandemic. *Journal of Educational Technology and Online Learning, 3*(3), 211–223.

Mogaji, E. (2019). Branding private universities in Africa: An unexplored territory. Available at SSRN 3457571.

Moshtari, M., & Safarpour, A. (2023). Challenges and strategies for the internationalization of higher education in low-income East African countries. *Higher Education*, 1–21.

Muftahu, M. (2020). Higher education and Covid-19 pandemic: Matters arising and the challenges of sustaining academic programs in developing African universities. *International Journal of Educational Research Review, 5*(4), 417–423.

Mulvey, B. (2021). Conceptualizing the discourse of student mobility between "periphery" and "semi-periphery": The case of Africa and China. *Higher Education, 81*(3), 437–451.

Nega, M., & Kassaye, M. (2017). *Research and PhD capacities in sub-Saharan Africa* (Ethiopia Report). British Council & German Academic and Exchange Service.

Ndofirepi, A. (2017). African universities on a global ranking scale: Legitimation of knowledge hierarchies? *South African Journal of Higher Education, 31*(1), 155–174.

Nyerere, J., & Obamba, M. (2018). Constructing transnational partnerships: New forms and spaces for internationalization in East African universities. In

*The future agenda for internationalization in higher education* (pp. 48–58). Routledge.

Oanda, I., Jon, J. E., & Blanco, G. (2022). Mobility for academic collaboration post-COVID-19. *International Journal of African Higher Education, 9*(3), 83–104.

Oketch, M. (2016). Financing higher education in sub-Saharan Africa: Some reflections and implications for sustainable development. *Higher Education, 72*, 525–539.

Sehoole, C., & Jowi, J. (2018). Internationalization of Higher Education, Africa.

Shabani, J., Okebukola, P., & Oyewole, O. (2014). Quality assurance in Africa: Towards a continental higher education and research space. *International Journal of African Higher Education, 1*(1).

Sooryamoorthy, R., & Scherer, C. (2022). Doctoral training in Africa: Taking stock. In *Doctoral training and higher education in Africa* (pp. 1–17). Routledge.

Spagnoli, P., Molino, M., Molinaro, D., Giancaspro, M. L., Manuti, A., & Ghislieri, C. (2020). Workaholism and technostress during the COVID-19 emergency: The crucial role of the leaders on remote working. *Frontiers in Psychology, 11*, 620310.

Tamrat, W., & Fetene, G. T. (2022). The achilles-heel of doctoral education in African higher education institutions: An Ethiopian university in perspective. *Higher Education Research & Development, 41*(4), 1294–1308.

Tayo Tene, C. V., Boiral, O., & Heras-Saizarbitoria, I. (2021). Does quality management improve the internalization of environmental practices? An empirical study in Africa. *Business Strategy and the Environment, 30*(7), 3053–3064.

Teferra, D. (2008). The international dimension of higher education in Africa: Status, challenges, and prospects. *Higher Education in Africa: The International Dimension, 5*, 44–79.

Teferra, D. (2013). Funding higher education in Africa: State, trends and perspectives. *Journal of Higher Education in Africa/Revue de l'enseignement supérieur en Afrique, 11*(1–2), 19–51.

Teferra, D. (2016). Conclusion: The era of mass early career academics and aging faculty–Africa's paradox. *Studies in Higher Education, 41*(10), 1869–1881.

Teferra, D. (2021). The treacherous adventure of ranking African universities. In *Research handbook on university rankings* (pp. 399–412). Edward Elgar Publishing.

Uetela, P. (2017). *Higher education and development in Africa*. Springer.

Van't Land, V. (2016). *The changing nature of doctoral studies in sub-Saharan Africa: Challenges and policy development opportunities at six universities in sub-Saharan Africa*. International Association of Universities (IAU).

Woldegiorgis, E. T., & Doevenspeck, M. (2015). Current trends, challenges and prospects of student mobility in the African higher education landscape. *International Journal of Higher Education, 4*(2), 105–115.
Woldegiorgis, E. T., & Scherer, C. (Eds.). (2019). *Partnership in higher education: Trends between African and European institutions*. BRILL.
Ye, W. (2022). Fragmented soft power: Bureaucratic politics and China's foreign aid in education to Africa. *Journal of Contemporary China*, 1–17.
Zeleza, P. T. (2019). Leveraging Africa's global diasporas for the continent's development. *African Diaspora, 11*(1–2), 144–161.
Zhu, X., & Chikwa, G. (2021). An exploration of China-Africa cooperation in higher education: Opportunities and challenges in open distance learning. *Open Praxis, 13*(1), 7–19.
Zygierewicz, A. (2019). Cultural heritage in EU discourse and in the Horizon 2020 programme.

CHAPTER 4

# Conceptualizing Research Infrastructures to Advance Science Systems in Africa

*Chux Daniels, Pearl Akazue, George Essegbey, Abena Yalley, Flora Tibazarwa, Jonathan Mba, and Damtew Teferra*

## Introduction

The African Union (AU) Agenda 2063 articulates the long-term development aspirations and targets expected to propel the continent to desired transformations in various areas, including science, technology, and innovation (STI), peace and justice, education, sustainability, gender, and inclusive development. Accordingly, research infrastructures (RIs) are needed to underpin the excellence in science and research that contribute to realizing Agenda 2063 and the transformations that Africa aspires to achieve.

C. Daniels (✉)
University of Sussex, Falmer-Brighton, UK
e-mail: c.u.daniels@sussex.ac.uk

Department of Engineering and Technology Management, University of Pretoria, South Africa

P. Akazue
Stittsville, ON, Canada

G. Essegbey
CSIR-Science and Technology Policy Research Institute, Accra, Ghana



D. Teferra (ed.), *Research and Innovation in African Higher Education*,
https://doi.org/10.1007/978-3-031-92909-0_4

As the Continental Education Strategy for Africa (CESA 16-25) highlights, there is increased recognition, at policy level, of the importance of research infrastructures (RIs) in achieving Africa's socioeconomic development objectives. This improved awareness and recognition are essential to strengthening and prioritizing the development of RIs across the continent. In realization of the critical importance of RIs, the second Strategic Objective (SO) of CESA 16-25 emphasizes the need to "build, rehabilitate, preserve education infrastructure and develop policies that ensure a permanent, healthy and conducive learning environment in all subsectors and for all, so as to expand access to quality education" (AUC, 2016, p. 8). Nevertheless, ambiguities with respect to what constitutes RIs exist at different levels. Evidence from literature reveals that it is unclear what RIs are in Africa, what constitutes "adequate" RIs, and how best to map, categorize, conceptualize, co-locate, or share RIs. Also, it is unclear how best to formulate, implement, evaluate, and govern policies, strategies, and frameworks on RIs at regional and continental levels to ensure mutually reinforcing and complementary benefits for countries in Africa.

To this end, this chapter seeks to address one main research question: in what ways can we (re)conceptualize RIs to enhance the resilience of science systems in Africa? To address this question, we (1) unpack the concept of RIs by exploring practices, impact, and policy to deepen our knowledge and understanding of how RIs are understood within Africa's science, research, and innovation ecosystems; (2) discuss strategies to further strengthen RIs across these ecosystems and explore policy directions that may help steer progress in RIs towards transformative

A. Yalley
University of Konstanz, Konstanz, Germany

F. Tibazarwa
EcoTek Tanzania Limited, Dar es Salaam, Tanzania

J. Mba
Association of African Universities, Accra, Ghana

D. Teferra
School of Education, University of KwaZulu-Natal, Durban, South Africa
e-mail: teferra@ukzn.ac.za

change in Africa (Daniels et al., 2021); and (3) propose a framework for conceptualizing RIs.

## RIs in Practice: Definitions, Categorizations, and Conceptual Framings

In practice, the role of RIs in scientific and technological advancement are well understood by the key actors in STI fields and beyond. However, the concept of RIs is still an emerging field of study, requiring further research and empirical evidence to justify the relevant definitions and categorizations proposed and improve our knowledge on the topic (Daniels et al., 2023; Hallonsten, 2020, forthcoming). As Hallonsten (2020, p. 2) notes, the "political hype around RIs has, however, not been matched by any comprehensive definitional or categorization work". This provides a strong justification for this research.

Broadly, and in the global ecosystem, *research infrastructures comprise facilities, resources and related systems of services which enable research communities to conduct their unique and top-level activities* (ESFRI, 2011). However, as Daniels et al. (2022, forthcoming) argue, this broad definition and the slight variations, widely adopted in existing literature, are inadequate for mapping—that is, providing a robust inventory of—RIs across multiple institutions, for example, universities, in order to ensure effective management, co-utilization (sharing of RI facilities, resources, expertise, or costs) (Kozlowski et al., 2020; van Ommen et al., 2014) and governance of RIs in Africa. To this end, Daniels et al. (2023, forthcoming) extend this definition, referring to RIs as "an aggregate of facilities, resources and services used by the scientific community in various disciplines to research the generation, preservation, application and dissemination of knowledge. Examples include (major) facilities—physical or virtual, equipment, sets of instruments, archives, databanks, collaborative networks and partnerships among the critical actors of the innovation system" ([see Zakaria et al., 2021, p. 4], which adopts the European Strategy Forum on Research Infrastructure (ESFRI)'s definition of RI, list other examples as "knowledge-based resources such as collections, archives, or structures for scientific information; enabling Information and Communications Technology-based infrastructures such as Grid, computing, software and communication, or any other entity of a unique nature essential to achieve excellence in research. Such infrastructures may be 'single-sited' or 'distributed'" [p. 4]). According to the authors, this definition underscores the importance of research and science ecosystems in African countries' contexts. In this paper, we adopt this definition in proposing the conceptual framework (see Section "The Concept of Research Infrastructures in Africa"), which helps address the gaps in definitions, categorization, and conceptual framings on RIs.

Related to these definitions, various categorizations (or classifications) of RIs have been advanced, as summarized in Table 4.1. More importantly, these definitions, categorizations, and the underpinning conceptual framings, which often are unsystematic and do not reflect the complexities in RIs, have shaped the ideas, narratives and discourses on RIs. Building on these definitions and varied and vague categorizations on the global scene, the concept of RIs is used to cover a myriad of both minor and major scientific equipment (such as Large Hadron Collider (LHC) at CERN) or sets of instruments, including telescopes or accelerators; knowledge-based resources such as collections, archives, or structures for scientific information, enabling ICT-based infrastructures such as grid and high-performance computing, software, and high-speed communication networks (also referred to as e-Infrastructures) among others (Hallonsten, 2020; PAERIP, 2019).

In the Second Action Plan of the Joint Africa-EU Strategy (JAES) (2011–2013), RIs were recognized as a priority focus for Africa-EU science and technology cooperation. In this regard, PAERIP was initiated from 2011 to 2013 to examine how Africa-EU RIs partnerships could be enhanced as part of the overall Africa-EU S&T partnership to advance sustainable development. PAERIP was coordinated by South Africa's Department of Science and Innovation (DSI) with part funding from the EC. They identified and assessed RIs available on the two continents, existing and potential collaboration and the related issues for research and partnerships (PAERIP, 2019). Although there were no scientific and technological outputs from the implementation of PAERIP, the project produced significant outcomes and important policy recommendations. These include:

- Research infrastructures should focus on bi-regional Africa-EU cooperation in science, technology, and innovation.

**Table 4.1** Examples of RIs definitions, categorizations, and conceptualizations

| | | |
|---|---|---|
| Definitions | "Facilities, resources, or services of a unique nature that European research communities have identified to conduct top-level activities in all fields | ESFRI (2011, 2018) |
| | Facilities, resources, and related systems of services which enable research communities to conduct their unique and top-level activities | ESFRI (2011), Wood et al. (2013), Hallonsten (2020), Ramoutar-Prieschl and Hachigonta (2020) and UKRI (n.d.) |
| | An aggregate of facilities, resources, and services used by the scientific community in various disciplines to conduct research for the generation, preservation, application, and dissemination of knowledge | Daniels et al. (2023, forthcoming) |
| Categorizations and conceptual framings: RIs can be... | Single-sited, distributed, or virtual" | ESFRI (2011, 2018), Hallonsten (2020) and UKRI (n.d.) |
| | Small equipment, departmental equipment, medium-sized infrastructure, or large-scale RI | DST (2016) |
| | Single-site, digital, and distributed RIs | Larsson (2017) and Larsson et al. (2018) |
| | Dedicated, public experimental, or public interest | Xu et al. (2017) |
| | "Mission-oriented and devoted to single disciplines, or multidisciplinary and open-ended" | Hallonsten (2020) |
| | According to the purpose and site (location): single-sited vs multiple-sited (distributed) and single-purpose vs multi purpose | Hallonsten (2020) |
| | According to functional types: Instrument, Observatory, Repository, or Vessel | Hallonsten (2020) |

(continued)

**Table 4.1** (continued)

| | | |
|---|---|---|
| | Classified according to thematic areas covering five scientific domains (i, Humans and society; ii, Health, biological, and food security; iii, Earth and environment; iv, Materials and manufacturing; and v, Energy [DST, 2016]); functionality and complexity (see Table 4.2) | Ramoutar-Prieschl and Hachigonta (2020) |
| | "Single-sited" or "distributed" | Zakaria et al. (2021) |
| | Physical or virtual | Daniels and Yalley (2025) |

*Source* Authors

- The emphasis on global partnerships as an essential component for developing research infrastructures; individual countries or regions cannot do it alone.
- Research infrastructures should be harnessed for scientific advancement and innovation on both continents (PAERIP, 2019).

Besides the European Commission, as discussed above in the Africa-EU partnership (PAERIP, 2019), the UK and other global actors are actively involved in prioritizing RI to promote innovation, enhance economic growth, and address the SDGs (UKRI, n.d.). In addition, a growing number of countries have established national frameworks for the prioritization of RIs. Such prioritization has helped budget allocation, allows for long-term financial commitment and improves political support for RIs (Toom & Miller, 2018). Long-term success on RIs is dependent on sustainable funding (López-Ballesteros et al., 2018) that is not constrained by changes in government research allocations due to economic hardships or short-termism of research investments (Atuahene, 2011; Zakaria et al., 2021).

**Table 4.2** Typology of RIs and functionality—the case of South Africa

| *Type of RI* | *Description* | *Examples* |
|---|---|---|
| 1. Research laboratory equipment | This is the minimum level of equipment and facilities that need to be in place as a necessary requirement for conducting basic research and training graduate students | Analytical NMR spectrometers; equipment for chromatography; and powder X-ray diffractometers |
| 2. Scientific equipment | Equipment enabling research tools that are fundamental for conducting competitive research and training the next generation of researchers. Scientific equipment refers to dedicated, immovable, free standing, large, networked, multi-user and multidisciplinary research equipment including all necessary ancillary components such as computers and specialized software, among others | A suite of mass spectrometers based at the Institute of Wine Biotechnology at the University of Stellenbosch in the Western Cape useful in understanding the biology of wine-associated organisms, ecology, physiology, molecular and cellular biology of grapevine, wine yeast/bacteria |
| 3. Specialized facilities | Dedicated research institutions that house large, unique, and highly specialized physical RIs that provide a controlled environment for ensuring the optimal performance of the research equipment as well as conducting highly specialized experiments | Specialized microscopy facilities, e.g. high-resolution microscopy; bio-repositories; radio-telescopes; research-focused forensic laboratories; biosafety, biohazard, and radiation containment facilities |
| 4. High-end infrastructure | Specialized platforms or laboratories that support (a) the transition from R&D to commercialization and (b) scalability and reproducibility of products and processes | Pilot plants, incubators, technology demonstrators and semi-commercial test facilities |

(continued)

**Table 4.2** (continued)

| *Type of RI* | *Description* | *Examples* |
|---|---|---|
| 5. Global Research Infrastructures | These are the critical enablers for advancing scientific knowledge, research outputs, and innovations, as well as accelerating the training and development of the next generation researchers; may be (i) "single-sited", that is, a single resource at a single location; (ii) "distributed" [a RI that is part of a network of distributed resources, such as ocean, earth, or seafloor observatories]; or (iii) "virtual" | The Large Hadron Collider (LHC), the Square Kilometre Array (SKA) project, Southern African Large Telescope (SALT) |
| 6. Cyber-infrastructure | These are ICT-based infrastructures comprising, among others (i) high-performance computing; (ii) broadband research networks; (iii) data storage and management systems; and (iv) grid and cloud computing infrastructures | The Centre for High-Performance Computing (CHPC), South African National Research Network (SANReN), the Data Intensive Research Initiative of South Africa (DIRISA) |

*Source* Based on Ramoutar-Prieschl and Hachigonta (2020) (also see DST, 2016)

## Research Methodology

This chapter is based on a review of academic journals (research articles, literature reviews, and opinion papers), books, and grey literature (reports, online sources, policies, and regulations). The grey literature reviewed included conference proceedings, organizational frameworks, and relevant research infrastructures in Africa. The literature search utilized controlled vocabulary and free-text terms combining components (inclusion criteria) such as "research infrastructure", "physical", and "virtual". The search strings were filtered with terms that include, for example, "government", "industry", "university", "practice", "policy", "impact", "funding", "management", and "sustainability". The online sources and databases search utilized Google Scholar, Science Direct, Scopus, and national and international websites. Figure 4.1 presents the literature search strategy.

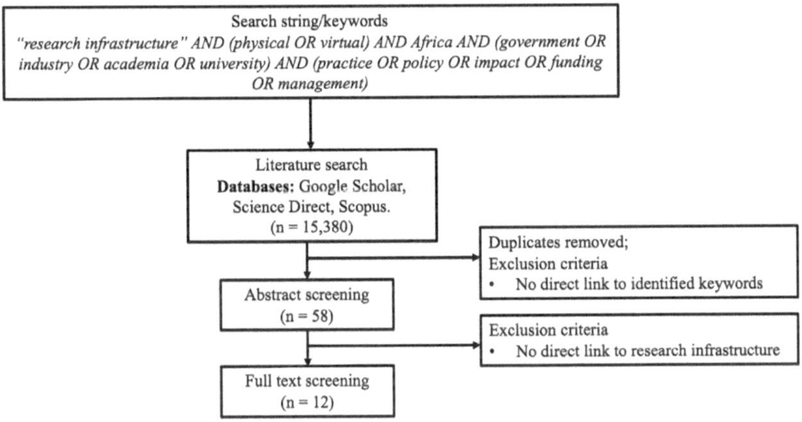


**Fig. 4.1** Flowchart illustrating the literature search process

The literature review was complemented by (a) online surveys, which helped to gather data on what respondents considered vital to identifying gaps, opportunities, and scope for strengthening RIs in Africa, and (b) five case studies on STEM African Centres of Excellence (CoEs) that were involved in the First Phase of the ACE Project. The survey covered 28 African countries and had 130 respondents. Combined, the survey and case studies provided rich insights that enhanced the robustness of the and the findings and conclusions reached.

Data analysis was guided by the National Systems of Innovation (NSI) (Freeman, 1987; Lundvall, 1992, 2010; Nelson, 1993) and Triple Helix (TH) (comprising of University, Industry and Government [U-I-G]) (Daniels et al., 2017; Etzkowitz, 1996; Jacob & Meek, 2013; Ranga & Etzkowitz, 2013; Sumberg, 2005) frameworks. Universities and industry actors are two major users of RIs as they utilize RIs to conduct research, generate knowledge, incubate technologies and innovation, support technology transfer, and foster entrepreneurship. These activities drive economic development (Daniels et al., 2021; Jacob & Meek, 2013; Twiringiyimana et al., 2021). University and industry actors are also key sources of human capital for scientific research. With RIs discussed in the context of education and innovation, these frameworks, therefore, are useful and relevant in the selection and analyses of the data. Alongside universities and industry as NSI stakeholders, government—through policies and regulations—also shapes and influences RIs in various ways, thereby making the government a third key actor in the research and STI ecosystems. The interactions, collaborations, and the strength of the linkages among these stakeholders determine to what extent research and innovation contribute to economic development and transformations as exemplified in Africa's Agenda 2063 and the sustainable development goals (SDGs) (AUC, 2014, 2015a, 2015b; Daniels, Byrne et al., 2020, 2021).

## The Concept of Research Infrastructures in Africa

RIs provide immense opportunities to train scientists and engineers while facilitating knowledge, technology transfer, and innovation, especially in HEIs. The efforts to ensure STI drives socioeconomic development must begin with establishing and redeploying robust RI in universities and other TH and NSI actors, focusing on science systems strengthening (Daniels & Gebhardt, 2021). The current definitions and framing of RIs in Africa have largely followed the ideas and conceptualizations by global actors, which considers RI as facilities, resources, and related services. There is a need to contextualize these ideas, definitions, and framings. And ensure that they are meaningful and relevant to African HEI ecosystems.

Any initiative to map RI in Africa needs careful conceptualization, planning, and execution to effectively address the key challenges and ensure a valuable exercise for the purposes intended. Such mapping can be informed by some of the works already done. For example, Brown et al. (2017) undertook mapping food and health research infrastructures in Europe. This study highlighted the challenging nature of identifying and classifying RIs as there appears to be no objective measure. With the increasing pace of technological advancement, RIs are dynamic and constantly developing (Brown et al., 2017). For the domain of the study, that is, food and health research, the highly multidisciplinary scientific nature brings additional complexities. Yet, there are opportunities for adaptability, flexibility, and innovation, especially as new demands for research emerge in various directions, including processes and products to address the global food and health challenges.

To address the challenges in identifying and classifying RIs, a study of RIs needs a well-formulated set of criteria to guide the process. Such a set of criteria is best determined with reference to the context of the study. However, the basic constitution of the RI is a fundamental criterion. For example, to qualify as an RI, a facility must be a built laboratory with the full complement of scientific equipment, network facilities, and the requisite utilities—water, electricity, and internet connection. A good team of human resources to ensure functionality is also a necessity. However, a number of questions arise, beginning with issues of limitation or scope and extending to standards/quality and scientific thematic focus. How large should the built laboratory be to qualify or be identified as an RI? What are the standards for the equipment in the laboratory?—A 1990 electron microscope versus a 2020 electron microscope brings out clearly the contrasts in sophistication and functionality.

Besides the age gap, other factors such as functionality, precision, and sophistication in delivery of the tasks matter. In terms of human resources, what level of staffing of the scientific workforce is acceptable? The total number of scientists and technicians in full employment or with part-timers and interns? Furthermore, context comes into play when utility supplies are considered—a 4G internet connection or 5G? What range of bibliographic databases should qualify the RI to be identified and classified? Clearly, for this study led by the AAU, an important precursor is the formulation of criteria to guide the identification and classification of the RIs. To help unpack these further, we explore different types of RIs, using the case of South Africa.

### *Types of Research Infrastructures*

RIs can be classified into six main types based on their functionality and complexity. Table 4.2 helps to illustrate the nature and diversity of RIs that are essential in building science systems and provides a basis for classifying RIs.

The efforts to promote RIs in Africa and create an enabling environment for their establishment, maintenance, and development have been ongoing at national, sub-regional, and international levels for some years. For example, in November 2013, an inception workshop on "Addressing Equipment Challenges in Development-related Scientific Research in Africa" was organized by the International Foundation for Science (IFS) and the African Academy of Sciences (AAS). The workshop followed a conference held in Nairobi in May 2012, titled "Getting and Using Equipment for Scientific Research in Africa". Country studies were conducted in Kenya, Ethiopia, and Ghana, leading to significant policy recommendations on scientific equipment for the consideration of African governments (Awuni & Essegbey, 2014; IFS, 2012, 2014).

The country studies highlighted the challenges and gaps in institutional arrangements and processes for acquiring, operating, maintaining, and developing scientific equipment. The findings revealed that the countries studied had built reasonably good S&T systems to facilitate national development. Nigeria, for example, has a science system composed of about 170 universities and research institutions at the Federal and State levels as well as a responsible Ministry for Science, Technology, and Innovation. Similar systems exist in the countries that the IFS and AAS partnered in the study of scientific equipment—Nigeria, Madagascar, Kenya, Ethiopia, and Ghana. In particular, the institutional frameworks for research and development (R&D) in these and other African countries have been established with a range of scientific equipment in their laboratories to undertake their required activities. However, the fundamental challenges, such as addressing the SDGs, which the R&D institutions are expected to impact significantly on, are still prevalent. It is not a lack of formulation of STI policies but a lack of effective implementation and governance of those policies (Essegbey et al., 2015).

The country case studies on scientific equipment highlighted that African science systems need additional equipment. The ecosystem for the proper functioning of these scientific equipment requires significant improvements. There were challenges surrounding the acquisition and use of scientific equipment. Thus, making it difficult to realize the dream of facilitating national development through the application of STI. To achieve the goals and objectives of the national development plan and realize socioeconomic development through science, various recommendations are advanced (see Section "RI in Practice: Policies, Regulations, Standards and Frameworks in Africa").

## RI in Practice: Policies, Regulations, Standards, and Frameworks in Africa

Several continents and countries have put in place policies, frameworks, and roadmaps and made other efforts (for example, establishing networks, institutions, and organizations on RIs, consortiums such as the European

Research Infrastructure Consortium (ERIC), or creating expert groups such as Senior Officials on Global RIs) to strengthen their RIs. ESFRI (2011, 2018) provides an example of roadmaps in Europe, while the South Africa Roadmap on RIs (DST, 2016) provides an example from Africa. In the remainder of this section, we unpack RIs in practice, focusing on Africa's policies, regulations, standards, and frameworks.

### *The Continental STI Policy Regime*

At the continental level, one may go back in history to the efforts at committing African nations to concrete STI-focused programmes and initiatives to enhance socioeconomic development. For example, there was the Lagos Plan of Action of 1980 and the Consolidated Plan of Action of 2003 signed in Maputo. These were among the efforts to bring STI-focus into economic development planning. Although these policies have been typified by weakness, providing a policy framework is essential to harnessing and applying research and STI in national and regional development efforts.

CESA 16-25 and STISA 2024 are the African continental policies with the primary goals of facilitating the achievement of the AU 2063 Agenda through education and STI, respectively. In terms of STISA 2024, there are six key areas giving policy directions to the AU member countries, including eradicating hunger and achieving food security, preventing and controlling diseases, and living together by building the society and creating wealth. STISA 2024 is further anchored on four main pillars, namely, (i) building and upgrading research infrastructures, (ii) enhancing professional and technical competencies, (iii) promoting entrepreneurship, and (iv) providing an enabling environment for STI development. It is important to state the mission of STISA 2024, to "Accelerate Africa's transition to an innovation-led and knowledge-based economy". Therefore, STISA 2024 provides the framework for analyzing the building and operations of science systems and the formulation and implementation of STI policies in the African countries. To deepen the discussions in this section, we shift attention to policies, regulations, strategies, and frameworks at the level of AU Regional Economic Communities (RECs), starting with West Africa.

## West Africa: ECOWAS, *ECOPOST*

The same recognition of STI policy relevance is manifested at the African sub-regional level. For example, in West Africa, the ECOWAS Commission adopted in 2012 the ECOWAS Policy on Science, Technology, and Innovation (ECOPOST), which provides a framework for the member countries to elaborate their policies and programmes on STI. ECOPOST encourages member countries to, among other objectives, increase their Gross Expenditure on Research and Development (GERD) to at least 1% (which is in consonance with the continental strategies), create a national fund for STI to enable researchers to work on research priorities of the country, equip research laboratories including with ICTs, facilitate the dissemination of modern information technology infrastructure to facilitate teaching, training, and research and promote collaboration (for more discussions on the importance of research collaboration, see, for example, (Park et al., 2021) between the knowledge institutions and industry in the country.

ECOPOST responds to the expectations of a region aspiring to advance beyond the developing country status. It addresses development challenges in the key sectors of agriculture, health, environment, and education. To achieve the aims and objectives of ECOPOST, the ECOWAS Commission also developed a 10-point strategic action plan, which came into effect in 2013. The actions include strengthening the (a) institutional framework for the development of STI policy and associated action plans, (b) scientific and technological institutions financial capacity, and (c) human and technical capacity in S&T. Others are (d) development and transfer of technology, (e) popularization of research results, (f) promotion of scientific and technological culture, local knowledge, and intellectual property protection, (g) involvement of the private sector for S&T development, (h) development of environment conducive for scientific and technological research creativity, (i) regional and international cooperation, (j) data management and indicators elaboration and promotion, and (k) mainstreaming of S&T in sectorial policies to meet basic human needs.

However, the key issue is implementation and the commitment of resources to conduct the relevant activities to attain the goals and objectives stated in ECOPOST. Implementation has not materialized as expected. At the level of the member countries, greater effort could be made given that implementation is about decision-making around resource allocation in alignment with national priorities and policy agenda. What is encouraging is the extent to which member countries have established ministries to oversee the portfolio of STI.

### *National STI Policy and Institutional Frameworks*

Nigeria stands out in respect of defining an institutional framework for STI policy formulation, implementation, monitoring, and evaluation. There is a sole ministry for STI. Other countries have a ministry for STI either in combination with environment or education. The Nigerian STI policy was formulated and approved in 2012 by the Federal government to transform the country's socioeconomic and technological circumstances. The establishment of the National Research and Innovation Council (NRIC) is one of the essential implementation actions carried out in relation to the STI policy. The NRIC sets R&D priorities, coordinates STI activities, and facilitates fund-raising to support innovative activities. The policy also outlines Nigeria's commitment to at least 1% of GDP to R&D through the establishment of the National Research and Innovation Fund (NRIF). However, the goal of attaining 1% of GDP is yet to be realized as currently, the GERD of Nigeria is about 0.22% (Essegbey et al., 2021).

In addition to oversight functions, various ECOWAS member countries have formulated specific STI policies or plans. For example, Benin formulated the Higher Education and Scientific Research Development Plan (2013–2017), which was adopted in 2014. The plan projects the vision that by 2025, Benin would have a sub-sector of Higher Education and Scientific Research, which provides qualified human resources and research results adapted to national development problems (Essegbey et al., 2021). Similarly, Burkina Faso has formulated the National Scientific and Technological Research Policy (2013–2025) that highlights priority areas for research and the aims of linking research to industry. Senegal does not have an explicit STI policy, but has adopted the "Plan Senegal Émergent" (PSE), which provides the framework for economic and social development by 2035. This plan is based on three pillars, namely (1) the structural transformation of the economy; (2) the promotion of human capital; and (3) good governance. Even though there are no specific STI-focused policies, Senegal is implementing STI-related programmes under the PSE. For example, significant investment is dedicated to acquiring laboratory equipment, a super intensive parallel computer, and the construction of the City of Knowledge to promote scientific culture (Essegbey et al., 2021).

Liberia has an interesting example in STI policy formulation. The Ministry of Posts and Telecommunication has formulated the National ICT Policy (2018–2023) to define the policy goals, objectives, and essential strategies to boost ICT applications and digitalization in the country. Given that the primary focus is ICT, it is not the conventional STI policy. However, Liberia has established the Liberia Innovation Fund for Entrepreneurship (LIFE), which became operational in 2015. It is one of the key programmes initiated to foster innovation and entrepreneurship in the country. LIFE is interesting as it gives impetus for innovators and entrepreneurs to contribute to socioeconomic development. However, the strategies for research and defining the institutional arrangement for driving research are important, and this must be better amplified in LIFE (Essegbey et al., 2021).

## North Africa

The North African region also shows strong efforts in building research infrastructures for the respective countries. For example, Egypt being an agricultural country, one of its leading research establishments is the Agricultural Research Center (ARC), which operates under the Egyptian Ministry of Agriculture and Land Reclamation auspices. The ARC serves as the research and development arm of the ministry and focuses on conducting applied research to produce technologies and innovations for increased productivity in the agricultural sector. The ARC also facilitates technology dissemination and adoption, drawing on government extension services to get technology to farmers, monitoring end users' adoption, and continuously developing human capital (see https://www.worldfishcenter.org/agricultural-research-center-egypt). The ARC contributes to the development of new crop varieties for farmers, improved agronomic practices and better food processing techniques. The research work by the ARC cuts across the agricultural value chain.

In Egypt, RIs are, however, spread in the universities and the research centres. For example, the American University in Cairo has established the Science and Technology Research Centre, which conducts a variety of nanoscience- and technology-oriented projects. Research activities are centred on generic imaging, analysis and fabrication equipment, and nanomaterials characterization and design and fabrication of micro-opto-electromechanical systems (see https://www.aucegypt.edu/research/research-centers). In addition, the Center of Nanoelectronics and Devices (CND) in Egypt has the goal to create an environment in which the electronics industry can thrive in the region. The ambitious vision is to become an internationally leading education and research centre supporting the growth of the electronics and devices industry in the region (see https://sse.aucegypt.edu/centers/CND). Thus, there is a diversity of research establishment for different sectors, including agriculture, industry, health, and the environment. Furthermore, Egypt seeks to develop nuclear research capabilities for other areas besides defence applications.

Egypt's Atomic Energy Authority (AEA) is one of its leading research establishments with nuclear research infrastructures. The Nuclear Threat Initiative (NTI), a non-profit organization committed to peaceful nuclear research, presents Egypt as having potential for peaceful nuclear research. NTI envisages nuclear research contributing to global biosecurity in terms of developing new outcomes to prevent catastrophic outcomes by instituting systems for bio-surveillance and pandemic forecasting (see https://www.nti.org/about/biosecurity/). The NTI programme hosts research focused on eliminating Cesium 137 blood irradiators, one of the most lethal sources of radiological materials. Although used widely in biomedical research and treatment, Cesium 137 blood irradiators still pose a threat on account of the potential of this isotope in producing "dirty" bombs (Iliopulos & Boyd, 2019).

Egypt has the capability to contribute to nuclear medical health research. Other North African countries have their research agendas with the required RIs and operate under prescribed government ministries. In Algeria, the Ministry of Higher Education and Scientific Research (MHESR) oversees research establishments that include 50 universities, 20 university centres, and ten research institutes. Morocco's University of Al-Karaouine is considered the oldest continuously operating academic degree-awarding institution in the world. The MHESR coordinates research in the Kingdom. In addition, the ministry implements the Moroccan Innovation Strategy and supports research in advanced technologies and the development of smart cities in Frez, Rabat and Marrakesh.

### *The South African Policy Dynamism*

The Southern African region illustrates how STI policy formulation and implementation have contributed to the present science systems, with South Africa representing a good example of the dynamism in the region. In 1996, South Africa formulated the White Paper on Science and Technology with a focus on three pillars of investment: (i) innovation; (ii) science, engineering, and technology, emphasizing human capital development and transformation; and (iii) creating an effective national science and technology system.

The progression in STI policy formulation in South Africa was the National R&D Strategy for South Africa published in 2002. It elaborated on key recommendations including the importance of scientific instrumentation in advancing research, economic growth, and human capital development. The strategy's priorities include the importance of modern, well-maintained equipment as a pre-requisite for high-quality research. Emphasis is on the considerable economic impact of equipment, particularly in the manufacturing sector, and in the educational sector for nurturing curiosity-driven research. Furthermore, the strategy recognizes value in developing requisite skills for undertaking world-class research and supporting the advancement of modern industry (DST, 2002).

In 2010 South Africa produced another relevant policy—the Research, Development, and Innovation Infrastructure Funding Framework. The focus on funding is exemplary as funding is one of the key ingredients usually missing in STI policy implementation. The framework identified five investment areas namely: (i) scientific equipment; (ii) high-end infrastructure; (iii) specialized facilities; (iv) access to global infrastructures; and (v) cyber-infrastructure. The last two investment areas—access to global infrastructure and cyber-infrastructure—are pre-requisites for participation in global science, enabling South Africa's participation in cutting-edge scientific research projects such as the SKA (Ramoutar-Prieschl & Hachigonta, 2020).

In 2016, South Africa launched the South Africa Research Infrastructure Roadmap (SARIR). SARIR provides a framework for delivering RIs necessary for a sustainable NSI. This roadmap articulates the commitment of the South African government to RI development in the country. The investment in SARIR reflects a deep understanding of the importance of RI as a critical enabler for undertaking excellent research (Chataway & Daniels, 2020). The roadmap identifies 13 potential investment areas of interest in RI, classified according to thematic areas (Ramoutar-Prieschl & Hachigonta, 2020). Clearly, the dynamism of the R&D and STI policy cycle has impacted the strength of the South African science system. The White Paper (WP) on STI, developed in 2019, spells out the long-term policy approach of the STI sector. The WP on STI emphasizes the core themes of (i) inclusivity (ii) transformation, and (iii) partnerships. In addition, the WP expands the investment in RIs, cyber-infrastructure and access to global research facilities (Ramoutar-Prieschl & Hachigonta, 2020). This helps to illustrate the commitment to research and STI for national development.

*Illustration at National Level: Using South Africa*
In South Africa, RIs for STI are organized at three levels: "(i) government and policy level; (ii) the funding agency level; and (iii) the implementation level, at research-performing institutions" (Ramoutar-Prieschl & Hachigonta, 2020, p. 5). RIs for STI in South Africa's HEIs are characterized by unequal funding; skewed demographic profile of students and staff. Academic staff are inadequately skilled or trained to lead research projects and/or supervise postgraduates. Institutional histories compounded by varying levels of support from industry as well as regional and local communities surrounding universities, and varying impacts of the evolving social discourses and national policy priorities all contribute to the inequality (Ramoutar-Prieschl & Hachigonta, 2020, p. 11). Efforts to rebalance the ecosystem must adopt a systems of innovation approach that considers gaps across multiple sectors, systems, and societies.

## RIs: Enhancing the Resilience of Science Systems for Development Impact

As discussed in preceding sections, research infrastructures are fundamental to excellence in research (Chataway & Daniels, 2020; Daniels, Byrne et al., 2020; Kraemer-Mbula et al., 2020; Tijssen & Kraemer-Mbula, 2018) and innovation, which in turn support economic growth, sustainable development, and transformative change (Daniels, Schot et al., 2020; Schot & Steinmueller, 2018). Given the importance of RIs, strengthening RIs in Africa can enhance the resilience of the science systems and lead to development impact in multiple dimensions: it can improve opportunities for greater impact from research and science systems, enhance collaboration in research (Jacob & Meek, 2013; Sumberg, 2005), increase research capacity and outputs (Teferra & Altbach, 2004), contribute to governance (Ryan, 2015) and improve the prospects of sustainability and resilience in ways that support long-term socioeconomic development.

In addition, RIs can help foster transformative change, that is, achieving economic progress alongside addressing social and environmental challenges (López-Ballesteros et al., 2018). In the modern world of research, science, and innovation, RIs are essential for human resource development, training and capacity building, mobility in the sciences, technology transfer, and knowledge circulation (Jacob & Meek, 2013). RIs that enable high-quality research, teaching, and learning in HEIs is essential to strengthening science systems across the continent and achieving the continental Agenda 2063 and the SDGs. Excellence in research and science is crucial if Africa is to realize its transformation aspirations. As COVID-19 has shown, world-class research and strong science systems provided the basis for the development of vaccines by countries like the UK (involving HEIs such as the University of Oxford, University College London, and industry actors). Progress in these areas was made possible by the advanced levels of RIs—physical and virtual, human resources, funding, policies and regulations, and enabling ecosystem. Furthermore, the many opportunities that science and technology, entrepreneurship, innovation and the commercialization of technologies (Daniels & Amadi-Echendu, 2021) and digitalization present to Africa may not be realized in the absence of excellent research and science systems facilitated by robust infrastructures.

There are various ways the existing infrastructure foster research in HEIs, innovation and capability and competence building, research collaboration, and technology transfer. Nevertheless, gaps in RIs across HEIs in Africa continue to hinder HEI research, innovation, and capability/competence building; research collaboration and technology transfer; exacerbate brain drain (good scientists leaving Africa to other continents with better RIs); and contribute to low involvement in STEM disciplines which do not meet market demand. Beyond funding, other challenges contribute to limiting Africa's research output. Research priorities in Africa have generally focused on health sciences, social sciences, agriculture, education and engineering, and however health research has dominated the research system in the past ten years. The majority of the research has focused on malaria, HIV/AIDS and maternal health and this, to a large extent, is influenced by the high degree of infectious diseases on the continent. This dominant research focus on health, in part, reflects the interests of funders such as Bill and Melinda Gates Foundation whose funding objectives go more into health research. In terms of research relevance, past studies have demonstrated a misalignment between research in HEIs and national agendas.

Despite these challenges and gaps in RIs across Africa's HEIs, strengthening RIs in Africa can foster transformations that transcend sectors, systems, and societies; enhance opportunities; contribute to governance; and improve the prospects of sustainability and resilience. To realize this potential, it is essential that gaps in physical and virtual research infrastructure, especially data and high-end computing facilities, poor digital skills among African academics and paywalls behind journal articles that restrict access to information are urgently addressed.

With respect to the role of data and e-infrastructure, using the Energy Sector as the illustrative case, "two-thirds of energy infrastructures report a 'significant e-infrastructure/data require mentor component'. E-infrastructure is seen as necessary by the sector to address the challenges of capturing data, undertaking complex modelling and the simulation of various subsectors / subsystems to ultimately simulate the entire energy system. E-infrastructure is needed for applied solutions to real sector issues, such as the real-time monitoring of remote facilities (e.g. wind farms) which is valuable for performance checks, early detection of faults and errors and ensuring the system's security is intact. Three-quarters of energy infrastructures consider that e-infrastructure and data will become more relevant over five to ten years. In the energy sector, data are a particularly valuable resource that can inform models, improve accuracy of forecasting and cost optimization, inform policy interventions, and help businesses develop. Data comes in many forms, such as individual user data, weather data for prediction of peaks and troughs in electricity production, systems performance and control data needed for maintaining grid stability and market data for ensuring optimum efficiency for suppliers and consumers. Researchers, businesses, and aggregators must have sufficient access to data to enable informed decisions. Hence, data are a valuable asset and are legally protected both as company property and the property of the individual customer" (UKRI, n.d., p. 95).

### *Opportunities for Greater Impact from RIs*

RIs can contribute to transformation in many ways and result in positive impacts at the system, national, regional, and continental levels. Areas of opportunities where VRIs can contribute to development include computing and communications, health, pharmaceuticals, agriculture, energy, policies, and regulations (UKRI, n.d.). Examples to help contextualize opportunities for RIs contribution to socioeconomic activities and development include:

- Enhancing collaboration, joint research projects and sharing of good practices.
- Boosting Africa's research outputs, publications, citations, patents and innovations.
- Improving linkages and interactive learning among researchers, and the wider NSI ecosystem actors and stakeholders. Strong university-industry linkages are vital for innovation, entrepreneurship and socioeconomic development (Assefa, 2016; Daniels & Gebhardt, 2021; Daniels et al., 2021).
- Foster knowledge sharing, peer learning or group work and networking that improves the prospects of idea generation and circulation that are essential to new projects and product development, conceptualization (of research, science and innovation projects and programmes) and funding applications.

To help realize these opportunities, specific challenges, particularly in relation to digital/virtual RIs will need to be addressed. These include, addressing gaps in:

- Low broadband and internet speed issues (Daniels et al., 2022).
- Absence of common standards and approaches to e-learning in Africa's HEIs.
- Access to mobile data access and connectivity (Faraj, 2020). For instance, some students are forced to access broadband services late at night or during off-peak hours. Others live in areas where connectivity is sporadic or inaccessible due to cost issues, while a third group does not have internet access.

- Energy (electricity) access and reliability: often, HEIs (staff and students) struggle to access consistent and reliable electricity to power their devices.
- Low internet penetration rates. COVID-19 pandemic has been a stark reminder that Africa's internet penetration is still under 40%, well below the global average. COVID-19 has highlighted the need to move towards technology for blended learning. Universities are expected to deploy management systems that house learning materials. This ensures that students can submit their assignments via digital platforms. This poses a challenge due to poor digital infrastructure.
- Systemic infrastructural and funding issues have meant that universities across sub-Saharan Africa have been slow to meet demand in Science, Technology, Engineering and Maths (STEM)-related fields (Akuru, 2019). The survey results on the impact of COVID 19 on researchers in Africa suggest a fractured system exacerbated by a global pandemic. While 83% of respondents reported experiencing disruption to their ongoing learning, 39% said they enrolled in institutions offering e-learning options. 17% of West African respondents reported being at institutions with e-learning options, compared to 43% of East African respondents and 41% of respondents in Southern Africa.
- Skilled e-learning practitioners and lecturers that are skilled in the use of ICT. This is a major barrier to the successful integration of e-learning and ICT infrastructure in Africa's HEIs.

### *Governance of RIs*

The good governance of RIs is important for the following reasons. RIs contribute to research and innovation that support many economic sectors—from public policies, health, energy and manufacturing to agriculture, computing, aerospace and transportation (UKRI, n.d.). In addition, RIs are needed in all fields of science, and no single institution can provide all her RIs. Nations need to have quality RIs that are open to all and ensure that such RIs adheres to the principles of good governance. This helps to improve the attractiveness of RIs to researchers and funders from other countries (DST, 2016, p. 7).

Good governance of RIs is essential to strengthening relevant ecosystems. Harnessing the opportunities outlined above requires effective governance frameworks and mechanisms. In strengthening RIs, careful attention must be paid to the appropriate ecosystems, for example, HEIs. A key part of strengthening the ecosystem is improving governance—to help address weaknesses in coordination, collaboration, accountability, and quality controls. Investments in RIs must target ecosystem building in ways that enhance collaboration. An investment in RIs ecosystem strengthening is an investment in generating evidence and not simply upgrading scientists' careers, which by itself is important.

Strong financial, technical, and human resources rationales provide justifications for collaboration between universities in Africa. While good examples of cooperation exist, the arrangements for cooperation are frequently ad-hoc. Opportunities for more systematic cooperation arrangements need to be supported by regional networks and intermediary organizations. If effectively harnessed, opportunities for collaboration among universities in Africa can help build the region's collective capacity for higher education. Reasons for collaboration include engaging in joint research, peer learning on organizational and transformation processes, learning about degree programmes, developing joint degree programmes or courses, students and faculty exchanges, and capacity building.

One of the major challenges for STI to thrive in Africa is the condition of the ecosystem within which scientific and technological activities are carried out. Fundamentally, conditions must be supportive of these activities especially from the economic and commercial perspectives. For example, venture capital must enable technology companies to overcome market entry challenges and take roots. Where these companies are linked to the institutions with robust RIs, they contribute to the sustainability and growth of the STI institutions. There are only a few venture capital enterprises on the continent with substantial resources to support start-ups to take root in the marketplace, and most of them are not indigenous. A review of the top ten prominent venture capitalists on the continent shows that their operations support business ventures in various areas, including agriculture, telecommunications, e-business and industry. They operate in several countries such as South Africa, Ghana, Nigeria, Kenya, and Mauritius. However, their investments are yet to directly buttress operations of the excellent RIs; and this needs addressing.

Linked to ecosystem enhancement is the operation of technology and innovation hubs and centres (Dosso et al., 2021; Martins et al., 2021). Currently, these hubs and centres are opening up and operating in several African countries. What remains to be seen is the strong linkages to the knowledge institutions—the universities and research institutions—with excellent RIs. Knowledge institutions, such as universities, generally have established their technology transfer centres. However, where private sector technology hubs are operating and connecting with the knowledge institutions, they provide a more entrepreneurial approach to commercialization of locally developed technologies, which must be encouraged.

### *Sustainability and Resilience*

Research infrastructures are long-term investments; hence sustainability of research infrastructure is of utmost importance. For sustainability, stable financial support and a long-term investment plan are required (López-Ballesteros et al., 2018; Zakaria et al., 2021). African countries with thriving research infrastructure rely on funds from the national government and international donors (Vicente-Crespo et al., 2020). However, with funds from international donors accounting for a large share of the R&D and STI funding portfolio, this raises sustainability issues with implications for the long-term resilience of the research and science systems.

STISA-2024 highlights how African countries can sustainably finance their STI programmes, including building or strengthening research infrastructures. If implemented, the AU recommendation to invest 1% of GDP on R&D can amount to substantial financial resources to support the development of RIs. For example, with total GDP of Nigeria being 52 billion USD; 1% of GDP is 5.2 billion USD. For Egypt, the 1% of GDP is 2.46 billion USD and for Angola it is 1.23 billion USD (AUC, 2014, p. 43). These are substantial financial resources that could contribute to improving RIs on the continent. The AU and various African countries must implement the recommendation to commit 1% of their GDP to R&D.

### *Conceptualizing Research Infrastructure*

Earlier in this paper, we discussed some of the gaps in RIs in Africa, covered definitions, categorizations and conceptual approaches. We also provided detailed discussions on the role of policies, demonstrating why policies and appropriate transformative innovation policy. Daniels and Dosso (2021) interventions are needed to address the current gaps and ensure that RIs are redirected towards a sustainable development pathway. The pivotal role of agricultural research as a vehicle for sustainable economic growth in Africa is discussed by Sumberg (2005) in particular, the evolving architecture of agricultural research in Africa. Sumberg (2005), highlights core issues that need to be addressed, including the conceptualization of RI at national level which does not reflect the realities of the state of agricultural research. According to Sumberg (2005), policy changes played a major role in the decline in agricultural research in Africa in the past two decades, contributing to the radical reforms in the role of government (through structural adjustment programmes, transforming independent research centres into national research centres and broadening funding base, and downsizing in staff strength) and changes in research priorities and approaches (to focus more on poverty reduction programmes rather than productivity). With the current challenge of low agricultural productivity, exacerbated by climate change and water scarcity in Africa, RIs that support cutting-edge research and science systems across the continent is vital to addressing this challenge.

In line with the arguments by Sumberg (2005) and other scholars, like Hallonsten (2020), we argue that a first and key step, is to develop a Conceptual Framework for Mapping RIs in Africa (see Fig. 4.2a,b). In particular, this should start with RIs in HEIs. Such a conceptual framework will help the continent to (a) improve clarity on what is meant by RIs in the context of Africa, (b) determine what RIs are currently in place in relevant organizations, (c) assess the status and functionality of RIs—including factors such as availability, accessibility, usability, interoperability, resolution, format, and quality (for more discussion on these see for example, López-Ballesteros et al. [2018]), (d) group RIs into single-sited vs multiple-sited, and single-purpose vs multiple-purpose categories, (e) understand how RIs maybe be shared (co-utilized) and co-funded among multiple institutions, government or other NSI actors and (f) aspects where physical RIs hinder virtual RIs. The insights gained from mapping RIs in Africa, using the framework proposed in this chapter, will contribute to the development of appropriate innovation and STI policies.

As discussed in the preceding sections, although the concept of RIs has been used in most policy discourse and academic literature, what

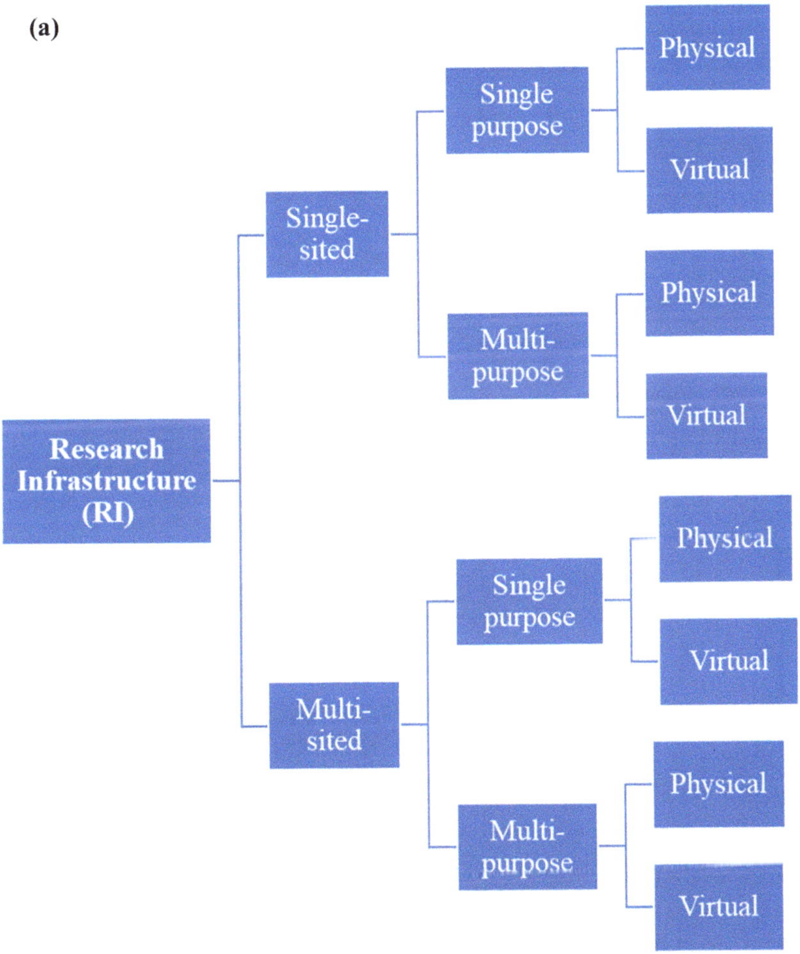


**Fig. 4.2** **a, b** Conceptual framework for mapping RIs in Africa. *Note* Texts highlighted in yellow are particularly relevant to Africa (*Source* Authors)

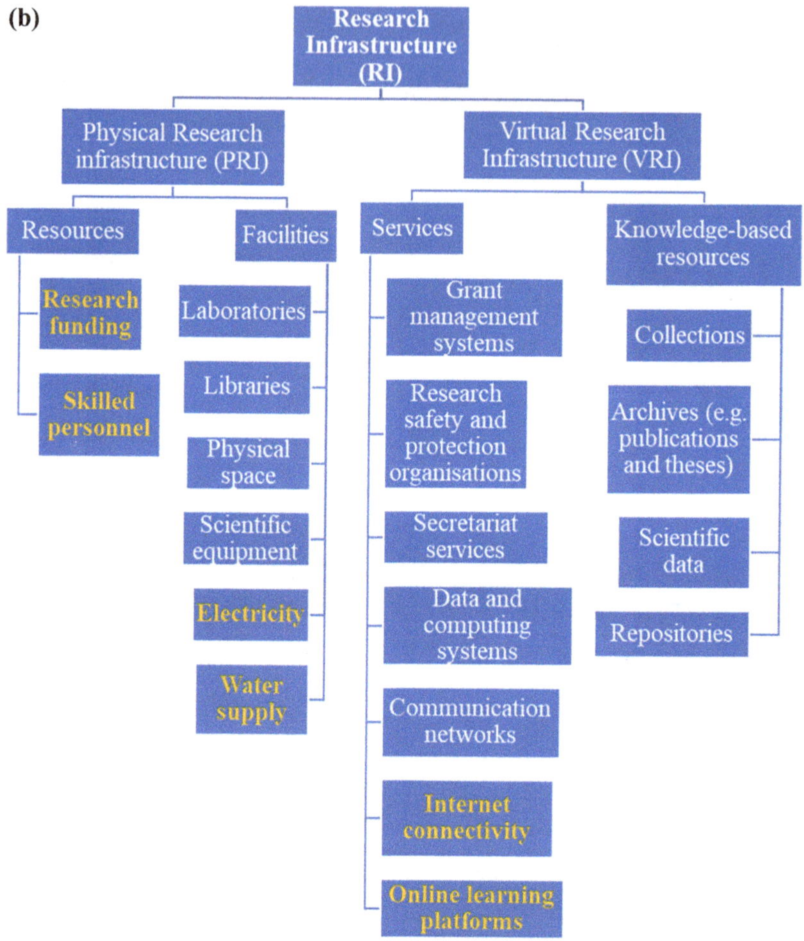


**Fig. 4.2** (continued)

constitutes RIs and how the concept is defined, categorized, and conceptualized requires further empirical research to deepen our understanding. Figure 4.2a,b are an attempt to conceptualize the concept of RIs to provide greater clarity on the categories and help to map (conduct inventories of) RIs. Mapping is useful for systematizing RIs, and essential to capturing key information that supports the evaluation of impacts from

RIs. In addition, mapping of RIs can underpin the management and development of governance and funding mechanisms and help establish sustainability measures and strengthen research, science, and innovation systems across Africa. Figure 4.2a is the basic framework while Fig. 4.2b highlights aspects particularly relevant to RIs in Africa.

The Frameworks proposed above has been designed to be used by all NSI actors—including universities, governments, private sector, research think-tanks, and civil society organizations—and in various organizational and country contexts. We believe the framework proposed can help improve functionality while reducing the complexity surrounding it. The framework enriches our knowledge and understanding of what constitutes RIs and what "RIs" mean.

## Conclusion: Policy Directions for RIs in Africa

### *The Policy Environment for RIs in Africa*

Policy is a crucial instrument for achieving developmental goals. African countries have developed Education and STI policies at the sub-regional, continental levels to strengthen education, research, and the STI environment. The Continental Education Strategy for Africa (CESA 16-25), for example, notes that the quality and relevance of university education have emerged as serious concerns of the sector for some time now. Furthermore, postgraduate education remains underdeveloped, and its contribution to research and innovation remains minuscule (AUC, 2016, p. 19). Although CESA appears to focus on schools rather than HEIs, the current continental policy, Science, Technology, and Innovation Strategy for Africa 2024 (STISA 2024), is a culmination of African countries' STI policy aspirations that emphasize HEIs. This is in line with harnessing STI to achieve an Africa based on the knowledge economy. The realization of this goal must be underpinned by research and STI, both of which require adequate RIs. The policy concerns of various African countries and the extent to which they can build resilient science systems depend largely on their RIs.

Discussing RIs policy is given dedicated emphasis as it is vital to guiding future development, funding, and influence on PE considerations, including institutions, structures, ideas, narratives, and actors' interests. By adopting this approach, we hope to highlight the importance of policies, regulations, strategies, or frameworks—at continental, regional, national levels, and organizations (for example, universities)—in redressing the gaps in RIs in Africa. In line with the NSI and TH frameworks, we emphasize that industry and other actors also have important roles in the advancements needed in strengthening RIs to enhance the resilience of science systems in Africa. Aspects, where industry and others can play key roles include funding, sharing, management and governance of RIs.

As the discussions on CESA 16-25 show, there is now increased recognition, at high policy levels, of the importance of RIs in achieving Africa's socioeconomic development objectives. This improved awareness and recognition are essential to strengthening and prioritizing the development of RIs across the continent. Nevertheless, it is far from clear how best to formulate, implement, evaluate and govern policies, strategies and frameworks on research infrastructures at regional and continental levels to ensure mutually reinforcing and complementary benefits for countries in Africa.

In the preceding discussions, we noted that policy frameworks on research and development had witnessed some change in recent years. These changes are linked to establishing new bodies to manage and fund research or policy frameworks that mandate investment in capacity. Some of the key policy frameworks include national STI policies by various governments and the creation of ministries of S&T or STI, such as the Ethiopian Ministry of Science and Technology (2013). Other changes include the development of Strategies, for example, by the Kenyan government (2010), the Emerging Senegal Plan (2014), the South African Research Infrastructure Roadmap (SARIR, 2016), and others.

The significant concepts of internationalization (Jacob & Meek, 2013), research relevance to socioeconomic needs, and human capacity building are core concerns in national research agendas across Africa. These issues are similar, for instance, when compared with the German Research Infrastructure (GRI) roadmap. However, unlike the GRI roadmap, which follows EU Roadmap, RIs in African countries are more fragmented and do not necessarily follow the African Union STISA 2024. Further developments of STI in Africa require upgrading RIs and establishing world-class STI infrastructure. This includes research and innovation facilities such as laboratories (for teaching, engineering and clinical trials), teaching hospitals, ICT equipment and infrastructure, Innovation Spaces, Living Labs and NRENs.

Existing physical and digital infrastructure and resources must be leveraged and networked to increase utilization efficiency at a national and regional level and reduction in maintenance and operating costs through shared services. NRENs will facilitate coordinated collaboration by education and research institutions and with Innovation Spaces and Living Labs, thus strengthening both the overall Research and Innovation Ecosystems and the scale and quality of training and support available to entrepreneurs and other innovators (AUC, 2014). The important point is made about the continent producing its scientific equipment.

At the continental level, establishing the African Observatory for Science, Technology and Innovation (AOSTI) in Malabo was intended to provide a robust framework for monitoring and evaluating Africa's STI. Efforts at implementing programmes to this effect include the ASTII Survey conducted in two phases—2007–2010 as phase I and 2010–2014 as phase II. This, however, proved unsustainable as international donors funded the pilot, and the member countries could not fully fund the subsequent surveys. Africa needs to take the fate of its RI, research, and STI seriously and begin to invest in the entire policy cycle, formulation, implementation, monitoring and evaluation, and governance to realize the dream of driving on the wheels of STI to socioeconomic advancement.

In concluding this section, we provide recommendations to help guide the formulation, implementation, evaluation, and governance of new policies and practices, as they relate to research infrastructure definitions, categorization, conceptualization, management, governance, and sustainability in Africa, with implications for practice in academia, industry, and development partners.

## *Recommendations*

Recommendations to African governments, higher education institutions, industry (private sector), development partners, and donors are outlined below.

### *Recommendations to African Governments*

i. Formulate criteria to guide the categorization of RIs in Africa, using the proposed conceptual framework, considering Africa's peculiarities rather than adopting a westernized framework that might not address its unique challenges.

ii. Develop RI roadmaps and investment plans to guide progress in RI at national, regional and continental levels. Also, to increase education, research, and R&D funding, starting with the agreed 1% GERD and 4% investment in education.
iii. Foster networking and collaboration among (a) faculty and students in HEIs in Africa, (b) among HEIs within and outside Africa, and (c) between HEIs and the private sector, thereby promoting innovation. It would be necessary to address governance challenges—coordination, collaboration, and accountability and structural barriers that disincentivize interactions, co-creation, and co-learning among HEIs. Also, avenues to improve the contributions of the African Diaspora in RIs development, management, and governance should be actively explored.
iv. Work with HEIs and innovation ecosystems actors and stakeholders to close the gaps in research infrastructure, particularly in virtual infrastructure (starting with data, broadband and internet connectivity, costs, reliability, and access). It is also crucial to improve stakeholders' knowledge of the political and economic factors that influence the sharing of research infrastructure funding, human resources development, policies and regulations, and related factors.
v. Address the gaps in implementing current policies that relate to HEIs and innovation; in doing so, emphasize the centrality of RIs. Where applicable, revise/update current policies and deepen understanding of underlying issues that hinder RIs in HEIs across Africa.
vi. Examine the (dis)incentives for private sector actors to engage in research infrastructure development, management, and governance. For example, the use of policy instruments such as R&D tax credits or avenues to enhance co-purchasing, colocation, co-hosting, and sharing facilities between industry and HEIs.

*Recommendations to HEIs*

i. Formulate and implement RI roadmaps and plans for mapping RIs, and the development and maintenance of RIs across HEIs in Africa. Mapping should focus on functional RIs especially, but also knowledge of non-functional ones, and why this is the case, is important for implementing effective RI development and management strategies.

ii. Initiate, under the auspices of relevant university governing bodies (such as, Ghana Tertiary Education Commission, in Ghana or National Universities Commission [NUC], in Nigeria), inter-institutional RIs that are shared and jointly used among neighbouring HEIs. This is vital in cases of high-end and expensive RIs. And establish adequate institutional arrangements to ensure effective governance, implementation, and M&E of RIs roadmaps and plans in HEIs.
iii. Create internal funding sources and mechanisms for RIs development and maintenance within individual HEIs at regional and national levels.
iv. Develop a long-term strategy for enhancing competence and knowledge of academic and other relevant staff in educational technologies and virtual applications.
v. Address the "ivory tower" mentality in academia that hinders effective collaboration with industry and other RI and innovation ecosystems actors and stakeholders.
vi. Seek out and exploit avenues for co-development, co-funding, co-sharing, co-development, co-management and joint governance of RIs with industry (private sector). And develop strategies for active engagements and collaborations with industry in R&D that results in mutual benefits, including joint patents, innovations, and commercialize products.

*Recommendations to Private Sector*

i. Adopt an open-minded approach to R&D, in collaboration with HEIs that aligns to national contexts and development goals.
ii. Invest in RIs that contribute to innovation in individual industry's and organization's lines of business. For example, the case of Guinness, Ghana, which uses local sorghum in the development of drinks and beverages.
iii. Be willing to open research and innovation facilities for capacity building to HEIs in areas such as training and internships; while at the same time, benefiting from the knowledge transfer that emanates from HEIs to industry.
iv. Establish strategies for active engagements and collaborations in research with HEIs.

v. Foster greater appreciation of the role of HEIs in research and innovation that underpins production and industrial growth; and the importance of RIs in the processes involved. With this in mind, work with HEIs to expedite RI development, co-funding, colocation, co-hosting and sharing of facilities.

*Recommendations to Development Partners/Donors*

i. Include components for building or improving relevant RIs in research funding calls. Taking this approach to funding reflects the priority on RIs and helps to highlight the importance of RIs to national governments and other ecosystem actors.
ii. In fostering international collaboration in research projects, which contributes to enhancing capacity and competence in African HEIs, increase efforts to address contextual challenges and the roles RIs can play in this regard.
iii. Strengthen engagements with government, private sector, and other key stakeholders as this is crucial to enhancing the sustainability of research and RIs in Africa.
iv. In funding research projects in Africa, encourage joint applications involving HEIs and industry actors.
v. Include RIs, as dedicated thematic areas, in research project calls and funding.

**Acknowledgements** This chapter is based on a deliverable for a project on Research Infrastructure in Higher Education Institutions (RI in HEIs) in Africa funded by the International Development and Research Centre (IDRC) through the Association of African Universities (AAU) (IDRC project grant number: 109506-001). The content of this chapter does not reflect the official opinion or position of the IDRC. The information and views expressed in the chapter are entirely the authors' responsibility. The authors acknowledge the useful feedback from members of the RI project team on the report that informed this paper.

## References

A4AI (Alliance for Affordable Internet), 2020 report. https://a4ai.org/affordability-report/report/2020/

African Union Commission (AUC). (2014). *Science, technology and innovation strategy for Africa 2024*. AUC.

African Union Commission (AUC). (2015a). *Agenda 2063, Africa we want, popular version*. AUC.

African Union Commission (AUC). (2015b). *Agenda 2063, First Ten-year Implementation Plan 2014–2023*. AUC.

African Union Commission (AUC). (2016). *Continental Education Strategy for Africa (CESA) CESA 2016–2025*. AUC. https://au.int/sites/default/files/documents/29958-doc-cesa_-_english-v9.pdf

Akuru, U. B. (2019). Research funding issues in African universities: Penalties and pathways. *Journal of Sustainable Development Studies, 12*(2), 305–327, https://doi.org/10.28924/ip/jsds.1911

Assefa, A. A. (2016). University-industry linkage practices, determinants and challenges theoretical and empirical article review: Lessons for effective and successful collaboration. *International Journal of Research in Management, Economics and Commerce, 6*(3), 1–16. www.indusedu.org

Atuahene, F. (2011). Re-thinking the missing mission of higher education: An anatomy of the research challenge of African universities. *Journal of Asian and African Studies, 46*(4), 321–341. https://doi.org/10.1177/0021909611400017

Awuni, S., & Essegbey, G. O. (2014). *Developing an enabling scientific equipment policy in Africa: The Ghana Country Study* (A Report Submitted to IFS and AAS, CSIR-STEPRI, Accra).

Brown, K.A., Timotijević, L., Geurts, M., Arentoft, J. L., Dhonukshe-Rutten, R. A. M., Fezeu, L., Finglas, P., Laville, M., Perozzi, G., Ocké, M., Poppe, K., Slimani, N., Snoek, H. M., Tetens, I., van't Veer, P., Vors, C., & Zimmermann, K. L. (2017). Concepts and procedures for mapping food and health research infrastructure: New insights from the EuroDISH project. *Trends in Food Science & Technology, 63*, https://doi.org/10.1016/j.tifs.2017.03.006, https://www.researchgate.net/publication/314465231_Title_Concepts_and_procedures_for_mapping_food_and_health_research_infrastructure_New_insights_from_the_EuroDISH_project. Accessed 6 February 2021.

Chataway, J., & Daniels, C. (2020). The Republic of Science meets the Republics of Somewhere: Embedding scientific excellence in sub-Saharan Africa. In E. Kraemer-Mbula, R. Tijssen, M. L. Wallace, & R. McLean (Eds.), *Transforming research excellence: New ideas from the global south* (pp. 39–58). African Minds. https://doi.org/10.5281/zenodo.3607326

Daniels, C., & Amadi-Echendu, J. (2021). Entrepreneurship, innovation, and technology commercialisation for transformative change in Africa: Perspectives, policies and practices. https://doi.org/10.1007/978-3-030-58240-1_1

Daniels, C., Byrne, R., Hanlin, R., Pointel, S., & Numi, A. (2020). *Updating the case studies of the political economy of science granting councils in sub-Saharan Africa, research project technical report*. https://idl-bnc-idrc.dspacedirect.org/handle/10625/59314

Daniels, C., & Dosso, M. (2021). Mapping the potentials for transformative innovation policies in Africa: Evidence from Cote d'Ivoire and Nigeria. https://doi.org/10.1007/978-3-030-58240-1_13

Daniels, C., Dosso, M., & Amadi-Echendu J. (Eds.). (2021). *Entrepreneurship, technology commercialization, and innovation policy in Africa*. Springer Nature. https://doi.org/10.1007/978-3-030-58240-1

Daniels, C., Erforth, B., & Teevan, C. (Eds.). (2022). *Africa–Europe cooperation and digital transformation* (1st ed.). Routledge. https://doi.org/10.4324/9781003274322

Daniels C., Essegbey G., Yalley A., Mba J., Akazue P., & Tibazarwa, F. (2023, forthcoming). Research infrastructures resilience in higher institutions in Africa.

Daniels, C., & Gebhardt, C. (2021). Special issue: Higher education, science and research systems for transformative change in Africa—What role for innovation policy? *Industry and Higher Education*. https://doi.org/10.1177/09504222211029901

Daniels, C., Schot, J., Chataway, J., Ramirez, M., Steinmueller, E., & Kanger, L. (2020), Transformative innovation policy: Insights from Colombia, Finland, Norway, South Africa, and Sweden. In *Innovation policy at the intersection global debates and local experiences*. Cele MBG, TM Luescher and AW Fadiji, HSRC.

Daniels, C. U., Ustyuzhantseva, O., & Yao, W. (2017). Innovation for inclusive development, public policy support and triple helix: Perspectives from BRICS. *African Journal of Science, Technology, Innovation and Development, 9*, 513–527. https://doi.org/10.1080/20421338.2017.1327923

DST (Department of Science and Technology). (2002). *South Africa's National Research and Development Strategy*. Department of Science and Technology, Pretoria. https://www.gov.za/sites/default/files/gcis_document/201409/rdstrat0.pdf

DST (Department of Science and Technology). (2016). *South African research infrastructure roadmap* (1st ed.). DST. https://www.dst.gov.za/images/Attachments/Department_of_Science_and_Technology_SARIR_2016.pdf. Accessed 15 November 2021.

Dosso, M., Braoulé Méïté, F., Ametepe, G., Gbogou, C., Guiella, G., & Oulaï D. (2021). New entrepreneurial narratives in urban West Africa: Case studies of five innovation hubs and communities. In C. Daniels, M. Dosso, & J. Amadi-Echendu (Eds.), *Entrepreneurship, technology commercialisation, and innovation policy in Africa*. Springer. https://doi.org/10.1007/978-3-030-58240-1_8

Essegbey, G., Diaby, N., & Konte, A. (2015). West Africa. In *UNESCO science report towards 2030* (pp. 470–497). UNESCO.

Essegbey, G., Konte, A., Sawadogo, N., & Siyanbola, W. (2021). West Africa. In *UNESCO science report 2020*. UNESCO.

ESFRI. (2011). *Strategy report on research infrastructure roadmap 2010*. European Strategy Forum on Research Infrastructures (ESFRI). https://www.esfri.eu/sites/default/files/esfri-strategy_report_and_roadmap_2010.pdf. Accessed 10 February 2021.

ESFRI (European Strategy Forum on Research Infrastructures). (2018). *Roadmap 2018*. Strategy Report on Research Infrastructures, http://roadmap2018.esfri.eu/media/1060/esfri-roadmap-2018.pdf. Accessed 10 February 2021.

Etzkowitz, H. (1996). The Triple Helix: Academic–industry–government relations. *Annals of the New York Academy of Sciences, 787*, 67–86. https://doi.org/10.1111/j.1749-6632.1996.tb44849.x

Faraj, G. (2020). *The impact of COVID 19 on universities in Africa* (online) (viewed January 2021). https://www.accord.org.za/analysis/the-impact-of-covid-19-on-universities-in-africa/

Freeman, C. (1987). Technology, policy, and economic performance lessons from Japan.

Hallonsten, O. (2020). Research infrastructures in Europe: The hype and the field. *European Review, 28*(4), 617–635. https://doi.org/10.1017/S1062798720000095

IFS (International Foundation for Science). (2012). *Addressing equipment challenges in development-related scientific research in Africa*. IFS Briefing Document 1/2012. http://www.ifs.se/IFS/Documents/Publications/Briefing%20Documents/IFS%20Briefing%20Document%201-2012.pdf

IFS (International Foundation for Science). (2014). *An enabling scientific equipment policy in Africa*. http://www.ifs.se/ifs-news/an-enabling-scientific-equipment-policy-in-africa.html

Iliopulos, I., & Boyd, C. (2019). *Preventing a dirty bomb: Case studies and lessons learned*. Nuclear Threat Initiative.

Jacob, M., & Meek, V. L. (2013). Scientific mobility and international research networks: Trends and policy tools for promoting research excellence and capacity building. *Studies in Higher Education, 38*(3), 331–344. https://doi.org/10.1080/03075079.2013.773789

Kraemer-Mbula, E., Tijssen, R., Wallace M. L., & McLean, R. (Eds.). (2020). *Transforming research excellence: New ideas from the global south*. African Minds.

Larsson, A. (2017). The need for research infrastructures: A narrative review of large-scale research infrastructures in biobanking. *Biopreservation and Biobanking, 15*(4), 375–383. https://doi.org/10.1089/bio.2016.0103

Larsson, A., Savage, C., Brommels, M., & Mattsson, P. (2018). Structuring a research infrastructure: A study of the rise and fall of a large-scale distributed biobank facility. *Social Science Information, 57*, 196–222. https://doi.org/10.1177/0539018418761848

Kozlowski, H. N., Farkouh, M. E., Irwin, M. S., Radvanyi, L. G., Schimmer, A. D., Tabori, U., & Rosenblum, N. D. (2020). COVID-19: A pandemic experience that illuminates potential reforms to health research. *EMBO Molecular Medicine, 12*(11). https://doi.org/10.15252/emmm.202013278

López-Ballesteros, A., Beck, J., Bombelli, A., Grieco, E., Lorencová, E. K., Merbold, L., & Saunders, M. (2018). Towards a feasible and representative pan-African research infrastructure network for GHG observations. *Environmental Research Letters, 13*(8). https://doi.org/10.1088/1748-9326/AAD66C

Lundvall, B.-Å. (1992). National systems of innovation: Towards a theory of innovation and interactive learning.

Lundvall, B.-Å. (2010). *National systems of innovation toward a theory of innovation and interactive learning*. Anthem Other Canon Economics. Anthem Press.

Martins, R. M., Park, E., Hain, D. S., & Jurowetzki, R. (2021). Mapping entrepreneurial ecosystem for technology start-ups in developing economies: An empirical analysis of Twitter networks between start-ups and support organizations of Nairobi's digital economy. In C. Daniels, M. Dosso, & J. Amadi-Echendu (Eds.), *Entrepreneurship, technology commercialisation, and innovation policy in Africa*. Springer. https://doi.org/10.1007/978-3-030-58240-1_4

Nelson, R. R. (1993). *National innovation systems: A comparative analysis*. Social Science Research Network.

PAERIP. (2019). *Final report summary—PAERIP (Promoting African—European Research Infrastructure Partnerships)*. https://cordis.europa.eu/project/id/262493/reporting. Accessed 6 February 2021.

Park, J. J. H., Mogg, R., Smith, G. E., Nakimuli-Mpungu, E., Jehan, F., Rayner, C. R., & Mills, E. J. (2021). How COVID-19 has fundamentally changed clinical research in global health. *The Lancet Global Health*. https://doi.org/10.1016/S2214-109X(20)30542-8

Ramoutar-Prieschl, R., & Hachigonta, S. (2020). *Management of research infrastructures: A South African funding perspective*. Springer. https://doi.org/10.1007/978-3-030-37281-1

Ranga, M., & Etzkowitz, H. (2013). Triple Helix systems: An analytical framework for innovation policy and practice in the knowledge society. *Industry and Higher Education, 27*(4), 237–262.

Ryan, L. (2015). Governance of EU research policy: Charting forms of scientific democracy in the European Research Area. *Science and Public Policy, 42*, 300–314. https://doi.org/10.1093/scipol/scu047

Schot, J., & Steinmueller, W. E. (2018). Three frames for innovation policy: R&D, systems of innovation and transformative change. *Research Policy, 47*, 1554–1567. https://doi.org/10.1016/j.respol.2018.08.011

Sumberg, J. (2005). Systems of innovation theory and the changing architecture of agricultural research in Africa. *Food Policy, 30*(1), 21–41. https://doi.org/10.1016/J.FOODPOL.2004.11.001

Teferra, D., & Altbach, P. G. (2004). African higher education: Challenges for the 21st century. *Higher Education, 47*(1), 21–50. https://doi.org/10.1023/B:HIGH.0000009822.49980.30

Tijssen, R., & Kraemer-Mbula, E. K. (2018). Research excellence in Africa: Policies, perceptions, and performance. *Science and Public Policy*, 45(3), 392–403. https://doi.org/10.1093/scipol/scx074

Toom, K., & Miller, P. F. (2018). Research infrastructure. In *Research management: Europe and beyond* (pp. 205–212). https://doi.org/10.1016/B978-0-12-805059-0.00009-2

Twiringiyimana, R., Daniels, C., & Chataway, C. (2021). STI policy and governance in sub-Saharan Africa: Fostering actors' interactions in research and innovation. *Industry and Higher Education*. https://doi.org/10.1177/09504222211026218

UKRI. (n.d.). *The UK's research and innovation infrastructure: Landscape analysis*. https://www.ukri.org/wp-content/uploads/2020/10/UKRI-201020-LandscapeAnalysis-FINAL.pdf. Accessed 10 February 2021.

van Ommen, G.-J. B., Törnwall, O., Bréchot, C., Dagher, G., Galli, J., Hveem, K., & Zatloukal, K. (2014). BBMRI-ERIC as a resource for pharmaceutical and life science industries: the development of biobank-based expert centres. *European Journal of Human Genetics 2015, 23*(7), 893–900. https://doi.org/10.1038/ejhg.2014.235

Vicente-Crespo, M., Agunbiade, O., Eyers, J., Thorogood, M., & Fonn, S. (2020). Institutionalizing research capacity strengthening in LMICs: A systematic review and meta-synthesis. *AAS Open Research, 3*, 43. https://doi.org/10.12688/aasopenres.13116.2

Wood, J. V., León, G., Von Gruenewaldt, G., & Botha, A. P. (2013). *A South African research infrastructure roadmap* (online) (viewed January 2021). https://www.dst.gov.za/images/pdfs/SARIR%20Report%20Ver%202.pdf

Xu, W., Xu, Y., & Li, J. (2017). A study of RI clusters based on symbiosis theory. *Sustainability, 9*, 396–408. https://doi.org/10.3390/su9030396

Zakaria, S., Grant, J., & Luff, J. (2021). Fundamental challenges in assessing the impact of research infrastructure. *Health Research Policy and Systems, 19*(1). https://doi.org/10.1186/S12961-021-00769-Z

CHAPTER 5

# The Role of the Diaspora in Advancing Research and Graduate Education in Africa

*Ayenachew Aseffa Woldegiyorgis*

## Introduction

The role of the African diaspora in the continent's development has garnered increasing attention in recent years. Since the beginning of the century, organizations like the World Bank and the United Nations have implemented programs and funding schemes aimed at harnessing diaspora contributions to African development. These organizations also advocated for African governments to adopt diaspora policies (Mangala, 2017). A landmark moment occurred when the African Union designated the diaspora as the continent's "sixth region," underscoring its strategic role in Africa's development agenda (Adisa, 2017).

An increasing number of African nations have since formulated national diaspora policies, broadening the focus beyond traditional remittances and foreign direct investment to include intellectual remittances, public diplomacy, technology transfer, and entrepreneurship. Although the degree

A. A. Woldegiyorgis (✉)
Center for Comparative Education and Policy Studies, Addis Ababa University, Addis Ababa, Ethiopia
e-mail: ayenachew@gmail.com



D. Teferra (ed.), *Research and Innovation in African Higher Education*,
https://doi.org/10.1007/978-3-031-92909-0_5

to which these policies are supported by institutional infrastructure and resources varies across countries, it is observed that engagement with the diaspora has expanded at local and institutional levels. As Brinkerhoff (2019) noted, diaspora policy frameworks are not exclusively rooted in state-led governance; rather, local governments, NGOs, and cultural or religious organizations often engage with the diaspora, though less formally and often on an ad hoc basis.

Such engagement is especially evident in higher education—specifically in research and graduate education. Diaspora involvement in these areas frequently occurs in fragmented forms at institutional, departmental, or individual levels (Amagoh & Rahman, 2016). Often reliant on personal networks and connections to alma maters, these collaborations typically begin informally and evolve over time (Woldegiyorgis, 2021). However, this informal and ad hoc nature of engagement undermines the contribution of diaspora to African graduate education and research, not only through lack of proper institutional support and resourcing, but also due to lack of proper documentation of initiatives and their outcomes.

This chapter features the role of the African diaspora to the advancement of research and graduate education in the continent. Drawing from literature, a major previous work of the author, and personal communications and professional encounters with members of the African academic diaspora, the chapter begins with establishing the rationale for the engagement of the African diaspora in higher education, particularly in graduate education and research. It highlights the different ways in which advanced expertise and experiences among the diaspora can be applied in supporting developmental efforts in Africa. Lastly it explores what enables and deters the engagement of diaspora in higher education.

## Rationale: Why Engage the Diaspora in Research and Graduate Education?

The rationale for the engagement of the diaspora in advancing research and graduate education in Africa can be explained from two perspectives. First is the current state of research and graduate education in Africa, which calls for coordinated efforts and commitment of resources for capacity building. Second is the unique potential of the African intellectual diaspora to contribute to these efforts.

There is a general agreement that Africa's research contribution is far less than its potential. According to the SCImago Journal and Country

Ranking (n.d.), for example, Africa contributed only 2.2% of the world's research documents from 1996 to 2021. South Africa, the highest-ranked African nation, placed 35th globally, with Africa's collective research production amounting to only one-tenth of that of the United States (1.49 million vs. 14.41 million). These figures, while limited to one database, highlight the need for Africa to expand its research capacity—not solely to improve rankings but to address regional challenges through innovation.

Similarly, graduate education in Africa is also limited, mainly owing to historical reasons (Hayward & Ncayiyana, 2014). Recent expansion efforts of graduate education across the continent are also faced with multiple challenges (British Council & DAAD, 2018; Cloete et al., 2015; Khodabocus, 2016). Limited institutional capacity, resource, and funding, supervision, facilities, diversity, and quality assurance are often cited as common challenges of graduate education in the continent (Woldegiyorgis, 2020). Institutions struggle to meet growing demand while dealing with these constraints.

In many studies the African intellectual diaspora has been identified as a valuable resource for addressing capacity constraints in higher education (Amagoh & Rahman, 2016; Foulds & Zeleza, 2014; Ogachi, 2016; Teferra, 2003, 2010; Zeleza, 2004, 2013). Although precise figures are elusive, the significant number and caliber of African-origin academics and researchers globally position the diaspora as a potent partner in higher education capacity building. Recognizing this potential, an increasing number of institutions are actively engaging diaspora academics in various roles, from supervising graduate students, teaching courses, and research collaboration to strategic leadership positions. As African higher education institutions aim to rise in the global knowledge system, the diaspora can play a pivotal role in leveraging their expertise, networks, and global visibility to mobilize resources from Western sources, including universities, foundations, and international organizations (Zeleza, 2013). However, it's important to acknowledge the inherent bias that often puts more trust on academics based in Western institutions for funding and partnerships.

Engaging the African diaspora in international collaborations offers unique advantages. First, many diaspora academics volunteer their services, often covering part or all of their costs, reducing the overall cost of initiatives. Second, their linguistic and cultural competence enables them to navigate bureaucratic hurdles and institutional practices with much ease (Agunias & Newland, 2012). Third, the sense of belonging and duty that many highly educated diaspora members carry (Zeleza, 2013) strengthens their commitment to the success of the projects they engage in. This lies in the nexus between professional benefits of international practices facilitated through social and cultural ties and the personal affective causes of staying close to home (Woldegiyorgis, 2021). Diaspora academics also possess a unique understanding of both academic worlds. They are familiar with the "as is" of African higher education, and the aspirations to be part of the state of global academic exercise. Therefore, it can be argued that they are better positioned to serve as effective mentors for graduate students and emerging researchers.

In addition, short-term engagements can serve as a catalyst for more significant and sustained contributions from diaspora academics, including permanent return or the facilitation of broader international collaborations. As Western institutions and international organizations increasingly prioritize African higher education, diaspora academics are assuming a pivotal role as interlocutors in establishing and leading collaborative partnerships. As Teferra (2010) noted, Western institutions are continuously acknowledging the contributions of their foreign born faculty as mediators of their espoused relations with the rest of the world, under initiatives such as internationalization efforts. This is also getting recognition by funding institutions who are increasingly inclined to support initiatives that involve the diaspora.

In sum, as African institutions strive to enhance their research and graduate education capacities, they increasingly turn to the academic diaspora for expertise and resources. To elevate their global standing, these institutions leverage the diaspora's unique insights and networks to foster international collaborations. Simultaneously, diaspora academics are motivated by both professional and personal reasons to engage with their home institutions. Their linguistic and cultural competence, coupled with their understanding of both African and global academic contexts, positions them as valuable intermediaries and mentors in the advancement of African higher education.

## Modes of Engagement

The engagement between local and diaspora academics can take different forms. Previous studies have employed diverse approaches to analyze the forms of engagement. Based on case studies from multiple countries,

Agunias and Newland (2012) identified three general categories that delineate the potential roles of diaspora academics in their countries of origin.

(A) *Diasporas as practitioners who fill critical knowledge gaps*: Diaspora professionals can fill critical knowledge gaps by providing expertise in areas where local capacity is limited. To leverage this potential, African governments and institutions must identify priority areas requiring specialized knowledge, locate diaspora experts in those fields, and establish appropriate institutional and policy frameworks, including incentive schemes. Outreach programs are crucial to connect with diaspora members, inform them about these initiatives, and encourage their participation.

The COVID-19 pandemic offers a compelling example of this approach. As countries grappled with the crisis, many turned to their diasporas for expertise. Task forces and response teams were formed, bringing together diaspora and local experts to develop policies, prevention guidelines, treatment protocols, and macroeconomic strategies. Diaspora professionals contributed their scientific knowledge, international experiences, and insights to inform public health campaigns and research initiatives. These experiences underscore the valuable role that diaspora experts can play in addressing critical challenges and advancing national development (Woldegiyorgis & Adamu, 2022).

*Diasporas as partners/collaborators:* This approach promotes collaborative engagement in research and other projects between local and diaspora academics. While it is quite common that such partnerships/collaborations occur at individual levels and in an informal manner, institutional and professional networks play an important role. Formal government arrangements create conducive policy environment and resource commitments for such partnerships to happen at scale. A good example of this form of engagement is the Chinese 111 project, which allows top scholars in the diaspora to team up with local researchers to work in selected innovation centers across the country. This approach is a suitable avenue for technology transfer as well as development of local capacities (Welch & Zhen, 2008).

(B) *Diasporas as members and leaders of scientific and technical networks*: Many countries establish online and web-based networks to bring together local and diaspora experts to address specific scientific, technical, and business issues. Advisory boards and councils to government offices or departments composed of diaspora and local experts can provide valuable insights and guidance. For instance, Ethiopia's Advisory Council for the Ministry of Education and the Independent Council of Economic Advisors—under the purview of the Office of the Prime Minister—purposefully combine diaspora and local academics and professionals. These councils facilitate collaboration between local and diaspora experts through task forces and committees, enabling the sharing of expertise and the development of innovative solutions. Similar initiatives have been implemented in other African countries with varying degrees of success.

Another approach to classifying the forms of engagement is proposed by Zeleza (2013) which looks at the major functions of a university—teaching, research, and service—as the framework to identify the different modes of engagement. Specific activities that can fall in the three major functions of a higher education institution can be summarized as follows (Table 5.1).

It is important to underscore that these various forms of engagement are not to be seen as separate, much less mutually exclusive. Mostly, engagements, even at the individual level, occur in multiplicity of activities. Diaspora academics frequently engage in multiple activities during a single visit to their home country, such as conducting research, teaching short courses, delivering public lectures, and participating in advisory bodies. It is even the case that one trip covers multiple institutions. Longer-term engagements, often furnished with leave and resources from home institutions, research is the driving engagement with other activities scheduled around it.

Another way of classifying the modes of engagement is to mix the two—the roles-based and the functions-based—approaches. Teferra's (2010) approach to identify the following five major forms of engagement can be understood as such, with a focus on research.

**Table 5.1** Types of diaspora engagement with African higher education institutions

| *University function* | *Types of engagement* |
|---|---|
| Teaching | student exchanges, study abroad programs, short courses, summer classes, curriculum development, supervision of graduate student dissertations |
| Scholarship and professional activities | joint research and grants, publishing and manuscript reviews, donations of books, journals and equipment, building data bases and digital archives, performance evaluations for promotion cases and as external examiners, and mentoring |
| Services (for higher education) | establishing or providing critical leadership for higher education institutions and networks including centers, institutes, foundations, and universities |

*Source* Adapted from "*Engagements between African diaspora academics in the US and Canada and African institutions of higher education: Perspectives from North America and Africa*" by P. Zeleza (2013), Carnegie Corporation of New York, p. 10

(i) *Joint research programs*—Joint research programs involve collaboration between diaspora and local academics to pursue shared research agendas. These partnerships can boost the research productivity of African researchers and help build a critical mass of researchers within African institutions. However, two key challenges should be noted. First, research is both time- and resource-intensive. Diaspora academics often engage in these partnerships during sabbatical leave, and research requires substantial institutional support or third-party funding, both of which are often limited. As a result, joint research programs tend to be less frequent compared to other forms of engagement. Second, such partnerships are not always set on equal footings for diaspora and local partners. In some cases, the local researcher's role may be reduced to providing support for the diaspora researcher, undermining the capacity-building objective of the collaboration.

(ii) *Contributions to publications*—Diaspora academics can significantly elevate local publications by contributing articles, reviewing manuscripts, and serving on editorial boards. They also frequently co-author articles with local scholars. A common example of this collaboration occurs when graduate students or early-career academics share drafts or raw data with diaspora scholars for feedback. Through iterative reviews and revisions, these collaborations often evolve into co-publications.

(iii) *Sharing knowledge resources*—perhaps there isn't a more stark difference between institutions in the center-periphery dichotomy than in academic resources. Academics in the diaspora can be key in addressing that gap by sharing current information and resources in their respective fields. They can also be engaged in mobilizing knowledge resources on behalf of African institutions. This has become easier and cheaper due to recent advancements in communication technology and growing interest in open access distribution of academic resources. The COVID-19 pandemic has also opened up some opportunities for academic resources to be made partially or fully available for free.

(iv) *Professional guidance and advice*—members of diasporas can be on professional advisory boards and support local academics in their activities by providing them access to their expertise and networks. Diaspora academics as members and honorary members of professional associations in Africa, provide critical leadership in their disciplines.

(v) *Endowment programs and chairs*—endowments and chairs are rare practices in Africa. Universities may encourage members of the diaspora to establish such schemes that target motivating local scientists and channeling resources in this unique form.

Analyses of diaspora engagement reveal three key elements. First, most engagement initiatives start at the individual level through personal connections that might be established in professional, personal, or social links (Teferra, 2010; Woldegiyorgis, 2021; Zeleza, 2013). These existing relationships are important resources around which formal and institutional partnerships form and flourish. Striking a working balance between the personal and the institutional and the formal and informal relationships is important.

Second, the role of communication technology is essential for any form of engagement (Amagoh & Rahman, 2016; Teferra, 2003; Zeleza, 2004). The physical and temporal divide between diasporas and their home countries has been diminished by the use of communications technologies. Therefore, countries that make better investments in communication technology infrastructure and institutions with better facilities are likely to reap more from the engagement of the academic diaspora. This difference can even go to the level of individuals: those who are more adaptable to the use of technology can have better access to academics in the diaspora and their resources. It is worth noting that the COVID-19 pandemic, halting any in-person interactions, created an impetus for a greater use of information communication technology in higher education across the world. This was also the case in diaspora engagement: many academics connected virtually with institutions in their home countries to collaborate on regular activities as well as COVID-19 response efforts.

Third, professional and diaspora networks play a crucial role. It has long been established that networks are instrumental in the flow of knowledge and other resources from migrants to their home countries (Findlay, 1990). Although maintaining networks is often difficult (Meyer, 2001) they remain crucial in facilitating easy communication between experts and coordinating collaborative projects. Experts connected through professional networks can easily find each other and easily identify who to work with based on existing interactions through the networks. Cognizant of the vital benefits, Aikins and White (2011, pp. 55–58) suggested a four-stage approach to managing networks of diaspora academics towards effective engagement. (i) *research* to identify members of the diaspora with strong connections and a willingness to mobilize others; (ii) *cultivation,* to create awareness and inform of interests and initiatives; (iii) *solicitation*, to recruit key diaspora members who can be passionately involved and be able to use their social and professional stature to mobilize others; and (iv) *stewardship*, to provide ongoing communication, feedback, performance tracking, and recognition to sustain networks and enhance their effectiveness.

In general, diaspora engagement in higher education takes diverse forms. Scholars suggest various frameworks to identify and analyze modes of diaspora involvement, particularly in graduate education and research. One approach classifies engagement activities by the specific roles diaspora members play, while another examines the functions these activities serve within universities. A third, mixed approach combines these perspectives to provide a fuller understanding. Such analyses, paired with studies on how connections form and evolve, offer African institutions a clearer strategy to harness diaspora resources effectively. Additionally, the COVID-19 pandemic has, in some areas, expanded opportunities for African institutions to strengthen their connections with intellectual diaspora networks.

## Enablers, Mediators, and Champions

While the motivation and commitment of the diaspora are essential, successful transnational engagement in higher education relies on a combination of many factors. Key among these are broad macro-environmental forces, including international political and diplomatic relations, global economic conditions, and the availability of funding. Within this context, certain elements serve as enablers, mediators, and champions, each playing a critical role in facilitating these engagements.

### *Enablers*

What can be called enablers are the foundational elements within the operating environment that facilitate diaspora engagement. Primarily, these include policies, strategies, institutions, and bureaucratic tools designed by countries to attract, support, and incentivize diaspora involvement in key national priorities. Gamlen (2006) notes that over half of UN member states have established some form of diaspora institution. In some countries, these institutions hold ministerial portfolios; in others, they function as departments within ministries or operate as independent entities solely focused on diaspora engagement. This trend extends to Africa, where, over the past two decades, many countries have implemented diaspora policies or strategies and established dedicated institutions (Mangala, 2017).

Such policies are designed to foster mutual benefits for both diasporas and their countries of origin across economic, political, and cultural spheres. Gamlen (2006) classifies diaspora policies into three broad categories based on their primary objectives (Table 5.2).

The first area, capacity building, encompasses two primary goals: (a) fostering a transnational identity connected to the home country and (b) establishing an institutional framework to engage and manage relationships with the diaspora. The latter goal often involves coordinated efforts to unify diverse diaspora stakeholders and organizations. Gamlen (2006, p. 6) describes these capacity-building policies as "symbolic nation building" and "institutional building," respectively. Both are essential to

**Table 5.2** Typology of diaspora engagement policies

| | | |
|---|---|---|
| Capacity Building | Symbolic nation building | Inclusive rhetoric & symbols; Cultural promotion & induction; Shaping media & PR; Conferences & conventions |
| | Institution building | Ministerial level agency; Dedicated bureaucracy; Monitoring efforts; Building transnational networks; Consular and consultative bodies |
| Extending Rights | Political incorporation | Special membership concessions; Dual nationality (no vote); Must return to vote; Embassy voting; Postal voting; Indefinite, unconditional vote; Parliamentary representation; Can run for office |
| | Civic and social rights | Tourism services; Welfare protection |
| Extracting Obligations | Investment policies & lobby promotion | Mandatory payments; Special economic zones; Remittance and FDI capture; Knowledge transfer programs Promoting expat lobby |

*Note* Adapted from "*Diaspora engagement policies: What are they and what kinds of states use them?*" by A. Gamlen (2006), Working Paper No. 32, Centre on Migration, Policy and Society, University of Oxford, p. 9

shaping a policy landscape that establishes the rhetoric and institutional foundations necessary for transnational engagement.

The second policy area focuses on extending rights to citizens living abroad, including political participation through dual citizenship or voting rights and access to civil and social rights. States often weigh the risks associated with these rights, such as the financial strain of providing social and civic services and the potential for influence—or even interference—from host countries with substantial diaspora populations (Gamlen, 2006). This risk can be heightened in many African nations, which may face both significant diaspora opposition to the government (Enoh, 2014) and limited economic and institutional capacity to support rights across multiple international locations.

The third area of diaspora policy, termed "extracting obligations" by Gamlen (2006), focuses on how governments seek to generate and maximize benefits from their diasporas' resources. Gamlen argues that the success of this approach depends on the reciprocal benefits offered to the diaspora. If a country focuses solely on extracting obligations, the relationship will remain unbalanced and can only last for so long. Eventually, the country must offer various incentives to encourage ongoing engagement and participation from the diaspora.

The policy instruments outlined above provide broad mechanisms for engaging with diasporas. However, more specific policies and strategies are required based on the unique characteristics of the targeted diaspora group and the needs and priorities of the home country, within the broader context. One such area where many African countries are developing engagement mechanisms is the highly educated segment of their diasporas, which falls under the third category of policies described earlier. Additionally, it is important to note that while many countries create policies targeting their intellectual diasporas, these diasporas are often actively involved in the development of policies across all three categories.

### *Mediators*

Mediators are organizations that facilitate diaspora engagement by acting as intermediaries between the diaspora and institutions in their countries of origin. These include professional associations, networks, nonprofits focused on specific causes, hometown or regional associations, and religious or cultural organizations. While many of these organizations concentrate on broader humanitarian and development goals, with education being one component, they typically prioritize K-12 education. In contrast, professional associations and networks tend to focus more specifically on higher education, particularly research and graduate education.

The Association of Nigerian Physicians in the Americas (ANPA) is a prime example of a professional diaspora organization with significant involvement in research and graduate education in the home country. Established in 1995 as an educational, scientific, and charitable organization, ANPA currently has nearly a thousand members. The association runs a variety of initiatives aimed at building capacity in medical education, research, and practice in Nigeria. One of its key missions is to "seek collaborative research opportunities in the international medical community" to improve healthcare in Nigeria (ANPA, n.d.). This mission has led to collaborations between ANPA, medical schools in Nigeria, and institutions in North America, providing specialist resources for research, education, and training.

ANPA not only supports graduate medical education in Nigeria, but it is also a certified Continuing Professional Development (CPD) provider in the medical field. Through a multidisciplinary approach and collaborative research programs, ANPA brings together Nigerian medical professionals, diaspora members, and other international medical experts. These efforts help streamline engagement between Nigerian diaspora medical professionals and their counterparts back home, reducing—for the former—the need to navigate bureaucratic hurdles.

Another type of mediator in diaspora engagement includes third-party organizations such as private foundations, non-profit organizations, and government-funded projects in countries with substantial African academic diaspora populations. These organizations not only connect diaspora members with institutions and academics in Africa but also provide resources and technical support for effective engagement in specific areas of higher education. One of the most well-known examples is the Transfer of Knowledge Through Expatriate Nationals (TOKTEN), an initiative of the United Nations Development Program (UNDP). Launched in 1977, TOKTEN has reached over 30 countries, including many in Africa, that are heavily impacted by the loss of highly skilled and experienced citizens (Wescott, 2006).

With its primary goal of capacity building, TOKTEN offers diaspora experts the opportunity to return to their home countries on a voluntary, short-term basis to engage in activities such as consultancy, training, and research in areas prioritized by the benefiting country. While the long-term impact is debated, participating host institutions are generally expected to benefit by forming lasting relationships with the visiting experts (Muneer, 2011). Many African higher education institutions have benefited from this initiative. Although individual cases show that TOKTEN has led to repeated volunteer efforts and longer-term relationships (Woldegiyorgis, 2021), the extent to which these engagements have generated lasting benefits for institutions remains largely unexamined.

Another noteworthy example is the Carnegie African Diaspora Fellowship Program (CADFP), funded by the Carnegie Corporation of New York and administered by the Institute of International Education (IIE). CADFP is a large-scale initiative uniquely focused on building capacity in African higher education. Since its launch in 2013, the program has awarded 665 fellowships, benefiting nearly 192 institutions in nine African countries (D'souza, 2024).

The program provides support for African diaspora academics in North America to spend time in African institutions (in selected countries) to engage with local faculty in the following areas:

- Research collaboration—the research collaboration proposed by potential hosts and fellows should demonstrate long-term impactfulness and positive contribution to the technical and research skills of faculty at host institutions.
- Graduate training and mentoring—looks for innovative approaches and methods that can enhance the technical and research skills of graduate students at host institutions
- Curriculum co-development—fellows collaborate with local faculty of host institutions in co-developing or reviewing curricula. Projects are encouraged to employ innovative approaches in designing and implementing courses, particularly to focus on strengthening online instructional capacities of host institutions.

CADFP takes a demand-driven approach, evident in its two-part application process. Eligible African institutions can submit project requests to host an African-born scholar based in the U.S. or Canada, specifying a preferred scholar or leaving the selection open. If no scholar is named, IIE will match the project with suitable candidates from its roster. Meanwhile, African-born academics in North America can apply for the fellowship either through a partnership with a specific host institution or by joining the general roster. In the latter case, applicants remain on the roster until a project aligned with their expertise is submitted by a host institution. This process ensures that the host institutions' needs, as expressed in their project requests, guide the scholar matches made by CADFP.

### *Champions*

Champions are individuals and organizations that actively advocate for the engagement of the diaspora in higher education. These champions can include local faculty and researchers, university officials, members of the African diaspora, and professionals from various backgrounds. Likewise, advocacy efforts can come from a range of organizations, including professional associations, networks, nonprofits, academic and research institutions, government-affiliated bodies, and diaspora organizations. Champions may work to influence policy broadly or provide targeted support to ensure the success of specific projects, strengthening the role and impact of diaspora engagement in African higher education.

Alliance for Brain-gain and Innovative Development, an Ethiopian non-governmental and non-profit organization better known by its acronym ABIDE, is one of the earliest and prominent organizations advocating for the greater utilization of skills resources in the diaspora to support development efforts. Since its establishment in 2006, ABIDE collaborates with stakeholders to establish institutional mechanisms, systems, and policies that streamline the involvement of skilled Ethiopians abroad in addressing local knowledge, skills, and technology gaps, ultimately contributing to sustainable development (Bishaw, 2010, p. 143). Over the years, ABIDE has championed the creation of a dedicated Ethiopian institution and integrated policy for diaspora engagement, particularly in the knowledge sector. Its activities have included organizing events, consulting with government offices, proposing action plans, forming networks, and engaging with Ethiopian professionals domestically and abroad. ABIDE's efforts have significantly advanced diaspora involvement in Ethiopian higher education and research.

Securing champions, such as university officials, senior faculty members, or others with the influence to support a project, is essential for success. Champions can also include institutions with aligned interests. For example, when a U.S.-based professor sought to establish a graduate program in Anthropology at a Tanzanian university, he faced significant resource limitations and skepticism about the project's viability. To overcome this, he strategically partnered with two non-university entities. By aligning the program with the needs of the Police Department (for forensic anthropology) and the National Parks Authority (which had understaffed and underused research facilities), he generated national interest and mobilized substantial resources. This example highlights how diaspora-led initiatives in research and graduate education can thrive by securing champions and aligning with the interests of supportive institutions.

## Challenges of Engagement

While challenges vary across engagement initiatives and their specific contexts in both home and host countries, research shows that certain obstacles are common across borders. Infrastructural, logistical, economic, political, social, and cultural factors all influence both the challenges and successes of these initiatives (Teferra, 2005, 2010). With this in mind, four major categories of common challenges in engaging academic diaspora emerge: the focus of initiatives, institutional processes, environmental factors, and attitudinal issues.

### *Clarity of Focus*

Clarity of focus is essential in designing effective engagement strategies. Wickramasekara (2011) emphasized the need to separate the euphoria about the diaspora's potential from the realistic scope for their contributions. While there is broad agreement on the African diaspora's potential as a resource, their actual impact depends heavily on the clarity of focus an engagement plan works with. Not all diaspora members have the necessary conditions in their own environments to make substantial contributions. According to Aikins and White (2011), one of the main reasons initiatives fail is their inability to identify and retain champions who are willing to persist through challenges. They describe this as the "mile wide – inch deep versus inch wide – mile deep" dilemma (p. 14).

In this regard, Larner (2007 p. 341) suggested a balanced approach, combining the "alumni model"—which mobilizes large numbers around a cause—with the "overachievers model," focusing on a small group of highly motivated, influential individuals who can rally others. The academic diaspora forms a small, specialized subset within a country's broader diaspora community, and identifying these members and securing their engagement through a targeted strategy is crucial. Mass mobilization efforts are generally less likely to be effective in the context of the academic diaspora, a common error in many engagement efforts and strategies.

Clarity of focus is also crucial in setting priorities that align with the home country's specific needs. Instead of a broad call for diaspora members to "come and serve," a targeted approach that identifies priority areas, alongside a clear strategy and incentive framework, can more effectively attract academic diaspora members to roles where they are genuinely needed. This clarity allows diaspora academics to integrate their engagement with their existing research, teaching objectives, and career plans, making their involvement both feasible and sustainable.

For example, Ethiopia's recent differentiation of its higher education system—assigning specific focuses to various institutions—provides an enabling environment for targeted diaspora contributions. This structured approach helps identify where diaspora academics with particular specializations and levels of experience can be most impactful, making it easier for them to find meaningful roles aligned with their expertise.

### *Institutional Processes*

Academic engagement with African higher education often relies heavily on informal, individual relationships initiated by diaspora members (Ogachi, 2016). However, sustainable and effective engagement requires robust institutional infrastructure that can adapt to evolving circumstances (Tejada, 2012). Diaspora academics frequently report frustrations over discrepancies between promised support and actual experiences when they arrive at African universities, encountering gaps in access to necessary facilities, resources, and appropriate scheduling (Zeleza, 2013). To attract, retain, and effectively utilize diaspora expertise, universities need formalized engagement plans that are integrated into their operations. While personal connections and advocacy from champions can temporarily bridge these gaps, lasting success relies on solid institutional backing.

### *Environmental Challenges*

These barriers can arise both in the home and host countries. In home countries, lack of clear policies, institutional support, and infrastructure—alongside political instability, corruption, weak governance, and limited information systems—significantly hinder effective engagement (Modupe, 2016). In host countries, factors such as local policies and the stability of diaspora members' professional and personal lives affect their motivation and capacity for engagement (Tejada, 2012; Tejada et al., 2014). Zeleza (2013) found that career trajectories, gender, and the pattern of diasporization play key roles in the engagement of African diaspora academics in North America. Woldegiyorgis (2021) found similar results. Senior or tenured professors, who have greater access to resources and institutional support, often find it easier to engage than adjunct or pre-tenure faculty focused on career advancement. Similarly, those affiliated with research-focused institutions that prioritize international collaboration are more likely to engage than those in teaching-focused institutions. Female academics, particularly, may face additional challenges due to family responsibilities and systemic gender biases. Additionally, diaspora members with traumatic experiences, such as political exiles, may be less inclined to engage. Recognizing these contextual factors is essential for developing realistic and supportive diaspora engagement strategies.

### *Attitudinal Issues*

Attitudes among both diaspora academics and local counterparts can create barriers to successful engagement. Some diaspora academics express enthusiasm for engagement in African institutions but may lack the genuine commitment to follow through. In some cases, engagement with African institutions is added to research projects or sabbatical plans primarily to enhance personal academic profiles, securing grants or promotions rather than genuinely supporting African institutions (Teferra, 2010). Nesbitt (2003) highlights how some African academics abroad adopt a "neo-colonial" mindset, equating Western standards with superior quality, potentially leading to unrealistic expectations from African institutions and colleagues. This mentality can hinder collaboration, as diaspora members accustomed to well-funded, resource-rich institutions may underestimate the limitations faced by their counterparts in Africa, affecting the mutual respect and adaptability necessary for meaningful partnership.

On the other hand, attitudinal challenges are often stronger and more common among African academics in home institutions (Agunias & Newland, 2012; Modupe, 2016; Teferra, 2005; Zeleza, 2004, 2013). One prominent sentiment is resentment towards diaspora academics for having "abandoned" or even "betrayed" their country in difficult times (Skeldon, 2008; Zeleza, 2004). There is also a prevailing mistrust and insecurity that diaspora academics might look down on local scholars, assuming a superiority over an academic culture perceived as underdeveloped—evident in the scarcity of publication, conference participation, and research grants within African institutions. This tension is further intensified by financial disparities; many diaspora academics receive financial support through government or international sponsorship—often seen as unfairly much higher than the locals—creating a perception of inequality, even though in numerous cases, diasporas work on a voluntary basis or receive only basic expenses (Agunias & Newland, 2012).

Modupe (2016) documented experiences in Nigeria where local academics expected financial benefits at each stage of their interaction with diaspora colleagues, reflecting unrealistic expectations about the material resources diasporas could bring. Misunderstandings about research funding processes can also lead to disagreements, as local academics and institutions may assume these grants are directly accessible for institutional use. Moreover, power dynamics complicate the relationship, as diasporas may struggle to offer constructive criticism without it being perceived as arrogance, creating a barrier to honest academic discourse (Zeleza, 2013).

Another aspect of the challenge in engaging the African academic diaspora is its almost exclusive focus on those residing in the global North. There is limited information and documentation regarding the diaspora's presence and impact within the continent. The lack of comprchensive data on the number, distribution, areas of expertise, and status of the intellectual diaspora makes it difficult to design targeted and effective engagement strategies. Moreover, academic diaspora engagement has not been a major research topic, and as a result, there is limited scholarship on the subject (Zeleza, 2013). This knowledge gap, combined with fragmented engagement efforts, has hindered the potential of the diaspora in strengthening higher education and research across Africa. However, there is a growing trend, as well as a positive shift in attitudes, towards mobility and knowledge circulation within the continent, supported by regional and continental institutions (Ogachi, 2016). These developments present a promising opportunity for future growth, offering new strategies and frameworks for more effective diaspora engagement within the continent.

In general, the importance of engaging the academic diaspora in the development and capacity enhancement of institutions in home countries is convincingly established among all stakeholders. However, there are several challenges that need to be addressed in the design and implementation of engagement initiatives.

## Concluding Remarks

Engaging the African academic diaspora in higher education across the continent is highly justified for several reasons. The growing demand for research and graduate education, combined with the exposure of diaspora academics to resource-rich and culturally diverse academic environments, fuels a strong interest in contributing to institutions in their countries of origin. Research and practical examples highlight the many ways diaspora experts can collaborate with individuals and institutions in their home countries.

These engagement efforts are more effective when supported by enabling policies and institutional arrangements. Mediators such as intergovernmental organizations, private foundations, professional associations, networks, and nonprofits play a crucial role in connecting the demand and supply sides of diaspora engagement. Additionally, individuals and institutions advocating for the broader role of the diaspora in development, including higher education, or for the success of specific projects, add another critical layer to the process. Importantly, these three groups—enablers, mediators, and champions—are not mutually exclusive. Instead, they work more effectively when coordinated, and an individual or institution may simultaneously play multiple roles.

The engagement of the African diaspora in higher education faces various challenges, including those related to the attitudes and experiences of individual academics and external environmental forces, such as interactions with local counterparts. Two key points emerge: First, challenges can be overcome (and even transformed into opportunities) by creatively aligning projects with the interests of various stakeholders. Second, diaspora engagement should not be viewed as a one-size-fits-all solution. Each case has its own contextual background and may contribute differently, potentially with its own set of limitations.

Finally, this chapter, like much of the existing literature, focuses on the African diaspora in the West (particularly North America) as the "typical" example. However, it is important to recognize that significant diasporic communities exist within Africa itself, each with its own unique experiences, characteristics, and capacities. Future research should explore the potential of these communities to support research and graduate education, both in their home countries and across the continent.

## References

Adisa, J. (2017). The African union perspective on diaspora. In J. Mangala (Ed.), *Africa and its global diaspora: The policy and politics of emigration* (pp. 39–57). Palgrave Macmillan.

Agunias, D. R., & Newland, K. (2012). *Developing a road map for engaging diasporas in development: A handbook for policymakers and practitioners in home and host countries*. International Organization for Migration and Migration Policy Institute.

Aikins, K., & White, N. (2011). *Global diaspora strategies toolkit: Harnessing the power of global diasporas*. Impress Printing Works.

Amagoh, F., & Rahman, T. (2016). Tapping into the potential of academic diaspora for homeland development: The case of Nigeria. *Journal of International Migration and Integration, 17*(1), 35–53. https://doi.org/10.1007/s12134-014-0410-5

Association of Nigerian Physicians in the Americas [ANPA]. (n.d.). *National projects*. https://www.anpa.org/project/national-projects/

Bishaw, T. (2010). Mobilizing Ethiopia's vital diaspora resources for capacity building and social change. *Ethiopia E-Journal for Research and Innovation Foresight, 2*(2), 139–149.

Brinkerhoff, J. M. (2019). Diaspora policy in weakly governed arenas and the benefits of multipolar engagement: Lessons from the Coptic Orthodox Church in Egypt. *Journal of Ethnic and Migration Studies, 45*(4), 561–576. https://doi.org/10.1080/1369183X.2018.1447360

British Council & German Academic Exchange [DAAD]. (2018). *Building PhD capacity in Sub-Saharan Africa*. British Council.

Cloete, N., Bunting, I., & Maassen, P. (2015). Research universities in Africa: An empirical overview of eight flagship universities. In N. Cloete, P. Maassen, & T. Bailey (Eds.), *Knowledge production and contradictory functions in African Higher Education* (pp. 18–31). African Minds.

D'souza, J. (2024). *A decade of building sustainable academic collaborations: The legacy of the Carnegie African Diaspora Fellowship Program*. https://tinyurl.com/2ex2fxbd

Enoh, R. A. A. (2014). Interactions between the government and diasporas: The West-African case of Cameroon. *Diaspora Studies, 7*(2), 75–87. https://doi.org/10.1080/09739572.2014.900604

Findlay, A. (1990). A migration channels approach to the study of high-level manpower movements: A theoretical perspective. *International Migration, 28*(1), 15–23. https://doi.org/10.1111/j.1468-2435.1990.tb00137.x

Foulds, K., & Zeleza, P. T. (2014). The African academic diaspora and African higher education. *International Higher Education, 76*(Summer), 16–17.

Gamlen, A. (2006). *Diaspora engagement policies: What are they and what kinds of states use them?* (Working Paper No. 32). Centre on Migration, Policy and Society, University of Oxford. https://tinyurl.com/2bsn76vv

Hayward, F. M., & Ncayiyana, D. J. (2014). Confronting the challenges of graduate education in Sub-Saharan Africa and prospects for the future. *International Journal of African Higher Education, 1*(1), 173–216.

Khodabocus, F. (2016). Challenges to doctoral education in Africa. *International Higher Education, 85*, 25–27.

Larner, W. (2007). Expatriate experts and globalizing governmentalities: The New Zealand diaspora strategy. *Transactions of the Institute of British Geographers, 32*(3), 331–345. https://doi.org/10.1111/j.1475-5661.2007.00259.x

Mangala, J. (2017). Engaging diasporas in development: Contours and outcomes of international policymaking. In J. Mangala (Ed.), *Africa and its global diaspora: The policy and politics of emigration* (pp. 3–37). Palgrave Macmillan.

Meyer, J. B. (2001). Network approach versus brain drain: Lessons from the diaspora. *International Migration, 39*(5), 91–110. https://doi.org/10.1111/1468-2435.00173

Modupe, A. F. (2016). Nigeria and outsourcing for sustainable development: The performance challenges of diaspora Nigerians. *Global Journal of Human-Social Science Research, 16*(3), 11–23.

Muneer, S. E. T. (2011). Transfer of knowledge through expatriate nationals (TOKTEN) as a gender-sensitive development assistance modality in patriarchal societies: An example from Kassala State, Eastern Sudan. *Journal of the Saudi Society of Agricultural Sciences, 10*(2), 89–94. https://doi.org/10.1016/j.jssas.2011.06.002

Nesbitt, F. N. (2003). African intellectuals in the belly of the beast: Migration, identity and the politics of African intellectuals in the north. *Critical Arts: A Journal of South-North Cultural and Media Studies, 17*(1–2), 17–35. https://doi.org/10.1080/02560040385310111

Ogachi, I. O. (2016). Engaging the African academic diaspora: How ready are universities in Africa? *International Journal of African Higher Education, 2*(1), 25–53.

Skeldon, R. (2008). International migration as a tool in development policy: A passing phase? *Population and Development Review, 34*(1), 1–18. https://doi.org/10.1111/j.1728-4457.2008.00203.x

Teferra, D. (2003). Unleashing the forces of the diaspora: Capitalizing on brain drain in the era of information and communication technologies. In R. Barré, V. Hernandez, J. B. Meyer, & D. Vinck (Eds.), *Diasporas Scientifiques—Scientific diasporas, Part II* (pp. 226–243). IRD Editions.

Teferra, D. (2005). Brain circulation: Unparalleled opportunities, underlying challenges, and outmoded presumptions. *Journal of Studies in International Education, 9*(3), 229–250. https://doi.org/10.1177/1028315305277618

Teferra, D. (2010). Deploying Africa's intellectual diaspora: Potentials, challenges, and strategies. In D. Teferra & H. Greijn (Eds.), *Higher education and globalization: Challenges, threats and opportunities for Africa* (pp. 89–100). Maastricht University Centre for International Cooperation in Academic Development (MUNDO).

Tejada, G. (2012). Mobility, knowledge and cooperation: Scientific diasporas as agents of development. *Migration and Development, 10*(18), 59–92. https://doi.org/10.1080/17437199.2012.673819

Tejada, G., Hercog, M., Kuptsch, C., & Bolay, J. C. (2014). The link with home country: A comparative analysis of host country environments for diaspora engagement. In S. Sahoo & B. K. Pattanaik (Eds.), *Global diasporas and development: Socioeconomic, cultural, and policy perspectives* (pp. 39–68). Springer.

Welch, A. R., & Zhen, Z. (2008). Higher education and global talent flows: Brain drain, overseas Chinese intellectuals, and diasporic knowledge networks. *Higher Education Policy, 21*, 519–537.

Wescott, C. G. (2006). Harnessing knowledge exchange among professionals. *International Public Management Review, 7*(1), 30–69.

Wickramasekara, P. (2011). *Circular migration: A triple win or a dead end?* (Discussion Paper No. 15). Global Union Research Network (GURN). https://tinyurl.com/7ts55v97

Woldegiyorgis, A. A. (2020). Challenges of development of doctoral education in Africa. In M. Yudkevich, P. G. Altbach, & H. de Wit (Eds.), *Trends and issues in doctoral education: A global perspective* (pp. 213–237). SAGE Publishing India.

Woldegiyorgis, A. A. (2021). Transnational diaspora engagements in higher education: A case of Ethiopian-born academics in the US. *International Journal of African Higher Education, 8*(2), 43–64.

Woldegiyorgis, A. A., & Adamu, A. Y. (2022). Ethiopian higher education and the COVID-19 pandemic: Opportunities, challenges and lessons. In F. Netswera, A. A. Woldegiyorgis, & T. Karabchuk (Eds.), *Higher education and the COVID-19 pandemic: Cross-national perspectives on the challenges and management of higher education in crisis times* (pp. 24–41). Brill.

Zeleza, P. (2004). The African academic diaspora in the United States and Africa: The challenges of productive engagement. *Comparative Studies of South Asia, Africa and the Middle East, 24*(1), 261–275.

Zeleza, P. (2013). *Engagements between African diaspora academics in the US and Canada and African institutions of higher education: Perspectives from North America and Africa*. Carnegie Corporation of New York. https://tinyurl.com/9xsnxw4t

CHAPTER 6

# Centres of Excellence for Research Development

*Frejus Ariel Kpedetin Sodedji, Achille Ephrem Assogbadjo, and Moses Osiru*

## List of Acronyms/Abbreviations

| | |
|---|---|
| AAU | Association of African Universities |
| ACE | Africa Higher Education Centres of Excellence |
| ADEA | Association for the Development of Education |
| AESA-RISE | The Alliance for Accelerating Excellence in Africa Regional Initiative in Science and Education |
| AFD | French Development Agency |

F. A. K. Sodedji (✉) · A. E. Assogbadjo
Laboratory of Applied Ecology, Faculty of Agronomic Sciences, University of Abomey-Calavi (UAC), Cotonou, Benin
e-mail: frejusariel@gmail.com

A. E. Assogbadjo
e-mail: assogbadjo@gmail.com

M. Osiru
World Bank, Kampala, Uganda
e-mail: mosiru@worldbank.org



D. Teferra (ed.), *Research and Innovation in African Higher Education*,
https://doi.org/10.1007/978-3-031-92909-0_6

| | |
|---|---|
| AMSEN | African Materials Science and Engineering Network |
| AU | African Union |
| AUDA | African Union Development Agency |
| CEGLA | West African-German Centre of Excellence for Governance for Sustainable and Integrative Local Development |
| CERM-ESA | East and South African-German Centre of Excellence for Educational Research, Methodologies and Management |
| CESAAM | Centre of Excellence in Sustainable Agriculture and Agribusiness Management |
| CoE | Centre of Excellence |
| DAAD | German Academic Exchange Service |
| DIGI-FACE | Digital Initiative for African Centres of Excellence |
| ECOWAS | Economic Community of West African States |
| KEMEREM | Kenyan-German Centre of Excellence for Mining, Environmental Engineering and Resource Management |
| NGCL | Namibian-German Centre of Excellence for Logistics |
| PeriPeri U | Partners Enhancing Resilience for People Exposed to Risks |
| RCU | Regional Coordination Unit |
| RFU | Regional Facilitation Unit |
| RISE | Regional Initiative in Science and Education |
| RISE-AFNNET | African Natural Products Research Network |
| RSIF | Regional Scholarship and Innovation Fund |
| RUFORUM | Regional Universities Forum for Capacity Building in Agriculture |
| SABINA | African Biochemistry and Bioinformatics Network |
| SA-GER-CDR | South African-German Centre of Excellence for Development Research |
| SASSCAL | Southern African Science Service Centre for Climate Change and Adaptive Land Management |
| SIG | Science Initiative Group |
| SSAWRN | African Water Resources Network |
| STEM | Science, Technology, Engineering, and Mathematics |
| STI | Science, Technology, and Innovation |

| | |
|---|---|
| TGL | Tanzanian-German Centre of Excellence for Legal Studies |
| TRANSCRIM | South African-German Centre of Excellence for Criminal Justice |
| UAC | University of Abomey-Calavi |
| UNA | National University of Agriculture |
| WAC-SRT | West African-German Centre of Excellence for Sustainable Rural Transformation |
| WASCAL | West African Science Service Centre on Climate Change and Adapted Land Use |
| WCRU | World-Class Research Universities |
| WIO-RISE | African Coastal and Marine Science Network |

## Introduction

Comprising 55 countries, with a population of over 1.2 billion and endowed with abundant resources, Africa constitutes one of the largest and most rapidly growing regions in the world. The United Nations projects that by 2100, two out of every five people on earth will be African (UN, 2022). At the same time, the region is faced with significant challenges such as food insecurity, malnutrition, persistent unemployment, that are further exacerbated by climate change, and regional conflicts (AU, 2014; Fonn et al., 2018; Mweetwa et al., 2020). Thus, Africa is home to more than one-third (418 million) of the world's undernourished (FAO et al., 2021). By 2030, "it is estimated that up to 118 million extremely poor people will be exposed to drought, floods and extreme heat in Africa, if adequate response measures are not put in place" (WMO, 2021). Despite its low greenhouse emissions, Africa feels the impact of climate change acutely, as 95% of its agricultural production depends on rainfall (Gangwar & Bassett, 2020; WMO, 2021). Significant advancement is required to meet the vision of the African Union's Agenda 2063 of "A prosperous Africa based on inclusive growth and sustainable development" and indeed the Global Sustainable Development Goals 2030.

Enhancing industrialization on the continent requires building a scientific system of innovation which is currently hampered by a lack of skilled human resources at the postgraduate level, weak research infrastructure and equipment, inadequate "know-how" and financing as well as an inadequate pipeline of skills (AU, 2015). For example, Africa's gross tertiary education enrolment ratio is 9.4%, which is far below the global average of 38% (Gangwar & Bassett, 2020). Significantly increasing this ratio, would also highlight structural challenges in the job market. Acceleration of postgraduate training therefore requires more than just research infrastructure and financing, but also relies strongly on faculty with doctoral degree and experience in supporting local postgraduate training and research, which is often lacking in strategic areas, and strong private sector engagement. Various approaches, models and mechanisms have been explored, with varying results, to promote the production and effectiveness of high level skills for stimulating industrial led growth (AU, 2014; NEPAD, 2017; Mugwagwa et al., 2019).

Globally, the concept of Centres of Excellence (CoEs) has become an important part of the policy mix of development (Hellström, 2018). It promotes standards of conduct in research, innovation and learning for economic development (Hellström, 2013). The objective of creating CoEs is always service driven (Tadwalkar, 2008), providing unique solutions to specific challenges. Given that the development processes in most countries around the world is centred on a knowledge-based economy, which translates into creativity and innovation (Al-Youbi et al., 2021); the adoption of the CoE approach presents both a business model and a research development opportunity. In Africa, the integration of the CoE approach in research training models can be traced back to 2004, fuelled by the need to accelerate knowledge output in a background of scarce human, infrastructural and other resources (Mohamedbhai, 2015). Since then, various "centres of excellence" initiatives have been launched across Africa, proliferating more recently with multilateral and bilateral funding arrangements. This chapter explores the status, trajectory, contribution and impact of the CoE approach in Africa and provides reflections and implications on their future use to meet Africa's development ambitions.

## Science Technology and Innovation as a Driver for Growth

Over the past decades, there has been a growing recognition of the critical need to advance industrialization in Africa through science, technology, and innovation (STI). Africa is one of a few regions where urbanization has occurred without corresponding industrialization (Mugwagwa et al., 2019; Mugwagwa et al., 2022). Thus cities are growing quickly in population, but the formal jobs and economic opportunities that typically come with industrialization have not kept pace. Industrialization relies on science led innovation, and requires a robust STI system, and a skilled workforce. Significant and sustained investment in the education sector is essential to strengthen tertiary training institutions to build this critical mass.

Enhancing skills yields benefits beyond knowledge generation and innovation. According to UNICEF (2022), each additional year of education boosts a person's income by 10 per cent and increases a country's GDP by 18 per cent. Countries that invested more in education as a proportion of GDP between 1990 and 1999 experienced faster growth in the subsequent decade (Carmignani, 2016). A prime example of how education can drive economic growth is the South Korea's economic expansion known as the "Miracle on the Han river[1]". Following the Korean War, the country prioritized education, reducing illiteracy rate, which dropped from 78 to 4 per cent in ten years (Yoon, 2022). Africa could potentially replicate similar growth with strategic investments in education (ADEA, 2021).

Significant investment in research, coupled with greater coordination can accelerate sustainable prosperity in Africa (WEF, 2020). Research enables evidence-based actions to address key societal challenges and enhances country's economic performance. Research contributes to national and regional GDP through knowledge creation, human capital development and revenue generation via technology trade. Adopting proven "models" for organizing research and innovation is critical for developing countries. However, challenges such as a low number of PhD-qualified staff, weak postgraduate training, inadequate financing,

[1] "The Miracle on the Han River" characterizes the unprecedented speed of South Korea economic growth https://www.korea.net/AboutKorea/Economy/The-Miracle-on-The-Hangang.

limited relevance of training to the private sector, and a high demand for undergraduate training limit the role of universities in supporting industrialization.

## Role of Universities in the Development Space

The African university must transition away from the "ivory tower" mentality to generate innovative solutions in direct response to industry needs and critical societal challenges (Atiase et al., 2020). The knowledge produced by universities and the skills of their graduates are thus very crucial in promoting economic growth and social welfare (Jowi et al., 2013). However, further advancement is needed by some African universities away from colonial legacies that focused on supply driven systems to feed public sector needs (Peters, 2017; AKEC, 2020) towards solving the challenges of local communities and to grow the private sector. These universities may need to restructure, including their incentive systems, to respond proactively to current socio-economic and development needs.

The restructuring of African universities gained pace in 1972, with the Association of African Universities (AAU) conference and the Accra Declaration, which urged Africa universities to become "development universities"(Osiru et al., 2016). Despite this, many remain focused on traditional and theoretical training, compounded by high demand for undergraduate training. Consequently, Africa's contribution to the global research output remains low, at 1.5 to 3% (Fonn et al., 2018). Additionally, there is a mismatch between graduate skills and job market requirements. The rapid expansion and establishment of new universities to address transformation needs have introduced new challenges such as inadequate staffing, poor infrastructure, especially in science disciplines, low learning and quality and substandard student life (Mohamedbhai, 2008; Osiru & Adipala, 2016). Further, the higher education sector in Africa faces insufficient funding, limiting its transformative potential (Mohamedbhai, 2008; Jowi et al., 2013).

As the job market evolves in response to a knowledge economy and pervasive technology (Fomunyam, 2020), African universities must transform to develop high level skills essential to support economic growth. Atiase et al. (2020) argue that universities in developing countries need to shift from merely diffusing knowledge from advanced nations to actively building indigenous knowledge to meet local needs and enhance global competitiveness. This transformation requires effective private sector participation, with universities leading partnerships, particularly with industries, to secure funding for training centres. These centres should focus on research, innovation, and producing high-quality graduates to become more relevant and autonomous. However, a significant challenge remains on how to accelerate both undergraduate and postgraduate training and knowledge production without sufficient PhD-qualified staff experienced in research and innovation.

## Research Universities in Africa

Research universities (or research-intensive universities) focus their governance, management and other systems to prioritize knowledge generation and its transfer and are characterized by emphasis on postgraduate training and research. Evidence of research universities transforming breakthrough research into commercial applications is not unique to the Western world, and African research universities also demonstrate notable successes. Examples include Mohammed V University's enhancement of Argan oil processing in Morocco, which has created business opportunities and promoted sustainable conservation of the Argan tree (IDB-UNESCO, 2014), Makerere University's revolution in the soybean value chain (Tukamuhabwa et al., 2019), and the Smart Mini-Grid innovation by the University of Witwatersrand (Fokazi, 2021). These examples illustrate that research universities in Africa are actively contributing to regional development. Elite research institutions are characterized by highly qualified faculty, excellent research outcomes, quality teaching systems, substantial funding from various sources, international and talented student bodies, academic freedom, autonomous governance, and well-equipped facilities. The CoE approach aims to identify and nurture clusters within existing institutions to develop into knowledge production hubs by fostering these conditions.

The Centres of Excellence (CoEs) approach is based on concepts from creation of World-Class Research Universities (WCRU), which include: a) the picking winners approach, b) the hybrid formula, and c) the clean-slate approach. The picking winners approach involves upgrading selected universities with high potential. The hybrid formula encourages the merger of existing institutions to form a new "anchor" university, achieving synergies typical of world-class institutions. The clean-slate approach involves creating new world-class universities from scratch.

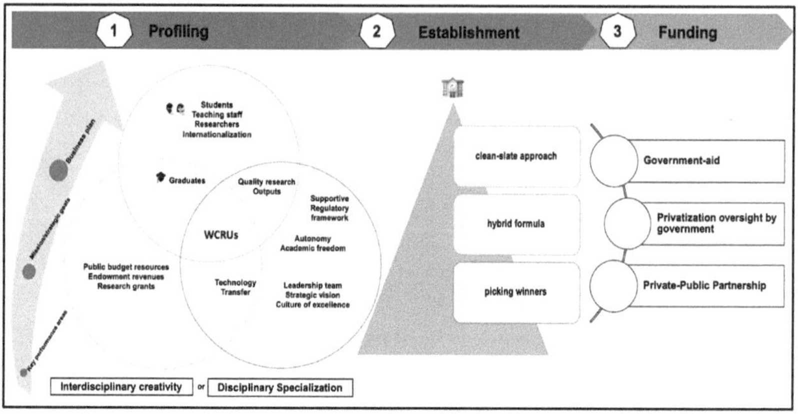


**Fig. 6.1** Road-map for establishment of world-class research universities[2] (WCRUs)

Funding for these WCRUs should adopt a systemic approach, building coalitions among innovation system agents, policy and governance structures, and funders to support emerging technologies and innovations (Mugwagwa et al., 2022). Privatization may also play a role in establishing WCRUs in Africa, as seen in the US, where half of the top 50 research universities are private, and two-thirds of the rest are state-aided (Brint, 2005). African governments could consider privatization supported by inclusive regulations. The CoE approach allows for leveraging existing successful segments within larger universities, enabling a more rapid path to excellence.

## The CoE Approach—What Is It and What Does It Offer?

In a broad sense, Centre of Excellence (CoE) is the combination of "emerging business model" and technologies, and defines any organization striving to create and use excellent state of the art technology to provide innovation and service in a competitive environment (Tadwalkar,

[2] The Venn diagram in Fig. 6.1 was adopted from Zaini et al. (2015).

2008). In that context, the CoE approach represents a duplicable impact-oriented, management and resources development tool that can be borrowed at different organization levels and types including corporates, governments, regional and global human organization to achieve sustainable impact. To illustrate this, the UK Government has introduced the establishment of departmental CoEs as a measure of improving project delivery capability in government departments programmes (O'Leary & Williams, 2008). When applied to the higher education sector, the CoE approach describes a formalized and documented relationship between the following components, i.e. education and research, the educational institution (s) and a third party (e.g. industry, development and investment partners...etc.) to bring to the partnership a special expertise of strategic and societal importance (Gnap et al., 2010). Various interventions of this kind are currently on-going to strengthen higher education in Africa and its impact on the continental transformation.

The CoE approach nurtures a team of specialized experts and organizational environment to carry out outstanding research, education and training, providing leadership service and best practice models (Fekadu et al., 2021), which attracts investments in the thematic areas of focus of the institution to generate new knowledge, innovation and services of high societal value (Hellström, 2013). Fekadu et al. (2021) highlighted that the ambition of excellence, i.e. the desire to be a world-class institution in the area of interest, should be reflected in the CoE goals. The adoption of the CoE approach in higher education helps to achieve various outcomes: i) relevant research agendas, ii) breaking down barriers between disciplines to enable multidisciplinary collaboration, iii) organic integration of activities related to research, product development and commercialization, iv) increased training capacity and quality of graduates v) technology centralization, sharing of best practices and knowledge for timely decisions, which offers competitive advantage vi) rapid delivery of solutions to society issues by leveraging expertise and vii) Increased technology usage and innovation development and their impact on the overall functioning of the CoEs (Tadwalkar, 2008; Beerkens, 2009; Hellström, 2013).

## CoE's in Africa

The creation of networks of institutions promotes excellence in research and training, and provides an effective and cost-efficient mode of strengthening institutional research capacity (Madhani, 2021). To date, we document at least 10 CoE networks championed by various initiatives: African Union CoE networks, USAID-funded Periperi U network, Regional Initiative in Science and Education (RISE) networks, Regional Universities Forum for Capacity Building in Agriculture (RUFORUM), DAAD (German Academic Exchange Service) CoE networks, and the World Bank CoE networks (Table 6.1, 6.2). The different networks are often the fruit of collaborations and funded primarily by multilateral, bilateral or joint efforts (Table 6.2). However, international cooperation prevails over regional (continental) collaboration in many of these networks, e.g. the DAAD networks (Table 6.2) highlighting the current disparity in science capacity between the continent and outside. The networks have led to significant impacts as presented in Table 6.3.

It is worth noting that the creation of these CoE networks was nurtured by various declarations, agenda and strategic plans, including: the AU Science Technology and Innovation Strategy for Africa (AU, 2014), and its predecessor African Science and Technology Consolidated Plan of Action (NEPAD, 2006); the Comprehensive African Agricultural Development Programme (CAADP) (AU, 2021); the Joint Ministerial Declaration to implement the Southern African Science Service Centre for Climate Change and Adaptive Land Use (SASSCAL), the declarations from African Ministers' Council on Water (AMCOW), the AU Agenda 2063 (AU, 2015), among others.

### *African Union CoE Networks*

#### *AUDP-NEPAD Networks of CoEs in Science & Technology*

The African Union Development Agency (AUDA) previously known as the New Partnership for Africa's Development (NEPAD) has the mandate to implement African Union policies. In 2019, the African Heads of State and Government approved the establishment of five Centres of Excellence (COEs) in the five African sub regions (Central Africa, East Africa, North Africa, Southern Africa and West Africa) (AUDA-NEPAD, 2021). These five CoEs are focused on different but interconnected themes,

**Table 6.1** Mission of the key CoE networks in Africa

| *CoE networks* | *Mission/Goals* |
|---|---|
| AUDP-NEPAD CoEs in science and technology | To play a catalytic role in knowledge management and supporting programme delivery at national and regional levels |
| NEPAD-STI hubs | To build the capacity of AU Member States in STI, including providing technical assistance, creating an enabling policy and regulatory environment for new technologies, and engaging in resource mobilization – especially in health, agriculture and education to support the vision of the AU Agenda 2063 |
| PeriPeri U ('Partners Enhancing Resilience for People Exposed to Risks) | To strengthen disaster risk related teaching and learning capacity in institutions across East, West and Southern Africa |
| African Union Pan African University | To develop innovations, stimulate undergraduate and/or graduate programmes to generate applied research outputs |
| RUFORUM | To strengthen the capacities of universities to foster innovations responsive to demands of small-holder farmers through the training of high-quality researchers, the output of impact oriented research and the maintenance of collaborative working relations among researchers, farmers, national agricultural research institutions and governments |
| RISE networks | To increase the population of qualified university academic staff, with a longer-term goal of building science, technology, and innovation capacity to stimulate economic development |
| DAAD Centres of African Excellence | To significantly contribute to the quality and relevance of selected disciplines at African universities, create research capacities, and establish networks between African universities and research institutes, including German partners |

(continued)

**Table 6.1** (continued)

| *CoE networks* | *Mission/Goals* |
|---|---|
| WASCAL | To provide information and knowledge at the local, national, and regional levels to its West African member countries to cope with the adverse impacts of climate change and devise integrated mid and long-term options to build up resilient and productive socio-ecological landscapes |
| SASSCAL | To strengthen the regional capacity to generate and use scientific knowledge products and services for decision-making on climate change and adaptive land management through research management, human capital development and services brokerage |
| East and Southern Africa CoEs | To strengthen selected Eastern and Southern African higher education institutions to deliver quality postgraduate education and build collaborative research capacity in the regional priority areas |
| West Africa CoEs | To promote regional specialization among participating universities in areas that address regional challenges and strengthen the capacities of these universities to deliver quality training and applied research |

which reflects the diversity and knowledge capacity building needs of the continent, and include the following networks:

(1) **The AUDA-NEPAD Centre of Excellence on Climate Resilience**: anticipates, prepares for, and responds to hazardous events, trends, or disturbances related to climate change and environmental sustainability.

(2) **The Centre of Excellence on Rural Resources and Food Systems:** provides access to a highly developed pool of knowledge in food systems and rural resources, including land systems, energy, water and trade.

**Table 6.2** Key CoE networks in Africa and their characteristics

| *CoE networks* | *Number CoEs* | *Years of activity* | *Geographical coverage* | *Thematic areas* | *Funding source* | | | *Participants* |
|---|---|---|---|---|---|---|---|---|
| | | | | | *Govs* | *Donors* | *Joint* | |
| AU NEPAD CoEs in science and technology | 5 | 06 (2019–to date) | Africa | Climate Resilience, Foods Systems, STI, Economy, Human Capital and Development | ✓ | | | AU, Academia, private sector, civil society organizations, AU |
| NEPAD-STI Hubs | 1 | 22 (2003–2025) | Africa | Health, Agriculture, Water, STEM | | | ✓ | Higher Education and Research institutions, TVETs, UE, AU, UNESCO |
| PeriPeri U | 1 | 20 (2005–to date) | Africa | Risk and Disaster | | | ✓ | Higher Education, Research Centres, Governments, USAID, UNDP |

(continued)

**Table 6.2** (continued)

| *CoE networks* | *Number CoEs* | *Years of activity* | *Geographical coverage* | *Thematic areas* | *Funding source* | | | *Participants* |
|---|---|---|---|---|---|---|---|---|
| | | | | | *Govs* | *Donors* | *Joint* | |
| AU Pan African University | 5 | 09 (2016–to date) | Africa | Water and Energy Sciences, Technology and Innovation, Life and Earth Sciences, Governance, Humanities and Social Sciences, Space Sciences | | | ✓ | Higher Education, Research Centres, Governments, |
| RUFORUM | 1 | 21 (2004–to date) | Africa | Agriculture, STI | | | ✓ | Higher Education, Research Centres, Governments, NGOs, Civil Society |
| RISE networks | 5 | 8 (2009–2017) | SSA | Materials Science, Engineering, Natural Products, Biochemistry, Bioinformatics, Coastal and Marine Science | | ✓ | | Universities, Governments, private Sector, Carnegie Corporation of New York |

| *CoE networks* | *Number CoEs* | *Years of activity* | *Geographical coverage* | *Thematic areas* | *Funding source* | | | *Participants* |
|---|---|---|---|---|---|---|---|---|
| | | | | | *Govs* | *Donors* | *Joint* | |
| DAAD CoEs | 10 | 15 (2008–to date) | West Africa, East Africa, South Africa | Education, Logistics, Law, Development, Mining, Environment, Engineering, Resource Management, Environment, Governance Agriculture, ICT, Climate Change, Land Use | | ✓ | | Universities, Governments, Private Sector, Germany |
| WASCAL | 1 | 12 (2013–to date) | West Africa | Climate change, Renewable Energy and Green Energy | | ✓ | | Universities, ECOWAS, Germany, private Sector |
| SASSCAL | 1 | | South Africa | Agriculture, Biodiversity, Climate, Forest, Water | | ✓ | | Universities, governments, EAC, Germany, Private Sector |

(continued)

**Table 6.2** (continued)

| *CoE networks* | *Number CoEs* | *Years of activity* | *Geographical coverage* | *Thematic areas* | *Funding source* | | | *Participants* |
|---|---|---|---|---|---|---|---|---|
| | | | | | *Govs* | *Donors* | *Joint* | |
| East and Southern Africa CoE | 24 | 11 (2014–2025) | East and Southern Africa | Agriculture, Health, Industry, Education and Statistics | | | ✓ | Universities, Governments, World Bank, Private Sector, EAC, ECOWAS, AAU, AFD |
| West Africa CoE | 53 | | West Africa | Agricultural sciences, health and STEM | | | ✓ | |

Govs=Governments, Donors= International/ Private Donors, Joint= Govs + Donors

(3) **The AUDA-NEPAD Centre of Excellence in Science, Technology and Innovation (STI)**: is established at Stellenbosch University (SU) in South Africa in cooperation with the South African Council for Scientific and Industrial Research (CSIR). It envisions to be a leader in data analytics, innovation and technology towards supporting innovative programme incubation on the continent within the dynamics of the Fourth Industrial Revolution.

(4) **The Centre of Excellence on Human Capital and Institutions Development**: is initiated to partnering academia with civil society organizations, the private sector, governments and development partners for strengthening human and institutional capacity required to drive the implementation of Agenda 2063.

(5) **The Centre of Excellence on Supply Chain and Logistics:** envisions to support initiatives linked to economic integration in Member States including Free trade, partial or full abolition of tariffs, common external tariffs, common market implementation, and granting Africa products a competitive advantage in the markets and on the global scene.

These five CoEs benefit from the expertise of the earlier established NEPAD Science Technology and Innovation (STI) Hubs.

*The NEPAD-STI Hubs*

Industrialization, Science, Technology and Innovation (ISTI) is one of the four investment programmes of the NEPAD Agency, which addresses new and emerging development trends in Africa, guided by the African Union (AU) mandate. Various science, technology and innovations hubs were initiated under the auspices of this programme (Mohamedbhai, 2015; Mugwagwa et al., 2022; NEPAD, 2017), including:

(i) ***The NEPAD Africa Biosciences Initiative (ABI):*** is one of the flagship programmes of the African Science and Technology Consolidated Plan of Action (NEPAD, 2006), and focuses on research and development (R&D) in the areas of biotechnology, biodiversity, indigenous knowledge systems and technology. Four biosciences regional networks were established under ABI based on geographical delineations: The Southern Africa Network for Biosciences (SANBio) for Southern African countries; the Biosciences Eastern and Central Africa Network (BecANet) for Eastern and Central African countries; West Africa Biosciences Network (WABNet) for West African countries and North Africa Biosciences Network (NABNet) for North African countries. Other Networks under ABI include: i) the African Biosafety Network of Expertise (ABNE); ii) the Alliance for Accelerating Excellence in Science in Africa (AESA); ii) the African Science, Technology and Innovation Indicators (ASTII) network. Implementation of these networks has been varied.

(ii) ***The NEPAD Water Centres of Excellence (NEPAD Water CoE):*** is a network of Higher Education and Research institutions from 17 countries that conduct high-end scientific research on water and related sectors, to provide policy guidelines to governments. Three CoE networks are part of this initiative. First, the Southern African Network of Water Centres of Excellence (SANWATCE) is hosted by Stellenbosch University with 11 university/research institutions participants from seven countries (Malawi, Zimbabwe, South Africa, Mauritius, Botswana and Mozambique). Second, the Western African Network of Centres of Excellence, which consists of five institutions from four western Africa countries (Senegal, Nigeria, Ghana and Burkina-Faso), and coordinated by University Cheikh Anta Diop in Senegal. Third, the Central/East African Network of Centres of Excellence, currently consists of four institutions from countries in the Central/Eastern African Region (Kenya, Uganda, Sudan and Ethiopia).

*USAID-Funded Periperi U Network*

Periperi U ('Partners Enhancing Resilience for People Exposed to Risks) is a partnership of African universities that spans across the continent and is committed to building local disaster risk related capacity. Established in 2006, with five original members, the partnership has grown to include universities from twelve countries including Algeria, Cameroon Ethiopia, Ghana, Kenya, Madagascar, Mozambique, Nigeria, Senegal, South Africa, Tanzania, and Uganda. The initiative receives financial support mainly from USAID for its activities, which include research and training with sizeable impacts (Table 6.3).

**Table 6.3** Key impacts of established CoE networks in Africa

| *Networks* | *Participating Countries* | *Key impacts* | *Beneficiaries* |
|---|---|---|---|
| AUDP-NEPAD CoEs in science and technology | 55 | Over 40 knowledge-based innovations identified, a state-of-the-art COVID-19 vaccine management platform developed | –Participating –governments, –Universities, –Research Institutions, –students, –Private sector, –Local communities |
| NEPAD-STI | 55 | Innovations, Policies, Research grants, Capacity building | |
| PeriPeri U | 12 | 2425 students trained, 50 Disaster short courses, 100 disease risk related outputs, 50 Disaster related Short Courses, reaching over 1500 professionals | |
| African Union Pan African University | 55 | 417 graduates, 9 patents, 600 Scientific publications, 2582 research grants and Scholarships awarded, | |
| RUFORUM | 38 | > 3735 students supported; 300 publications, 490 scholarships and research grants | |
| RISE networks (Phase 1, ended 2017) | 12 | 188 students trained and 15post-docs | |
| DAAD Centres of African Excellence | 12 | 1064 persons trained, 59 innovations, 1120 Research grants and Scholarships | |
| WASCAL | 11 | 262 persons trained, 15 Research Projects, 300 Scholarships; > 1000 Short course and conferences supported | |
| SASSCAL | 5 | 80 Research grants, 400 Scholarships, Scientific publications | |

(continued)

**Table 6.3** (continued)

| *Networks* | *Participating Countries* | *Key impacts* | *Beneficiaries* |
|---|---|---|---|
| West Africa CoEs | 11 | 54,947 students (4877 PhD & 19,732MSc); 4,836 publications, 89 programmes accredited; over 30,000 professional short course participants; 11,019 internships/ exchanges; Gene sequencing work and virus rapid testing kits, COVID-19 testing, Maternal health care, Water filtering techniques; 90 improved crop varieties developed | |
| East and Southern Africa CoEs | 8 | 16,950 students (1,485 PhD & 5746 MSc); 9719 persons trained; > 3692 publications; > 299 MoUs Partnerships, > 3184 internships and exchanges, 27 programmes accredited | |

*Pan African University (PAU) CoE Network*

The Pan African University (PAU) was inspired and driven by major policy frameworks of the African Union Commission, including the Vision of the African Union, the Second Decade of Education, and the Consolidated Plan of Action for Science and Technology. It was established by the African Union Commission in 2012. PAU is hosted by five leading institutions, equally distributed across the five Africa sub regions, and hosted by Algeria (Université Abou Bekr Belkaid), Cameroon (University of Yaoundé II), Kenya (Jomo Kenyatta University of Agriculture and Technology), Nigeria (University of Ibadan) and South Africa (Cape Peninsula University of Technology), respectively. PAU also comprises the African Virtual and E-University, which operates as the open, distance and e-learning arm of PAU. PAU covers five thematic areas: i) Water and Energy Sciences (PAUWES, Algeria); ii) Basic Science, Technology and Innovation (PAUSTI, Kenya); iii) Life and

Earth Sciences (including Health and Agriculture) (PAULESI, Nigeria); iv) Governance, Humanities and Social Sciences (PAUGHSS, Cameroon); and v) Space Sciences (PAUSS, South Africa). These networks make significant contribution in training human resources in the specific thematic areas in Africa (Table 6.3). The initial selection of CoEs was determined by regions, and each CoE was matched with a financing partner outside Africa, including the African Development Bank (AfDB), Germany, India, and Japan.

*RUFORUM*

The Regional Universities Forum for Capacity Building in Agriculture (RUFORUM), established in 2004, is a consortium of 170 universities in 40 African countries. This network works to strengthen capacity of the universities to drive sustainable and inclusive agricultural development to feed and create prosperity for Africa (Table 6.3). RUFORUM has used a Centre of Excellence / "centre of leadership" approach to accelerate training of Masters and PhD students, by harnessing existing capacity across the continent in its development and implementation of MSc and PhD programmes. PhD programmes adopted one year of course work, recognizing that students being trained would come from diverse MSc programmes across the continent and need strong theoretical underpinning. In 2008, RUFORUM launched these CoE coursework-based doctoral regional training programmes in various thematic areas. The RUFORUM regional CoE's include four key elements of i) course-work based learning that involve the use of staff exchange and visiting lecturers to access available expertise for teaching; but also enhance theoretical underpinning of the program; ii) Academic research at the host university and home countries; iii) skills enhancement training course on scientific data management, personal mastery, journal publications and proposal development etc., usually delivered using a "caravan" approach; iv) internships and field attachments. These programmes have supported training of over 420 doctoral students who are now contributing to the development of the African continent in different capacities in the agricultural sector and leadership positions. As part of building institutional capacity and recognizing excellence, some of the programmes have become part of the World Bank-supported Africa Higher Education Centres of Excellence (Mweetwa et al., 2020).

*The World Bank's Africa Higher Education Centres of Excellence*
The Africa Centres of Excellence (ACE) programme comprises regional higher education initiatives designed to enhance postgraduate education, training, and applied research in key priority areas such as science, technology, engineering, mathematics (STEM), agriculture, health, and industry (World Bank, 2016). Supporting over 81 centres in 21 countries, this is far the largest CoE network on the continent with an investment of over $650 million from the World Bank (an additional $72 million co-financing was provided by AFD to the West Africa ACE Impact Project). By fostering regional collaboration, these projects enable the pooling of resources to address critical skills and applied research needs shared by multiple countries. The ACE projects complement national higher education efforts and among other objectives aim to achieve a significant increase in the highly skilled workforce and applied research output across the SSA region.

In 2014, the first phase of the project, ACE I, was launched with an investment of $165 million, with the establishment of 22 ACEs across eight countries (Benin, Burkina-Faso, Cameroon, Côte d'Ivoire, Ghana, Nigeria, Senegal and Togo) in three priority sectors of STEM, Agriculture, and Health. By 2018, the implementation ACE I achieved 21,341 students' enrolments; 2,559 publications, 70 programmes accredited; and 3,583 faculty trained. Some of the innovations developed through this initiative include: rapid virus testing kits, COVID-19 testing, Water filtering techniques, and 90 improved crop varieties developed, and increased students linkage with industry (Worldbank, 2018).

ACE II is a six-year (2016–2022), $148M project aimed at strengthening selected Eastern and Southern African higher education institutions to deliver quality postgraduate education and build collaborative research capacity in regional priority areas. Building on the ACE I experience, the second phase ACE seeks to strengthen the capacity of 24 ACEs in eight East and Southern Africa countries (Ethiopia, Kenya, Malawi, Mozambique, Rwanda, Tanzania, Uganda, and Zambia) in delivering quality postgraduate education and build collaborative research capacity in five regional priority areas: industry, agriculture, health, education and applied statistics. By 2023, the project had already made noticeable impact: 4535 students' enrolments; 3120 persons trained; more than 2461 publications; 1618 Faculty and Students participation in exchange programmes, and 220 programmes accredited. An additional financing of

$70 million was provided for six centres in agriculture (5 in Malawi and 1 in Mozambique).

As a follow on to the ACE I in West Africa, the ACE III or "ACE impact" was initiated to establish new and scale up well-performing existing ACEs for development Impact; foster Regional Partnerships, and to enhancing national and regional level project facilitation. The World Bank provided $274 million supporting 53 Regional CoEs (18 from ACE 1 and 25 new) in various areas. AFD provided $72 million co-financing to ACE Impact. The Association of African Universities (AAU) is the Regional Facilitation Unit (RFU) of the first and third ACE Projects, while the Inter University Council for Eastern and Southern Africa (IUCEA) is the RFU for ACE II.

The ACEs are achieving significant results both in terms of enrolments, research outcomes and impacts on higher education institutions. At a higher level, the ACEs are encouraging the system to reflect more on postgraduate education and offering a model of what postgraduate facilities should look like. The program supports infrastructural growth including development of laboratories and demonstration centres that previously have not been supported. Importantly, the Program has improved the image of the institutions as postgraduate training centres through strengthening programs, quality assurance, international accreditation, and attracting higher quality international partnerships.

The World Bank ACEs make use of a results-based financing to enhance achievement of targets through pre-agreed disbursement linked indicators. This requires that centres sequence the timing of results in a way that ensures the consistency, efficiency and impact of financing.

*RISE Networks*

The Regional Initiative in Science and Education (RISE) is a project established in 2008 by the Science Initiative Group (SIG), an organization dedicated to fostering science in developing countries, and based at the Institute for Advanced Study, Princeton, New Jersey, in the United States. RISE receives financial support from the Carnegie Corporation of New York, and it was initially implemented in five African countries (Botswana, Mozambique, South Africa, Uganda, and Zimbabwe). Five networks were developed under this project in the areas of: Materials Science and Engineering (AMSEN), Natural Products (RISE- AFNNET), Biochemistry and Bioinformatics (SABINA), Water Resources (SSAWRN) and Coastal and Marine Science (WIO-RISE). The first phase of the project ended in 2017 and trained 188 students including 93 master's degrees and 95 doctorates, and nine had completed postdoctoral work. The second phase of the RISE project is housed at the African Academy of Sciences as a postdoctoral fellowship program, with three-year postdoctoral grants (AESA-RISE fellowships) awarded to seven RISE doctoral graduates to conduct research in Africa in collaboration with international partner institution (Madhani, 2021).

*DAAD CoE Networks*

The DAAD (German Academic Exchange Service) has supported African universities to establish CoEs to improve the quality of the education service, and increase their research capacities, enabling future decision-makers in Africa to be trained in line with international standards. From 2008 to date, DAAD interventions has yielded 10 CoEs and, two Science Service Centres (WASCAL and SASSCAL) with interconnected thematic areas (Table 6.1, 6.2 and 6.3) to drive high-quality training, research and innovations in Africa.

**DAAD Centres of African Excellence**

The "Centres of African Excellence" is a DAAD flagship programme. This programme, which started in 2008, has supported 10 CoEs which bring expertise from universities in eight African countries (Ghana, Senegal, Congo, Namibia, South Africa, Tanzania, Kenya, Mali and Niger) in partnership with world-class universities to champion change in their field of interest (DAAD, 2021). They have trained 1064 persons generated over 59 innovations, with 1120 Research grants and scholarships to support students and researchers (Table 6.3).

The CoE networks include: (i) the West African-German Centre of Excellence for Development Studies (GGCDS), (ii) the Congolese-German Centre of Excellence for Microfinance (CCAM), which has a tailor-made modern curriculum for training experts in microfinance (iii) the Namibian-German Centre of Excellence for Logistics (NGCL) (iv) the South African-German Centre of Excellence for Development Research (SA-GER-CDR); (v) the South African-German Centre of Excellence for Criminal Justice (TRANSCRIM); (vi) the Tanzanian-German Centre of Excellence for Legal Studies (TGL); (vii) the East and South African-German Centre of Excellence for Educational Research,

Methodologies and Management (CERM-ESA); (viii) the Kenyan-German Centre of Excellence for Mining, Environmental Engineering and Resource Management (CEMEREM), (ix) the West African-German Centre of Excellence for Sustainable Rural Transformation (WAC-SRT); (V) the West African-German Centre of Excellence for Governance for Sustainable and Integrative Local Development (GEGLA). Five of these CoEs (CCAM, TRANSCRIM, SAGER-CDR, TGL and GGCDS) were first established in 2008, followed by NGCL in 2009, CERM-SEA in 2014, CEMEREM in 2016, and CEGL and WAC-SRT in 2017. DAAD has also enabled the establishment of the "Digital Initiative for African Centres of Excellence" (DIGI-FACE) where the centres are working together to digitalize their teaching and learning opportunities and to offer cross-curricular courses.

### WASCAL

The West African Science Service Centre on Climate Change and Adapted Land Use (WASCAL) is a network of twelve universities from 11 countries (Ghana, Mali, Benin, Burkina-Faso, Cabo Verde, Côte d'Ivoire, Gambia, Niger, Nigeria, Senegal and Togo), funded by the government of Germany through its Academic Exchange Service (DAAD). WASCAL is a large-scale research-focused climate service centre that contributes to strengthening the research infrastructure and capacity in West Africa related to climate change. WASCAL runs 16 Graduate Studies Programme (GSPs) including 10 doctoral and 2 master's programmes in Climate Change, and 4 international master's programmes in energy and green hydrogen (WASCAL, 2020). The network has trained over 262 African experts and attracted funds to support 15 Research Projects, 300 Scholarships; and over 1000 short courses and conferences (Table 6.3).

### SASSCAL

The Southern African Science Service Centre for Climate Change and Adaptive Land Management (SASSCAL) is a joint initiative of Germany and five African countries (Angola, Botswana, Namibia, South Africa, Zambia) in response to demographic change, climate change and the globalization of economic systems, which affect the global community. The creation of SASSCAL was endorsed by the 2012 Namibia Joint Ministerial declaration. SASSCAL envisions to be a leading regional centre in integrated climate change and adaptive land management science services for improved quality of life in southern Africa. An overview of SASSCAL activities (SASSCAL, 2019) demonstrates its progress towards achieving this vision. SACCAL has awarded 80 research grants, 400 Scholarships with significant scientific contributions.

## Key Lessons from On-Going CoE Networks in Africa

We categorize key lessons from CoEs in Africa within important areas of **strategy**, **excellence**, **collaboration, governance collaboration**, **sustainability**, **regionality** and **response to COVID-19**.

### *Strategy*

The overview of the CoE networks revealed that over the two decades a large range of networks have been established in Africa. Although they differ in thematic focus (Table 6.1), funding arrangements and establishment strategies (Table 6.2) and impacts (Table 6.3), they are all committed to accelerating high level human capital development, knowledge generation and innovation in Africa (Table 6.1). The networks leverage expertise from international partnerships, which helps to close the gaps in terms of quality of research, teaching and outreach, mentorship as well as access to research infrastructure.

### *Excellence*

Excellence denotes a relative status of prominence, superiority, and uniqueness, accompanied by tangible growth (Fekadu et al., 2021). Salmi (2016) defined an "excellence initiative" in tertiary education as a substantial infusion of additional funding by a national government, aimed at rapidly upgrading existing universities. This is facilitated by key factors in World-Class Research Universities (WCRUs): i) a high concentration of talented faculty and students, ii) ample resources resulting in a rich learning environment and advanced research, and iii) governance structures that promote strategic vision, innovation, and flexibility, enabling efficient decision-making and resource management. Our observations indicate that all Centres of Excellence (CoEs) networks established in Africa prioritize "excellence" in their vision, as evidenced by their growth and the impact of their activities (Table 6.3). Notably, there has been an increase in the number of accredited training programmes under some initiatives, while others have developed research and publication policies. However, excellence is typically a recognition of an already achieved status (Mohamedbhai, 2015). Some CoE networks discussed in this chapter are newly established and are working towards their milestones, whereas others have been operational for over a decade with tangible outcomes. Despite these efforts, achieving excellence remains a critical goal requiring further efforts from these networks. Measuring excellence poses a challenge, as no African universities are ranked among the top 200 globally, and the continent's contribution to the global knowledge economy remains minimal.

### *Collaboration*

The existing Centres of Excellence (CoEs) networks, primarily established through a hybrid formula (bringing together multiple departments or institutions to create a distinguished entity), have facilitated the consolidation of institutions into anchor institutions in their priority areas. This consolidation has bolstered both north–south and south-south collaborations, fostering experience sharing among regions and countries, and attracting international partnerships and investments.

A significant aspect of the implementation roll-out has been the enhancement of international collaborations, which has substantially impacted the CoE's capacity to accelerate postgraduate training, particularly in strategic areas where initial capacity was limited and where the programmes have adopted course work as part of training. The CoE networks have also strengthened public–private partnerships and industry linkages, as evidenced by the patents and internship opportunities offered to students within some networks (Table 6.3), although progress varies among centres and more effort is needed in this area. It appears that the character of the private sector in SSA may require more innovation in engagement.

CoEs have supported African higher education institutions in deepening the internationalization of their programmes by attracting students from other countries and regions and engaging a broader range of staff in teaching, supervision, and mentorship. This "talent concentration" is a crucial outcome of the CoEs. Collaboration has been instrumental in improving curricula and its delivery, supporting the implementation of short training programmes, and enhancing pedagogy in general. The regional approach of CoEs, which brings students from across the continent, necessitates a strong theoretical underpinning for research to ensure robust academic foundations. Collaboration has also enhanced the capacity for course delivery where the CoE lacks in-house the full range of teaching capabilities required. The use of technology has enabled greater participation of international partners in teaching, research, and mentorship, broadened supervision capacity, and increased publication output.

### *Governance*

The scoping of the literature available on these networks revealed that they are endorsed by different continental and regional regulations. Also, most CoEs have clear organizational structure, rules and policies, with governing and advisory committee which promote sustainable growth. However, governance was often "superimposed" within a larger institutional framework that could lead to friction and other management challenges. This addition of "new patch" on an "old cloth" requires a rethink in the longer-term for management of CoEs, particularly when the initial programme funding comes to an end. It also has led to "wet" (or well-funded) and "dry" (poorly funded) departments within the same institutions. Furthermore, the governance and management approach in some of the host universities of these networks relies heavily on procedures that often led to delays in implementation of training programmes. There is also weak participation of some countries and institutions (Table 6.3), especially those from North Africa, in some of these networks, which could be a hindrance in the pursuit of the regional goal of eradicating poverty and hunger in Africa. The different networks work along with gender governance policies (e.g. ratio of scholarships awarded to women and people from conflict countries), which promote equity and equality.

### *Sustainability*

All the CoE networks are "owned" and led by Africans and institutions in Africa, which promotes ownership of the mission, service, and the generated outcomes. Financial sustainability is likely to continue to be an issue due to reliance on externally driven funding arrangements for most of the CoEs. The World Bank CoEs for example, highlight the importance of sustainability within the programme structure and have focused on external generation of finances, largely through proposal writing, as a key indicator to complement existing financing. Many networks have attracted funds from philanthropy and international development partners. However, the fund-raising capacity is still very low in some of the networks, which may require them to invest efforts in resource mobilization for the long-term running of their activities. It also highlights the limitations to donor funding that is often tied to specific foci and may limit support for certain elements such as infrastructure and salaries. Additionally, incentive schemes are built on models external to host institutions that will require significant changes at the institution to integrate the CoEs into their institutional frameworks.

***Regionality***

The establishment of CoE networks reduces boundaries between countries, enabling free people and knowledge movement and duplicable innovations through mobility programmes and jobs. The headquarters and or host institutions of different networks are fairly distributed across the continent, which promotes inclusion. Moreover, some of the CoE networks contribute in the development of capacity in conflicts and post-conflicts countries. For instance, the Centre of Excellence in Sustainable Agriculture and Agribusiness Management (CESAAM), a network established under the ACEII project and hosted by Egerton University, Kenya offered 30% of its fellowships to applicants from regional post conflict countries (Burundi, Rwanda, South Sudan and Uganda) and fragile states (Guliye et al., 2016). This sort of initiative can support inclusion and support maintenance capacity for fragile states. It highlights a strength of the model that improves the sharing of regional capacity for building a wide range of capacities and knowledge in areas strategic for the region, and rationalizes investments in these areas. The CoEs will also play an important role in supporting the implementation of the Africa Continental Free Trade Area that brings closer 1 billion people in 55 countries of the African Union and eight Regional Economic Communities (RECs).

Conversely, prior experiences with this model underscore certain risks, emphasizing the crucial necessity for well-defined risk mitigation strategies within all CoE initiatives to attain the anticipated outcomes.

For example, during the more prosperous periods of the East African Community, Makerere University was designated to host a Centre of Excellence in Social Sciences. However, this initiative was severely impacted by the dissolution of the East African Community, which coincided with the rise to power of the late Idi Amin Dada, former President of the Republic of Uganda. The substantial investments and resources allocated to this programme were lost amid the ensuing civil conflict in the country, which also had repercussions for the broader region.

### COVID-19 Impacts on CoEs

The COVID-19 pandemic plunged the world into a state of chaos, profoundly affecting lives and economies on a global scale. Numerous development sectors were halted and are still in the process of recovery, with the impact being particularly pronounced in fragile or emerging economies. For example, school closures were more prevalent in Africa compared to other regions of the world (UNESCO, 2021). Predictably, the pandemic disrupted activities in some networks while necessitating significant operational and financial adjustments in others. Simultaneously, these networks have played pivotal roles in responding to COVID-19, underscoring their importance in the development process in Africa. Notable success stories include: (i) the sequencing of the COVID-19 genome in Africa through the collaboration between the West Africa Centre for Cell Biology of Infectious Pathogens (WACCBIP) and the African Centre of Excellence for Genomics of Infectious Diseases (ACEGID) in Nigeria; and (ii) the partnership between the AUDA-NEPAD Centre of Excellence on Science, Technology and Innovation and Vodacom-Mezzanin to develop a state-of-the-art vaccine management platform across all African Union member states.

## Conclusions and Recommendations

A country's ability to generate, adapt, utilize and commercialize knowledge is essential for addressing local challenges, fostering wealth and prosperity, and ensuring economic growth (AfDB, 2023). Research and innovation capacity and relevant systems are therefore pivotal in accelerating economic growth and development. The adoption of CoE networks has significantly contributed to Africa's STI ecosystem and its advancement. This review identified more than 115 CoEs that have been established across Africa, aligning with key continental priorities despite variations in thematic focus, funding, and governance arrangements. Most CoEs, with few exceptions, have been supported by external donors, including World Bank credits and grants. The impact of these networks is substantial, as CoEs have demonstrated their capacity to accelerate research outputs, including publications and address key research and training challenges.

The CoE networks have facilitated enhanced engagement between private and public sectors and strengthened industry linkages within higher education. This is evidenced by the generation of patents and the provision of internship opportunities for students within some networks (Table 6.3). Additionally, CoEs have bolstered the internationalization of programmes by establishing necessary infrastructure, staffing, and systems that promote student mobility across countries and regions, and involving a broader range of staff in teaching, supervision, and mentorship. CoE collaborations have also significantly improved teaching and research capacities, resulting in a critical mass of talent concentration, which is a notable outcome of CoEs.

The review also revealed a strong reliance on both south-south and north–south collaborations and some industry linkages to achieve their goals. However, governance issues and weak sustainability, primarily due to inadequate financing strategies, hinder the long-term viability of CoEs. To ensure broader impact and rapid growth in Africa, it is recommended that countries build suitable incentive systems for CoEs, including income generation and sustainability. Furthermore, enhancing the participation of the private sector, particularly in financing knowledge generation, is crucial. This will ensure that research directly contributes to the productivity and growth of the private sector, and should be aligned to the national and regional development growth strategies thereby fostering sustainable development.

## References

ADEA. (2021). *Development of country policy on provision of quality STEM education at the basic learning levels in Africa* (Vol. Policy Brief N° 1). Association for the Development of Education in Africa.

AFDB. (2023). *African economic outlook 2023. Highlights. Mobilizing private sector financing for climate and green growth in Africa*. African Development Bank.

AKEC, J. A. (2020). Envisioning the future of the African University: Needed reform, and adjustments to respond to the emerging challenges *African Journal of Rural Development*, *5*(3), 1–31.

Al-Youbi, A. O., Zahed, A. H. M., Nahas, M. N., & Hegazy, A. A. (2021). The roles of universities in development. In *The leading world's most innovative universities* (pp. 1–8). https://doi.org/10.1007/978-3-030-59694-1_1

Atiase, V. Y., Kolade, O., & Liedong, T. A., 2020. The emergence and strategy of tech hubs in Africa: Implications for knowledge production and value creation. *Technological Forecasting and Social Change*, *161*. https://doi.org/10.1016/j.techfore.2020.120307

AU. (2014). *Science, technology and innovation strategy for Africa 2024*. African Union.

AU. (2015). *Agenda 2063 of African Union: The Africa we want in 2063.The Africa we want in 2063*. African Union

AU. (2018). *The 2nd High Level Dialogue on enhancing policies and practices to promote STEM- focused TVET for Women and Girls has called on Member States to contribute to the vision of Agenda 2063*. Ethiopia: African Union

AU. (2021). *The comprehensive african agricultural development programme*. Retrieved 19 April from https://au.int/en/articles/comprehensive-african-agricultural-development-programme

AUDA-NEPAD. (2021). *AUDA-NEPAD 2021 annual report*.

Beerkens, E. (2009). Centres of excellence and relevance. *Science, Technology and Society, 14*(1), 153–175. https://doi.org/10.1177/097172180801400106

Brint, S. (2005). Creating the future:'New directions' in American research universities. *Minerva, 43*(1), 23–50.

Carmignani, F. (2016). Does government spending on education promote economic growth? *The Conversation Africa* https://theconversation.com/does-government-spending-on-education-promote-economic-growth-60229

DAAD. (2021). *Fachzentren Afrika – Centres of African excellence*. www.african-excellence.de

FAO, Ifad, UNICEF, WFP, & WHO. 2021. The State of Food Security and Nutrition in the World. (2021). Transforming food systems for food security, improved nutrition and affordable healthy diets for all. *FAO*. https://doi.org/10.4060/cb4474en

Fekadu, A., Oppenheim, C., Manyazewal, T., Nislow, C., Woldeamanuel, Y., Hailu, A., Belete, A., Wondimagegn, D., Hanlon, C., Gebremariam, T., Collins, A., Larson, C. J., Gebreyes, W., Aklilu, E., Muula, A. S., Mugus, S., Caffrey, C. R., Giday, M., Yimer, G., Makonnen, E. (2021). Understanding the key processes of excellence as a prerequisite to establishing academic centres of excellence in Africa. *BMC Medical Education*, *21*(1), 36.

Fokazi, S. (2021). Wits University energy innovation may alleviate load-shedding woes. *Times Live*. https://www.timeslive.co.za/news/south-africa/2021-06-24-wits-university-energy-innovation-may-alleviate-load-shedding-woes/

Fomunyam, K. G. (2020). Agenda 2063: Science, technology, engineering, and mathematics (STEM) education to the rescue. *International Journal of Engineering Research and Technology, 13*(7). https://doi.org/10.37624/ijert/13.7.2020.1603-1609

Fonn, S., Ayiro, L. P., Cotton, P., Habib, A., Mbithi, P. M. F., Mtenje, A., Nawangwe, B., Ogunbodede, E. O., Olayinka, I., Golooba-Mutebi, F., & Ezeh, A. (2018). Repositioning Africa in global knowledge production. *The Lancet, 392*(10153), 1163–1166. https://doi.org/10.1016/s0140-6736(18)31068-7

Gangwar, M., & Bassett, R. M. (2020). *Covid19 coronavirus response*. https://thedocs.worldbank.org/en/doc/837811591117062566-0090022020/render/OneAfricaTEandCovid05292020.txt

Gnap, J., Kalasova, A., Gogola, M., & Ondrus, J. (2010). The centre of excellence for transport service and control. *Communications - Scientific letters of the University of Zilina, 12*(3A), 116–120. https://doi.org/10.26552/com.C.2010.3A.116-120

Guliye, A. Y., Owuor, G., Ouma, J. P., Omwamba, M. N., Mwonga, S. M., & Ogendo, J. O. (2016). Centre of excellence in sustainable agriculture and agribusiness management (CESAAM): An Eastern and Southern Africa higher education centres of excellence project at Egerton University, Kenya. In *Fifth African higher education week and RUFORUM Biennial Conference 2016" Linking agricultural universities with civil society, the private sector, governments and other stakeholders in support of agricultural development in Africa, Cape Town, South-Africa.*

Hellström, o., 2013. *Centres of Excellence as a Tool for Capacity Building.*

Hellström, T. (2018). Centres of excellence and capacity building: From strategy to impact. *Science and Public Policy, 45*(4), 543–552. https://doi.org/10.1093/scipol/scx082

IDB-UNESCO. (2014). *Africa's minds build a better future: African science, technology & innovation success stories*. https://unesdoc.unesco.org/ark:/48223/pf0000227858

Jowi, J. O., Obamba, M., Sehoole, C., Barifaijo, M., Oanda, O., & Alabi, G., 2013. *Governance of higher education, research and innovation in Ghana, Kenya and Uganda* (Innovation, Higher Education and Research for Development (IHERD), Issue. https://www.oecd.org/sti

Madhani, N. (2021). *Investments in higher education and research in Africa 2010–2019*. https://www.carnegie.org/publications/investments-in-higher-education-and-research-in-africa-20102019/

Marginson, S. (2011). Global perspectives and strategies of Asia-Pacific research universities. In N. C. Liu, Q. Wang, & Y. Cheng (Eds.), *Paths to a World-Class University. Global perspectives on higher education* (Vol. 23). SensePublishers. https://doi.org/10.1007/978-94-6091-355-6_1

Mohamedbhai, G. (2015). *Regional, continental and international collaboration: Foundations for emerging centres of excellence in Africa* Regional, Continental and International Collaboration: Foundations for Emerging Centres of Excellence in Africa, Kigali.

Mohamedbhai, G. T. G. (2008). *The effects of massification on higher education in Africa*. Association of African Universities. https://books.google.ci/books?id=IQ_opwAACAAJ

Mugwagwa, J., Banda, G., Ozor, N., Bolo, M., & Oriama, R. (2022). Optimising governance capabilities for science, research and innovation in Africa. *Technology in Society, 68*. https://doi.org/10.1016/j.techsoc.2021.101804

Mugwagwa, J., Banda, G., Ozor, N., Bolo, M., & Oriama, R. N. (2019). *New approaches for funding research and innovation in Africa*. African Technology Policy Studies Network.

Mweetwa, A. M., Okori, P., Rukarwa, R. J., Waswa, M., & Adipala, E. (2020). Building higher level skills to drive development in Africa: The case of the RUFORUM doctoral regional training programmes. *African Journal of Rural Development, 5*(3), 33–52.

NEPAD. 2006. <*Africa's Science & Technology Consolidated Plan of Action_E.pdf*>. http://archives.au.int/handle/123456789/5941

NEPAD. (2017). ISTI Consolidated Programme Brochure. In (pp. 15).

O'Leary, T., & Williams, T. (2008). Making a difference? Evaluating an innovative approach to the project management Centre of Excellence in a UK government department. *International Journal of Project Management, 26*(5), 556–565. https://doi.org/10.1016/j.ijproman.2008.05.013

Osiru, M., & Adipala, E. (2016). *Responding to key gaps in Africa's Higher Agricultural Education: Lessons from the Regional Universities Forum for Capacity Building in Agricultu* Fifth RUFORUM Biennial Regional Conference Cape Town, South Africa.

Osiru, M., Nampala, P., & Ekwamu, A. (2016). *African Faculties of Agriculture within an Expanding University Sector*. https://doi.org/10.2499/9780896292123

Peters, M. A. (2017). Manifesto for the postcolonial university. *Educational Philosophy and Theory, 51*(2), 142–148. https://doi.org/10.1080/00131857.2017.1388660

Salmi, J. (2016). Excellence initiatives to create world-class universities: Do they work? *Higher Education Evaluation and Development, 10*(1), 1–29.

SASSCAL. 2019. *Annual Report*

Tadwalkar, S. V. (2008). Create centre of excellence (CoE) for better business. *Ubiquity*, *March*, 1–9.

Tukamuhabwa, P., Obua, T., Namara, M., Okii, D., Kabayi, P., & Yiga, G. (2019). *Soybean research and development in Uganda: Highlights 2002–2018. Makerere University, Kampala, Uganda*. Centre for Soybean Improvement and Development, College of Agricultural and Environmental Sciences (CAES), Makerere University.

UNESCO. (2021). *UNESCO figures show two thirds of an academic year lost on average worldwide due to Covid-19 school closures*. Retrieved 20 April 2022 from https://en.unesco.org/news/unesco-figures-show-two-thirds-academic-year-lost-average-worldwide-due-covid-19-school

Unicef. (2022). *Education: the most powerful investment in our future*. https://blogs.unicef.org/blog/

United Nations. (2022). *World population prospects*. https://www.un.org/development/desa/pd/sites/www.un.org.development.desa.pd/files/wpp2022_summary_of_results.pdf

WASCAL. (2020). *2020 annual report*.

WEF. (2020). *The global competitiveness report 2019*. www.weforum.org/gcr.

WMO. (2021). *Climate change triggers mounting food insecurity, poverty and displacement in Africa*. World Meterological Organization. Retrieved 21 April 2022 from

WoldBank. (2016). *ACEII Eastern & Southern Africa higher education centers of excellence project: A regional solution to transform science and technology education in Africa*. http://www.ace2.iucea.org

Worldbank. (2018). *Implementation completion report (ICR) review* ICRR0022604).

Yoon, S. (2022). *This is how South Korea can become a global innovation hub*. WEF. Retrieved 12 April 2022 from https://www.weforum.org/agenda/2022/01/startups-in-south-korea-are-thriving-this-is-why/

Zaini, R. M., Lyan, D. E., & Rebentisch, E. (2015). Start-up research universities, high aspirations in a complex reality: a Russian start-up university case analysis using stakeholder value analysis and system dynamics modeling. *Triple Helix*, *2*(1). https://doi.org/10.1186/s40604-014-0016-8

CHAPTER 7

# Research and Academic Collaborations in Africa: Imperatives, Potentials, and Risks

*Damtew Teferra*

## Introduction

Modern academic collaboration, involving structured partnerships among institutions, was catalyzed in the twentieth century by technological advancements and global challenges, like those during and after World War II. In the last two to three decades, academic collaboration has intensified across the world with the ushering of the world into what is called a "knowledge society" that rides on a knowledge economy (Teferra et al., 2022). Kwiek (2017) holds that international academic, particularly research, collaboration has captivated the imagination of the academic profession and informed governments' research policy across the world. Marginson (2022) affirms that few human activities are more globally integrated and interconnected than science and the academic enterprise.

Scientific research productivity has been closely linked to high levels of collaboration (De Solla Price & Beaver, 1966; Lee & Bozeman, 2005; Lewis et al., 2012) and consequently, many developed countries seek

D. Teferra (✉)
School of Education, University of KwaZulu-Natal, Durban, South Africa
e-mail: teferra@ukzn.ac.za



D. Teferra (ed.), *Research and Innovation in African Higher Education*,
https://doi.org/10.1007/978-3-031-92909-0_7

to stimulate collaboration through a mix of research grant schemes and grant criteria. Thus, academic collaboration has evolved into a critical and increasingly sought practice for institutions and individuals striving for excellence and distinction. The status and ranking of academic institutions—now more vital than ever—(Hazelkorn, 2016) are significantly influenced by the breadth and depth of research partnerships and collaborations they cultivate and maintain. These collaborations are not just a marker of prestige but a fundamental strategy for enhancing research output, fostering innovation, and expanding global influence. As a result, institutions are systematically pursuing collaborative efforts to bolster their reputation and achieve academic excellence (Altbach, 2011).

Academic collaboration has witnessed massive growth as the interest in tackling global issues and challenges have taken center stage. There is a robust understanding and hence practice of undertaking massive multinational, multi-institutional collaborative research to tackle major challenges often unencumbered by national borders and artificial boundaries (Teferra et al., 2022).

Institutions are often driven by a multitude of intentions to engaging in academic collaborations mainly dictated by necessities. The imperatives of academic collaboration are many and different and are attributed to generating resources, enhancing academic capacities, exchanging experiences, and enhancing institutional profile. Institutions also engage in collaboration to pursue mega initiatives such as human genome project and the Hadron collider and tackle major global challenges such as climate change or COVID-19 (Teferra, 2022a).

Such endeavors largely occur within the framework of North–North and, to some extent, North–South collaboration. However, the same cannot be said of South-South collaboration, which Marginson (2022) describes as "periphery-to-periphery networking." Although the established trend of North–South collaboration appears to be shifting in these regions, the conventional center-periphery paradigm has become increasingly less relevant in capturing the evolving dynamics of global academic partnerships, since it was noted by Gopinathan and Altbach (2005).

For decades, academic collaboration has been hailed as a powerful tool for knowledge creation and capacity building, particularly in the Global South. However, much of this narrative has been framed from the perspective of the Global North, with traditional North–South collaborations dominating the landscape. In response to growing calls for a shift away from this dependency, this chapter explores the imperatives of academic collaboration in the context of Africa, while also drawing insights from the broader South. South-South collaboration—cooperation among institutions in Africa, Asia, and Latin America—has remained comparatively underdeveloped, despite its critical role in regional and global development.

Recently, interest in this form of collaboration has been gaining momentum, driven by the recognition that shared experiences and common developmental challenges can be more effectively addressed through direct partnerships between these regions. This growing focus aims to build research capacity, foster regional innovation, and reduce reliance on traditional North–South partnerships (Teferra et al., 2022).

## Conceptual Underpinning

The literature on research collaboration is extensive and reflects diverse interpretations, often accompanied by a degree of conceptual ambiguity. Research collaboration encompasses a broad spectrum of relationships, including those between individuals, organizations, and hybrid interactions where individuals engage with organizations. These relationships typically involve key elements such as resource sharing, effective communication, and task coordination (Bozeman et al., 2013).

At the individual level, research collaboration often manifests as partnerships between scholars, researchers, or practitioners working toward shared objectives, such as co-authoring papers, conducting experiments, or developing innovative solutions. On the organizational front, collaboration may include joint research programs, institutional partnerships, or alliances fostering interdisciplinary innovation. When these dimensions intersect—such as individuals within one organization collaborating with external institutions—hybrid collaborative models emerge, further enriching the collaborative landscape.

The conceptual ambiguity arises because collaboration can vary significantly in scale, scope, and intent. It can range from informal knowledge-sharing networks to formalized agreements involving significant investments and complex governance structures. Furthermore, collaboration may be driven by diverse motivations, including enhancing research impact, accessing specialized resources, capacity building, addressing global challenges, or fostering cross-cultural exchanges.

Understanding research collaboration as a multifaceted phenomenon underscores its critical role in advancing knowledge, fostering innovation, and addressing complex problems that transcend disciplinary, institutional, and geographical boundaries. This complexity highlights the need for nuanced frameworks to analyze and enhance collaborative efforts in research ecosystems.

Katz and Martin (1997) hold that the concept of collaboration "has been taken for granted as though we all know exactly what is meant by the term" and defined the term as "the working together of researchers to achieve common goal of producing new scientific knowledge." They recognize research collaboration as very "fuzzy" with ill-defined border without the precise location of its boundaries across institutions, fields, sectors, and countries as well as over time. In this chapter the term academic and research collaboration—and its variants, such as cooperation and partnerships, are used rather loosely and interchangeably to encompass typical joint academic and scholarly engagements and tasks—of teaching and learning, research, publication/communication—within one's border and/or across the world.

## The Realm of Academic Cooperation in the Global South

Sa e Silva (2009, in du Toit et al., 2017) notes that South-South collaboration has probably existed since the very first independence movements in colonized nations, though it acquired an institutionalized character only in the 1940s. The author goes on to describe the eras of South-South Collaboration in the twentieth century in three phases. These include Self-reliance and Political Strengthening (1949–1979), Demobilization (1980–1998) and Best Practice Transfer (1999–present).

*Self-reliance and political strengthening* imply that all countries are at a certain stage on one, single development continuum, and that underdeveloped countries therefore need to follow the path that has been followed by the ex-colonial powers. This era, the period immediately after World War II, was characterized by technical consultants and multilateral agencies, with the rise of the influence of multinational corporations such as the Bretton Wood institutions of the International Monetary Fund (IMF) and the World Bank "created in 1944 to help restore and sustain the benefits of global integration, by promoting international economic cooperation" (IMF). In what Hydén (2016) calls the "first wave," to describe the period of 1960s and 1970s, it parallels Sa e Silva's first phase where the massive support to higher education consisted largely of three components: first, for "bricks and mortar," second, technical assistance, and third scholarships.

In *Demobilization*, Western neoliberal economic policies gained dominance, effectively overshadowing the political and economic ideologies previously championed by the Eastern bloc. These Western policies, particularly through the structural adjustment programs (SAPs) enforced by the International Monetary Fund (IMF) and the World Bank, imposed stringent economic reforms on partner countries. These reforms mandated austere policy measures, often leading to severe budget cuts in critical sectors such as health, education, particularly higher education and other social services.

In developing regions, especially in the Global South and notably in Africa, these policies had disproportionately negative impacts. The reduction in public spending on social services, such as education and heath, exacerbated inequalities and eroded access to essential services for vulnerable populations. Although designed to stabilize economies, Structural Adjustment Programmes (SAPs) often undermined development prospects and worsened socio-economic conditions in many African countries (Samoff, 1994). It was also in this era that the infamous, and unfavorable study sanctioned by the World Bank erroneously declared higher education as having a lower rate-of-return—with major consequences for the sector (Teferra, 2009b). Most development partners withdrew their support toward higher education and research for Africa on the basis of the study, which later officially renounced (Bloom et al., 2006; World Bank, 2002).

On the account of the study, higher education and research in Africa were declared a luxury that the continent affords the least—with massive repercussions for the sector. To make matters worse, this was the time when SAPs were in full gear impacting social services as health and education, a further blow to the sector. This study had three immediate impacts on higher education development on the continent: It (a) immediately affected lending institutions directly, (b) constrained other (bilateral) development partners, and, moreover, (c) prevented individual countries from supporting their own institutions and systems (Teferra, 2005). Woodhall (2003, p. 45) writing on financing and economics of higher education in Africa concurs that the conclusion of the study made "considerable influence, not only on World Bank lending policies but also on investment and aid strategies of other international agencies and donors." This period aligns with what Hydén (2016) calls "the reversal" where in the 1980s and 1990s higher education fell out of favor with the development community, where also African governments adopted the same attitude.

Far from fostering growth and stability, the austerity measures intensified inequality and hardship in many developing nations, particularly in Africa and Latin America. The negative socio-economic impacts from these policies prompted a renewed interest in South-South Cooperation (SSC), which had previously emerged as an alternative model for development. SSC focused on mutual support among developing nations, emphasizing shared experiences and indigenous solutions to local challenges rather than adherence to Western economic models that often exacerbated existing problems. Sa e Silva (2009, in du Toit et al., 2017) goes on to state that the transfer of best practice policies and programs in this era of South-South collaboration as useful for discussion among other developing nations to share similar domestic situations, problems, and possible advantages rejecting the linear development path so characteristic of modernist views earlier in the twentieth century.

The third phase, *Best Practice Transfer* highlights the disillusionment that arose in the developing world with both socialism and the doctrines of free-market economics. After initial hope in socialism faded, many Southern countries shifted toward neoliberal policies, guided by the Washington Consensus. However, the outcomes of adopting these SAPs fell far short of the economic prosperity promised by neoliberal advocates. Instead, these policies led to high levels of unemployment, persistent poverty, and decreased access to vital social services. This phase aligns with what Hydén (2016) calls "the second wave" to note the return of the involvement of the development community in supporting higher education that economic benefits to society are taken for granted now that knowledge apparently "equals power."

Buchert (1998) held that since the 1990s, agency-determined and project-oriented aid, which has been severely criticized for counteracting holistic and systemic educational development in a given country, are increasingly being replaced by sector programs. A decade after Buchert's observation, Teferra (2009b) notes that the donor-recipient dynamics were changing, albeit slowly and that "Donors—as complex and diverse as they are—have over the years manifested different responses to the multitude of criticisms and concerns, some with considerable sensitivity, and others with little adjustment, largely because the primary tenet that drives their giving is simply not guided by altruistic desire alone."

Since Sa e Silva's analysis over a decade and a half ago, the global landscape has undergone profound shifts, marked by instability reminiscent of the *Demobilization* phase. Multilateralism has weakened, with legacy alliances faltering, giving rise to a multipolar world where new economic and political power centers, such as China, India, and other regional players, are reshaping international relations. At the same time, the global economic and political outlook remains bleak with persistent economic stagnation, compounded by challenges such as climate change, disease, rising populism, persistent poverty, and geopolitical tensions which have deepened uncertainty and inequality across the world. These current global realities present significant challenges in international cooperation and development efforts, making it increasingly difficult to coordinate responses to shared global issues, particularly in the South and Africa, in particular.

This transformation has disrupted global governance, as the dominance of Western powers is increasingly challenged by these emerging actors. As a result, the landscape of global cooperation has become more robust but also more complex, particularly in the realms of development cooperation and academic and research engagements. Countries in the Global South now have a broader array of partnership opportunities, though these options come with intricate geopolitical considerations and maneuvering. This diversification introduces both opportunities and challenges, with nations needing to navigate competing interests while advancing their own developmental goals.

In the majority of the countries in Southeast Asia, South Asia, Latin America and Africa, patterns of collaborations follow historical ties. This is evident where former colonial powers continue as custodians of reputable centers of higher education where they anchor numerous key collaborations with those in the South. The pattern of links of Latin American universities follows the colonial past with Europe and the influence of North America, and is limited by the inability of a large part of the academic community to manage in another language (other than Spanish or Portuguese), which leaves international relations to an endogenous and intra-regional scenario. The same could be said about Africa except the issue of language where the continent uses four international languages in academic and research transactions: Arabic, English, French, and Portuguese. Thus while the potential of South-South cooperation is evident, it has not had the necessary development to establish strong links that would allow it to transcend hegemonic cooperation schemes (Teferra et al., 2022).

The most dominant form of academic collaborations in the Global South tends to be vertical in nature, i.e., North–South, except for Latin America where inter-regional collaborations are prominent. Mostly driven by resource flows and further consolidated by intense pressure and lofty ambition and interest to collaborate with institutions in the North, institutions in the South often overlook collaboration among equals in the South. The narrative and the discourse around quality, rankings, and prestige—some of the driving forces for collaboration—are important factors in looking out for a stronger and prominent partner which happens to be based in the North (Teferra et al., 2022).

On the other hand, horizontal, i.e., South-South, collaborations are few and far between and when they exist, they lack visibility, sustainability, and impact. South-South partnership dates back to the 1970s on the adoption of the Buenos Aires Plan of Action for Promoting and Implementing Technical Cooperation among Developing Countries (BAPA) by 138 UN Member States in Argentina, on September 18, 1978. This was a time when the global socio-economic climate entangled with Cold War politics, where developing countries began seeking ways to chart the course of their own development as alternative to the existing economic and political order (UN, 1998).

South-South Cooperation are conceived as horizontal partnerships, where activities are based on trust, mutual learning, and equity and conceived to establish long-term relationships (OECD, 2011). Notably, on this basis, South-South academic collaborations may not be solely based or primarily driven by the need for higher education institutions to improve institutional image/reputation and for higher education system to improve on a rating scale.

It is important not to underestimate the effort by many public-funded universities in the more developed higher education systems in the Global South to initiate research and publication activities with other countries in the less-developed South based on common goals and mutual learning, and the broader societal purpose of universities. In this respect, the agenda for inclusive and socially responsible universities (GUNI, 2022) on an inter-regional context underpins South-South academic collaboration.

These South-South academic collaborations are primarily driven by individual universities' sense of commitment to improving collaboration with universities in the South. But more often, these are facilitated through intra-regional associations comprising countries of the Global South such as the Association of Southeast Asian Nations (ASEAN), the South Asian Association for Regional Cooperation (SAARC), the Association of African Universities, and recently Association of Research Universities in Africa (ARUA), among others. Furthermore, inter-regional governmental arrangements on collaboration and cooperation in higher education and cultural spheres exist. UNESCO, for instance, has been known to promote partnership and exchanges among countries of the Global South based on common goals and objectives. In fact, an important milestone in the advancement of African higher education was the birth of the Association of African Universities in 1962, supported by UNESCO, to promote cooperation among them (Teferra et al., 2022). That said, the impact of some of these institutions have been heavily constrained by dwindling resources.

While South-South academic collaboration is being actively promoted and pursued, the role of intermediaries (described as midwives discussed later) in the Global North play a vital role in mediating collaboration (Morshidi, 2017; Teferra, 2016, 2022b). Admittedly, South-South academic collaboration is more practical and effective at the institutional level based on a broader agreement at the inter regional or inter-governmental level. But even then, there are discernible patterns in these collaborations (Teferra et al., 2022).

Furthermore, historical and language ties are important factors that influence the direction and nature of South-South collaboration. Anglophone countries, for instance through the Association of Commonwealth Universities that enjoy English-language sphere of influence and the African and Malagasy Council for Higher Education, for French speaking Africa are notable examples.

Increasingly, three-way partnerships in the form of North–South-South collaborations are emerging as a dynamic model in a global academic and research cooperation scene. This arrangement typically involves an institution from the Global North coordinating and often funding the collaboration, alongside two or more partner institutions from the Global South. The Southern partners may be located within the same continent or span across different regions in the Global South, enriching the partnership with diverse perspectives and shared experiences. This tripartite model offers a unique opportunity to address some of the systemic inequities in global academic collaborations though elements that continue to sustain the power imbalance still persistently prevail in favor of the Northern partner.

## Academic and Research Collaboration: African Realities

Higher education in Africa has a very long history that goes back 1,000 years. While Africa can claim an ancient academic tradition, its traditional centers of higher learning all but disappeared or were destroyed by colonialism (Teferra & Altbach, 2003). The most important of the colonial powers in Africa, Britain, and France, left their lasting impact not only in terms of the organization of academe and the continuing links to the metropole, but in the language of instruction and communication (Teferra & Altbach, 2003)—key tools of collaboration. This historical legacy remains key in anchoring the partnership and collaboration dynamics in contemporary African higher education.

Contemporary higher education in Africa, from the outset, has been a manifest of international engagement without regard to the route and history in which this institutional tenet was assumed. For the most part, this feature was attained through colonial legacies when newly liberated countries sought to establish universities through international cooperation. Historically, the colonial powers served as "international gateways" to the colonial entities for matters, big and small, including higher education (Teferra, 2009b). That said, pre-colonial Africa had had a long history of international engagement at a time when a few countries attracted intellectuals from beyond the continent. Universities of Timbuktu (in the current day Mali) and Al-Azhar University in Egypt were some of the centers of intellectual hubs which attracted scholars from outside the continent.

Post-independence, Africa has become a central front in international development and cooperation in higher education attracting a host of players including bilateral and multilateral organizations and foundations, particularly US-based ones. Multilaterals, such as the World Bank and UNESCO, bilaterals such as DAAD, NORAD, SIDA, and foundations such as Ford and Carnegie Corporation of New York played a pivotal role, some with chequered history, in promoting international cooperation in the advancement of African higher education.

Currently, Africa has the most marginalized and the least competitive higher education system internationally—as measured for instance in research output and expenditure. And yet, the continent has the most highly connected internationalized system—if not by choice, by necessity, if not by design, then by legacy. Even the most parochial higher education institutions exhibit their international dimension in the language of instruction they use; by the books, journals, and other published resources they utilize; by the methodologies they pursue; and/or by the resources they deploy. As the weakest global higher education system, it relies heavily on the discourse, paradigms, and parameters set by others, rendering it vulnerable to global whims and idiosyncrasies (Teferra, 2008b).

Collaborations are paramount in advancing higher education and revitalizing the knowledge systems in Africa, which currently enrolls some 20 million students in the sector (Teferra, 2017). A multitude of factors drive the interest in collaborations and partnerships in the continent as the sector is growing fast and its needs—and challenges—are mounting. This development was conditioned on major and shifting discourses in higher education and the knowledge domain as espoused by UNESCO (2021), UNESCO/World Bank (2000), and the World Bank (2002, 2004, 2009, 2010), and Commission for Africa (2005).

One of the main rationales for academic collaborations in Africa is to solicit resources that typically requires partnership between institutions in Africa and the Global North. This remains the primary imperative for academic collaboration by African countries. This noted, the implications of heavy reliance on resources and discourses generated or dominated by external entities have been a subject of numerous regional and global dialogues, contestations, and resolutions (Teferra, 2013).

Collaborations require solid and sustained financial resources and much-needed academic and research competence, as well as enhanced intellectual capital and confidence. They also help address academic isolation and marginalization typical in the Global South, and Africa in particular. Academic and research collaborations with researchers and academics in the Global North often generate publications in high-impact journals, making research institutions and their personnel more visible. This can lead to more grants, more research and publications, faster promotion for academics and institutions, and more invitations to major conferences and meetings (Teferra, 2009a). These enviable tenets continue to drive academics and their enterprises to continue to seek international collaboration.

African higher education depends heavily on external resources—both in monetary terms and discourses—as described, a key rationale for research collaboration. Typically, considerable resources originate in rich industrialized countries through bilateral and multilateral arrangements and (to a lesser extent) foundations. The low global research productivity in Africa—which accounts for 13.5% of the global population but less than 1% of global research output (Fonn et al., 2018)—is attributed to the systemic and critical scarcity of funds for research and academic cooperation in the continent.

A typical African university maintains a long list of partnerships mostly, if not exclusively, with institutions in the Global North mostly sealed by resources deployed from there. For instance, in Ghana, the three most research productive organizations were highly dependent on collaboration to sustain their levels of research production and for the most recent period (2006–2013), respectively, 98% and 92% of research articles by government and the public universities would not have materialized without any collaboration (Boshoff & Owusu-Nimo, 2017).

It is quite common to find that many, if not most, African universities maintain a large number of both active and, mostly, inactive/dormant partnerships as sealed in memoranda of understanding. For instance, the University of Ibadan, Nigeria, as of October 2009, maintained partnerships and had links with over 100 institutions around the world where these partnerships had been in the form of exchanges of staff members and students, collaborative research, development of internationalized curricula, increasing joint internships, and other policies (Materu et al., 2011).

That noted, partnerships in African institutions with the Global South are pretty minimal. For instance, at the University of Nigeria, of the over 70 collaborations (as broadly considered from study destination of students to research) only about 20% are recorded within the Global South and most of them in Africa (https://www.unn.edu.ng/collaborations/).

Ilon (2003) eloquently states that the story of development partners' (donor) assistance to African higher education is a story of waxing and waning resources and commitments. It is closely linked to the interplay of development ideology, the perceived role of education within that ideology, and the geopolitical position of Africa as articulated earlier by Sa e Silva (2009, in du Toit et al., 2017). Each of these forces has changed with the shifting political and economic climate of the world economy and as such, the story of why development partners' monies have fallen off during some periods and increased during other periods, needs to be understood in the framework of evolving development ideology.

Samoff and Carrol (2002) hold a simple but powerful analogy that foreign aid to education in Africa is a small animal with a loud roar. They hold that for nearly all African countries the major source of funds for education is the national treasury. With a few exceptions, foreign funding is a very small portion of total spending on education. And yet, it has come to seem not only obvious but also unexceptional that new initiatives and reform programs require external support, and therefore responsiveness to the agenda and preferences of the funding agencies with a concomitant result of aid dependence. Aid dependence is not about education systems whose principal funding comes from abroad. Rather, aid dependence is the internalization within those education systems of the notion that improvement and change require external support, advice, and often personnel. That internalization makes the policies and preferences of the foreign funders far more consequential than can be explained by the volume of their assistance.

The discourse-shaping dialogue regarding higher education's development is still dominated by external forces, either through their own internal think-tanking or by alliances with powerful players that influence local institutions toward a favored policy track. For better or worse, external forces will remain one of the main, if not the main, powerful forces of internationalization on the continent through their financial and technical muscle, their backing of particular policies, and their promotion of terms by which discourse can occur (Teferra, 2008a). As noted elsewhere the marketplace of development discourse has now effectively diversified with multiple actors, benefactors, and beneficiaries involved chipping away the key role of legacy players.

The next key imperative of African interest in academic cooperation falls in what is typically called capacity building. African academic institutions typically face critical shortages of well-trained and qualified academics with PhDs—key players in collaboration; and the massive expansion of the sector has in fact exacerbated the situation. Even in a typical flagship university in Africa, the PhD holders are minorities though increasingly countries, such as Kenya, Nigeria, and Uganda, are enacting legislations restricting academic staff employment only to those with PhDs.

As a result of this massive scarcity, in the face of sector expansion, academic institutions in Africa often seek to train their academic staff through international, and to a limited extent regional, academic partnership schemes. Because an academic staff training is often packaged in an academic cooperation schemes supported within a framework of bilateral and/or multilateral arrangement, it is often extended to joint research and joint publication. Therefore, African academic institutions draw on academic cooperation to train their academics, typically, to a PhD level, funded by external resources, as part of their academic development programs. The massive input of Norwegian, Swedish, and German development cooperation in this endeavor in the continent is worth noting.

Increasingly the destination of African students seeking postgraduate studies, particularly PhDs, has diversified through own and government resources. The US and Europe have been important destinations for African students. But China (ICEF, 2021),India, and, of recent, Turkey are fast emerging as the new frontiers of foreign study for African students also augmented by scholarship opportunities. Russia and the states of the former USSR are also bidding to attract students from the continent after losing their lot following the end of the Cold War. While it is true that such government-sanctioned and individual-driven endeavors may not be directly gauged as academic collaboration, they are however seeds for future engagements and partnerships—and a nucleus for deploying soft power (Teferra et al., 2022).

## The Summits

Since Africa graduated from the "Hopeless Continent" in 2000 to "Africa Rising – The hopeful continent" in 2011 and later elevated to "Aspiring Africa – The world's fastest-growing continent" in 2013, according to *The Economist*, the continent has seen a plethora of high-level bilateral-multilateral conventions. The list includes Canada-Africa, China-Africa, France-Africa, Germany-Africa, India-Africa, Japan-Africa, Korea-Africa, Russia-Africa, Turkey-Africa, and US-Africa Summits, Conferences, and Compact (Teferra, 2019); and recently Italy-Africa and Saudi-Africa Summits joined the growing company. To this end, similar patterns are also evident at a multilateral level including the EU-AU Summit where these conventions invariably narrate the multiple areas of partnerships and collaborations, including higher education.

In analyzing the declarations of the different summits and conferences, their "linearity"—i.e., engagements narrowly conceived as a one-to-one rendezvous—becomes starkly evident. This linear pattern in the partnership landscape comes with implications for the "polygamous" partner, in this case Africa, as it strives to accommodate the multiple and typically discrete partnership and collaboration schemes that tend to lack coherence and exhibit competition with each other (Teferra, 2022b). As Marginson (2022), for instance, observes China-US competitions and tensions in science and technology as possibly disrupting autonomous global collaboration by national agendas forcefully, with implications for a much smaller players in the ring, as China is emerging a powerful player in African political, economic, education, and diplomatic arenas. The burden of managing this partnership schemes ultimately lies in the court of African institutions who often are short in the human, financial, and technical resources, skills and support to handle them (Teferra, 2022b). More on this in Polygamy section.

While many external stakeholders increasingly adopt consultative methods to better align policies, enhance coordination, build mutual understanding, and collaboratively implement programs, the depth of these efforts often varies. For instance, in Ethiopia the Development Partners Group (DPG) initially established in 2001, as the Development Assistance Group (DAG) comprised 30 bilateral and multilateral partners. It "was established to foster and catalyse policy dialogue and to coordinate and harmonize development partners' support for the Government of Ethiopia's preparation, implementation, monitoring and evaluation of the national development plan and the SDGs" (UNDP). Without structured commitments, consultations may remain superficial, with minimal engagement or actionable outcomes. Furthermore, these efforts frequently preserve the interests of the external parties involved and depends on the goodwill of each participant, which can sometimes limit their openness to policies or practices that could challenge their strategic or economic positions.

In Paris in 2005 and in Accra in 2008, two key conventions, respectively, culminated in major declarations: the Paris Declaration on Aid Effectiveness and the Accra Agenda for Action. The Paris Declaration and the Accra Agenda are founded on five core principles, born out of decades of experience of what works for development, and what doesn't. These principles have gained support across the development community, changing development cooperation paradigms presumably for the better. The principles include ownership, alignment, harmonization, result-focused, and mutual accountability (Teferra, 2019). The 2015 Addis Ababa Action Agenda also calls for "providers of ODA [overseas development assistance] and South-South cooperation to further increase the effectiveness of their development cooperation and to share knowledge about their respective efforts." It is notable that the Addis Ababa Action Agenda anticipates South-South Cooperation through the interventions of the Global North (ODA).

Yet still, in the study "Modes and Premises of Transnational Mobility and Collaboration at the Intersection of International Development Aid and Global Science Regimes – The Case of Mozambique and Tanzania," which analyzed the North–South partnership dynamics in the context of the Swedish International Development Agency support, Fellesson and Mählck (2017) observed the frequently unclear and inferior role of participation in international collaboration and "token presence" of Africans in Global North research projects. And that access to and knowledge of funding opportunities became an early determinant in the "pecking order" of the partners involved in the collaboration. They also observed the African researchers lack of insight and access to funding opportunities in the Global North which significantly reduced their ability to influence and shape collaborative research projects.

That noted, the recent review of the policies and guidelines governing research collaborations in various bilateral and multilateral development cooperation agreements with Africa reveals considerable shifts in this practice. For instance, partnerships have evolved to emphasize, and even demand, the need for a leadership role of Africans in a partnership as principal investigators. In many cases, African researchers are increasingly expected to take a leadership or co-leadership roles in research initiatives for instance in the Norwegian-supported schemes; further, a practice that ensures the allocation of a sizeable amount of partnership funds to Southern institutions is also growing. These shifts mark a positive step toward ensuring that research agendas and outcomes are more relevant to the local context and responsive to African priorities—important in achieving equitable partnerships.

However, while the growing emphasis on African leadership and larger portion of funds flowing to the African institutions are notable, the conditions that embed the Northern institutions' ideologies and values remain strong. While the intention behind addressing these issues may be laudable, the approach can sometimes appear idealistic or disconnected from the local cultural, social, political, and educational realities of the African context. For instance, some external agencies make it imperative for a partnership scheme to have an equal number of female partners, when, in actual fact, their numbers in these establishments in most of Africa remain small. The infusion of these perspectives, though well-meaning, can still overshadow African values, realities, voices, and priorities in the process undermining the essence of equity and equality—consequently the dynamics of power in the relationship.

Finally, the prime reason for African universities seeking partnership lies in their dire quest for financial, material, infrastructural, and human resources. Therefore, the drive for collaboration—a key aspect of internationalization—in the continent is fraught with scarcity—and driven by coercion (Teferra, 2020b). The imperatives of equitable collaboration may only become a reality if the trend in the need for, compliance and interest in genuine co-creation take a deeper root. Thus, while there is progress in promoting African leadership in research collaboration schemes, the challenge remains ensuring that such partnerships are truly collaborative and aligns with Africa's own vision and context, without imposing external ideals that may not align with local needs, realities, or values. This calls for a more nuanced and balanced approach to research partnerships, where African perspectives are at the forefront.

## Pursuing Equity in Polygamy

In the context of development cooperation, the analogy of "polygamous partnerships" may better illustrate how relationships between multiple stakeholders—whether nations, institutions, or organizations—are fraught with similar tensions. Just as in polygamous marriages, where resentment and competition may arise between partners vying for attention or resources, countries engaged in multifaceted partnerships often experience competing interests, mistrust, and imbalances in power dynamics. This can result in fragmentation, with partners prioritizing their own strategic interests, leading to strained cooperation and undermining collective efforts. Moreover, the lack of trust and transparency between partners can stifle collaboration and hinder the realization of shared goals in development.

Naseer et al. (2021) in an article "Exploration of Polygamous Marriages: A Worldview" observed that polygamous marriages are often characterized by issues such as jealousy, poor marital satisfaction, unhealthy competition, and a lack of trust. These issues serve as useful metaphors for the challenges inherent in multilateral and multipartner development cooperation, as in the case in Africa. Multiple polygamous partnerships operating in a similar landscape, unless they are systematically and ably managed, could be a cause for tension and frustration as they create competing and unhealthy dynamics in institutions. It requires seasoned institutional actors to manage multiple external partners, especially when these tend to be, less friendly and hostile to each other or intend to exercise undue influence and power—with implications to disrupting the partnership ecosystem. At a high-level visit to an African university some years ago, a team including this author, witnessed contrasting government/institutional behaviors manifesting in a number of contradictory ways. The team observed equipment and resources commissioned by a partner country from Asia which demanded every piece of equipment conspicuously emblazoned with its name while the other next door, from Scandinavia, which firmly insisted against it (Teferra, 2022b)—leaving a contrasting, even contradictory, institutional terrain carved by the dictate of external benefactors.

This metaphor of polygamy sheds light on the often-complicated nature of development cooperation, where multiple partnerships can be both advantageous and fraught with challenges, requiring careful negotiation and diplomacy to achieve sustainable outcomes. In the same way that healthy relationships within polygamous marriages demand clear communication and equitable treatment, successful development cooperation relies on transparency, mutual respect, and shared objectives.

Much have been said and officially declared on the need to change the dominant form of collaboration paradigm in higher education research and innovation in favor of equitable relationship; and yet commensurate political will to effectively materialize it has so far been largely elusive. This once again calls for the need for more progressive discourses on academic collaboration in the developing world. The lofty spectacle of the summits and compacts stated earlier and the frequency in which they take place underscores the need for Africa to carve its own path as it engages with a multitude of new as well as historical partners in light of its changing status. That the "polygamous" nature of collaborations, particularly in the context of Africa, may require a deeper and more extensive analysis of the mode and experience of research and academic collaboration in the expanding partnership landscape (Teferra, 2022b).

## Intermediaries as Cooperation Midwives

It is essential to recognize the "hidden" actors who serve as intermediaries or "midwives" in development cooperation between the Global North and the African continent. While multiple partnership modalities have evolved over time, many of these collaborations are often facilitated through national institutions or home-based NGOs, think tanks, and other organizations based in the North. These entities play a crucial role in shaping the nature and, more so practice, of partnerships, determining how resources, expertise, and knowledge are exchanged.

Despite the introduction of newer, more direct partnership models, the persistence of intermediaries reflects the deeply entrenched organizational behaviors—and vested interests—that have taken root over decades of development cooperation. Intermediaries, according to Guston (2000 in Veletanlić & Sá, 2020), though effectively execute policy goals and objectives through the design of programs and the allocation of resources that are then pursued by agents, their role and the complexity of their mandates induce tensions in their relationships with the principal (government) and the agents (beneficiary research organizations). These tensions stem partly from ensuring that policy objectives from governments are addressed while maintaining scientific norms and adhering to institutionalized practices that guide the research enterprise.

These intermediaries, which often consist of national institutions, NGOs, and think tanks based in the North, can create significant barriers to the transformation and modernization of the partnership landscape. More concerning, their dominance often stifles the growth of similar or competing entities within African countries, limiting local ownership of development processes. For instance, NGOs and think tanks based in the Northern capitals continue to dominate the consultancy and administrative landscape of development partnerships on the account of competence, proximity to the principal, executing capacity, and safeguarded presence. This leaves little room for other African entities to compete, and even less so to prevail.

It is important to note with concern that these institutions sometimes aggressively position themselves to maintain influence, often maneuvering African institutions into submission—both subtly and aggressively. For instance, this may involve insisting on embedding their representatives within African offices, thereby undermining the autonomy and agency of local organizations. While these intermediaries can offer structure, oversight, and accountability, their involvement frequently reinforces existing power imbalances, hindering the establishment of more equitable, direct partnerships. By maintaining control over critical aspects of development cooperation, they perpetuate a model that serves their own interests more than those of their African counterparts, undermining growth and sustainability.

To overcome these challenges, a concerted effort is required to streamline collaboration and foster transparency. Prioritizing the needs and voices of all partners, particularly those from Africa, is essential to building equitable, sustainable partnerships. A shift toward empowering local institutions, reducing dependency on external intermediaries, and ensuring greater decision-making autonomy for African partners is key to addressing these power asymmetries—both at a macro (policy) and micro (operational) level—and fostering meaningful, mutually beneficial collaboration in the development arena.

## The Emergence of a New Charter

In response to the entrenched and dominant discourse in development cooperation, a transformative initiative has emerged—the *Africa Charter for Transformative Research Collaborations*. A critical effort to reshape the global development landscape, it is intended to promote more equitable, inclusive research partnerships. The Charter emerged as a significant outcome of the Conference of Rectors, Vice-Chancellors, and Presidents of African Universities (COREVIP), organized by the Association of African Universities, held in July 2023 in Windhoek, Namibia. Under a theme "Advancing Excellence in African Higher Education," the conference brought together key stakeholders from across Africa and beyond to discuss the critical challenges facing higher education and research on the continent.

The discussions emphasized the need for collaborations that go beyond traditional, often extractive models of North–South engagement, advocating instead for partnerships that are more just, reciprocal, and inclusive. The Charter now endorsed by multiple stakeholders from both the Global South and North, it represents a collective move toward fostering a pluriversal approach to global scientific efforts, where diverse worldviews and knowledge systems are recognized and valued.

One of the key drivers of the Charter is to counterbalance the historically unequal relationships between African institutions and their global counterparts, where research collaborations have often been dictated by the interests and agendas of the Global North. Recognizing that this imbalance undermines the full participation and leadership of African researchers in global scientific efforts, the Charter calls for transformative partnerships that prioritize co-creation, mutual respect, and shared leadership. These principles aim to ensure that African institutions play a central role in defining research agendas, shaping methodologies, and determining the outcomes of collaborative efforts.

The Charter calls for a global scientific effort that spans across disciplines, recognizing Africa's rightful place in shaping the future of knowledge production. It seeks to challenge the conventional notion of African institutions as mere recipients of knowledge and instead positions them as equal contributors and co-creators in the global research landscape. This shift aims to foster a richer, more diverse global scientific community that leverages Africa's unique perspectives, challenges, and prospects. By embracing the principles outlined in the Charter, African universities and research institutions are intended to lead transformative collaborations that contribute to sustainable development, knowledge equity, and the advancement of excellence in higher education across the continent and globally.

The development of the Charter at this point in time is both a reflection of Africa's intellectual heritage and a response to the pressing need for more just and equitable global partnerships in research. For decades, African intellectual thought has challenged colonial legacies and systemic inequalities that persist in global research collaborations. While earlier efforts have made progress, the present moment—marked by an acute awareness of unmitigated global injustice and the urgent need to address collective crises—demands more profound change, the Charter states.

The Charter, the work of multiple African organizations and a UK partner, arises from a global consciousness that the traditional, often exploitative models of South-North partnerships must be dismantled. These older paradigms frequently positioned African institutions as recipients rather than equal participants in global knowledge production. By reinforcing this imbalance, they perpetuated hegemonic systems that stifled Africa's intellectual agency and hindered its potential to lead transformative research.

Now, the imperative to undo these unjust legacies is clearer than ever. The world is facing unprecedented global crises that require radically different approaches—solutions that can only emerge through inclusive, diverse, and equitable collaboration. The Charter represents a timely shift toward a new framework for research relations, emphasizing co-creation, mutual benefit, and shared leadership between Africa and the Global North.

The *Africa Charter for Transformative Research Collaborations* symbolizes the "change whose time has come." It is a declaration that Africa is no longer willing to play a peripheral role in global scientific efforts. Instead, it is asserting its place at the center of knowledge production, seeking to influence the global research agenda in ways that better serve the continent's unique challenges and opportunities. The timing of the Charter is significant because it coincides with a global reckoning on systemic inequities and the urgent need for a new, more equitable world order. This moment provides the ideal backdrop for a fundamental transformation in research relations—one that will redefine how Africa engages with the world and how the world engages with Africa (Perivoli).

## Conclusion

Institutions in the Global North have been manifestly dominant in partnerships with the South—leading, managing, and coordinating them—often exclusively. This has been one of the most chronicled and criticized aspects of academic partnerships attributed to the Global North's (often sole) ownership, closer proximity, and implicit entitlement to the resources (Teferra, 2016). These attributes are deeply manifest and embedded in the imperatives of collaboration—with massive implications.

In an increasingly globalized and competitive world, the production of knowledge is not just a pathway to economic development but a critical factor for survival and global relevance. African nations, while advocating for education as a means to build human capital, frequently overlook the vital role that research plays in driving innovation, solving local challenges, and enhancing global competitiveness. Without a robust research ecosystem, the promise of education alone falls short, and the continent risks falling behind in science, technology, and innovation. Bridging this gap between education and research investment is imperative for Africa's sustainable development and for positioning itself in the global knowledge economy.

The investment in research in the continent is negligible, even as it grapples with the urgent need for a robust homegrown knowledge production. This disconnect between the rhetoric of building a knowledge society and the actual investment in creating knowledge remains alarmingly wide. It is both deeply unsettling and incomprehensible why a large majority of African states allocate a substantial portion of their national budgets to education, while they often fail to extend even minimal financial support to research and innovation in higher education.

It is crucial to challenge and rethink the prevalent "donor-recipient" phraseology in development cooperation, as it is premised on a simplistic and monetized view of international relations. This phraseology continues to dominate the landscape presumably because what is considered to be donated or received is inequitably claimed, inappropriately monetized, and unfairly expressed. The reality is that no donor gives without receiving, just as no recipient benefits without contributing in some way in pursuit of a sustainable development for a sustainable planet. The "donor-recipient" discourse persists largely due to an inequitable valuation of what is being exchanged, where what is considered donated (often financial resources) is monetized, while other forms of contributions—such as human capital, raw materials, knowledge, and cultural exchange, to mention some—are undervalued or ignored. This imbalance perpetuates a hierarchical relationship that undermines genuine cooperation and stifles the potential for sustainable, mutual development. Furthermore, this transactional model fails to capture the complexity of partnerships that should be based on shared values, mutual respect, and common objectives, rather than on financial alone. The pressing global issues that unite nations—climate change, public health, the environment, and education—demand a more equitable partnership model where all stakeholders collaborate as equals (Teferra, 2020a).

South-South and South-South-North Partnerships are growing in importance as their significance is gaining more traction. Yet, these partnerships themselves are often financially augmented by resources generated from the North, and often steered by them, typically in Africa. There is now near unanimity—and a renewed call—for South-South collaboration though however often with token support for its implementation. The great need for more "progressive" discourses on academic collaboration among partners in the South cannot be overemphasized

(Teferra, 2019) and that initiatives, such as the Higher Education Forum for Africa, Asia and Latin America (HEFAALA), spearheaded by the International Network for Higher Education in Africa, based at the University of Kwazulu-Natal, are aimed at fostering exactly that.

In a piece "COVID-19 – A vindictive messenger for multilateralism" Teferra (2020a, UWN) observed

> The COVID-19 pandemic has shattered the deeply-seated notion of invincibility, supremacy and affluence of the Goliaths of the world. The power of the invisible virus has not only demonstrated our collective vulnerability, but has humbled the most powerful nations, their people and their institutions. This pandemic – mercilessly and indiscriminately – strikes at the time when the new world order, as peddled by its most powerful architects, has been dangerously marching towards unilateralism. Enter COVID-19: the infinitesimal multilateralist, which brought together the gigantic unilateralists in a search for redemption.

The imperative for collaboration in a bid to the advancement of human civilization and sustainable co-existence could not probably be illustrated more vividly.

There is also a financial reality behind the imperative for collaboration. Altbach (2007, pp. 13–14) notes "With the rising costs of university research due to expensive laboratories and equipment, large interdisciplinary scientific research teams, and other factors, raising funds to support research in the sciences grows more difficult. Even large and well-funded universities in the industrialized countries struggle to support cutting-edge research. In some fields, only the richest institutions can support frontier scientific research." Recognizing this critical insight and the persistent challenges it underscores, countries in the Global South, particularly in Africa—especially those with smaller, emerging higher education and research ecosystems—must forge stronger, collaborative alliances to address monumental national and international issues. By pooling resources, expertise, and experiences, often lacking in these nations, these countries can create synergies that amplify their collective ability to overcome such barriers often difficult to confront in solo undertakings.

It is important to underscore that the imperatives of collaboration are fraught with challenges, risks, and threats to those in Africa and the Global South in general—in matters such as ownership, dependency on external finances, and agenda setting and priorities. Papatsiba (2013) points out that collaboration is a contested practice and acknowledges two long-standing camps of champions and skeptics who dominated the debate about the collaborative phenomenon. Citing Beaver and Rosen (1978, p. 66), she remarks that studies attempting to establish the significance of collaboration for science are "strongly polarized between those which see teamwork as bane and those which see it as boon. Both views are stereotypical, reflecting different assumptions about the nature of scientific activity and discovery."

Therefore, the global community must move toward a model of collaboration that genuinely values the contributions of all partners equally by confronting the systemic and entrenched adverse discourses against them. This shift is essential for fostering research and innovation to advance an inclusive and sustainable development. By recognizing the full spectrum of contributions—whether financial, intellectual, or social—research collaboration can become more meaningful, fruitful and effective, advancing the shared goals of all involved. The principles embedded in *Africa Charter for Transformative Research Collaborations*, among comparable others, offer a promising alternative in the realization of these critical values.

## References


Altbach, G. P. (2007). Empires of knowledge and development. In P. G. Altbach & J. Balan (Eds.), *Transforming research universities in Asia and Latin America: World class worldwide* (pp. 1–28). John Hopkins University.

Altbach, G. P. (2011). The past, present, and future of the research university. In P. G. Altbach & J. Salmi (Eds.), *The road to academic excellence: The making of world-class research universities* (pp. 11–32). World Bank.

Bloom, D. E., Canning, D., & Chan, K. (2006). *Higher education and economic development in Africa*. World Bank.

Boshoff, N. & Owusu-Nimo, F. (2017). Research collaboration in Ghana: Patterns, motives and roles. *Scientometrics, 110*(3), 1099–1121. https://doi.org/10.1007/s11192-016-2221-x

Beaver, D., & Rosen, R. (1978). Studies in scientific collaboration: The professional origins of scientific coauthorship. *Scientometrics, 1*, 65–84.

Bozeman, B., Fay, D., & Slade, C. P. (2013). Research collaboration in universities and academic entrepreneurship: The-state-of-the-art. *The Journal of Technology Transfer, 38*(1), 1–67.

Buchert, L. (1998). Education sector analysis in Africa: An evolving case in mutual North-South learning. *Prospects, 28*, 353–363. https://doi.org/10.1007/BF02736810

Commission for Africa. (2005). *Our common interest* (Report of the Commission for Africa).

De Solla Price, D. J., & Beaver, D. (1966). Collaboration in an invisible college. *American Psychologist, 21*(11), 1011–1018.

du Toit, L., Couper, I., Peersman, W., & Maeseneer, J. D. (2017). South-South cooperation in health professional education: A literature review. *African Journal of Health Professions Education, 9*(1), 3–8.

Fellesson, M., & Mählck, P. (2017). Untapped research capacities? Mobility and collaboration at the intersection of international development aid and global science regimes. *International Journal of African Higher Education, 4*(2), 1–24.

Fonn, S., Ayiro, L. P., Cotton, P., Habib, A., Mbithi, P. M. F., Mtenje, A., Nawangwe, A., Ogunbodede, E. O., Olayinka, I., Golooba-Mutebi, F., & Ezeh, A. (2018). Repositioning Africa in global knowledge production. *The Lancet, 392*(10153), 1163–1166. https://doi.org/10.1016/S0140-6736(18)31068-7

Gopinathan, S., & Altbach, P. G. (2005). Rethinking centre-periphery. *Asia Pacific Journal of Education, 25*(2), 117–123. https://doi.org/10.1080/02188790500337882

GUNI. (2022). GUNi International Call for Action (2022–2025). Rethinking Higher Education Institutions (HEIs) for sustainable and inclusive societies. https://acesse.dev/Df0D1

Hazelkorn, E. (Ed.). (2016). *Global rankings and the geopolitics of higher education. Understanding the influence and impact of rankings on higher education, policy and society.* Routledge.

Hydén, G. (2016). The role and impact of funding agencies on higher education and research for development. In T. Halvorsen & J. Nossum (Eds.), *North–South knowledge networks towards equitable collaboration between academics, donors and universities* (pp. 1–39). African Minds.

ICEF. (2021). *China emerging as a major destination for African students.* https://acesse.dev/D7SdF

Ilon, L. (2003). Foreign aid financing of higher education in Africa. In D. Teferra & P. G. Altbach (Eds.), *African higher education: An international reference handbook* (pp. 61–72). Indiana University Press.

Katz, J. S., & Martin, B. R. (1997). What is research collaboration? *Research Policy, 26*, 1–18.

Kwiek, M. (2017). International research collaboration and international research orientation: Comparative findings. *Journal of Studies in International Education, 22*(2), 136–160. https://encr.pw/NLLJA

Lee, S., & Bozeman, B. (2005). The impact of research collaboration on scientific productivity. *Social Studies of Science, 35*(5), 673–702.
Lewis, J. M., Ross, S., & Holden, T. (2012). The how and why of academic collaboration: Disciplinary differences and policy implications. *Higher Education, 64*(5), 693–708. https://doi.org/10.1007/s10734-012-9521-8
Malaysia. (2015). *The Malaysian education blueprint (higher education), 2015–2025.* Ministry of Education.
Marginson, S. (2022). What drives global science? The four competing narratives. *Studies in Higher Education, 47*(8), 1566–1584. https://encr.pw/FWLKS
Materu, P., Obanya, P., & Righetti, P. (2011). The rise, fall, and reemergence of the University of Ibadan, Nigeria. In P. G. Altbach & J. Salmi (Eds.). *The road to academic excellence: The making of world-class research universities* (pp. 195–227). World Bank.
Morshidi, S. (2017). ASEAN's flagship universities and regional integration initiatives. *Higher Education Evaluation and Development, 11*(2), 68–80. https://encr.pw/qmSWx
Naseer, S., Farooq, S., & Malik, F. (2021). Causes and consequences of polygamy: An understanding of coping strategies by co-wives in polygamous marriage. *ASEAN Journal of Psychiatry, 22*(9), 1–10.
OECD. (2011). *Task team on south-south co-operation.* https://encr.pw/HQ3Rq
Papatsiba, V. (2013). The idea of collaboration in the academy: Its epistemic and social potentials and risks for knowledge generation. *Policy Futures in Education, 11*(4), 436–448. https://doi.org/10.2304/pfie.2013.11.4.436
Perivoli Africa Research Center, Bristol University. https://l1nq.com/iKoF4
Samoff, J. (1994). Financial crisis, structural adjustment, and education policy in Tanzania. Prepared for presentation at the Annual Meeting of the American Educational Research Association, New Orleans, 4–7 April 1994.
Samoff, J., & Carroll, B. (2002). The promise of partnership and the continuities of dependence: External support to higher education in Africa. *Report presented at the 45th Annual Meeting of the African Studies Association*, Washington, DC.
Teferra, D. (2005). Financing higher education in sub-Saharan Africa. In *The financing of universities* (pp. 153–164).
Teferra, D. (2008a). Internationalization of higher education: Legacy and journey in the African landscape. In D. Teferra & Jane K. (Eds.), *Higher education in Africa: An international dimension* (pp. 553–558). Boston College and the Association of African Universities, Ghana.
Teferra, D. (2008b). The international dimension of higher education in Africa: Status, challenges, and prospects. In D. Teferra & J. Knight (Eds.), *Higher education in Africa: An international dimension* (pp. 44–79). Boston College and the Association of African Universities, Ghana.

Teferra, D. (2009a). *African research collaborations must be fair and equal*. https://l1nq.com/RXhJm

Teferra, D. (2009b). Higher education in Africa: The dynamics of international partnerships and interventions. In R. M. Bassett & A. M. Maldonado (Eds.), *International organizations and higher education policy: Thinking globally, acting locally?* (pp. 155–173). Taylor & Francis.

Teferra, D. (2013). Introduction. Funding higher education in Sub-Saharan Africa. In D. Teferra, *Funding Higher Education in Sub-Saharan Africa* (pp. 1–12). Palgrave MacMillan.

Teferra, D. (2016). Shifting grounds in higher education partnerships. https://l1nq.com/YSx7Z. Accessed on 4 August 2022.

Teferra, D. (2017). African flagship universities in the era of "massification." In D. Teferra (Ed.), *Flagship universities in Africa* (pp. 1–16). Palgrave Macmillan.

Teferra, D. (2019). *A proliferation of summits—What role for universities?* https://acesse.dev/9MUBs

Teferra, D. (2020a, April). *COVID-19—A vindictive messenger for multilateralism*. University World News. https://acesse.dev/pXIG7

Teferra, D. (2020b). The irrelevance of the re-configured definition of internationalisation to the Global South: Intention versus coercion. *International Journal of African Higher Education, 7*(2). 157–172. https://acesse.dev/v6zJt

Teferra, D. (2022a). Editorial: Academic collaboration in Africa, Asia and Latin America in the post-COVID world. *International Journal of African Higher Education, 9*(3), 1–12.

Teferra, D. (2022b, March). *Prospect or burden? Managing Africa's linear partnerships*. University World News—Africa Edition. https://l1nq.com/hPkiV

Teferra, D., & Altbach, D. (Eds.). (2003). *African higher education: An international reference handbook*. Indiana University Press.

Teferra, D., Sirat, M., & Beneitone, P. (2022). The imperatives of academic collaboration in Africa, Asia and Latin America. *International Journal of African Higher Education, 9*(3), 13–35.

UN. (1998). *Buenos Aires Plan of Action*. https://unsouthsouth.org/bapa40/documents/buenos-aires-plan-of-action/

UNESCO. (2021). *UNESCO Institute for Statistics*. https://data.uis.unesco.org/

Veletanlić, E., & Sá, C. (2020). Implementing the innovation agenda: A study of change at a research funding agency. *Minerva, 58*, 261–283 https://l1nq.com/PIVsg

Woodhall, M. (2003). Financing and economics of higher education in Africa. In *African higher education* (pp. 44–52).

World Bank. (2002). *Constructing knowledge societies: New challenges for tertiary education*. World Bank.
World Bank. (2004). *Improving tertiary education in sub-Saharan Africa: Things that work*. World Bank. https://encr.pw/s0Hty
World Bank. (2009). *Accelerating catch-up: Tertiary education for growth in sub-Saharan Africa*. World Bank.
World Bank. (2010). *Financing higher education in Africa. The international bank for reconstruction and development*. The World Bank. https://encr.pw/E2tnv
World Bank/UNESCO. (2000). *Higher education in developing countries: Peril and promise*. World Bank.

CHAPTER 8

# Industry-University Partnership in African Science: Status, Barriers, and Opportunities

*Bright I. Nwaru, Eman Sobh, Olu Akanmu, and Charles Ayo*

## Introduction

Science aims to generate knowledge, understand, and solve societal, technical, and environmental challenges. The impact of the science economy is increasing with the advent of new technologies. However, this influence is either hidden or underestimated (MacIlwain, 2010), probably due to poor scientific metrics (Lane, 2010). There is no argument about the benefits of science for economic development, although only a few studies

B. I. Nwaru (✉)
Krefting Research Centre, Institute of Medicine, University of Gothenburg, Gothenburg, Sweden
e-mail: bright.nwaru@gu.se

E. Sobh
Faculty of Medicine for Girls, Al-Azhar University, Cairo, Egypt

O. Akanmu
Lagos Business School, Lagos, Nigeria

C. Ayo
Trinity University, Lagos, Nigeria





D. Teferra (ed.), *Research and Innovation in African Higher Education*,
https://doi.org/10.1007/978-3-031-92909-0_8

have described the economic benefits of science and the low efficiency of research and innovation in low-income regions (Rodríguez-Navarro & Brito, 2018). Science generates the required knowledge for all sources of economic development and creates new methodologies, technologies, innovations, or models for problem-solving. Besides, science drives communication and interaction network and helps to develop solutions that are essential for the economic networks and productivity in several aspects of life (Bornmann, 2012; Brooks, 1994; Lesjak, 2019). Science participates in human capital development by creating skilled and trained graduates (Chen et al., 2015).

In general, a university serves three fundamental purposes: generation, communication, and advancement of knowledge. The ultimate goal is to turn theoretical knowledge that underpins the core activities that go on within the four walls of a university into practical products for the development of society. Without the transformational aspect in which theories are converted into practical solutions for society, the goal of the university is defeated. The process through which ideas are converted into tangible deliverables for society has been generally known as innovation. The university is the epicenter of all sorts of research activities (Ugnich et al., 2017). The innovation process then involves the translation of the generated research into quantifiable outputs that add value to the improvement of goods and services and their delivery to society, whether in the economic, health, technological, or social spheres (Kaloudis et al., 2019). The research-innovation spectrum then ensures that the university remains central to societal development and nation-building (Kaloudis et al., 2019). However, the university's drive toward the translation of research ideas into innovation is not a trivial process. Consequently, a degree curriculum at the university, particularly the postgraduate curriculum, must imbibe and teach students the essence of knowledge translation as a core mandate for their studentship.

University-industry collaboration (UIC) is the process that links knowledge developed in universities with that applied in industries (Alrajhi & Aydin, 2019). It involves all aspects of interactions between the university and industry, leading to knowledge and technology exchange (Bekkers & Bodas Freitas, 2008), including knowledge transfer and strategy development, investment in infrastructure, and human capital development (Alrajhi & Aydin, 2019). This collaboration certainly will go beyond money gains for both sectors. Furthermore, most of the world-class university ranking agencies, for example the Times Higher Education

World University Ranking (THEWUR), recognize industry partnership/ income as one of the parameters for ranking world-class universities. The THEWUR parameters are often divided into teaching (30%), research (30%), research citations (30%), international outlook (7.5%), and industry Income (2.5%). In addition to the research outputs from the universities, industry income measures the university's ability to help the industry with innovations, inventions, and consultancy. Essentially, these parameters seek to capture knowledge-transfer activities between universities and industries adjusted for purchasing power parity (PPP) scaled against the number of academic staff it employs (THE, 2021). In recent decades UIC in knowledge transfer and intellectual property, in the form of patents, has gained interest as a measure of successful collaboration for society and economic development (Bertoletti & Johnes, 2021).

Usually, the university must not act alone in its pursuit of innovation-based knowledge that can spur development across different sectors of the society. Engagement with the industry is important for the translation of knowledge generated at the university into research output and/or product development (Ćudić et al., 2022). UIC is important for societal development through solving societal problems by combining university theories and knowledge with industry skills and resources (de Wit-de Vries et al., 2019). This engagement is called the third mission of the university—its efforts toward meaningful contribution to societal development (Compagnucci & Spigarelli, 2020). Knowledge transfer and engagement are significant higher education institution (HEI) activities (Bertoletti & Johnes, 2021). In addition to the industry, the government is a key player in creating success in the university-industry partnership through the creation of policies and an enabling environment that helps the partnership to thrive. This three-way partnership can be a game changer in the success of UIC in opening opportunities and solving challenges (Young, 2013). Effective UIC results in mutual benefits as the partnerships give the possibility to promote the creation of new synergies and models for growth.

For the university, an opportunity is created to address its research ideas in a real-world context. Through this, tangible benefits are bound to accrue, for example, university staff can acquire new skills in the implementation of science, data, and technology or equipment, and have access to new resources and technologies (Ankrah & AL-Tabbaa, 2015). Beside increased publications (Verreynne et al., 2021), and improved research visibility (University-Industry-Collaboration, n.d.), there are also opportunities for increased funding, student industrial attachment for training and career development opportunities, economic development, quick utilization of research findings, increased citation, and improved ranking of universities (Org, 2012; University-Industry-Collaboration, 2021). UIC may also result in the development of new curricula that match the career market. UIC may be one solution to the brain drain problem. Many university faculty experts often leave universities due to low salary issues, unfavorable work environments, and the lack of resources for research and innovation (World Economic Forum, 2018). Long-term UIC can lead to changes in university strategic management and organizational structure that fit the collaborative culture. For the industry, the knowledge gained from the partnership provides a web of scenarios that can lead to improvement in business performance and outputs. This can come through the development of new technologies, research-oriented investment based on real-life evidence, and the increase and extension of industry capabilities on its own. The industry will have access to new resources and the human power of experts that give them a competitive advantage (Org, 2012). Patents and innovative products and reduced costs for knowledge transfer are outcomes of collaborative projects (Verreynne et al., 2021). Furthermore, UIC will enhance the image and recognition of both entities and improve community development (Ankrah & AL-Tabbaa, 2015).

In recent decades, there has been an increase in university-industry partnerships, most of these happening in high-income countries, where tangible data exists to measure the trends in these partnerships. As university-industry partnerships are crucial for catalyzing innovation, there is a clear correlation between increased university-industry partnerships and national and societal development. This remains a model being operated by many industrialized nations, resulting in increased innovation outputs through joint research and development (Bertoletti & Johnes, 2021; Davey et al., 2018). University-industry-government collaboration in the United States (US) results in increased investment in innovation, education, and commercialization of research-driven products. Additionally, these types of collaboration can lead to lowering costs through sharing facilities and exchange consultations (Young, 2013). However, progressive partnerships between universities and industry appear very minimal, and in some contexts non-existent in Africa (Mugabe, 2011). This chapter discusses university-industry partnerships in Africa. Taking the triple helix model as a basis, the chapter considers the government as a key player in the success of university-industry partnerships in any context. The benefits of partnership—to the university, industry, and society at large, particularly for societal development and nation-building—are discussed. The status of university-industry partnerships in Africa is highlighted and key steps are proposed for improvement. The chapter concludes by proposing a shift from the triple helix model to a quadruple model to derive maximum benefits for the partnership.

## Science, Technology, and Innovation in Africa

Africa shares a small percentage of global scientific outputs. However, over the last few years, scientific production in Africa, measured as the share of global scientific publications, increased from 1.7% (2010) to 3% (2018) (Kahn, 2022). The minimal contribution of African countries to global scientific outputs is exacerbated by the fact that most African countries spend less than 1% of GDP on research and development. Although some Sub-Saharan African (SSA) countries adopted the Research Technology and Innovation (RTI) or Science, Technology, and Innovation (STI) for national sustainable development goals, its implementation has been low due to lack of both resources and government commitment, as well as poorly developed and implemented agenda (Kahn, 2022).

While most African countries attempt to focus on research and technology, they tend to neglect the part on innovation. The innovation ecosystems are a complex process that involves idea generation and knowledge translation into products and commercialization of the developed products (markets of tomorrow). Successful ecosystems depend on the presence of sound culture, collaboration, and administrative and regulatory processes (Schwab, 2019). Setting priorities and sustainable environments that facilitate this transformational process of research, innovation, and the invention of ideas into commercial products is important to maintain the innovation-business environment. But it is not a trivial process, perhaps the reason many African countries have often failed to achieve a continuous innovation goal. Governments need to support innovation goals and processes through funding, capacity building, and improved administrative and regulatory systems. No data are available on the transformation readiness of most African countries (Schwab, 2019). Most African countries have a low rank in the Global Competitiveness Index (GCI). South Africa, for example, has a low index for facilitation of the creation of markets of tomorrow: updating curricula, strengthening skills, incentivization, investment in Research & Development (R&D) (Schwab & Zahidi, 2020). Although Africa has had a long history of creativity, many African countries currently struggle to gain the full potentials of innovation. The innovation and Intellectual Property (IP) policies are growing in snail-pace, warranting the need to establish innovation and IP strategies for economic development across the continent. Although the GCI of some African countries is growing slowly, this creates an opportunity for these countries to capitalize on future development in knowledge translation and technology transfer (Gurry, 2015).

## The Triple Helix Model of Science and Society

In the 1990s, Henry Etzkowitz and Loet Leydesdorff introduced the Triple Helix Model as a framework for fruitful interaction between the university, industry, and government (Cai & Etzkowitz, 2020; Ranga & Etzkowitz, 2013). Although this framework has advanced to more complex interactions by including more stakeholders than the three originally articulated, the overarching goal has been to illustrate how key stakeholders in the society can interact to foster local economic and social development. This model emanated from the desire to shift the dominating dyad role of industry-government to a triadic one, involving a close relationship between university, industry, and government (Cai & Etzkowitz, 2020; Ranga & Etzkowitz, 2013). The triadic model was based on the premise that greater impact for innovation and economic development in a knowledge society is achieved in a triadic framework than in a dyadic one. In this relationship, each actor has its own unique and independent role (Fig. 8.1). The university remains the conduit for active research and knowledge generation. Taking the generated knowledge, the industry ensures its transfer to the production stage and provides the basis for using it for onward innovation and development. The government is the driving force that creates the enabling environment, through the design of relevant policies and incentives, facilitating the university and industry actors to develop a fruitful partnership. In essence, the relationship between the three actors is an interdependent one that ultimately nurtures a transformed society and catalyzes development.

The concept of entrepreneurial university is an offshoot of the triple helix model (Cai & Amaral, 2021; Feola et al., 2021; Klein & Pereira,

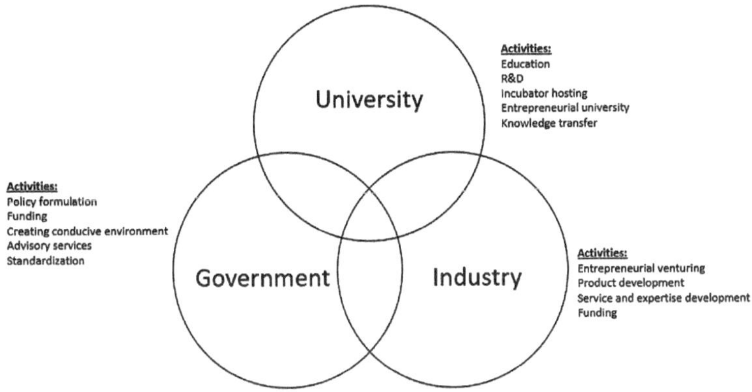


**Fig. 8.1** Triple helix framework ("balanced" framework) demonstrating the interactions between actors that create favorable environments for innovation. Adapted from Cai and Etzkowitz (2020)

2021). While the university's traditional missions are centered on education and research, a third aspect identifies the university as a channel to economic development through the transfer of outcomes of research from the laboratory to the market, innovation corridors, and economic systems. While education and research as the core mandate of the university represent internal missions, the entrepreneurial aspect represents an external function, which moves the university away from its comfort zone. This external migration, aimed at increasing the efficiency of the function of the university to better serve society, is not a trivial one. It is a radical change from the traditional conception of the institution to innovation, highlighting the value of knowledge-based entrepreneurship. A condition for a truly entrepreneurial culture of the university is that there is a clear prioritization of innovation and the dissemination of an entrepreneurial culture (Cai & Amaral, 2021; Feola et al., 2021; Klein & Pereira, 2021). The university undertakes a conscious awareness and a university-wide active training in entrepreneurial activities, which become essential ingredients for its outputs. Special emphasis is placed on developing entrepreneurial human capital and the development of competencies that enable the setting up of new projects. Regardless, the entrepreneurial university is believed to increase the university's competitiveness, economic growth, and wealth creation, making it attractive for partnership with the industry and government.

## Global Trends in Industry-University Partnership

Industry depends on research in developing its products, thereby creating a feedback system between the industry and university in a continuous innovation space. Failure to judiciously combine the research and business objectives is tantamount to suboptimal innovation or even failure: ultimately the society suffers from such failures. At no other time in human history has the need for innovative research at the universities and cordial relationships between the university and industry become more crucial than during the era of COVID-19. While the world struggled to muster a coordinated global response to the pandemic, the success of any solution at the local, national, and continental stages could only depend on the direction of the university-industry cooperation. As the COVID-19 pandemic remained a continuing reality for most societies across the globe, an important lesson learned and continues to be learned is that all hands must be on deck in order to muster an effective response and keep society safe. However, the global impetus and operation of the university-industry relationship historically and during times of emergency as the COVID-19 pandemic varies across contexts. Whether a gold standard of operation exists is unclear, but the intensity and dynamism seem to be encouraging in some developed settings, whereas several low- and middle-income countries appear to be playing a catch-up role. This section provides a brief overview of the historical and current trends in industry-university partnerships across the globe, highlighting contexts where the partnership is thriving and where it is poor. Further, the characteristics that differentiate thriving and poor partnerships will be described and contrasted.

In November 2020, Times Higher Education released its report on university-industry collaboration across the world, which was used for its 2021 World University Ranking, focusing on the role of technology companies' support for higher education research (THE, 2021). This report gave one of the most current insights into the trends in university-industry partnerships across the globe. In terms of industry research income that accrued to the university, the median annual amount was \$36,000 for the top 200 ranked universities and \$24,000 for the 201–300 ranked universities (more in Table 8.1). Many of the top ten ranked universities achieved or exceeded this target. For example, the California Institute of Technology, Stanford University, and Massachusetts Institute of Technology achieved over \$100,000. Apart from some universities in

South Africa that were ranked between 150 and 400 positions, most African universities were ranked starting from 501, which indicates that research income support from industry in Africa is among the least compared to any other region of the world. This income flow is attributed to a university's ability to help the industry with innovations, inventions, and consultancy, and in return, the industry supports and funds university research activities (THE, 2021). In its 2020 report, the UNESCO Institute for Statistics listed the top 15 research and development spending countries in the world and the share contributed by the industry, with South Korea, Japan, Switzerland, and the United States standing at the top (more in Fig. 8.2) (UNESCO Institute for Statistics, 2020). UIC in the United Kingdom resulted in increased number of joint articles as well as citations. However, the production of firms outweighs the number of published articles or citations. During the COVID-19 pandemic, the outcomes of UIC resulted in the development of the Oxford–AstraZeneca COVID-19 vaccine. This vaccine was produced in a short time, is cheap, effective, and can be stored at ordinary temperatures. The production of this vaccine contributed to fighting the spread of the COVID-19 infection and opened opportunities for vaccinations in low- and middle-income countries (LMIC) (Oxford University News, 2020).

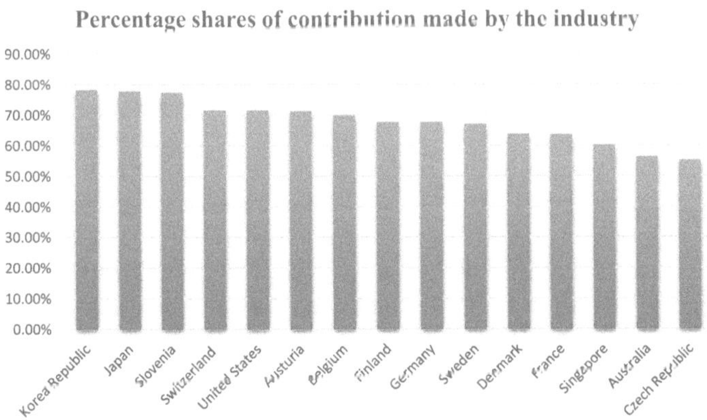


**Fig. 8.2** Top 15 countries spending most in R&D in the world (*Source* UNESCO Institutes for Statistics [2022])

**Table 8.1** Median research income from industry to university per academic staff based on Times Higher Education Ranking (USD)

| | |
|---|---|
| Top 200 | $36,000 |
| 201-300 | $24,000 |
| 301-400 | $14,000 |
| 401-500 | $9,000 |
| 501-800 | $8,000 |
| 801+ | $5,000 |

*Source* THE World University Rankings 2021 (https://cutt.ly/uFv7KNP)

China has had a rapid and continuous economic growth over the last few decades. This growth is accompanied by rapid growth in scientific outputs, especially in technology, engineering, and innovation (Chen et al., 2015). This economic and scientific evolution passed several stages, however. The positive impact clearly occurred after the application of several strategies that improved higher education funding, and communication, enhanced higher education (HE) institutions' link to social development, reform and promote HE research and development infrastructures. This is in addition to promoting the mobility of innovative talents, which moved thousands of China's innovative talents back to China to lead innovative projects (Chen et al., 2015). By providing financial incentives for working in several scientific fields such as engineering and digital technology (Xie et al., 2014), growth in scientific output and economy was associated with the evident improvement in education and the cultivation of a highly skilled workforce (Chen et al., 2015).

For most African countries, there were no tangible data to describe the industry's contribution to research and development. For example, in South Africa, according to research conducted by The Research and Innovation Strategy Group of Higher Education South Africa (HESA), a significant proportion of academic institutes and researchers have some way of engaging with industry. Nevertheless, this engagement involves the traditional, informal way, closely related to teaching and some sponsorship from industry to research, with less evident entrepreneurial activities and of low budget (Kruss et al., 2012). In Egypt, poor UIC (Elhadidi & Kirby, 2017) was claimed to be the main factor behind the declining competitiveness index in the last decades (Egypt Competitiveness Rank, 2022).

Another indication of the university-industry partnership highlighted by The Times Higher Education is the number of research publications co-authored between the university and industry, but the report focused on the six leading countries: the United States, The Netherlands, France, Switzerland, Germany, and the United Kingdom. In the latest year of the extracted information used (2019), universities in the Netherlands had more publications co-authored by industry partners proportional to all publications (5.8%) than universities in France (5.1%), Switzerland (5.1%), Germany (4.6%), United Kingdom (4.6%), and United States (4.3%) (Fig. 8.3). By considering a few of the leading global technology companies, the report highlighted that Microsoft, for instance, had over 7,900 co-authored academic publications between 2015 and 2019 in collaboration with over 2,400 universities globally: over 900 in Europe, over 670 in North America, and over 600 in East Asia. China's share is estimated to be over 200 universities, producing over 1,600 publications during this period. Another company described was Samsung, which published over 800 co-authored academic publications between 2015 and 2019 in collaboration with over 1,400 universities globally: over 540 in East Asia, over 430 in Europe, and over 380 in North America (THE, 2021). In these two examples of leading technology companies, there was no indication of the trends in Africa, despite the surge in product utilization from these companies in the continent.

## Frameworks of Industry-University Partnership

There are several forms of university-industry collaboration. The most common forms are: first, research & development, where universities conduct research projects, develop strategies, provide education, training, and support (Roger & Creso, 2009), and mobility of staff to implement research results on the industry side and academic and student entrepreneurship (Michel-Schneider, 2021). Second, management, where universities provide professional consultancy and expertise to build, drive, and enhance technologies and innovations, to provide solutions to problems in different aspects, and to improve the commercialization

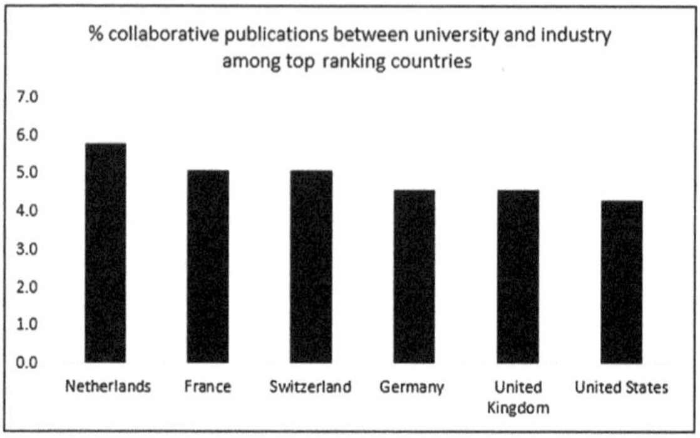


**Fig. 8.3** Percentage of university-industry publications among the six leading countries 2015–2019 (*Source* THE World Rankings 2021, THE: University Industry Collaboration [2020])

of products (Roger & Creso, 2009) is another form of university-industry collaboration. Third, universities and industry can collaborate in education for co-development, design, and improvement of curriculum, and industry funding of educational activities, mobility, and training of students (Michel-Schneider, 2021).

To fulfill these forms of collaboration, a framework for the whole process is important. Ultimately, an industry-university partnership represents an input in the process of innovation, with the desired outputs being productivity, robust innovation, growth, and healthy competitiveness, all of which, with enabling local policies, lead to economic development and an innovation state. However, the operation of industry-university partnerships is heterogeneous and complex across contexts. It is this variation that eventually differentiates thriving and not thriving partnerships and thus signals that different frameworks of partnerships may be in operation across settings. While recognizing the increasingly global nature of universities and industries in the current dispensation, this section reviews potential frameworks of industry-university partnerships from a global perspective that are adaptable to local situations. Ivascu and colleagues, proposing a business framework for university-industry collaboration in open innovation, observed that six areas are fundamental prerequisites for the university to have a successful partnership with industry (Ivascu et al., 2016). A university must have well-defined structures to support research projects implemented with industry as this gives confidence in the success of the project. There must be effective project management, including active and efficient communication and progress monitoring mechanisms. Young researchers should be involved both in project initiation and implementation, especially in identifying the features of the economic environment, as this provides a capacity-building opportunity for developing expertise in managing the partnership. There should be a platform for developing new partnerships and at the same time for supporting existing projects to create and launch new opportunities. The organizational culture that outlines its strategies for partnership is fundamental for the university to successfully engage industry partners, particularly the culture of openness. Finally, the university needs to have a strong dissemination strategy that helps the external communication of its research outputs, as well as market structures that help it to actively interact with new partners.

Aimed to develop a collaborative framework for efficient university-industry partnership, Awasthy and colleagues outlined a set of 14 generic best practices that are fundamental and, taken together, create a framework for building an enabling environment that results in effective collaborations (Awasthy et al., 2020).

The key features of the 14 basic practices are summarized below:

Before starting a partnership, it is crucial to understand the landscape of possible interactions and relationships that can exist between the university and industry in terms of type, degree, and duration of the interaction. This understanding will facilitate informed decision-making. Next, the identification of the precise stakeholders for partnerships. Strategic stakeholders share the vision and long-term goals and meet the local context needs of all parties. A long list of stakeholders for UIC exists and the motivation for UIC can be divergent from problem-solving, resource-sharing, or people's access to skills development through education. So, setting up the motivation for their collaboration and common areas of interest is a vital step before formal collaboration. This will help guide expectations and the development of strategies for success (Awasthy et al., 2020).

Following these initial steps, there is need to identify and appoint the partnership leadership team who will drive the partnership and ensure the achievement of expectations. This team involves people from both the university and industry who have the capability to contribute to openness to change, are willing to cooperate, and have a high level of trust working in collaboration with the respective leaderships of the university and industry.

Basic values and principles of the partnership should be ensured and agreed upon and an agreement drafted on those principles in a win–win scenario. Once an agreement of a working agreement is drafted, both actors need to devote a long-term commitment to it. Besides, efficient communication should be in place as a critical ingredient to the success of the relationship. Both the university and industry must develop communication channels and monitoring that will help enhance the evaluation of the progress of the partnership and stimulate future partnerships (Awasthy et al., 2020).

A dissemination strategy should be strengthened through which results emanating from the partnership can be distributed and share with actors outside the partnership. The university in particular should adopt a variety of channels for dissemination, particularly using elements of marketing for sharing the results of their research. The partnership should address any impending intellectual property concerns, avoiding extensive constraints on information and overprotection of intellectual property which can often become a stumbling block to potentially fruitful partnerships. The adaptation of internal and external policies that encourage and facilitate partnerships should be supported by both the university and the industry. Policies should be flexibly articulated to take care of the changing research environment while at the same time preserving academic and financial integrity. Policies that help the resolution of institutional conflicts and resolve gaps at the university-industry interface should be encouraged. At the same time, the partners should adopt strategies that will encourage collaboration within and between the actors. The partnership should adopt the various social capital resources, including trust, mutual obligations, common understanding, access to information, and opportunities, that are often important in leading to an effective relationship between actors and stakeholders in a collaborative endeavor.

Moreover, universities should set up processes for reward incentives for the university staff leading the partnership with the industry. Rewards and incentives help to drive the motivations and engagement levels of the representatives, thereby leading to a more effective partnership. The framework for managing the partnership needs to be agreed upon by both the university and industry so that set goals can be achieved within set times. Finally, by maintaining links with its alumni, the university has an opportunity to capitalize on the knowledge base of its previous students working in the industry to support their adventure in partnership with the industry (Awasthy et al., 2020) (Fig. 8.4).

To our knowledge, there are no frameworks for university-industry partnerships in Africa. The above-developed framework however provides a global perspective that can be adopted by African universities in engaging with potential industry partners to reach a successful and effective collaboration. Consequently, the need for collaboration should be identified; identify the win–win scenarios for both the university and industry; ascertain whether the university and industry have the right and qualified personnel to see through the collaboration; identify the bottlenecks to achieving a successful collaboration; and put the buffers in place to mitigate conflicts. All these aspects need to be put into perspective

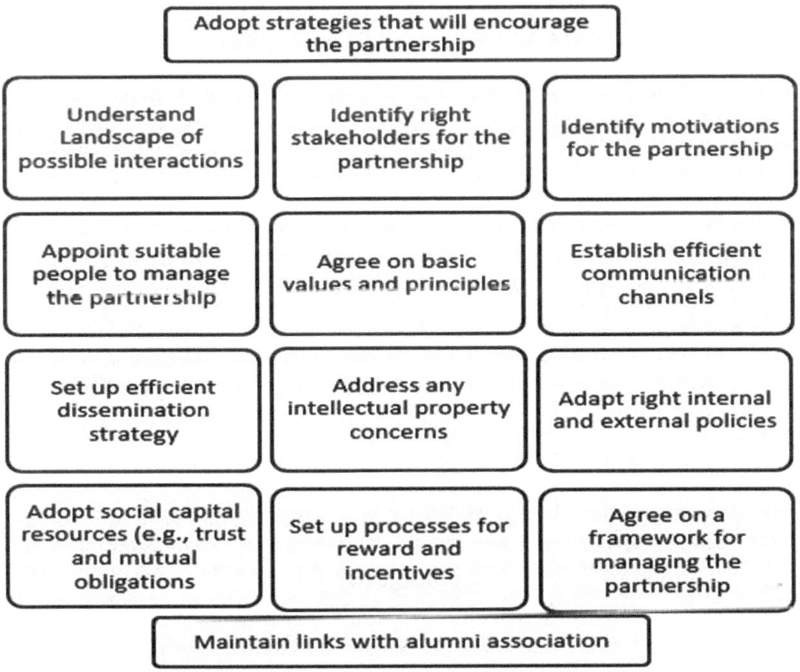


**Fig. 8.4** Framework for considerations for efficient university-industry partnership (*Source* Awasthy et al. [2020])

and the above framework provides extended ingredients that can help the university and industry to develop a seamless and fruitful collaboration.

## Current Status of University-Industry Partnership in Africa

Generally, there is a common understanding that university-industry partnership is poor in Africa (Mugabe, 2011). The extent to the validity of this claim is inhibited by a paucity of data to assess the trends in university-industry partnerships in the continent. It is commonly recognized that the nature of the African economies makes it unattractive for a widespread and efficient partnership that has the capacity to compete in global knowledge production and exchange. In particular, the African economy is primarily dependent on extractive and raw material industries, thus there is very limited attraction and potential for technological innovation. Many of the industries are usually subsidiaries of multinational companies that are headquartered in foreign counterpart countries, where significant partnerships are performed with universities in their countries of origin, leaving little or no such opportunities for African universities. According to Munyoki and colleagues (2011), "multinational firms rely more on imported technology than the indigenous firms, which supports the hypothesis that manufacturing firms rely more on imported technology than indigenous firms" (Munyoki et al., 2011).

The poor level of UIC in Africa may be attributed to the nature of the university organizational structure, lack of independence (Elhadidi & Kirby, 2017), and the complex process of collaboration. The industries also have a poor knowledge of the nature of research carried out at universities. Given the current limited landscape of activities, there is therefore increased consensus across Africa for improved university-industry partnership. The Association of African Universities report (Sá, 2012) described some exemplar university-industry partnerships across different countries in Africa, including the Education Partnership in Africa (2008–2011) funded by the UK government and involved a three-way partnership between universities in the United Kingdom and Africa and local industries in Africa; the Corporate Graduate Link at the University of Zambia funded by the German government to help bridge the gap between university graduates qualification and the needs of local industries; Incubator INNODEV established by five Senegalese universities and two agricultural institutes and funded by the French government to support innovative research results through identification and creation of enterprises; and Kenyatta University—Equity Bank partnership for Community Outreach and Extension Programmes (COEP) to provide training seminars and mentoring where Kenyatta University provided recruitment, training, supervision, and Equity bank provided funding and field training. Based on this successful UIC, a partnership with the University of Ottawa was established, where students of Ottawa went to Kenya for three weeks of community service, research, and training.

In recent times, some countries have taken national steps toward a proactive improvement in university-industry partnership. For instance, the South African-integrated Post-Graduate Industry Partnership is based on a White Paper on Science, Technology, and Innovation that aims to increase the partnership between government, business, and academia, thereby increasing human capabilities and expanding research enterprises (IPGIP, 2022). Recently, the Rwandan government, through the National Council for Science and Technology, announced up to 12 grants targeting academia-industry research and development collaboration (National Council for Science and Technology Rwanda, 2021). In Egypt, the government took several actions to remove the obstacles facing UIC through the facilitation of the Technology Innovation & Commercialization Offices (TICO) in all universities, promoting the culture of innovation and entrepreneurship among the scientific community through training and providing support to innovators (Academy of Scientific Research & Technology, 2022; Technology Innovation Commercialization Offices (TICOs), 2022).

A study involving the University of the Western Cape, South Africa showed that university partnership with stakeholders proved to have a high impact on the development of university infrastructure, research output, and teaching. It provides financial mobilization and capacity building for staff and students (Bidandi et al., 2022). The rapid growth of technology at the current time has great effect on the higher education industry and the universities try to tackle the problems of poor infrastructure, and high cost of technology and keep their competitiveness by partnering with the industry. These partnerships include developing co-curricular, training and capacity building, joint labs, and alignment of curricula with career market requirements. The UIC in education will provide opportunities for skills development, and career market shifts to provide more jobs and skilled job seekers, in addition to securing funding for education frameworks (Australian Government

Department of Education, Skills & Employment, 2021). In Egypt, university-industry-government partnerships have been established to provide digital resources for all stages of education through the initiative "Egyptian Knowledge Bank," This involves partnership with international publishers, training institutes, and technology companies. In addition, online and face-to-face training is provided to researchers, librarians, educators, and various employees to build their skills in research, publishing, and work-related skills. Educational materials and scientific resources are made freely available for all Egyptians. This initiative is primarily funded by the Egyptian government (EKB, 2022).

## Barriers and Facilitators to Industry-University Partnership

### *Global Perspectives on University-Industry Partnership*

Several barriers to UIC coexist. These barriers include the diverse cultures and organizational structure of the university and industry (The Chamber of Commerce of Metropolitan Montreal, 2012), the discrepancy in goals and expectations on both sides (Schulze-Krogh & Calignano, 2020) as academics are more concerned with short-term research outcomes, publications, recognition in the scientific community and have more strict timelines while industry focuses on long-term outcomes, financial gains, and marketing (Siegel et al., 2003) and do have more flexible timelines. Poor communication and lack of common language can act as a major hindrance to initiating or maintaining UIC (Verreynne et al., 2021). At the same time, several administrative and legal barriers have been reported, including the lack of institutional support, poor management strategies, the high costs of collaboration, the complex administrative process, and the poorly developed or absent strategies for technology transfer and property rights or copyrights (Verreynne et al., 2021). Project management frameworks and confidentiality agreements can be complex (Garnweidner-Holme et al., 2021) and inflexible and bureaucratic processes that can serve as important barriers for UIC (Verreynne et al., 2021).

In addition to the lack of confidence between universities and business partners or the inherent idea that this collaboration may be unethical can abort the UIC or even stop it at the stage of an idea (Mirza et al.,

2020). This is a common globally relevant barrier that is widely recognized to jeopardize potential partnerships. As the framework for successful partnerships proposed by Awasthy and colleagues (described above) indicated, a culture of trust, goal alignment, and capable management are prerequisites for a successful university-industry partnership (Awasthy et al., 2020). Also, the lack of institutional incentives, both from the university and industry, is an important barrier to a successful partnership. The inability to recognize and reward the contributions of key players in the partnership project may dampen morale and consequently weaken the strength of the collaboration. Other global barriers can also be described as the lack of entrepreneurial mindset of university staff involved in the partnership; lack of entrepreneurial skills knowledge, and competencies of university staff; lack of urgency and focus of the partnered projects; different ways of keeping progress between university and industry; and potential disagreements on the processes (Verreynne et al., 2021). The lack of industry partners' knowledge about the research process undergoing in universities is a barrier to initiating partnerships from the industry side and making the selection of a university to collaborate with a difficult process (Alrajhi & Aydin, 2019). Researchers also lack knowledge about the existing opportunities for collaboration, and strategies to advance the partnership agreements (Kleiner-Schaefer & Schaefer, 2022).

### *Barriers to University-Industry Partnership in Africa*

A report prepared for the Association of African Universities (Sá, 2012) identified seven barriers that inhibit university-industry partnership in Africa. That report was based on interviews of 32 informants from 13 African countries and two from France and Canada. The African informants were representative of the geographical landscape of the continent. The informants covered those from the university, industry, and government. One of the key barriers to a successful university-industry partnership is the presence of cultural differences between academia and industry. Both university and industry actors view each other from a somewhat negative perspective: there is a sense from the industry sector that the academia is egoistic, while the academia seems to think that the industry lacks an understanding of the culture of universities. Informants also believe that cultural differences between universities and industries emanate from perceived differences in goals and priorities. The second barrier identified was a lack of confidence in the industry actor in the ability of universities to meaningfully contribute to national economic development, consequently, the industry is not motivated to invest in research infrastructures at the universities. Thirdly, the nature and scope of the African economies represent a major barrier to university-industry partnership in Africa. Since many industries in Africa are branches of foreign multinational companies, many of the partnerships are performed with universities in the countries where the companies originated from, leaving little or no partnership opportunities for African universities. Consequently, results emanating from industry-based research or in collaboration with academia are usually exported into Africa from abroad.

The fourth and major barrier relates to what informants described as the weak institutional capacity of African universities, which includes limited human resources, poor infrastructure, and limited qualified personnel to productively engage with the industry. Fifthly, informants identified a lack of strong leadership at the universities as another major barrier to a successful engagement with the industry. There is a feeling that senior university administrators do not see their roles to include facilitating the establishment of partnerships with the industry. Without a clear leadership impetus from the university administration, it is impossible to make any tangible and meaningful progress with industry partnerships. The sixth barrier identified by informants concerns issues of bad governance and corruption at many universities in Africa. Some informants alleged mismanagement and misappropriation of resources at the universities, in some cases channeling the resources for personal gain. Finally, informants from some African countries highlighted the absence of national policies to promote university-industry collaboration, this being particularly because of a clear-cut definition of the role of the university in society and national development in most African countries.

To overcome these barriers all involved parties need to take urgent action. Governments should revise and design new policies and legal frameworks that support and facilitate the innovation culture. Universities need to establish and declare strategies for collaboration and provide capacity building for researchers and staff members on project management and partnerships. Involving stakeholders in discussions will pave the way for a favorable collaboration environment. Although decades passed since the identification of these barriers, it seems that there is little or no change in the African universities' policies to tackle these barriers.

### *Facilitators of University-Industry Partnership in Africa*

The informants were also interviewed regarding the perspectives on key facilitators of successful university-industry partnership. They believe that the role of the government in facilitating the partnership is crucial and this can be done through the creation of national policies, creation of an enabling environment, provision of some funding support, continuous institutional capacity development of staff through improvement in human resources, training, and recruitment of staff. Improvement in the university's external communication will put it in a place to improve engagement with the outside world. This will also provide an opportunity to engage in more economically relevant activities, thereby enhancing the employability of its graduates and attracting industry actors.

Globally, governments have challenges in providing resources to maintain access to higher education to the population due to limited resources and constrained budget allocation to education and research. Most higher education resources come from public sources and a little share from the private sector. With increasing demand to provide higher education to a greater number of citizens, there is a need to find and increase private sector investment in higher education in addition to science and research (THE: University Industry Collaboration, 2020). Governments worldwide exert efforts to enhance UIC to improve funding to universities and enhance economic development (Fan et al., 2019; Sá, 2012).

## The Quadruple Helix Collaboration (QHC) Model

Traditionally, the university, industry, and government have been the formally recognized agents in the research and development (R&D) ecosystem. Society has not been conceptualized as an active actor in the research process, but rather as the agent that receives the product of the research output or in other words the consumer of R&D. However, recent movements, represented, for example, by responsible research and innovation, seek to change this trajectory and move the involvement of the society in the R&D process to the mainstream (Cavallini et al., 2016). In this way, the values and expectations of society can be considered as part of the ingredients that shape R&D processes and decisions. The recognition of society as a key part of the R&D and innovation ecosystem motivated the extension of the traditional triple helix to the advocacy for a quadruple-helix collaboration (QHC) model for a fruitful UIC (Fig. 8.5).

**Fig. 8.5** Quadruple helix framework that integrates the civil society as one of the actors in the innovation process

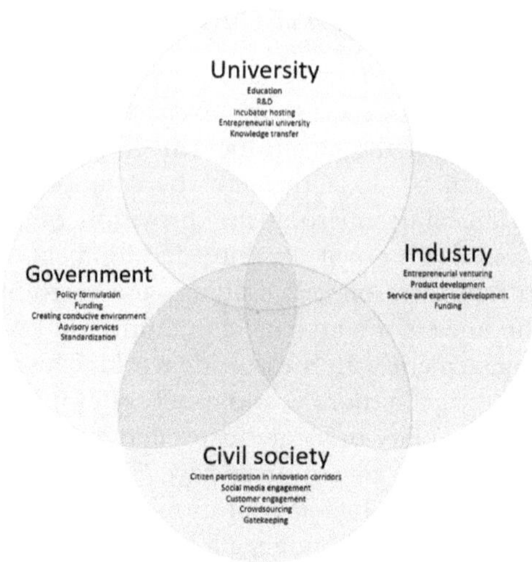


Over the last few decades, the QHC has gained increased attention as a result of its promise of increased efficiency and responsibility. Undoubtedly, R&D and innovation are complex endeavors, situated in a complex and dynamic society. Societal values and expectations are dynamic, and this should be captured in any effort that must adequately meet societal developmental needs. Therefore, all actors in society must be adequately represented in the R&D and innovation ecosystem to derive maximum benefits. Consequently, the traditional triple helix model that recognizes only the roles of the university, industry, and government can be said to be inadequate in delivering the fruits of collaboration between the actors in society in terms of R&D and innovation. By bringing the society on board in the mix of actors in R&D and innovation, QHC promises efficiency by providing extra problem-solving capacity, essentially when dealing with complex societal R&D and innovation problems (Head & Alford, 2013). Rarely can individual organizations or actors represented in the triple helix model alone solve complex societal problems in the absence of the society itself. In this context, QHC promises to provide the right solutions through the active collaboration of the four key actors in society (Fig. 8.5). In this model, efficiency is derived through the integration of expertise and value-driven behavior in which all four helixes make contributions. Beyond the creation of efficiency in the R&D and innovation ecosystem, QHC also promises that collaboration of the four helixes will create a more responsible innovation environment. In the literature, several authors have stressed the fact that it is only through the integration of the four helixes that the objective of responsible research and innovation be achieved (Hess et al., 2021; Owen et al., 2012). The consequence of this four-thronged collaboration is that value and minimization of risks will be integrated into the R&D and innovation pathways and thus, society will be better for it.

Although engagement of all four helixes in QHC is promising for R&D and innovation systems, it also carries some challenges as defining the roles of members of the society, the degree of their engagement, and the methods of communication can be challenging (Schütz et al., 2019). Nevertheless, in the QHC model, the university remains the conduit of research and knowledge generation. In the case of collaboration between the university and the industry, the generated knowledge is converted to innovation and further to implementation for development. The government's role remains the enabling actor by creating relevant policies and an environment that supports university-industry partnerships to thrive. The civil society then is the watchdog of the partnership—it provides context-specific information on the needs of the society, the impact interventions are making, and areas of urgency. Such a framework provides a comprehensive view of an efficient development-focused partnership.

## Future Insights and Conclusions

The increasing multi-sectoral nature of the global society and in particular the African society and economy and the persistent challenges inherent in the system signals a multi-system response. University-industry partnership remains crucial in making any tangible progress in STI as well as societal and economic development, but in societies where this partnership succeed, the government and the society, represented by non-governmental actors, have usually had significant roles to play. In this context, the triple helix model is inadequate. Moving to a quadruple framework, whereby civil society becomes a key actor in the research process and conversion of research into innovation, will help to spur societal development.

This chapter has provided perspectives on the current state of university-industry partnership, starting from the global perspective, and coming down to the situation in Africa. Clearly, most industrialized countries in the world continue to thrive in university-industry partnership and this is invariably reflected in the level of development such societies enjoy. But for this to happen, several factors form the ingredients for success. This chapter has reviewed some of these factors, providing a cogent framework for successful partnerships across any context. African countries, unfortunately, are far from deriving the benefits expected from the university-industry partnership, thanks to the invisible role of government in this interaction, mistrust between university and industry, lack of expertise on the part of the university in managing such partnership, and the nature of the African economy. All hope is not lost, however. Workable frameworks have been highlighted in this chapter. Key barriers, based on the perspectives of academia and industry, have been described, and factors that will facilitate improvement in university-industry partnership have been highlighted. So, it is now the responsibility of all relevant actors to take actions and design a road map for effective and fruitful UIC and engage in proactive conversations that will engineer a significant turn-around in the current situation.

The university in particular needs to understand the importance of the industry and its role in social development and economic growth. On the other hand, the industry must recognize its need for research in innovation processes, so that partnership with universities becomes a crucial journey the industry must undertake. Stakeholders and civil society can only play their role when they have the proper knowledge of the outcomes of these partnerships and have the motivation to play this role. African governments should make more effort to make UIC a strategic priority, facilitate the process of administration of agreements, and change the policies to support the mobility of university staff to industry and industry experts to universities to exchange knowledge and expertise.

## References


Academy of Scientific Research & Technology. (2022). http://www.asrt.sci.eg/

Alrajhi, A. N., & Aydin, N. (2019). Determinants of effective university–business collaboration: Empirical study of Saudi universities. *Journal of Industry-University Collaboration, 1*(3), 169–180. https://doi.org/10.1108/JIUC-05-2019-0011

Ankrah, S., & AL-Tabbaa, O. (2015). Universities–industry collaboration: A systematic review. *Scandinavian Journal of Management, 31*(3), 387–408. https://doi.org/10.1016/J.SCAMAN.2015.02.003

Australian Government Department of Education, Skills & Employment. (2021). Review of university-industry collaboration in teaching and learning.

Awasthy, R., Flint, S., Sankarnarayana, R., & Jones, R. L. (2020). A framework to improve university–industry collaboration. *Journal of Industry-University Collaboration, 2*(1), 49–62. https://doi.org/10.1108/JIUC-09-2019-0016

Bekkers, R., & Bodas Freitas, I. M. (2008). Analysing knowledge transfer channels between universities and industry: To what degree do sectors also matter? *Research Policy, 37*(10), 1837–1853. https://doi.org/10.1016/J.RESPOL.2008.07.007

Bertoletti, A., & Johnes, G. (2021). Efficiency in university-industry collaboration: An analysis of UK higher education institutions. *Scientometrics, 126*(9), 7679–7714. https://doi.org/10.1007/S11192-021-04076-W/TABLES/12

Bidandi, F., Ambe, Anthony, N., & Mukong, C. (2022). Collaboration and partnerships between South African higher education institutions and stakeholders: case study of a post-apartheid University. *Discover Education 2022, 1*(1), 1–14. https://doi.org/10.1007/S44217-022-00001-2

Bornmann, L. (2012). Measuring the societal impact of research. https://doi.org/10.1038/embor.2012.99

Brooks, H. (1994). The relationship between science and technology. *Research Policy, 23*, 477–486.

Cai, Y., & Amaral, M. (2021). The Triple Helix model and the future of innovation: A reflection on the Triple Helix research agenda. In *Triple Helix* (Vol. 8, Issue 2, pp. 217–229). Brill Academic Publishers. https://doi.org/10.1163/21971927-12340004

Cai, Y., & Etzkowitz, H. (2020). Theorizing the Triple Helix model: Past, present, and future. *Triple Helix, 6*, 189–226. https://doi.org/10.1163/21971927-bja10003

Cavallini, S., Soldi, R., Friedl, J., & Volpe, M. (2016). Using the Quadruple Helix approach to accelerate the transfer of research and innovation results to regional growth. https://doi.org/10.2863/408040

Chen, D., Zheng, S., & Guo, L. (2015). The impact of science and technology policies on rapid economic development in China.

Compagnucci, L., & Spigarelli, F. (2020). The Third Mission of the university: A systematic literature review on potentials and constraints. *Technological Forecasting and Social Change*, *161*, 120284. https://doi.org/10.1016/J.TECHFORE.2020.120284

Ćudić, B., Alešnik, P., & Hazemali, D. (2022). Factors impacting university–industry collaboration in European countries. *Journal of Innovation and Entrepreneurship, 11*(1), 1–24. https://doi.org/10.1186/S13731-022-00226-3/FIGURES/4

Davey, T., Meerman, A., Galan Muros, V., Orazbayeva, B., Baaken, T., Allinson, R., Plewa, C., Melonari, M., Tercanli, H., Paula Troutt, M., Japarashvili, N., Dreier, A., Serbin, D., Rosalinde Hofer, A., Perkmann, M., & Potter, J. (2018). The state of university-business cooperation in Europe. https://doi.org/10.2766/676478

de Wit-de Vries, E., Dolfsma, W. A., van der Windt, H. J., & Gerkema, M. P. (2019). Knowledge transfer in university–industry research partnerships: A review. *Journal of Technology Transfer, 44*(4), 1236–1255. https://doi.org/10.1007/S10961-018-9660-X/FIGURES/3

Egypt Competitiveness Rank. (2022). *Trading economins*. https://tradingeconomics.com/egypt/competitiveness-rank

EKB. (2022). https://www.ekb.eg/

Elhadidi, H., & Kirby, D. A. (2017). University–industry collaboration in a factor-driven economy: The perspective of Egyptian industry. *Industry and Higher Education, 3*, 195–204. https://doi.org/10.1177/0950422217705243

Fan, H.-L., Huang, M.-H., & Chen, D.-Z. (2019). Do funding sources matter? The impact of university-industry collaboration funding sources on innovation performance of universities. *Technology Analysis & Strategic Management, 31*(11), 1368–1380. https://doi.org/10.1080/09537325.2019.1614158

Feola, R., Parente, R., & Cucino, V. (2021). The entrepreneurial university: How to develop the entrepreneurial orientation of academia. *Journal of the Knowledge Economy, 12*(4), 1787–1808. https://doi.org/10.1007/S13132-020-00675-9/TABLES/7

Garnweidner-Holme, L., Lieberg, H. S., Irgens-Jensen, H., & Telle-Hansen, V. H. (2021). Facilitators of and barriers to collaboration between universities and the food industry in nutrition research: A qualitative study. https://doi.org/10.29219/fnr.v65.7874

Gurry, F. (2015). *Intellectual property for an emerging Africa*. WIPO Magazine. https://www.wipo.int/wipo_magazine/en/2015/si/article_0001.html

Head, B. W., & Alford, J. (2013). Wicked problems. *47*(6), 711–739. https://doi.org/10.1177/0095399713481601

Hess, D. J., Lee, D., Biebl, B., Fränzle, M., Lehnhoff, S., Neema, H., Niehaus, J., Pretschner, A., & Sztipanovits, J. (2021). A comparative, sociotechnical design perspective on responsible innovation: Multidisciplinary research and education on digitized energy and automated vehicles. *Journal of Responsible Innovation, 8*(3), 421–444. https://doi.org/10.1080/23299460.2021.1975377

IPGIP. (2022). https://www.ipgip.co.za/about-ipgip

Ivascu, L., Cirjaliu, B., & Draghici, A. (2016). Business model for the university-industry collaboration in open innovation. *Procedia Economics and Finance, 39*, 674–678. https://doi.org/10.1016/S2212-5671(16)30288-X

Kahn, M. J. (2022). The status of science, technology and innovation in Africa. https://doi.org/10.1177/09717218221078540

Kaloudis, A., Arild, A., Koch, P. M., Lauvås, T. A., Mathisen, M. T., Strand, Ø., Sørheim, R., & Aadland, T. (2019). How universities contribute to innovation: A literature review-based analysis.

Klein, S. B., & Pereira, F. C. M. (2021). Entrepreneurial university: Conceptions and evolution of theoretical models. *Revista Pensamento Contemporâneo Em Administração, 14*(4), 20–35. https://doi.org/10.12712/rpca.v14i4.43186

Kleiner-Schaefer, T., & Schaefer, K. J. (2022). Barriers to university–industry collaboration in an emerging market: Firm-level evidence from Turkey. *The Journal of Technology Transfer 2022, 47*(3), 872–905. https://doi.org/10.1007/S10961-022-09919-Z

Kruss, G., Aphane, M., Muller, L., & Manamela, A. (2012). *Promoting-higher-education-industry partnerships and collaboration*. https://www.usaf.ac.za/promoting-higher-education-industry-partnerships-and-collaborations/

Lane, J. (2010). Let's make science metrics more scientific. *Nature 2010, 464*(7288), 488–489. https://doi.org/10.1038/464488a

Lesjak, D. (2019). Measuring impacts of science and research on the society: Development, issues and solutions. *Mnagement, 14*(3), 219–236. https://doi.org/10.26493/1854-4231.14.219-236

MacIlwain, C. (2010). Science economics: What science is really worth. *Nature, 465*(7299), 682–684. https://doi.org/10.1038/465682A

Michel-Schneider, U. (2021). Challenges for university—Industry collaboration—A stakeholder view. In *Proceedings of Business and Management Conferences* (pp. 47–60). https://ideas.repec.org/p/sek/ibmpro/12713398.html

Mirza, H., al Sinawi, H., Al-Balushi, N., Al-Alawi, M., & Panchatcharam, S. M. (2020). Barriers to university-industry collaboration in an academic university department in London, United Kingdom. *International Journal of Pharmaceutical and Healthcare Marketing, 14*(3), 445–460. https://doi.org/10.1108/IJPHM-11-2016-0062/FULL/XML

Mugabe, J. O. (2011). Science, technology and innovation in Africa's regional integration. *Policy Research Series, 44*. http://www.acode-u.org

Munyoki, J., Kibera, F., & Ogutu, M. (2011). Extent to which university-industry linkage exists in Kenya: A study of medium and large manufacturing firms in selected industries in Kenya 1. *Business Administration and Management (BAM)*, *1*(4), 163–169. www.primejournal.org/BAM

National Council for Science and Technology Rwanda. (2021). https://www.ncst.gov.rw/

Org, U. (2012). A guide for successful institutional-industrial collaborations.

Owen, R., Macnaghten, P., & Stilgoe, J. (2012). Responsible research and innovation: From science in society to science for society, with society. *Science and Public Policy, 39*(6), 751–760. https://doi.org/10.1093/SCIPOL/SCS093

Oxford University News. (2020). *Oxford University announces landmark partnership with AstraZeneca for the development and potential large-scale distribution of COVID-19 vaccine candidate | University of Oxford*. The University of Oxford News. https://www.ox.ac.uk/news/2020-04-30-oxford-university-announces-landmark-partnership-astrazeneca-development-and

Ranga, M., & Etzkowitz, H. (2013). Triple Helix Systems: An analytical framework for innovation policy and practice in the knowledge society. *Industry and Higher Education, 27*(4), 237–262. https://doi.org/10.5367/IHE.2013.0165

Rodríguez-Navarro, A., & Brito, R. (2018). Technological research in the EU is less efficient than the world average. EU research policy risks Europeans' future. *Journal of Informetrics*, *12*(3), 718–731. https://doi.org/10.1016/J.JOI.2018.06.009

Roger, G., & Creso, S. (2009). *Tapping the riches of science; Universities and the promise of economic growth*. Harvard University Press.

Sá, C. M. (2012). Perspective of industry's engagement with African universities.

Schulze-Krogh, A. C., & Calignano, G. (2020). How do firms perceive interactions with researchers in small innovation projects? Advantages and barriers for satisfactory collaborations. *Journal of the Knowledge Economy, 11*(3), 908–930. https://doi.org/10.1007/S13132-019-0581-1

Schütz, F., Heidingsfelder, M. L., & Schraudner, M. (2019). Co-shaping the future in Quadruple Helix innovation systems: Uncovering public preferences toward participatory research and innovation. *She Ji: The Journal of Design, Economics, and Innovation, 5*(2), 128–146. https://doi.org/10.1016/J.SHEJI.2019.04.002

Schwab, K. (2019). The Global Competitiveness Report 2019. https://www3.weforum.org/docs/WEF_TheGlobalCompetitivenessReport2019.pdf

Schwab, K., & Zahidi, S. (2020). *The global competitiveness report special edition 2020*. World Economic Forum.

Siegel, D. S., Waldman, D. A., Atwater, L. E., & Link, A. N. (2003). Commercial knowledge transfers from universities to firms: Improving the effectiveness of university–industry collaboration. *The Journal of High Technology Management*

*Research, 14*(1), 111–133. https://doi.org/10.1016/S1047-8310(03)00007-5

Technology Innovation Commercialization Offices (TICOs). (2022). http://www.asrt.sci.eg/structure/pillars/ticos/

THE. (2021). *Methodology for overall and subject rankings for the times higher education world university rankings 2022.* https://www.timeshighereducation.com/world-university-rankings/world-university-

The Chamber of Commerce of Metropolitan Montreal. (2012). University-industry collaboration: Researchers weigh in.

THE: University Industry Collaboration. (2020). *The vital role of tech companies' support for higher education research.* https://www.timeshighereducation.com/sites/default/files/the_consultancy_university_industry_collaboration_final_report_051120.pdf

Ugnich, E., Chernokozov, A., & Filinkova, E. (2017). Problem of knowledge generation in terms of university innovation ecosystem development.

UNESCO Institute for Statistics. (2020). *Global investments in R&D a snapshot of R&D expenditure Figure 1. Regional R&D investments shares of world R&D expenditure (GERD) by region.* http://uis.unesco.org

UNESCO Institutes for Statistics. (2022). *How much does your country invest in R&D?* R & D Data. http://uis.unesco.org/apps/visualisations/research-and-development-spending/

University-Industry-Collaboration. (2021). https://www.elsevier.com/__data/assets/pdf_file/0008/1115396/university-industry-collaboration.pdf

Verreynne, M., Torres, de O. R., Mention, A.-L., & (with contributions from Lay J., N. T., F. S. and M. T. L. ). (2021) *Enablers and barriers to industry-research collaboration.* https://www.csiro.au/-/media/SME-Connect/21-00095_SER-SME_REPORT_IndustryUniCollaborators.pdf

World Economic Forum. (2018). *3 ways to nurture collaboration between universities and industry.* World Economic Forum. https://www.weforum.org/agenda/2018/11/3-ways-to-nurture-collaboration-between-universities-and-industry/

Xie, Y., Zhang, C., & Lai, Q. (2014). China's rise as a major contributor to science and technology. *Proceedings of the National Academy of Sciences of the United States of America, 111*(26), 9437–9442. https://doi.org/10.1073/PNAS.1407709111/SUPPL_FILE/PNAS.201407709SI.PDF

Young, M. (2013). IndustryAcademia. *Business Horizon Quarterly*, *7*, 17–21. https://www.uschamberfoundation.org/bhq/industry-academia-and-government-collaboration-game-changer-us-economic-future

CHAPTER 9

# Graduate Education and Knowledge Production in Africa in the Context of the Knowledge Economies

*Oanda Ibrahim Ogachi*

## The Status of Graduate Education in African Higher Education

Graduate education in Africa has significantly expanded in recent decades, with countries setting targets to invest in qualiy graduate education, expand enrolments and outputs from graduate level training. Part of the efforts have included national, regional, and pan-African commitments to increase public funding to graduate level education, support broadening of relevant international partnerships in support of graduate education, enhancing quality through faculty development and curriculum reviews,

The views expressed in this chapter are personal and do not represent the views of any of the organizations with whom he has a professional affiliation.

O. Ibrahim Ogachi (✉)
Nairobi, Kenya
e-mail: ibrahimoanda@gmail.com



D. Teferra (ed.), *Research and Innovation in African Higher Education*,
https://doi.org/10.1007/978-3-031-92909-0_9

upgrading research infrastructures, promotion of regional approaches to graduate training, and strengthening governance and regulatory frameworks to support the growth and sustainability of graduate education across the continent (African Union/European Union Summit, 2017; Bekele, 2022; Gumbo et al., 2024; Maassen, 2020; Oluwatomilayo et al, 2024; Molla & Denise, 2016; The Kigali Communique, 2014). In the context of the knowledge economies, the demand for skilled researchers to serve the expanding higher education systems and economies has attracted political commitment from African governments to invest in advanced research training as a strategy to create a culture of innovation and knowledge-driven socio-economic transformations (Molla & Denise, 2016). Despite these commitments, the status of graduate education in Africa is comparatively low, compared to other levels of education. Based on metrics such as percentage of public funding, capacity, quality, and efficiency and relevance of knowledge produced and consumed by policymakers and local communities, graduate education compares unfavourably.

The percentage of public resources allocated to support graduate education in Africa varies across countries, institutions, and disciplines. This variation, in itself is a cause of inefficiency and inequities determining on who gets to access graduate education and of what quality. Due to data limitations, a precise percentage of public resources committed to graduate education in Africa is difficult to determine. It is also the case that public resources to support graduate education are often calculated in terms of tuition costs. Not much thought is given to the fact that given the research and knowledge production orientation of graduate education, broad investments are required beyond tuition fees, to supporting research and knowledge production and dissemination infrastructures, regulatory institutions, and research uptake and policy institutions. Given the focus on only tuition expenses, graduate education across the continent largely remains underfunded. Recent data indicates that per capita public expenditure on all levels of education, including graduate education stagnated around $100 over the decade (UNESCO, 2023). A quality graduate education is supported by a well-funded research eco-system, both within and outside the universities. Public funding to establish strong research eco-systems has however been low. Although African countries have committed to 1% of their GDP on research and development (Caelers & Okoth, 2023), the 2021 UNESCO science report shows that Africa spends only 0.59% of its GDP on research and development, compared to a world average of 1.79% (UNESCO, 2021). The low expenditure on research has translated into low research output from African universities and researchers, accounting for just 1.01% of global research and development expenditures, 2.50% of global researchers, and 3.50% of scholarly publications (Pelser, 2024). Given the research orientation of graduate education, the low expenditures on research and low research outputs translate into poor environments for graduate education across the continent. Since these resources have to be shared between university and non-university research institutions, what remains within universities to sustain a quality research culture is negligible. To compensate for lack of public funding, institutions are forced to compete for external sources of funding, which if secured, is usually at the expense of losing control over the direction of graduate training and research to align with national and pan-African interests. Besides, the pipeline for graduate level training in most higher education institutions remains narrow, both in terms of percentage enrolments and nature of programs (Oluwatomilayo et al, 2024).

The ratio of graduate to undergraduate enrolments in African universities remains low. Historical data tracking the evolution of capacity of graduate level programs in African universities shows that enrolment in master's and doctoral programs as a ratio of undergraduate enrolments rose from 6.9% in 1997 to 9.3% in 2014 (Friesenhahn, 2014). Recently, data on graduate level enrolments compiled by the African Research Universities Alliance (ARUA) covering 16 of its member universities confirms the ratios have not changed much, considering ARUA member universities constitute the continent's foremost elite research universities. The data reveal that doctoral enrolment as a percentage of university enrolments averaged 4.49%, with the lowest enrolment being 0.70% and the highest 12% by 2021 (ARUA, 2022). The ratio of graduate enrolments however increases when master's level enrolments are included, ranging from a low of 9.3% to a high of 41.7% within the same period (ARUA, 2022). In terms of graduation trends, the ARUA data shows that the share of doctoral graduates as a percentage of all graduates from the 16-member universities averaged 3.12%, with the lowest being 0.8% and the highest 7.0% (ARUA, 2022). The trends show that graduate level enrolments in African universities are driven by expansion at the master's level of education, yet increased enrolments at a master's level are not serving as a critical pipeline to drive up doctoral enrolments. It is at the doctoral level that one's research and knowledge generation skills are deepened. When gauging how Africa can contribute to global knowledge economies, it is investments at the doctoral segment of graduate education that should be considered.

The low enrolment levels at the graduate level point to capacity constraints for doctoral education within the continent, understood both in terms of demand and supply. In terms of demand, available data does indicate an increasing number of students from Africa seeking tertiary education opportunities outside their countries. Eurostat data, for example reveals that 17% of the foreign students who were undertaking tertiary education within the European Union in 2021 were from Africa, with more than half (52.5%) foreign tertiary education students in France being from Africa (Eurostat, 2024). The same picture is replicated in the United Sates where students from Sub-Saharan Africa totalled 42,515, representing 4.5% of all foreign students in US universities and colleges during the 2012/2022 academic year (Open Doors, 2022). While specific data for graduate students from Africa aren't readily available, the percentage provide an idea of the capacity constraints that students in Africa who seek access at all levels of tertiary education face.

A related issue to supply is the availability and quality of staff to train and mentor graduate students. Across the continent, the percentage of PhD holders qualified to supervise graduate students, relative to undergraduate teaching and other commitments, is low. South Africa, with one of the most developed higher education systems in the continent, had 48.8% of academic staff with doctoral degrees by 2021 (Khuluvhe & Netshifhefhe, 2023). The target is to increase the percentage to 75% by 2030 through a number of interventions. Other countries are worse-off with PhD holders as low as 20%, with most serving in administrative positions with minimal direct support to graduate education.

The low numbers of PhD graduates pose various challenges to graduate education. An overworked staff that has to combine administrative work, undergraduate teaching, and graduate supervision does not constitute the best conditions for a quality graduate education. Studies show that among the challenges limiting the quality of graduate education in Africa is lack of a critical mass of senior staff to supervise and mentor graduate students, which impacts on supervision quality, leading to long time to graduation (Osiru et al., 2022).

The issue of capacity goes beyond physical spaces, to include funding capacities from governments and institutions, the quality of available programs and support systems. This capacity gaps however, have a history. In the 1990s, graduate education across the continent was affected by World Bank reform packages to African governments that led to reduced public spending in higher education. This change of policy impacted and continue to impact graduate education more compared undergraduate education, given the relative political clout of graduate level education to attract funding from the state. The politics of underfunding higher education in Africa in the 1980s affected the eco-system and pipeline for graduate education, including research and scholarly publishing in various ways. Institutional research funding for early career researchers that is critical for robust graduate education declined. The attendant decline in terms of service for academics pushed well-established scholars into overseas higher education markets or into the many local NGOs that had been established to provide a new vision for "African Development", thus denying younger academics the much-needed mentorship. The intrusion by the World Bank into higher education in Africa, and the subsequent economic crisis also resulted in the collapse of epistemic communities and disciplinary associations that nurtured graduate students around the continent, and in turn, continued to undermine knowledge production and scholarly publications from the universities (Olukoshi, 2007). University presses and bookshops for tertiary books, where they existed also collapsed together with local journals that provided a first step to scholarly publishing for young academics. In East Africa, for example, university-based journals, such as *East African Geographical Review, Tanzania Notes and Records,* and *Transafrican Journal of History* all ceased operations in the 1980s (Nyamweru, 2016).

In place of state support to graduate education, institutions have come to rely heavily on external partnerships to support graduate studies. The partnerships facilitate knowledge exchange, capacity building, and intra-African academic mobility. The external support takes various models, from full-time support for graduate studies, sandwich programs, grants and fellowships to support research training and post-doctoral fellowships.

The external partnerships range from international development agencies such as the World Bank and UNESCO; Consortium networks such as the Consortium for Advanced Research Training in Africa (CARTA), which support doctoral students and post-doctoral researchers with CARTA fellowships and research grants to enhance research capacity, university-to-university collaborations which secure funding for joint research projects and capacity building programs, and support from private foundations. Given the lack of central databases, it is often difficult to gauge the volume of support that targets graduate and post-graduate studies. Various reports and studies highlight external support as the single most source to graduate education in the continent. For example, in the 2010–2019 decade, the Carnegie Corporation of New York invested $134.43 million to strengthen higher education and research capacity in African universities, with 63% going directly to support graduate education as part of a strategy to advance the next generation of African academics (Carnegie Corporation of New York, 2021).

In terms of fellowships to support research and joint publications, data obtained from the University of Cambridge, under the university's North–South collaborations show that between 2013 and 2022, the University of Cambridge academics collaboratively published 3,850 academic works, with academic colleagues and researchers from universities in Sub-Saharan Africa. While the joint publications involved researchers from 42 countries, the largest share was concentrated in six countries: South Africa, Kenya, Nigeria, Uganda, Ghana, and Ethiopia. In terms of grants to support research fellowships, a key component of graduate education, the data from Global Cambridge shows that over £19 million project grants were disbursed to African partners between 2017 and 2022, with 25, 22, 19, 17, 9, and 8 per cent of the grants going to partners in Ethiopia, Kenya, Uganda, Ghana, other, and South Africa, respectively (Global Cambridge, 2023).

Partnerships as the main source of support for graduate education however, has not been adequate and often has led to some misalignment in instances where sectors critical to Africa's development do not attract the needed support from external partners. For example, recent studies in the area of health research show that there has been improved investment in PhD training across the continent in health research (Rivero, 2024). The gains from PhD level training have however not been matched by an expansion of training opportunities in the areas of technical, leadership, and transferrable skills that will empower graduate students develop their own ideas enriched by indigenous knowledge and prevailing local health needs, into compelling fundable research proposals (Rivero, 2024). Consequently, researchers in Africa who feel the research infrastructures in Africa offer less prospects for their career ambitions leave the continent, though the new knowledge produced by such African researchers working beyond their own countries and continent, is never attributed to Africa (Butler-Adam, 2017).

Besides the partnerships being unequal and promoting some forms of dependency, most of the partners foremost prioritize the research and knowledge interests of the funding partner. The call for Commonwealth PhD scholarships does, for example, indicate the overall objectives of the scholarships as the need to widen access to UK equipment and expertise for quality doctoral candidates from Commonwealth countries, but also contribute to UK and Commonwealth higher education and research through collaboration and partnerships. Given the dependency of funding, some scholars argue, graduate education in Africa, in the manner it is offered and funded cannot lead to equal higher education partnerships, unless Africa has the capacity to put its resources on the table with a clearly designed national and continental articulations of what research and innovation can do for African countries and the continent as a whole (Di Ciommo & Thijssen, 2019). While science is universal, the context in which it is applied matters.

Beyond the undercurrents in international partnerships and collaboration in graduate education, there are internal dynamics within African institutions that undermine the quality and vibrancy of graduate schools. For example, recent political support to increase the number of doctoral graduates from African universities with no public funding has led to a situation where graduate schools have been turned into income generation centres to generate income for the universities. The focus on graduate education on knowledge production and innovation has been relegated, as institutions prioritize on the capacity of graduate programs to attract fee paying students regardless of their preparedness for graduate studies. While this would be a global trend, prioritizing graduate education as a revenue generation stream in most African Universities has raised issues of the extent institutions have the capacity to invest in a quality graduate education for relevant knowledge generation and for revenue generation. The trend has also shifted institutional focus from investing in graduate programs that are core in driving socio-economic transformations and knowledge economies. A profile of the ARUA member universities in terms of masters' and doctoral enrolments does show that social science and humanities, and business, economics, and management tend to have more enrolments compared to other academic fields (ARUA, 2022).

The trend in commercializing graduate education as opposed to knowledge production has further deepened the problem of "deinstitutionalization" of research. The trend has also worsened the conditions for graduate training, especially for students coming from minority backgrounds and women. Most countries and universities in the continent do not have national co-ordination strategies on the development of young academics for local universities and some departments lurch from one staffing crisis to another. Yet, at the same time, the expectations are that universities have to produce and retain a new generation of academics and thus transform the academic workforce and society. Poor and/or lack of coherent strategies for graduate education has resulted to the decline in scientific production from the universities due to poor research infrastructure, poorly equipped libraries and limited access to new technologies or the lack of financing for graduate research. In a number of countries, the production of doctoral graduates is limited and this, coupled with the poor quality of basic research, hinders the proper training of PhD students who will make up the new generation of academics. Evidence from SCOPUS studies show that the share of research output from Africa's social scientists (including arts and humanities) occupy the smallest share of SSA's research output, although social science enrolments remain higher. The 2016 World Social Science report shows that between 1992 and 2013, SSA contributed only 3.2% of research publications in social sciences. Beyond providing teachers for their expanding higher education systems, African countries need graduate level researchers to contribute to the knowledge economy and help achieve targets set in the SDGs.

## Research Networks and Graduate Education in Africa

The reduced capacity of universities to support robust graduate schools has witnessed parallel pan-African research networks established outside the universities to support graduate students in an ideological and material sense. Some of the research networks are publicly owned, and therefore constitute sites for research training in a national, regional, and pan-African context. Other networks have been established independently as research centres, while others are external and quasi-public. The research networks outside the universities have over-time provide graduate students in Africa, and emerging researchers access to research training skills and knowledge dissemination outlets (Kitchen & Jay, 2019).

In the social sciences, the networks have included the Council for the Development of Social Science research in Africa (CODESRIA), the African Association of Political Science (AAPS) launched in Dar es Salam in 1974 as the continental parent body of political scientists in Africa, the African Institute for Economic Development and Planning (IDEP), the Organization for Social Science Research in Eastern and Southern Africa (OSSREA), the Association of African Women for Research and Development (AAWORD), the Southern Africa Political Economy Series (SAPES) Trust, and the African Economic Research Consortium (AERC). Recently, the Partnership for African Social and Governance Research (PASGR) was established in Nairobi to support graduate students with research skills to undertake interdisciplinary and multi-disciplinary policy-oriented research.

In the area of science and innovation and public health research, pan-African research institutions such as the African Population and Health Research Centre (APHRC), the International Centre for Insect Physiology and Ecology (ICIPE), the International Livestock Research Institute (ILRI), and the African Science Foundation (ASF), all located in Nairobi, do provide tailored research training and support for graduate students in specific areas. The research centres also have established linkages with graduate schools in public universities to ensure graduate programs and curricula benefit from latest developments in relevant areas of learning. The Africa Research Excellence Fund (AREF) funds locally led post-doctoral capacity training in health research in the areas of research leadership, grant writing skills workshops, mentoring, fellowship funding that support locally led research, and capacity building in African institutions.

There have also been support from governments at a pan-African level for graduate programs in science and technology. Some examples of these initiatives include The Regional Scholarship and Innovation Fund (RSIF), a flagship project of the Partnership for Skills in Applied Sciences, Engineering and Technology (PASET) program launched by the Governments of Senegal, Ethiopia, and Rwanda with support from the World Bank in 2013. The focus of RSIF is to train new doctoral students in applied sciences, engineering, and technology in competitively selected African universities partnered with international universities. Other initiatives under this category include the Regional Initiative in Science and Education (RISE), which supports graduate students and early career scientists in Africa through university-based, regional research and teaching networks in selected disciplines. The Regional Universities

Forum for Capacity Building in Agriculture (RUFORUM), a consortium of 170 African universities, provides doctoral and post-doctoral grants.

The pan-African research networks and centres do provide important support that continues to shape graduate education in the continent, though still heavily dependent on external funding. They provide important capacities in terms of structuring and organizing graduate programs in relevant disciplines in ways that fill important gaps in university-based training. By coupling training in research skills and training in academic publishing and knowledge dissemination, the centres and networks do strengthen indigenous research and publishing and enhance local research capacities while contributing to the development of a self-sustaining academic environment. By emphasizing on African-led research, the networks, research centres, and programs are responding to the quest for creating equitable research partnerships, and reshaping graduate schools to spearhead the challenges of decolonization in African knowledge eco-systems (Gumbo et al., 2024).

## Graduate Education and Knowledge Production in Africa: A Contested Space

Graduate education is central to research and production of new knowledge that are supposed to inform public policy. Graduate students undertake research, produce new knowledge which is published and disseminated thus, boosting Africa's place in the knowledge economies. However, the political economy of national and global knowledge production and dissemination often limit the opportunities available to graduate students from Africa to publish and disseminate their work. One of the continuing contestations in this area is on what type of graduate education should be promoted in the continent, given the unique challenges, and the necessity to avoid mimicking western models, while remaining globally competitive and locally relevant (Pelser, 2024). Concerns continue to be raised by academics and policymakers in Africa that reduced public investment in graduate education and research, coupled with lack of locally owned knowledge dissemination outlets, mean that knowledge produced by graduate students in Africa and its use is marginalized even when such knowledge is of high quality (Rivero, 2024). Despite the growth in digital publishing, the subsequent increase in the cost of journal article processing fees and subscriptions mean that the best ranked journals and dissemination outlets are out of reach for graduate students in Africa. The funding available to graduate students in Africa often does not include support for publications and dissemination. This means that knowledge produced by graduate students from their research does not often get disseminated in outlets that give the knowledge and the students visibility, as the students can hardly afford the journal publishing fees charged by most high visible journals (Mekonnen et al., 2022). The option such students have is to publish in journals with lower impact factors and visibility, and which are considered of lower quality, even when the outputs from their research is of high quality (Asare et al., 2021).

Graduate education in Africa, as a key node from where new knowledge is produced, is deeply embedded in forms of global, regional, and national ideologies and the politics of knowledge that inform graduate research landscape and knowledge dissemination outlets. An understanding of the nature and dynamics of knowledge publication and dissemination at the disposal of graduate students in African universities does illuminate the nature of opportunities available to graduate students in African universities, and how such opportunities ultimately shape the character of graduate schools, and universities, more generally.

Academic and scholarly publishing are central to documenting and distributing new knowledge accruing from graduate research. Undertaking research and publishing the results of such research through acceptable publication outlets remains central both to graduate students' academic careers and the development process. In Africa, fundamental questions persist about who produces knowledge, for what purposes, through which publication infrastructures it is created and disseminated, and who ultimately consumes it. These questions are central to shaping Africa's pursuit of socio-economic and political transformation. In the context of Africa's development vision, "Agenda 2063", academic publishing plays a central role in supporting graduate students and advancing the quest for "the Africa we want", while at the same time, contributing to strengthening research capacities and capabilities of individuals and institutions.

While it is true that infrastructures for disseminating knowledge in Africa have been shaped by colonial and post-colonial knowledge architectures, one has to take note of the emergence and resilience of indigenous/African-based academic publishing outlets. The trend towards indigenization emerged from the late colonial period, in the context of the decolonial movements of the 1940s and 1950s, which were often led by graduate students. During this period, indigenous African newspapers emerged outside the European controlled and sanctioned mission publications (Bodil, 2011; Fay, 1980). The newspapers became the first attempts at indigenous publishing in a number of African countries, depended on voluntary and political associations, and sidestepped the European-dominated print culture and created an anti-colonial counter-voice, espousing traditions of freedom of speech and against any forms of censorship (Fay, 1980). Since the emerging indigenous African publishing outfits were seen to be competing with colonial government-supported publishing houses, the indigenous outfits were often dismissed as contributing little to the independence movement, but instead, thrived on subversive attacks on government and irresponsible publications (Hachten, 1971: 202). The attempt at independent publishing by Africans as part of the struggle for independence also extended to metropole cities, where African students founded magazines and publishing houses. The best known of these initiatives include *Présence Africaine*, founded in 1949 by Alioune Diop, a Senegalese, in Paris, France (Graf, 2001). *Présence Africaine*, which celebrated its 70th Anniversary in 2019, brought together well-known black writers, poets, and intellectuals in a common course to support the formation of a new cultural, historical, and political identity of and for blacks, and still remains the world's oldest Black-owned independent publishing house (Graf, 2001). The indigenous African press in the pre-independence period, however helped to spread social and political ideas and to mobilize the African population in the struggle for independence (Scotton, 1975), and in the post-independent period, became the nucleus within which African governments organized national publishing houses.

From the 1960s, with African countries gaining independence, universities were nationalized and graduate education expanded as part of the project of development (Mkandawire, 2011). The expansion of graduate education, offered both locally and overseas, was seen as part of a strategy to indigenize the development of the newly independent countries and offer a democratic break from colonial practices (Samuel, 2015). The establishment of national universities went hand in hand with the nationalization of publishing houses and expansion of indigenous publishing outlets to ensure graduate students and African scholars generally had access to the new independent publishers giving a voice to Africa's own scholarship and perspectives (Kitchen & Jay, 2019). Strong centres of graduate education especially in the social sciences grew, such as the "Dar es Salaam and Ibadan schools of thought", which, besides training a new generation of graduate students along nationalist lenses, provide ideological and intellectual direction in the process of African development. The growth in graduate education offered locally was accompanied by growth in local academic publications, emergence of co-publishing and emphasis in locally relevant research processes (Kitchen & Jay, 2019). Foreign-owned educational publishers however continued to dominate academic publishing (Bgoya & Jay, 2013). This meant that despite the expansion of higher education in the first decade of independence, publishing decisions of work produced by the emerging African academics were largely being made in the North (Bgoya & Jay, 2013). But, African higher education institutions and academics didn't totally have control of what ideas or content they published and how it related to the development needs of the new nations.

From the 1990s, the implementation of structural adjustment programs resulted in the decline and in some cases, the collapse of the pipeline for graduate education in the universities. This decline in graduate enrolments, also witnessed a shift in academic publication dynamics. Instead of university-based publishing houses, journals and scholarly associations, new private scholarly publishing houses emerged outside the universities to support young academics. Some of these were and continue to be individual-driven efforts often focusing on non-scholarly academic books targeting the primary and secondary education markets. A database of African-based publishers of scholarly books developed by the International African Institute (IAI) in association with the African Books Collective, shows that the landscape is changing, with most of the publishers established after 1990. The data reveals that in Anglophone Africa, South Africa leads the scholarly publishing market with 11.6% of publishers; followed by Nigeria (8.2%), Kenya (6.6%), Ghana (4.1%), and Zimbabwe (3.6%). In Francophone countries, Algeria leads the scholarly publishing market with 6.1% of the publishers, followed by Cameroon (4.1%), Cote d'ivoire/Morocco (3.6%), and Senegal (3.1%). Angola leads the Luspohone market at 3.6% (https://tinyurl.com/3pc66wn6). This landscape in terms of the countries and regions where most scholarly publishers are located translates to countries whose issues are researched and get published in scholarly publications (Briggs & Weathers, 2016).

There have also been initiatives to establish African-based journals. Some of these are within the universities, while others are outside the universities. A study undertaken in 2017 did establish the existence of

52 university presses across the continent, besides the emergence of new journals that have embraced technology to promote the idea of the knowledge commons (Schalkwyk & Luescher, 2017). The Society of African Journal Editors (SAJE), founded in 2004, continues to work in mobilizing resource and support for the strengthening and growth of African journals, promoting the utilization of African journals by graduate students and within the development community and policymakers, besides enhancing the international visibility of African journals (Shehu & Ameh, 2005). African Journals Online, the world's largest collection of peer-reviewed, African-published journals, established in 1998 to increase the global and continental online access, awareness, quality, and use of African-published, peer-reviewed research carries 854 journals (602 open access) and 184,861 open access full articles across a range of disciplines (AJOL, 2024). The focus of AJOL is to support researchers and policymakers in Africa to have access to contextually relevant quality research publications from Africa to address the continent's challenges in health, education, climate change, and under-development. AJOL is obviously a critical resource that can shape graduate education and research in Africa.

The emergence of new publication outfits outside the universities, has been accompanied by efforts to distribute scholarly publications from Africa, outside the continent. The motivation here has been to ensure that African voices are heard outside the continent as a strategy to influence the manner the continent is perceived and change the politics of knowledge production on the continent. In 1989, a number of independent African-based publishers convened and founded the African Book Collective (ABC), a London based publisher and marketing company, to facilitate publication and distribution of scholarly books from Africa in Europe, North America, and the Commonwealth. While ABC continues to be instrumental in influencing the politics of knowledge production on Africa, outside Africa, it has had little support from African governments and other continental African bodies, perhaps, repeating the experiences of similar outfits in the past, which though vouching for the African voice, have attracted little political support. Other institutions that have been established to influence scholarly publishing outside the continent include *the Bellagio Publishing Network*, an informal association of organizations and individuals committed to strengthening indigenous publishing and book development in Africa, founded in 1991 with the support of the Rockefeller Foundation.

More recently, developments in open access, open science, and digitization have broadened opportunities for graduate students in Africa to disseminate their research and facilitate sharing of locally produced knowledge to wider audiences. It is an opportunity to make visible knowledge coming out of Africa and the contribution to the global knowledge. Caution however should be exercised in embracing the various available open access regimes if young academics in Africa have to avoid the traps from previous decades that have been discussed elsewhere in this chapter. Open access regimes and digitization will not be free from power hierarchies that have governed knowledge production previously. The open access situation in Africa cannot be isolated from the underside of the movement and its contribution to reproducing the global structure of knowledge production—of ideas, information, images, and knowledges (Meagre, 2021). For graduate education in Africa to contribute to the kind of knowledges that have the capacity to support Africa's socio-economic transformation, uncritical embrace of global trends in knowledge production and dissemination as the basis of organizing graduate education in Africa should be avoided.

Recent debates about equitable research partnerships, embracing of local knowledge in research and prioritizing knowledge needs in Africa have resulted to several partners supporting graduate education in Africa to also include aspects of research training, knowledge production, and publication to influence public policy. The idea is to couple together support to graduate education with a greater focus on equitable international research partnerships and locally led research, as African researchers are best placed to meet the challenges of improving sector policies in their countries (Rivero, 2024). For example, with support from Agence Française de Développement and the World Bank, the African Development Forum (ADF) book series has since 2009 been providing space for the publication of issues of significant relevance to Africa's social and economic development (Riviere, 2016). ADF provides graduate students, practitioners, and scholars with opportunities to publish their research in ways that can promote public policy and development thinking in Africa (Riviere, 2016).

To address the gap between funding for graduate education and support for academic publishing and knowledge dissemination skills, some funders are supporting initiatives focusing on time-bound short-term residential summer trainings. This has entailed supporting universities to set up centres for doctoral academies and organize short-term training in conceptualizing research problems in new areas of knowledge, research techniques, and data analysis using new IT software and techniques in journal article development, publication, and dissemination. Examples of these new approaches to supporting and improving the quality of graduate education and knowledge production in Africa include the Carnegie Corporation of New York supported Pan-African Doctoral Academy at the University of Ghana and the African Doctoral Academy at Stellenbosch University (Onyima, 2020). CODESRIA, intent on mobilizing the African academic diaspora has also established a college of senior academic mentors made up of senior African academics from the diaspora to support graduate students registered in African universities (Bangura et al., 2019). The college was set up to address the shortage of supervisory capacity in African universities, besides providing graduate students with critical methodological and epistemological considerations that they need in conceptualizing topics for research and executing fieldwork (Bangura et al., 2019).

The nature of academic publishing and knowledge dissemination infrastructures have therefore been part of factors that have and continue to shape the quality and capacity of graduate education in Africa. On one hand, there are indigenous research and academic publishing outlets that have continued to struggle alongside officially sanctioned and "internationally" recognized outfits (Mill et al., 2021). The current manifestation of this trend is the characterization of a large number of journals located within African universities as "predatory", with academics in African universities encouraged to publish in journals that are characterized as "international" and "prestigious" (Mckenna, 2018). Graduate students are therefore confronted with these contradictions, where attempts at producing, publishing, and communicating knowledge with the potential to support their academic growth is easily labelled "subversive" or of low quality in favour of academic publications that erode the very idea of knowledge sovereignty (Mckenna, 2018; Mill et al., 2021).

## Emerging Issues in Graduate Education and Research

### *Gender*

Although there has been a marked improvement in the percentage of women as undergraduate students in African universities, the pipeline for graduate education, research and innovation careers for women remain gendered across the continent's higher education and research institutions. The share of female students as graduate students at the doctoral level has shown a marked improvement in the last few years. Data from 16 universities that constitute part of ARUA show that an average of 40% doctoral students were female, while an average of 38% female students graduated from the 16 universities in 2021(ARUA, 2022). Hence, a slight increase in enrolment does not necessarily translate to similar graduation rates, signalling perhaps to the many barriers that female graduate students face. These inequalities often translate into inequalities in thematic issues in research, frameworks underlying research and the nature of knowledge produced. In terms of knowledge dissemination, existing practices contribute to limiting the extent gender/women issues are accorded space in scholarly publications, and enabling conditions for female graduate students to constitute an epistemic community as authors of various scholarly works published from the continent.

Research institutions that are less accommodating of the women academics, coupled with cultural expectations and lack of senior women to act as role models and mentors have limited prospects for gender equality in graduate education and research in Africa. This is turn has resulted to diminished visibility of the contributions from women researchers as measured by research and innovation outputs such as publications, patents, and citations (Rivero, 2024).

Given the resource constraints facing higher education institutions in the continent, most academics struggle to establish their careers at this level due to various institutional barriers, including resources and facilities for research, but most critically, lack of appropriate institutional cultures and attitudes to research which are needed to support, protect, and advance intellectual endeavour, support emerging scholarship, emphasize collegiality and communities of research, encourage vertical relationships within faculties, and set policies which protect and support early career academics, a situation which tends to affect female scholars more (British

Academy/Association of Commonwealth Universities, 2011). The reason for this, as several studies seem to show are that the pipeline for females to progress towards graduate and post-doctoral studies and into academic careers gets narrower as they climb the academic ladder. The situation of female early career academics in terms of academic and scholarly mobility is worsened by the increasing diverse metrics that universities in the continent have adopted in the context of ranking cultures, such as a record of research and scholarly publications in highly ranked journals. Female academics in Africa are comparatively under-represented as authors in available databases, in part a reflection of female academic's low overall participation in higher education across sub-Saharan Africa (Rose et al, 2019). UNESCO data for 2016 indicate that on average, just 24% of academic staff in tertiary education across sub-Saharan Africa were female (UNESCO, 2019). This situation translates to low rates of female academics as percentage of scholarly works published from Africa's higher education institutions.

### *Mentoring a New Generation of Researchers Through New Models of Research Training*

How can graduate schools contribute to producing the new generation of academics and scholars and advance a culture of excellence? How can the research and knowledge generated in graduate schools be locally contextualized while attracting global interest? Within the emerging culture of metrics and the imperative to contribute to the global knowledge pool, interventions to overcome barriers to quality graduate education and knowledge production need to be part of the culture of academic planning in African higher education institutions. Most institutions however lack resources and strategies to help young academics write more and better, and have their work accepted for publication in reputable and widely disseminated journals (British Academy/Association of Commonwealth Universities, 2011). Some studies have documented that whereas early career academics in Africa especially during their graduate studies produce valuable work worthy of publishing, rates of publication especially from these cohort of academics across the continent remain low (British Academy/Association of Commonwealth Universities, 2011). This is in part due to lack of institutional resources and support for which, among other things, would offer graduate student skills in negotiating the submission and peer review and publishing chain successfully, to ensure that their work makes it through to the scholarly community. On the other hand, inadequate resourcing for skilling early career academics in African universities to publish their work in reputable journals has predisposed them to be trapped into publishing in the rapidly growing open access publishing, funded by article processing charges with publishers and journals with highly questionable academic and peer review practices (Shen & Bjork, 2015). This situation only accentuates inequalities in knowledge production and consumption and deepens the misrepresentation and misunderstanding of African realities even within the academic and research institutions in the developed countries.

Supporting interventions to improve the pipeline for scholarly publishing in Africa will have the added advantage of enhancing mutuality in higher education partnerships and the potential for achieving transformational rather than individual transactional relationships and partnerships (Chrystal, 2017). Increased scholarly publication rates and dissemination of knowledge from graduate students in Africa will also contribute to minimizing "knowledge divides" (UNESCO, 2010).

### *The Politics of Peer Review, Location, and Generations*

The current status of research and publications in Africa is such that it remains concentrated in a few countries, disciplines, and a specific generation of academics in the universities. Dominant perceptions about scholarly research capacity in Africa often begin from a narrative of deficiency, leading to approaches that favour western ways of knowledge production and top-down approaches to capacity support that displaces contextualized knowledge and co-creation processes, including peer review and scholarly publication (Havemann et al., 2021). In terms of the opportunities available for graduate students to publish and develop their scholarship, this has been limited. The funding crises that higher education institutions in the continent have faced over the last three decades, has to a greater degree affected the quality and capacity of the new generation of academics, including graduate students to effectively serve in a broad range of knowledge production roles, including serving as peer reviewers and journal editors. This tends to create a generational gap, with for example, the older generation of academics still serving in editorial boards of journals. There are perceptions among the younger generation of academics, especially graduate students that the older generation of academics who serve in editorial boards and in research networks intentionally "gatekeep" to limit opportunities for graduate students (Fokwang, 2024). It is another power game, where a generation determines access to research and scholarly publication opportunities (Fokwang, 2024; Tempelhoff, 2020).

The peer review process and the role of editors in academic publishing and the opportunities this creates determine the quality of knowledge available to graduate students in Africa (Sebola, 2018). One of the important functions of peer review process is to detect fraud before publication (Ancker & McLellan, 2003: 1), even though such can still be detected by careful readers after material has been published (Sebola, 2018). But the peer review process often leads "to gatekeeping to regulate entry of new ideas and persons into scholarly fields" (Harley & Acord, 2011: 1; Mills et al, 2023). Peer review and publication in most visible journals are also determined by established networks of collaboration, a fact which favours the older generation of academics as they are the ones who most likely benefit from these networks compared to younger graduate students. A detailed study by Beaudry et al. (2018) on the state of the next generation of scientists in Africa does suggest persisting lack of support, collaboration, and mentorship as well as patronizing attitude from the older academics to young ones, which often translates to longer period to PhD completion and missing out on related career advancement opportunities like research and publications. The dominance of extractive mentorship relationships in the graduate education to academic publication support systems in Africa has also been variously documented (Beaudry et al., 2018; Fokwang, 2024; Mills et al, 2023). Published works from South Africa, for example, do suggest that despite recent increases in the proportion of black academics in the universities, scholarly publishing remains disproportionately white, due to the persisting legacies of apartheid, with 45% of the publications being accounted by academics aged 50 years and above (Wild, 2017). This signal both a persisting racial and generational problem. Studies have also pointed out at emerging strong network of gatekeepers to ensure that emerging ideas, especially from young scholars (graduate students) that challenge a dominant paradigm remain at the periphery of scholarship in which the new is often dismissed on the basis that it possesses only a little knowledge, which is seen as dangerous (Maserumule, 2012; Sebola, 2018).

A number of externally funded schemes do exist focusing on supporting research capacities and scholarly publications by early career academics in African universities. Some of the support is tied to graduate phase of training and rarely does the support encompass the post-doctoral level. Given the funding constraints in most universities, institutions continue to depend largely on various forms of external support and interventions to run graduate education programs, even when this external support has not resulted into internal capacities to manage graduate schools and undertake research of greater local relevance (Wenzel & Noémi, 2016). The emerging strong voices advocating for equitable research partnerships and local/African-led opens new opportunities to respond to the question of what kind of graduate education Africa needs and the interventions required to achieve this ambition.

Some of the external partners supporting graduate students and early career academics publishing capacities include the British Academy, the African Studies Association (UK), and the Germany Academic Exchange program (DAAD). The Consortium for Advanced Research Training in Africa (CARTA) and the Pan-African Doctoral Academy, a PhD training hub based at Stellenbosch University in South Africa, both funded by the Carnegie Corporation support research and scholarly publishing. Recently, *Open Research Africa*, an initiative by Science for Africa (SFA) Foundation, The African Academy of Sciences, and the Africa Research Excellence Fund (https://tinyurl.com/2t9duvrr) launched an open science publishing initiative targeting young scholars in Africa and in all disciplines. Open Research Africa publishes scholarly articles and other research outputs by researchers from affiliated institutions. Scholarly content published on Open Research Africa is fully open access and article processing charges (APCs) are funded centrally by platform partners. This means that researchers formally affiliated with partners can publish on the platform without direct cost to them. The initiative enables researchers to publish and share outputs of their research, and support reproducibility of such research.

## Conclusion

Analysing graduate education and knowledge production in Africa through a political economy lens reveals the dilemma that Africa faces in expanding graduate education with the ambition to gain from the global knowledge economies. While the ambitions to expand graduate education and increase the number of doctoral students has been well articulated, public resources to support these ambitions have not been forthcoming. Instead, graduate education, knowledge production, and dissemination are largely supported by external partnerships. While the partnerships provide the much-needed resources, they raise issues about the capacity of graduate schools to contribute to the production of younger academics who can conceptualize research and produce knowledge that addresses local contextual problems. Though a few knowledge production and publishing outfits such as CODESRIA remain supportive of graduate students, the lack of dedicated public funding from African governments to support their research and publication strategies leaves the institutions exposed. If African ambitions for knowledge and development sovereignty have to be actualized, including "Agenda 2063", African governments need to put more resources to support graduate education and boost relevant knowledge production in Africa. *The African Manifesto for Science, Technology and Innovation (2010)* did argue aptly for Africa's sovereignty in Science and technology through funding and socialization into African indigenous perspectives of knowledge production and use. This call has been echoed in subsequent policy documents such as STISA 2024 and the Continental Education Strategy for Africa (CESA). Graduate schools and programs need to be organized and delivered to respond to the priorities identified in these policy documents.

## References

African Union – European Union Summit. (2017, November). Abidjan Declaration on Investing in Youth. https://tinyurl.com/bdf8u44m

African Journal Online. (2024). https://www.ajol.info/index.php/ajol. Accessed on 29th December 2024.

Alliance of Research Universities in Africa (ARUA). (2022). Profiles of ARUA universities Report. ARUA.

Ancker, J. & McLellan, F. (2003). The Journal's role in scientific misconduct. A council of Science editors retreat. Landsdowner Resort and Conference centre, 7–9 November 2003.

Asare, S., Mitchell, R., & Rose, P. (2021). How accessible are journal articles on education written by Sub-Saharan Africa-based researchers? *Development and Change, 52*(3), 661–669. https://doi.org/10.1111/dech.12639

Bangura, A. K., Obando, J. A., Munene, I. I, & Shisanya, C. (Eds.). (2019). Conducting research and mentoring students in Africa CODESRIA College of mentors handbook. Dakar. *CODESRIA Working paper series.*

Beaudry, C., Mouton, J., & Prozesky, H. (2018). *The next generation of scientists in Africa.* African Minds.

Bekele, T. A. (2022). *Boosting African doctoral capacity needs national partnerships*. https://tinyurl.com/et8mmeuw.

Bgoya, W., & Jay, M. (2013). Publishing in Africa: From independence to the present day. *Research in African Literatures, 44*(2), 17–34. Indiana University Press.

Bodil Folke Frederiksen. (2011). Print Cultures, Nationalisms and Publics of the Indian Ocean. *Africa: Journal of the International African Institute, 81*(1), 155–172. Cambridge University Press.

Briggs, C. R., & Weathers, S. (2016). Gender and location in African politics scholarship: The other white man's burden? *African Affairs, 114*(460), 466–489.

British Academy/Association of Commonwealth Universities. (2011). Foundations for the Future: Supporting the early careers of African researchers. *A paper commissioned by the British Academy as part of the Nairobi Process.*

Butler-Adam, J. (2017). *Africa is establishing itself as global player in research but it's going unnoticed*. https://tinyurl.com/2scf3xh8

Caelers, D., & Okoth, D. (2023, December 14). Research funding in Africa: Navigating sustainability and shifting perspectives. *Nature Africa*. https://tinyurl.com/2hhb7v5t

Carnegie Corporation of New York. (2021). *Investment in Higher Education and Research in Africa, 2010–2019 Report*. Carnegie Corporation of New York.

Chrystal., G. M. (2017). Partner positioning: Examining international higher education partnerships through a mutuality lens. *The Review of Higher Education 41*(1), 33–60.

Di Ciommo, M., & Thijssen, S. (2019). Refresh and Reload: EU and Africa working together on Research and Innovation. ECDPM, Discussion paper No, 256.

The Kigali Communique. (2014). *Higher education for science, technology and innovation: Accelerating Africa's aspirations*. https://tinyurl.com/y3eev9n6. Accessed on 24th December 2024.

Eurostat. (2024). *Learning mobility statistics.*

Fokwang, J. (2024). Centring Africana Voices in Contemporary Publishing. Paper presented at the Workshop on Defiant Scholarship in Africa, Yaoundé, Cameroon, 18–20 June.

Friesenhahn, I. (2014). *Making higher education work for Africa: Facts and figures*. https://tinyurl.com/5fn66pyd

Gadsden, F. (1980). The African Press in Kenya, 1945–1952. *The Journal of African History,*(4), 515–535. Cambridge University Press.

Global Cambridge. (2023). *Annual report, 2022–2023*. Cambridge Africa. chrome-extension://efaidnbmnnnibpcajpcglclefindmkaj/https://www.cambidge-africa.cam

Graf, M. (2001). Roots of identity: The national and cultural self in Présence Africaine. CLCWeb. *Comparative Literature and Culture, 3*(2). https://doi.org/10.7771/1481-4374.1121

Gumbo, M. T., Knaus, C. B., & Gasa, V. G. (2024). Decolonising the African doctorate: Transforming the foundations of knowledge. *Higher Education, 88*, 1611–1627. https://doi.org/10.1007/s10734-024-01185-2

Hachten, W. A. (1971). *Muffled drums: The news media in Africa*. Iowa State University Press.

Harley, D., & Sophia, K. A. (2011). Peer review in academic promotion and publishing: Its meaning, locus, and future. Centre for Studies in Higher Education. http://escholarship.org/uc/item/1xv148c8

Havemann, J., Munene, A., Ngugi, J. W., Obanda, J., Owango, J., & Saderi, D. (2021). Best practices and innovative approaches to peer review in Africa. *The Scholarly Kitchen*.https://tinyurl.com/3mcuwpjn

Kitchen, S., & Jay, M. (2019). Decolonization and Co-publishing. A paper prepared for the European Conference on African Studies (ECAS). University of Edinburg, 12–14, June.

Khuluvhe, M., & Netshifhefhe, E. (2023). Are we producing enough doctoral graduates in our universities? Department of higher education and Training.

Maassen, P. (2020). Developing equal, mutually beneficial partnerships with African universities. Recommendations for a new European collaboration strategy (The Guild Insight Paper No. 1). Retrieved from The Guild of European Research-Intensive Universities' website: https://tinyurl.com/4d78rbz8

MacGregor, K. (2017, September 22). Network aims to strengthen African scholarly publishing. *University World News*. https://www.universityworldnews.com/post.php?story=20170921154031974

Maserumule, M. (2012). The new and the old in the complex of power relations in the politics of knowledge-a polemic editorial. *Journal of public Adminstration, 47*(1), 1–6.

Mckenna, S. (2018). Why developing countries are vulnerable to predatory journals. *Social Science Space*. https://tinyurl.com/5bjwffn5

Meagre, K. (2021). Introduction: The politics of open access—Decolonizing research or corporate capture? *Development and Change, 52*(2), 340–358.

Mekonnen, A., owns, C., Effiom, E. O., Kibaja, M., Lawes, M. J., Omeja, P., Ratsoavina, F. M., Razafindratsima, O., Sarkar, D., Stenseth, N. C., & Chapman, C. A. (2022). Can I afford to publish? A dilemma for African scholars. *Ecology Letters, 25*, 711–715. https://doi.org/10.1111/ele.13949

Mill, D., Branford, A., Inouyel, K., Robinson, N., & Kingori, P. (2021). *'Fake' journals and the fragility of authenticity: Citation indexes, 'Predatory' Publishing, and the African Research Ecosystem*. https://tinyurl.com/bdcvtmsv

Mills, D., Kingori, P., Branford, A., Chatio, S. T., Robinson, N., & Tindana, P. (2023). *Who counts?* Ghanaian academic publishing and global science.

Mkandawire, T. (2001). Thinking about Developmental States in Africa. *Cambridge Journal of Economics, 25*(3), 289–314.

Mkandawire, T. (2011). Running while others walk: Knowledge and the challenge of Africa's Development. *Inaugural Lecture*. London School of Economics and Political Science.

Moahi, K. H. (2012). Promoting Africa indigenous knowledge in the knowledge economy: Exploring the role of higher education and libraries. *New Information Perspectives, 64*(5), 540.

Molla, T., & Denise, C. (2016). In pursuit of the African PhD: A critical survey of emergent policy issues in select sub-Saharan African nations, Ethiopia, Ghana and South Africa. *Policy Futures in Education, 14*(6), 635–654.

Mwangi, C. A. G. (2017). Partner positioning: Examining international higher education partnerships through a mutuality lens. *The Review of Higher Education, 41*(1), 33–60.

Nyamweru, C. (2016). African based scholars in academic publishing: Q&A with Celia Nyamweru. http://blog.oup.com/2016/09/african-scholars-publishing-celia-nyamweru/

Olukoshi, A. (2007). From colonialism to the new millenium and beyond. *Institute of Development Studies Bulletin, 38*(2), 20–25.

Olukoshi, A., & Nyamnjoh, F. (2000). CODESRIA: Over 30 years of scholarly publishing. In Alois Mlambo (Ed.), *African Scholarly Publishing* (pp. 257–265). African Books Collective.

Oluwatomilayo, O., Udeme, S. M., Olumide, A. O., & Omowale, A. O. (2024). Exploring perspectives: A scoping review of the challenges facing doctoral training in Africa. *Higher Education*. https://doi.org/10.1007/s10734-024-01264-4

Onyima, B. N. (2020). Pan-African doctoral schools and knowledge production in Africa: Experiences, issues, and testimonials of participants. In S. Oloruntoba, A. Afolayan, and O. Yacob-Haliso (Eds.), *Indigenous Knowledge Systems and Development in Africa*. Palgrave Macmillan. https://doi.org/10.1007/978-3-030-34304-0_7

Open Doors. (2022). *Report on international education exchanges*. Institute of International Education (IIE). Department of State.

Osiru, M., Nguku, E., Nyagah, B., Oremo, C., Tambo, E,. Cheo, A, & Mainguy, G. (2022). PhD programs in Africa: The arrows, the targets and the archers. In *UNESCO world hire education conference (WHEC2022)*. https://repository.rsif-paset.org/xmlui/bitstream/handle/123456789/268/phD%20programs%20in%20Africa%20-%20the%20arrows,%20the%20target%20and%20the%20archers.pdf?sequence=1

Pelser, A.-M. (2024). Synergistic advancements: Fostering collaborative excellence in doctoral education. *Frontiers in Education, 8*, 1289424. https://doi.org/10.3389/feduc.2023.1289424
Rivero, C. (2024). There''s a science research gap in Africa. Here's how to fill it. https://tinyurl.com/5yajt5nw
Riviere, F. (2016). *How can research improve public policy in Africa?* https://tinyurl.com/5fds4evz
Rose, P., Downing, P., Asare, S., & Mitchell, R. (2019). *Mapping the landscape of education research by scholars based in sub-Saharan Africa: Insights from the African Education Research Database*. REAL Centre, University of Cambridge. https://doi.org/10.5281/zenodo.3242314
Samuel, A. M. (2015). How African doctorates and doctoral candidates are changing. *The Conversation*. https://tinyurl.com/3ubpu7s6
van Schalkwyk, F., & Thierry, L. M. (2017). Open Minds, Cape Town. The African University Press.
Scotton, J. F. (1975). Kenya's Maligned African Press: Time for a reassessment. *Journalism Quarterly, 52*(Fall), 30–56.
Sebola, M. P. (2018). Peer review, scholarship and editors of scientific publications: the death of scientific knowledge in Africa. *KOERS—Bulletin for Christian Scholarship, 83*(1). https://doi.org/10.19108/KOERS.83.1.2314
Shehu, B., & Ameh, E. A. (2005). The Society of African Journal Editors (SAJES). *Annals of African Medicine*.
Shen, C., & Björk, B. (2015). Predatory' open access: A longitudinal study of article volumes and market characteristics. *BMC Medicine, 13*, 230. https://doi.org/10.1186/s12916-015-0469-2
Tempelhoff, J. (2020). Peer review in academic journals: A Pandora's box. *South African Journal of Science, 116*(9–10).
UNESCO. (2010). *World social science report: Knowledge divides*.
UNESCO. (2019). *Women in science: Fact sheet no 55*. https://uis.unesco.org/sites/default/files/documents/fs55-women-in-science-2019-en.pdf
UNESCO. (2023). *Education Finance Watch: Special edition for the African Union Year of Education, 2024*. UNESCO.
UNESCO Science Report. (2021). The race against time for smarter development; Executive summary. UNESCO.
Wenzel, G. P., & Tousignant, N. (2016). Capacity as history and horizon: Infrastructure, autonomy and future in African health science and care. *Canadian Journal of African Studies / Revue Canadienne des Études Africaines, 50*(3), 349–359. https://doi.org/10.1080/00083968.2016.1267653
Wild, S. (2017). Black academics soon to outnumber white researchers in South Africa. *Nature*. https://doi.org/10.1038/nature.2017.23030

CHAPTER 10

# Graduate Research in African Universities: The State of Research Integrity

*Tesfaye Semela*

## Introduction

With the estimated population of about 1.6 billion, Africa constitutes 16% of the world population and owns a staggering 30% of the global mineral resources (AfDB, 2016). In flip side, however, Africa stands at the bottom of the hierarchy of world regions in terms of its contributions to the global scientific and technological innovations. According to World Economic Forum (WEF) (2023), Africa contributes just 2% of the global scientific and technological innovations. Many scholars and international institutions attribute Africa's marginal performance mainly to poor financing (e.g., WEF, 2023; Kahn, 2022) that prompted the African Union (AU) to come up with the *Science, Technology and Innovation Strategy of Africa 2024* (STISA-2024). The initiative is in line with the AU Agenda 2063 expected to capitalize on earlier agreements by 55 member states to set aside 1% of their GDP for the development of science, technology, and innovation (AU, 2014). Achieving the objectives

T. Semela (✉)
Hawassa University, Hawassa, Ethiopia
e-mail: tesfayes@hu.edu.et



D. Teferra (ed.), *Research and Innovation in African Higher Education*,
https://doi.org/10.1007/978-3-031-92909-0_10

could be far from realistic without accumulating a critical mass of scientists which could be materialized through quality postgraduate training supported by sufficient research infrastructure and funding. Yet, fully engaging in world class research and innovation is predicated on internationally accepted standards of ethical practices of responsible conduct of research (RCR). On the other hand, it should be recognized that Africa's Science, Technology and Innovation (STI) capacity has been curtailed not only by the size and quality of graduates, but also owing to lack of ethical standards of research undertaking at national and institutional levels.

### *Historical Overview*

For the larger part of its post-independence period, Africa went through lots of ups and downs which undermined the development of higher education. To make matters even worse, nearly two decades after independence, African states were forced by the World Bank and IMF to implement the infamous Structural Adjustment Program (SAP) which set several preconditions including investing more in basic education while cutting funds that should have otherwise been allocated to higher education (e.g., Hayward, 2010; Hayward & Ncayiyana, 2015; Mohamedbhai, 2013). After a decade of defunding higher education in Africa, the 1990s brought with it a new World Bank publication "Constructing Knowledge Societies" (World Bank, 2002) heralded the policy shift calling on expansion of higher education in Africa. However, the marginalization and under funding of the higher education subsector in the preceding two decades by itself posed considerable challenges, let alone compensating for the lost years. Thus, it can be argued that the status of graduate education resonates highly with Africa's poor performance in research and innovation relative to the rest of the world.

In light of the glaring problems of Africa's underperformance in the area of scientific research and innovation, giving due heed to the voices calling for reversing the depressing state of postgraduate training sets the necessary (e.g., Hayward, 2010; Hayward & Ncayiyana, 2015; Jowi, 2021; Mohamedbhai, 2013) but not sufficient condition for research and innovation to flourish without putting in place institutional structures that can ensure responsible conduct of research (RCR) (Bain et al., 2022). Because, no matter how qualified they may be, research and innovations produced by postgraduates and researchers are no longer valid, if they fail to fulfill the expected standards of ethical practice and scholarly integrity.

Thus, African higher education and research institutions should simultaneously assess where they stand in terms of cultivating a research culture which embraces universal ethical standards, as well as professional, and scientific integrity (e.g., Ndebele et al., 2014; Owunsu et al., 2022).

### *Antecedents of Research Capacity in Africa*

Africa has not been able to harness the benefits of scientific research mainly due to its inability to put in place quality graduate programs that could produce sufficient number of scientists in all fields. This partly explains why Africa stands as the least performer in terms of generating scientific knowledge and technologies through research and innovation. According to recent data sub-Saharan Africa's contributes less than 1% (0.44%) of the global expenditure on R&D (see Fig. 10.2), have 198 researchers per million population (UniRank, 2023). Africa's global share of scientific publications stood at 3% in 2018 showing slight increase from where it was in 2010 (1.7%) (Kahn, 2022). Furthermore, compared to other regions of the world Africa's share in the number of granted patents is small, which as of 2022, stood at just 9% (WIPO, 2023).[1] What that means is that African HEIs were, and still are, not able to develop a critical mass of academics and researchers to stand in par with the rest of the world (e.g., Teferra, 2003; Tijssen & Winnink, 2022). As illustrated in Fig. 10.1, the average size of researchers in sub-Saharan Africa was estimated to be 26 per million inhabitants. That accounts for about 0.2% of the world average which was about 1353 per million inhabitants as of 2022 (UNESCO-UIS, 2024; URL: http://data.uis.unesco.org/index.aspx?queryid=3685). A closer look at six selected African states indicate considerable differences across states with Nigeria (39), Ghana (87), and Ethiopia (90) having less than 100 researchers per million inhabitants while Kenya (227), South Africa (437), and Senegal (581) reported well over 200 researchers per million population (see Fig. 10.1). In contrast, the share of North African countries is visibly

[1] According to the World Intellectual Property Organization (WIPO), patent applications had increased from 10,700 in 2012 to 16,200 in 2022. Africa had submitted. Nonetheless, majority of the applications were submitted non-resident entities (i.e., entities that do not reside, in Africa). As a result the share of patents granted to resident applicants remained the same in 2012 (9%) and 2022 (9%), respectively, despite the significant increase in the number of patent applications.

higher ranging between 822 for Egypt to 1,081 researchers per million inhabitants for Morocco (UNESCO-UIS, 2024; URL: http://data.uis.unesco.org/index.aspx?queryid=3685).

One of the major reasons for the poor performance of African universities with respect to research productivity is partly attributable to small staff size with PhDs. This has been impacting not only the quality of graduate education, but also the growth and expansion of PhD training (British Council & DAAD, 2018; Jowi, 2021). This has made it difficult to bolster research productivity and knowledge generation in African HEIs at the world stage. To make matter worse, many African countries seem to lack the commitment to allocate financial resources (see: Fig. 10.2) as concluded in 8th Ordinary Session of the Executive Council of the African Union in 2006 in Khartoum (UNECA, 2018) to earmark 1% of their GDP for R&D.

As shown in Fig. 10.2, recent data is not uniformly available for all states including in the World Bank database. Thus, literature review was used to augment to get a general impression on current trends of funding scientific research as percentage of GDP for the selected countries. The average investment on R&D in Africa as a percentage of GDP in 2018 was 0.50% (UN-ECA, 2018). However, the R&D budget allocations by individual states vary considerably where some states contribute 0% while others spending very close to 1% of their GDP. For instance, as shown

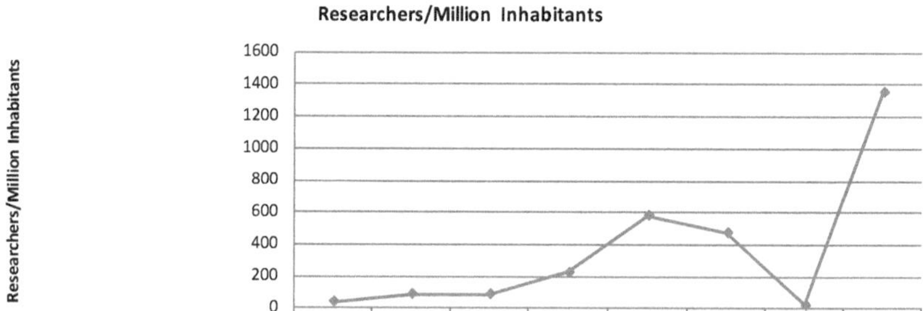


| | Nigeria (2007) | Ghana (2015) | Ethiopia (2017) | Kenya (2010) | Senegal (2015) | South Africa (2020) | Sub_Sahran Africa (2020) | World Average (2020) |
|---|---|---|---|---|---|---|---|---|
| Researchers/Million Inhabitants | 39 | 87 | 90 | 227 | 581 | 473 | 26 | 1353 |

**Fig. 10.1** Number of researchers per million populations in six African countries (*Source* UNESCO- Institute for Statistics (UIS). Available at http://data.uis.unesco.org/index.aspx?queryid=3685, accessed on February 28.2024)

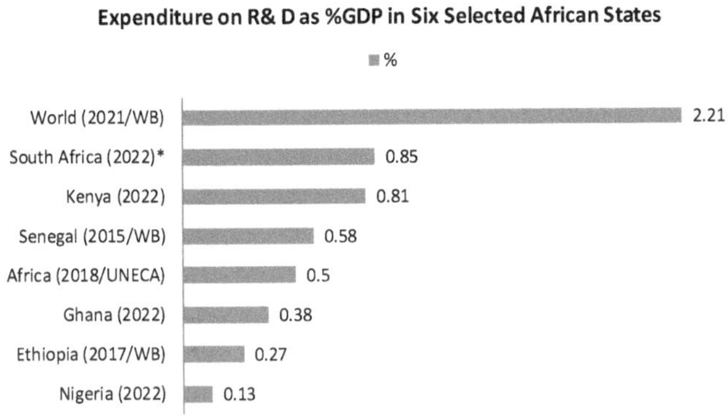


**Fig. 10.2** Expenditure on (R&D) as % GDP on selected African countries (*Source* World Bank. (November 27, 2023). Research and Development Expenditure (% of GDP). Available at https://tinyurl.com/mwsy4k74. Accessed February 28/2024. Kenya: expenditure on R&D as GDP share 2020–2022 | Statista https://tinyurl.com/5dns93yw; Ghana: expenditure on R&D as GDP share 2020–2022 | Statista https://tinyurl.com/5e2bsf35; Nigeria: expenditure on R&D as GDP share 2020–2022 | Statista https://tinyurl.com/4a246xkn; South Africa: expenditure on R&D as GDP share 2020–2022 | Statista https://tinyurl.com/mwks8r6d

in Fig. 10.2, Nigeria allocates the lowest (0.13%, 2022) followed by Ethiopia (0.27%, 2017), Ghana (0.38%; 2022), Senegal (0.58%, 2015) in that order. On the other hand, as reported in 2022, Kenya (0.81%) and South Africa (0.85%) are closing on 1% threshold.

In any case, regardless of the variations in the time frame, the values reported for the six selected countries show far lower investment when compared with the world average which stood at 2.21% of GDP in 2021.However, according to a report by Academy of Science of South Africa (2019), Kenya and South Africa reportedly contribute their respective GDPs while in contrast countries like Lesotho and Madagascar contribute 0%. To make matters difficult for researchers and policymakers, there is no data on 24 other African states regarding their R&D spending (Academy of Science of South Africa, 2019). Thus, it is safe to say that the majority of African states, governments spend very little on research projects undertaken by public universities. This is why public funding on graduate research and other researcher projects conducted by academic or research staff is largely dependent on external sources, especially those of Western partners and international donors.

The reminder of this chapter is as follows: In section two a brief conceptual clarifications on the fundamental notions RE/RI will be in order followed by theoretical frameworks explaining structures and interactions across institutional, national, regional/international RE oversights. Section three assesses the degree to which continental, national, and institutional structures and frameworks are in place so as to ensure responsible conduct of research (RCR) while section four specifically examines RCR at institutional level with particular reference to graduate research (i.e., Master's and PhD dissertations) including existing practices related to the state of research integrity (RI) the challenges surrounding contract cheating, and emerging technologies. Finally, section five presents the conclusion and policy implications.

## Conceptual Framework

The research ethics literature is diverse when it comes to the use of agreed upon concepts that made it difficult to maintain uniform message to researchers and the wider readership. Some of the terms and concepts are interchangeably used despite differences in their operationalization and scope. As such, it is important to start with a condensed clarification of the terms and concepts used in this chapter.

Research ethics is a very complex subject encompassing a wide range of activities throughout the entire process of research undertaking. Taking this into account, Resink (2018) defines:

> Research ethics is a type of applied (or professional) ethics that addresses the questions, dilemmas, and issues related to the ethical conduct of scientific research... Topics that fall within the domain of research ethics range from practical problems, such as assigning authorship, to more abstract questions, such as resolving conflicts between normative principles.

Elaborating on his definition, Resink (2018) identifies 12 dimensions which constitute research ethics (RE). These are: (a) *Honesty*: which indicates the need that researchers should communicate honestly with each other, research sponsors and institutions, government agencies, and the general public; (b) *Due care*: Researcher should be vigilant to avoid errors and reduce or control biases in research; (c) *Openness*: Scientists should share data, results, methods, and tools; (d) Fair credit: Researchers should fairly distribute credit for scientists involved; (e) *Respect* for colleagues and students; (f) *Respect for property*: Researchers should respect physical and intellectual property; (g) *Respect for research subjects*: Researchers should show respect toward human and animal research subjects; (h) *Respect for the law*: Researchers should be obey institutional policies and legal rules; (i) *Nondiscrimination*: Researchers must avoid unfairly discriminating peers or students. (j) *Stewardship of resources*: Researchers should make effective use of physical, financial, and other resources. (k) *Social responsibility*: Researchers should maximize benefits and minimize harms to society; and (l) *Freedom*: Researchers should respect the right to freedom of inquiry and debate (Resnik, 2018). However, as demonstrated below, Research Integrity (RI) used interchangeably with Research Ethics (RE) even though the former is broader in scope.

Rossouw et al. (2014) distinguish among three overlapping concepts frequently used in the literature namely, research ethics, research integrity, and responsible conduct of research (RCR). Rossouw et al. (2014) conceive "Responsible conduct of research" (RCR) as "an umbrella" term which encompasses issues related to authorship, plagiarism, research misconduct, whistle-blowing, research ethics guidelines, codes of conduct, conflict of interest, research ethics, and other training. However, in practice, the authors (Rossouw et al., 2014) argue, the line drawn between "research integrity" and "responsible conduct of research" is increasingly fading away. On the other hand, "research misconduct" is a notion which subsumes under "research integrity" and represents the manifestation of the former through individual or group behavior in research and publication process. These, according to Benos et al. (2005), include falsification, plagiarism, redundant and duplicate publication, conflict of interest, disagreement over authorship, and violation of animal and human welfare, among others. Scientific misconduct, on the other hand, is defined as fabrication, falsification, and plagiarism (Gross, 2016).

The notion of "responsible conduct of research (RCR)" is comprehensive yet, distinguishable from both RI and RE. RE often include the processes in terms of which a proposed research study is scrutinized via assessing its compliance with the desired values and principles that constitute ethical research while RI is conceived as to incorporate the implementation of the research processes and the behavior of the researchers. So much so, RI is not only the foundation for a credible research, but also a pre-requisite to ensure successful academic and research environment. As such, RI entails adherence to professional standards prescribed by oversight bodies such as governmental agencies, funding agencies, and professional associations as well as adherence to ethical principles and values that promote responsible conduct of research (RCR) (Rossouw et al., 2014).

## *Theoretical Framework*

A credible research process demands the instruments of ensuring RI/RE. In a university setting in particular, at least two important steps needs to be taken to ensure RCR. First, there should be RE/RI structure cascaded often from top to bottom to effectively monitor a research process. Second, within this structured environment, there should be a continuous learning and development among individual researchers and community of researchers since monitoring alone cannot establish credible research culture. In this connection, two widely employed theoretical frameworks are adopted to demonstrate how higher education institutions could establish effective institutional research culture. The first, comprehensive framework which draws on Turner's (2010, 2012) macro-meso-micro theories. This framework borrowed from discipline of sociology is important to decipher how the global, national, institutional environment, and individual researchers (individual actors) interact with each other in the research process. More specifically, the micro-meso-macro analysis enables us to explore who makes decisions on RE/RI standards, guidelines, and oversee the implementations at different levels, i.e., micro, meso, and macro. This approach allows what roles are played by individual researchers/graduate students, academic units (to which the student is affiliated), or unit/college level RECs, or independent bodies that are not affiliated to the university operating at national or regional levels.

According to Turner's (2010, 2012) macro-meso-micro theories, there are three different levels of social reality; and are defined as follows: (a) *Micro level*: The micro-level social reality encompasses the agent's (i.e., graduate student) face-to-face and indirect social interactions within or outside campus/university settings with other groups and institutions (e.g., research team, academic department, faculty/college administration, etc.) which are constrained by macro-level forces (e.g., Ministry of

Higher Education; Ministry of Health) in shaping postgraduates' ethical and moral principles in relation to research and academic integrity, (b) *Meso level*: This level of social reality focuses on higher education institutions and research centers where micro-level players i.e., postgraduate students, research teams, or department/faculty level research groups come in direct interaction with macro-level forces like national level policies on research ethics or research integrity. This level of social reality serves as a platform by bringing together the micro and macro-level realities which itself serving as a mediator between the more powerful macro structure and the less powerful micro-level players. (Turner, 2010), and (c) *Macro level*: Refers to national policies affecting individual students and meso-level social units through the policy provisions and guidelines related to RE/RI. In line with Turner (2010), the reciprocal interactions between the levels of social reality correlate very greatly with the amount of power held by the respective social spaces. Meaning, in more concrete terms, the macro-level social reality strongly impacts the meso (institutional) and micro social realities through the policies and guidelines developed at the top (macro) of the structure (see Fig. 10.3). For instance, international standards of RE/RI are often endorsed as integral part of national policies and guidelines are applicable to universities and research institutes (i.e., meso level). Consequentially, institutions cannot ignore meeting these standards of RE/RI. It follows that lower academic/research units and individual researchers (micro level) must comply with these policies. However, this does not mean that individual researchers or departments cannot voice their demands, needs, and concerns. They do have an impact on meso and macro levels even though the latter is more influential as it holds the highest decision-making authority. What this means in the context of RE/RI is that effective national oversight bodies are indispensable to ensure a functioning institutional Research Ethics Committees (REC) or Institutional Ethical Review Boards (IERB). Nonetheless, it is not enough to have effective national and institutional structures to ensure RI/RE. For instance, having an anti-plagiarism policy does not guarantee the absence of plagiarism in theses or dissertations. Instead, it is the well-nurtured students and researchers who can ensure RI as illustrated in the paragraph that follow using the Ecological System Theory (EST).

Unlike Turner's (2010) sociological analysis that seems to employ similar terminologies, the Ecological System Theory (EST) originated from the discipline of developmental psychology to understand how an

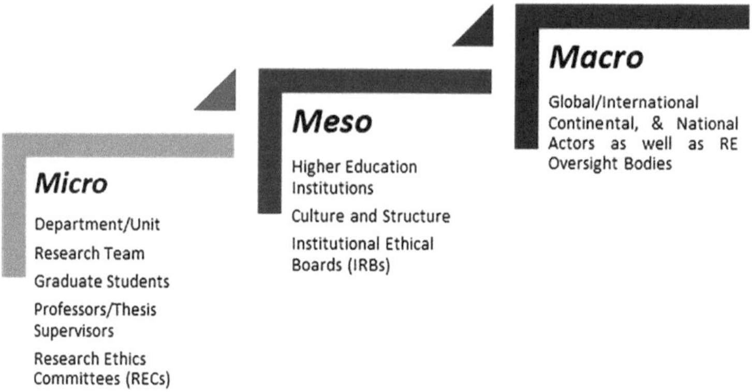


**Fig. 10.3** Oversight of a research process as a sociological interaction (*Source* Based on Turner's (2010) levels of sociological reality)

individual (referred to as "developing person") develops as a result of her/his direct or indirect interaction with proximal or distal environment. As such, the EST places the developing person (in our case a graduate student/researcher) at the center and examines how he/she undergoes change and development as a result of direct interaction with immediate (proximal) environment (e.g., peers, classmates, professors, thesis supervisors) and indirectly with relatively distant (distal) environmental influences (such as institutional guidelines or Policies of RE/RI, Institutional Research Ethics Board, etc.). EST has been widely applied to understand how university students develop in many situations and areas often adopting the Human Ecology framework (e.g., Conceicao et al., 2018; Renn & Smith, 2023) whose origin is the EST. The EST posits that the development of an individual is influenced by four environmental forces, namely the microsystem, mesosystem, exosystem, macrosystem, represented by circular layers and the fifth dimension being the chronosystem, which embodies the time component (Tong & An, 2024). The microsystem contains the developing person's immediate environment (Bronfenbrenner, 1994, p. 39) which constitutes the activities, roles, relationships, and experiences s/he acquires through direct face-to-face interactions. The microsystem also embodies social settings or institutions like family, university department where the individual is affiliated, as well as classmates, research group, among others. The second layer, *Mesosystem* embodies the sum total of microsystems—it is essentially a system of relationship between two or more sub-systems at least he/she is not a member in one of them (For example, the interaction between the department where the graduate student is enrolled and the research team in which she/he is part of). Bronfenbrenner (1994) illustrates that the Mesosystem "comprises the linkages and processes taking place between two or more settings containing the developing person" (p. 40). The third layer *Exosystem* on the other hand, is different from the previous two inner layers. The *Exosystem*, according to Bronfenbrenner (1994) refers to the "linkages and processes taking place between two or more settings, at least one of which does not contain the developing person, but in which events occur that indirectly influence" (p. 40). For instance, a graduate student is not a member of the department council and the research ethics committee (REC), at faculty/college level. Yet, decisions that are made by these entities have a direct impact on him/her. The outer most layer of EST, the *Macrosystem* encompasses the micro-meso-, and exosystems. The *Macrosystem* however goes beyond embracing these sub-systems; rather it dictates their functioning within the ecological system (Duerden & Witt, 2010; Friedman & Allen, 2019). For instance, the overarching societal or local culture, socio-economics or political systems are superimposed on other immediate contexts of the students or researcher in HEIs.

In contrast to the four EST dimensions, however, the *Chronosystem* functions almost independently of the Macrosystem. Bronfenbrenner (1994) conceives the Chronosystem as representing the time dimension that the developing person (a graduate student) experiences along the lifespan. This encompasses not only the acquisition of the knowledge, attitudes, and skills during their university stay, but also the values, moral and ethical principles upheld in the environment of higher education or research institutions. For instance, before the advent of the internet graduate students had to manually search for publications to do a literature review than those who wrote their dissertations using search engines like *Google Scholar* at their disposal. Today, researchers and postgraduates alike are confronted with the reality of how to ethically use new tools such as conversational AI like ChatGPT. As such, the whole ecological system is impacted by the historical developments that have transpired at national, regional, or global levels that have negative or positive influences on research process, institutions, and students alike.

In the sections that follow, the two major theoretical frameworks drawn from the fields of sociology and developmental psychology will inform the interpretation and analyses of researcher's (students') behavior and ethical conduct, institutional culture and practices related to RCR, as well as the macro-level RE/RI oversight.

## Robustness of RE Oversight at Macro-Level

As discussed in the preceding section, the existence of strong macro-level RE structures are necessary to develop relevant legal frameworks and policies governing research undertaking. As part of the macro-level continental oversight bodies play a critical role by helping national RECs to realign their policies, legislations, and guidelines with international/global norms and standards without necessarily infringing into their values and norms. However, looking at the situation at continental level, the activities surrounding establishing an Africa-wide structure which oversee national RECs to achieve common goals to ensuring RCR in all higher education systems and research institutions has been limited (Mwaka, 2017). However, in many African states there are legal frameworks that could serve as a point of departure to establish a working structure and organization of RE system for universities, research institutions, and centers of excellence in individual states. According to the Association of African Universities (AAU) and African Academy of Science (AAS) (2023) study in 10 selected African states, it was found that in all countries there existed structures that are concerned with research ethics (see Table 10.1). The entity which is entrusted to oversee RE is known as Research Ethics Committee (REC) in all countries considered. At the same time, there is considerable diversity in the nature and type of national level frameworks that govern RE. Accordingly, fewer countries have decentralized RECs (e.g., Ghana) while the majority still opt to maintain centralized systems (e.g., Ethiopia; Malawi; Mozambique; Namibia Rwanda, & Senegal). On the other hand, countries like Malawi, Tanzania, Uganda, and Zambia were better positioned than others (see Table 10.1) since they put in place "clear regulations that require the establishment and accreditation/registration of RECs in institutions that conduct human research" (AAU & AAS, 2023). Apart from the African states considered in AAU and AAS study, countries like Nigeria and South Africa reportedly have developed their own Research Ethics Accreditation Systems (REAS), which suggests that some states are at more advanced level compared to other counterparts (Moodley & Myler, 2007; cited in AAU & AAS, 2023).

In short, the national level RE oversight structures does exist in most African states. Yet, most of them are still at embryonic stage given the

**Table 10.1** Regulations supporting operations of RECs in selected countries and existing REC systems

| *Country* | *Regulations on RECs* | *Macro/National Frameworks* | *Scope of Oversight* |
|---|---|---|---|
| Botswana | Yes | National REC at MOH + decentralized RECs | Health + Social Science |
| Burkina Faso, Cote d'Ivoire, Malawi, Mozambique, Namibia, Rwanda, & Senegal | Yes | Centralized REC under MoH | Health Focus National Ethics Review Committee (NERC) |
| Ethiopia | Yes | Centralized | Health and related sciences |
| Ghana | Yes | Decentralized system | Health |
| Kenya | Yes | Accreditation by NACOSTI | Sci & Tech and Health |
| Tanzania | Yes | Accreditation system | Accreditation system |
| Uganda | Yes | Accreditation System | Accreditation System |
| Zambia | Yes | Registration of RECs | Registration of RECs |
| Zimbabwe | Yes | National REC. Centralized system with a registration system for institutional RECs | National REC. Centralized system with a registration system for institutional RECs |

*Note* MoH = Ministry of Health; N.A. = Not Available; NACOSTI = National Commission for Science, Technology & Innovation; REC = Research Ethics Committee. *Source* Association of African Universities (AAU) and the African Academy of Sciences (AAS). (2023). Deepening Knowledge and Implementation of Research Ethics in the African Context. AAU & AAS

scope and scale of expectations of the expanding postgraduate education that is ready to take on the challenges articulated in the AU's *Science, Technology and Innovation Strategy for Africa 2024* (AU, 2014).

### *Oversight at Institutional Level*

Higher education institutions are platforms where the macro-level RE/RI policies and RECs encounter micro social units like academic and research units, and individual researchers, lecturers, and masters' and PhD candidates in the process of undertaking, publication and dissemination. In other words, universities develop their own RE/RI policies and guidelines and organizational structures aligning with the broader national level RE/RI policies while at the same time taking into account the institutional objectives, needs, and priorities as well as the technical, scientific, and innovative capacity of their human resources as well as available financial and material resources. However, the starting point for responsible conduct of research relies heavily on the existence of institutional-level research ethics committees (RECs) and RE/RI policies. In order to get a general impression, we will review the status of RECs and REPs in sample of widely named universities in nine African countries geographically located in different sub-regions in terms of their institutional-level structure to oversee RE/RI. The countries include Egypt, Ethiopia, Ghana, Kenya, Nigeria, South Africa, Tanzania, Uganda, and Zambia. According to the data shown in Table 10.2, of the 16 universities, we found evidence that all have either Institutional Ethical Review Boards (IERBs) or Institutional Review Boards (IRB) depending on how they name their respective RECs. However, what majority of these universities share in common is the focus on medical, health, and biological research which involve human subjects. However, there are few exceptions, of the 16 universities, three including Kenyatta University (Kenya), Nnamdr Azikiwe University (Nigeria) which reported to have RECs for the fields of social science and humanities.

## Research Integrity (RI) in African Institutions

Extant studies demonstrate the degree to which African universities are challenged owing to the widespread research misconduct in the form of pervasive data fabrication, falsification, plagiarism in Masters' and PhD dissertations (e.g., Adeleyes & Adebamawo, 2012; Coughlin, 2015; Mireku et al., 2023; Sentleng, 2010; Stella-Maris, 2014) among other academic papers students submit to get credits. In this regard, a number of studies (e.g., Kibret & Kebede, 2016; Mireku et al., 2023) expressed their concern about the worsening situation of academic integrity in African higher education systems. Most of these studies focus on the extent and magnitude of research misconduct such as plagiarism, data fabrication, and falsification of data in graduate theses and dissertations (e.g., Adeleyes & Adebamawo, 2012; Anney & Moshe, 2015; Coughlin, 2015; Kibret & Kebede, 2016; Mireku et al., 2023; Okonta & Rossouw, 2012; Stella-Maris, 2014). A growing empirical evidence suggest that

**Table 10.2** Institutional research ethics and RE policy in selected African universities

| *Country* | *Name of Institution*[1] | *RE Frameworks and Oversight* | | *Description* |
|---|---|---|---|---|
| | | REP | REC | |
| Egypt | University of Cairo | unknown | Yes | Networks of Medical & Health Science Colleges |
| Ethiopia | Addis Ababa University; Jimma University, Hawassa University | N.A | Yes (e.g., Anti-Plagiarism Guidelines by Addis Ababa Uni; other Ethiopian Universities rely on Senate legislations and Graduate School Thesis and dissertation guidelines which only partially address limited issues of RE & RI) | - Colleges of Medicine & Health Sciences<br>- (IRBs)<br>- National Ethics Review Committee (NERC)<br>- Institutional IRBs |
| Ghana | University of Ghana University of Cape Cost | No National Policy[a] | Yes—IRBs | The two institutions have IRBs |
| Kenya | Kenyatta University; Strathmore University | University Research Policy | KU, Ethics Review Committee (ERC) | A national oversight—NACOSTI has a guideline for Institutional Ethical Review Committees (IERCs) |
| Nigeria | University of Ibiden; Nnamdi Azikiwe University | N.A | Yes | University of Ibiden, College of Medicine; College of Law & Social Science & Humanities are members of REC |
| South Africa | University of Kwa-Zulu Natal (UKZN), Pretoria University, University of Cape Town | N.A | Yes | Institutional Review Board (IRBs) are in charge in respective institutions |

(continued)

**Table 10.2** (continued)

| *Country* | *Name of Institution*[1] | *RE Frameworks and Oversight* | | *Description* |
|---|---|---|---|---|
| | | REP | REC | |
| Tanzania | Aga Khan University Tumalini University Makumira | Yes | Yes | Research Ethics Review Committee (RERC) |
| Uganda | Makerere University | Yes | Yes | School of Public Health |
| Zambia | The University of Zambia | N.A | Yes | Natural & Applied Sciences Research Ethics Committee (NASREC) |

*Note* [1]Institutional websites; [3]http://orid.ug.edu.gh/research-ethics; [a]Owunsu et al. (2022); MoH = Ministry of Health; N.A. = Not Available; NACOSTI = National Commission for Science, Technology & Innovation; REC = Research Ethics Committee

student research is deeply embroiled in research misconduct as observed in many African countries including Ethiopia (e.g., Kibret & Kebede, 2016), Ghana (Anaman & Agyei, 2021; Owusu et al., 2022), Kenya (Were et al., 2023), Nigeria (e.g., Adeleyes & Adebamawo, 2012; Okonta & Rossouw, 2012), Mozambique (Coughlin, 2015), South Africa (e.g., Mahabeer & Pirtheepal., 2019), and Tanzania (e.g., Anney & Moshe, 2015) to mention some. For instance, Coughlin (2015) examined the extent of plagiarism in graduate theses in five purposively selected universities in Mozambique. The finding shows that, of the total 150 theses which undergone a plagiarism check using Turtin and Urkund, 75% (102) turned out to constitute "significant plagiarism". Similar studies based on survey of the views and experiences of students or lecturers' confirms the findings that have been reported by studies which employed data using anti-plagiarism softwares (e.g., Adeleye & Adebamowo, 2012). For instance, a survey of postgraduates in Malawi (Selemani et al., 2018) reveals that students admitted to have plagiarized by "Copying word for word without acknowledging the source" (28.3%) being the most frequently mentioned to "Submitting a research work" (downloaded from the web) authored by another person as their own (17%) being the least frequently mentioned one. Kibret and Kebedes' (2016) survey of graduate students at Addis Ababa University indicated that 59.8% have violated the principle of "openness" by way of hiding books/materials from fellow student researchers, about 39% hiding their research topics while about 48% deliberately concealing the limitations of their research. Furthermore, some graduate students had reported that they were not as respectful to their respondents by way of covering up the real purpose of the research (14.7%) and giving false promises that they wouldn't be able to honor (20.1%). Kibret and Kebedes' (2016) survey of graduate students at Addis Ababa University, Ethiopia indicated that more than a third of postgraduates (35.9%) admitted that they had copied material form other people's work without acknowledging the sources. Besides, the study also found that 59.8% have violated the principle of "openness" (Resink, 2018) by hiding books/materials from fellow students, 39% concealing their research topics while about 48% intentionally failing to state the limitations of their research to their colleagues and supervisors. Furthermore, some graduate students had reported that they were not as respectful to their respondents by way of covering up the real purpose of the research (14.7%) and giving false promises that they wouldn't be able to honor (20.1%).

On the other hand, studies based on surveys of lecturers do not seem to differ much as one might expect. A survey on a sample of 132 academic staff in medical and dental sciences in Nigeria finds that 22.0% admitted to have violated RI by way of data fabrication, falsification, or plagiarism (Adeleye & Adebamowo, 2012). In addition, a similar study among Nigerian lecturers (Okonta & Rossouw., 2012) indicates that about 68.9% (n = 132) admitted to have committed at least one of the eight listed forms of research misconduct of which 42% admitted to have falsified data while 9.2% admitted to have plagiarized.

The most important reasons behind the growing research misconduct in the form of plagiarism, according to Selemani et al. (2018) include "pressure to get good grades" (86.7%) and "poor time management" (85%). The reasons for lecturers seem more or less similar when it comes to knowledge gap on RE/RI) except that lecturers mention "pressure to publish enough papers for promotion" as an important factor (Adeleye & Adebamowo, 2012). Nonetheless, an entirely different argument comes from a South African study (Mahabeer & Pirtheepal, 2019) that attributes increased plagiarism to uncontrolled expansion of higher education. The authors specifically contend that massification of higher education has led to large class size and poor student assessment practices which in turn resulted in increase in plagiarism.

### *Knowledge of Research Integrity*

Due to the limited scope and coverage of existing empirical studies in addressing what RI constitutes as concept in the context of African HEIs, this analysis is technically limited to some specific aspects owing to paucity of empirical data. Most importantly, as demonstrated in a recent study (e.g., Mireku et al., 2023), data related to research integrity (RI) focuses mainly on plagiarism. As reported by Mireku et al (2023), in the past decade alone (2012–2022), 171 research papers were published in sub-Saharan Africa. Nonetheless, there is considerable lack of uniformity across states in the methods employed that render data aggregation difficult. While the studies vary with respect to the kind of research design adopted (qualitative vs. quantitative), those which employed similar approach still vary with respect to the instrument of data gathering employed. For instance, some survey research assessing postgraduates' knowledge of plagiarism preferred to use standardized questionnaires (e.g., Okonta & Rossowu, 2012) while others opted to develop data gathering tools to tap the same construct (e.g., Clarke et al., 2023). Within these limitations, it is attempted to tap on the extent to which African postgraduate students have some basic knowledge of RI. In order to assess this, two questions were used to tap knowledge of plagiarism based on publications focusing on six African countries. The questions include: (a) "directly *copying some one's research work without crediting the source*" and (b) "*presenting or submitting one's work as your own downloading from the internet*". Based on data availability six SSA countries were considered for the analysis namely, Ghana, Kenya, Malawi, Nambia, Nigeria, and South Africa. In all the six countries considered, postgraduate students, regardless of their fields of specialization, were asked if "*directly coping others work without crediting the source*" is plagiarism? As it turned out, relatively more postgraduate students who participated in the respective studies in Ghana (67.8%) and Kenya (61%) endorsed "yes" as opposed to their counterparts in Namibia (28%), Malawi (27.3%), South Africa (27%), and Nigeria (21%) possessed the most rudimentary knowledge of about RI (see Fig. 10.4). Similarly, the proportion of postgraduates who reported that "*presenting or submitting one's work as your own downloading from the internet*" is a breach of RI vary considerably. In this regard, less than a third of postgraduates participated in cross-sectional surveys in Ghana (5.2%), Somaliland (19%), and Nigeria (24%) reported the act is a violation of RI while in contrast, from 60–89% of their counterparts in Kenya

(61%), Namibia (70%), and Rwanda (88.5%) reported that they aware of the fact that using or submitting others' work downloading from the internet is indeed a form of plagiarism (see Fig. 10.5).

Taken together, the findings in existing studies suggest that postgraduates' knowledge about and application of research integrity (RI) could vary from country to country or even from one institution to the other within the same country. Some scholars (e.g., Bain et al., 2022; Ndebele, 2020) attribute the problem to lack of adequate effort on the part of higher education institutions in creating the right environment that nurtures the culture of RCR. Specifically, Bain et al. (2022) argue that violations of RI are often the result of inadequate knowledge and awareness about RI and RE; lack of institutional structures, systems, and guidelines, marginalization of topics on RE and RE in research methodology courses. Thus, it can be argued that universities need to integrate the necessary regulations and practical guidelines into institutional structures to ensure ethical practice in HEIs. This among others include integrating Research Ethics (RE) as part of a mandatory research methodology course or as a standalone course for graduate students; putting in place a periodic training packages, and public lectures on the subject of RE and RI to help establish institutional research culture apart from establishing/strengthening Institutional Review Boards (IRB) as well as

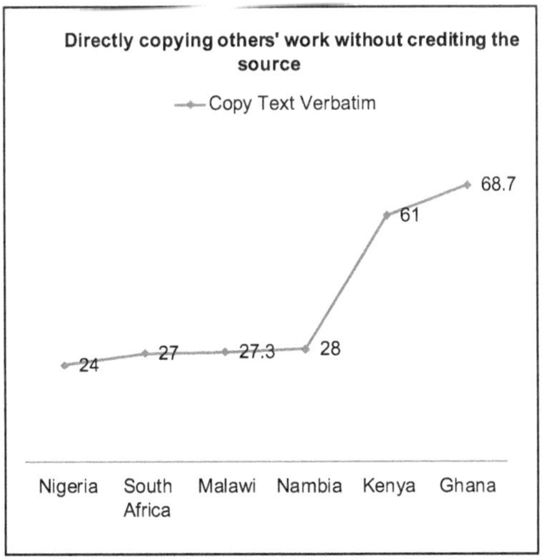


**Fig. 10.4** Proportion of postgraduates who know directly copying without crediting the source is plagiarism (%, Yes) (*Source* Ibegbulam and Eze (2015/ Nigeria); Chrysler-Fox & Thomas (2016/South Africa); Njeri (2016/Kenya); Selemani et al., (2018/ Malawi))

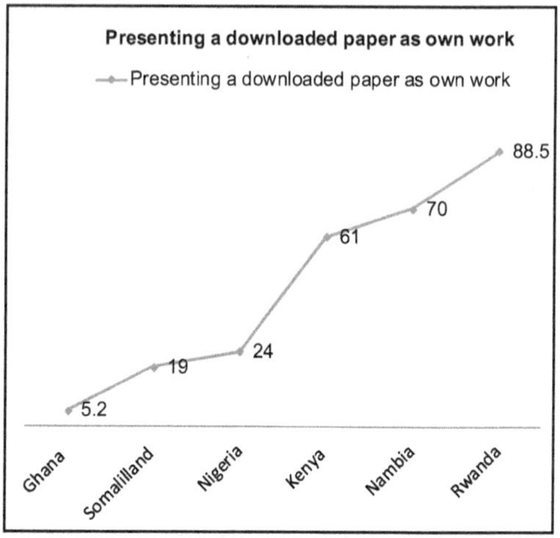


**Fig. 10.5** Proportion of postgraduates who know presenting a downloaded paper as own work is plagiarism (%, Yes) (*Source* Ibegbulam and Eze (2015/Nigeria); Clarke et al., (2023/Rwanda); Anaman & Agyei. (2021/Ghana); Chrysler-Fox & Thomas (2016/South Africa); Gebremariam et al., (n.d./Somaliland))

setting up college and department level research ethics committees that work hand in hand with IRBs.

### *Contract Cheating*

Even though a deeply ingrained institutional culture can help buffer the likelihood of violating the established codes of conduct, there is no guarantee that researchers are totally immune from the temptations of getting a degree without going through the bustle and hustle of completing a Masters' or PhD dissertation that entails a lot of time and hard work. Central to this is the ever expanding contract cheating or "dissertation mills" that are currently mushrooming in many African countries (e.g., Achuka, 2019; Mushawatu, 2022; Stella-Maris & Awala-Ale, 2017). It should be clear that the actors involved in contract cheating are many and ranges from individual contractors to business companies legally established under the guise of consultancy firms (e.g., Achuka, 2019; Bitrus-Ojiambo et al., 2022; Lubinga et al., 2023).

Contract cheating is now a major challenge of research ethics at global level. And, Africa is by no means immune from it. Instead, report from many African countries seem to suggest that many students get undergraduate and graduate degrees using dissertations "written" by registered firms or individuals (Achuka, 2019; Bitrus-Ojiambo et al., 2022; Lubinga et al., 2023; University World News, January 28/2023). For instance, Kenya is often mentioned when it comes to the contract cheating industry in Africa (Bitrus-Ojiambo et al., 2022; Walker, 2023). A number of international news outlets Blogs, and social media portray Kenya as a flashpoint of ghost writing whose tentacles are reaching out to American college students (Achuka, 2019; Bitrus-Ojiambo et al., 2022; Walker, 2019, 2023). However, this does not rule out the possibility that other African countries are not harboring individuals or firms involved in contract cheating. In Nigeria, contract cheating is reported to be rampant among postgraduate students. In this regard, Stella-Maris and Awala-Ale (2017, pp. 561–62) find that more than half of the respondents who participated in their study admitted to have had their assignments, essays, or theses written by "ghost writers". Similar findings are reported in South African context whereby contract cheating is posing clear and present danger undermining responsible conduct of research (e.g., Lubinga et al., 2023). Be that as it may, ghost writing is the fast growing predicament to ensuring research ethics as the "Ghosts" come in many forms and sizes.

According to *University World News* (2023/January 28), university students in Tanzania are contracting individuals and bureaus to write thesis and dissertations. The online newspaper went on to state:

> An investigation by *The Citizen* [a South African News Paper] has discovered a rising number of bureaus and individuals who survive by writing dissertations and research reports for postgraduates and undergraduates. This form of academic dishonesty is widespread among postgraduate students, most of whom are employed in the public as well as the private sectors. (University World News, January 28/2023)

Owing to the danger that contract cheating poses, scholars (e.g., Lubinga et al., 2023) advise African HEIs to introduce technologies that detect the authenticity of the authors apart from policies and guidelines that would help prevent and punish contract cheating.

### *AI and the Future of Research Integrity*

Apart from traditional plagiarism and other forms of research misconduct, there is a new challenge in the horizon. Ormond (2020) describes this new threat as "the ghost in the machine" to refer to the emergent role of Artificial Intelligence (AI).

At this juncture, it is revealing to cite what the renowned scientist in the field, Professor Hawking had to say.

> Success in creating AI could be the biggest event in the history of our civilization,
> But it could also be the last – unless we learn how to avoid the risks. Alongside the benefits, AI will also bring dangers like powerful autonomous weapons or new ways for the few to oppress the many (in Frutism Oct 20/2016; https://tinyurl.com/mw42d2ww)

Notwithstanding the widespread sense of bewilderment on how to come to terms with AI, others (e.g., Nolan, 2023) paint a more optimistic picture by capitalizing its significance especially in increasing research productivity in areas of science and engineering including in addressing the impending challenges such as climate change (Nolan, 2023). The recent OECD report (Nolan, 2023) went so far as to argue that Africa is at the forefront to benefit from AI to redress its long-standing capacity limitations (pp. 43–45). However, in connection with the impact of AI in future research; scholars (e.g., Van dis et al., 2023) did not shy away from expressing their concern about the threat represented by conversation AI or what collectively referred to as Large Language Models (LLM) which includes ChatGPT[2] ChatGPT has been made freely available since 2022. Since then, it seems to catch everyone by surprise—ranging from teachers, researchers, journal editors, etc. Particularly, it is highly concerning given students and researchers could use it to facilitate their write up, review literature, edit language or at worst, submit AI-generated content as their own work. Because, AI raises the question of transparency in producing an essay or manuscript which poses serious ethical issues since the material represents plagiarism as no one knows about the original source used (van Dis et al., 2023). And, given the difficulties of detecting the use of conversation AI such as ChatGPT may not be effectively prevented whereby there is not. Thus, even when universities and research institutions are willing to embrace Language Learning Models (LLM) such as ChatGPT, they would be challenged by the threat it poses on research integrity as does not reliably site original sources or authors (Van Dis

[2] According to van Dis et al. (2023), ChatGPT is a large language model (LLM), a machine-learning system that autonomously learns from data and can produce sophisticated and seemingly intelligent writing after training on a massive dataset of text (p. 234).

et al., 2023). As feared, at least in academics and research, AI is serving the unintended purpose of ghost writing term papers, essays, thesis, and dissertations for graduate students worldwide. Despite this danger, however, it is not yet clear how many institutional RI policies cover AI-generated content (Tarisayi, 2021). Nonetheless, van Dis et al. (2023) caution that academics and researchers should embrace AI before it is too late since its impact on future research is inevitable no matter how hard researchers and universities try to downplay the looming danger. The question remains, how would African countries have a level playing field while AI tools are less likely to be equally accessible as African scientists and researchers still suffer from the financial and technological inequality?

## Conclusion

As demonstrated earlier on, Africa has a long way to go with respect to putting in place credible centers of excellence in research and innovation within higher education. Universities running Masters' and PhD programs need to be provided with the necessary political support and resources to establish functional structures. Nonetheless, most universities do not have a well-organized institutional ethical review boards (IERBs) nor do the host countries have the necessary legal frameworks that took account of the range of disciplinary or multidisciplinary fields that are offered in their postgraduate programs. When such frameworks exist at national level, they are centralized where graduate research project proposals have to wait for long to get their ethical clearance certificate that would eat up a good portion of their research time. On the other hand, RECs in most African states focus on health or medical research giving lesser attention to other areas of research including science and technology, behavioral and social sciences, and humanities and cultural sciences. This trend seems to be replicated at institutional level where majority of universities give more emphasis to health and medical sciences.

The other important finding is that graduate research has been negatively impacted by lack of research integrity (RI) due to the growing research misconduct in graduate theses and dissertations. Data from countries like Ethiopia, Ghana, Kenya, Nigeria, Mozambique, Tanzania, and South Africa testifies to the fact that research works are marred by widespread plagiarism, data fabrication, and falsification among other kinds of violations of RI. Not only that, the integrity of graduate research has been challenged by the strong adversaries often physically located outside of university campuses or at times, omnipresent regardless of distance, thanks to the World Wide Web. These include entities involved in *contract cheating* where from private individual to legally registered companies are involved in writing masters' thesis and PhD dissertations. The other fresh challenge for graduate research is the advent of AI. The strong potential for misuse of AI in graduate research is in the horizon at best, or already in full swing at worst.

The findings show that research misconduct in graduate research is widespread though the extent and magnitude cannot be accurately determined based on the data garnered from secondary sources and scholarly publications. Nonetheless, the findings provided sufficient evidence that African graduate education is increasingly troubled by the growing variety and complexity of research misconduct including the threat posed by the apparent misuse of AI. Looking at the existing and future challenges, it is important to consider both short-term and long-term measures.

While regional, national, and institutional policies and guidelines are critical to ensure RCR, it cannot guarantee complete control over research misconduct and incidences of violation of RE altogether. The lessons drawn from the experience and practices of scientific research in the developed world which has put in place very effective systems and institutional-level oversight tells stories of utter violations of RCR by high profile academics and researchers. However, the presence of these structures not only minimize the likelihood of research misconduct, but also provide the space to cultivate the culture of research integrity and ethical practice among the majority of graduate students and researchers in universities and other centers of knowledge. Most importantly, creating an environment that nurtures a culture of research integrity and ethical practice should start early at undergraduate level the fact that internalizing ethical and moral standards happen gradually. Then, integrating RE and RI elements in research methodology courses will be effective on top of tailored training to all graduate students.

## References


Academy of Science of South Africa. (2019). African Open Science Platform - Landscape Study. https://doi.org/10.17159/assaf.2019/0047

Achuka, V. (2019, April 1). Kenya on the spot as cheating at varsity hits worrying levels. *Nation*. https://www.nation.co.ke/news/education/cheating-at-Kenyan-universities-worrying-/2643604-5052212-qjwcr4/index.html?fbclid=IwAR0_fBb-B02IMJBK9T09

Adeleye, O. A., & Adebamowo, C. A. (2012). Factors Associated with Research Wrongdoing in Nigeria. *Journal of Empirical Research on Human Research Ethics, 7*(5), 15–24. https://doi.org/10.1525/jer.2012.7.5.15

AfDB (African Development Bank). (2016). Catalyzing growth and development through effective natural resources management. African Natural Resources Center.

African Union (AU). (2014). *Science, technology and innovation strategy for Africa 2024*. African Union.

Anaman, A. A., & Agyei, F. (2021).Perception of and Attitudes towards Plagiarism among Graduate Students in Ghana. *Library Philosophy and Practice* (e-journal), 5201. https://digitalcommons.unl.edu/libphilprac/5201

Anney, V. N., & Mosha, M. A. (2015). Student's plagiarisms in higher learning institutions in the era of improved internet access: Case study of developing countries. *Journal of Education and Practice, 6*(13).

Association of African Universities (AAU) and the African Academy of Sciences (AAS). (2023). Deepening Knowledge and Implementation of Research Ethics in the African Context. AAU & AAS.

Bain, L. E., Tchuisseu-Kwangoua, L. A., Adeagbo, O., Nkfusai, N. C., Amu, H., Saah, F. I., & Kombe, F. (2022). Fostering research integrity in sub-Saharan Africa: Challenges, opportunities, and recommendations. *Pan African Medical Journal, 43*(182). https://doi.org/10.11604/pamj.2022.43.182.37804

Benos, D. J., Fabres, J., Farmer, J., Gutierrez, J. P., Hennessy, K., Kosek, D., Lee, J. H., Olteanu, D., Russell, T., Shaikh, F., & Wang, K. (2005). Ethics and scientific publication. *Advances in Physiology Education, 29*(2), 59–74.

Bitrus-Ojiambo, U. A., Mwangi, S. W., & Mwaura, I. W. (2022). Globalizing academic dishonesty: Western media frames of contract cheating by Kenyan graduates (Got Posho?). *African Multidisciplinary Journal of Research*, 15–35. https://journals.spu.ac.ke/index.php/amjr/article/view/111

British Council and DAAD. (2018). Building PhD capacity in sub-Saharan Africa. https://static.daad.de/media/daad_de/pdfs_nicht_barrierefrei/laenderinformationen/afrika/building_phd_capacity_in_sub-saharan_africa.pdf

Bronfenbrenner, U. (1994). Ecological models of human development. In M. Gauvain, & M. Cole (Eds.), *International encyclopedia of education* (2nd Ed.). Freeman

Clarke, O., Chan, W.-Y.D., Bukuru, S., Logan, J., & Wong, R. (2023). Assessing knowledge of and attitudes towards plagiarism and ability to recognize plagiaristic writing among university students in Rwanda. *Higher Education, 85*, 247–263. https://doi.org/10.1007/s10734-022-00830-y

Chrysler-Fox & Thomas. (2016), Managing plagiarism of South African postgraduate students: Does an intervention have any effect? A Paper Presented at The Higher Education Conference, in Amsterdam, The Netherlands.

Conceiçao, S. C., Mina, L., & Southern, T. (2018). Living and studying in the US: An ecological systems perspective. Adult Education Research Conference. https://newprairiepress.org/aerc/2018/papers/46

Coughlin, P. E. (2015). Plagiarism in five universities in Mozambique: Magnitude, detection, Techniques, and control measures. *International Journal for Educational Integrity, 11*(2). https://doi.org/10.1007/s40979-015-0003-5.

Duerden, M. D., & Witt, P. A. (2010). An ecological systems theory perspective on youth programming. *Journal of Park and Recreation Administration, 28*(2), 108–120.

Friedman, B. D., & Allen, K. M. (2019). Systems Theory. In Jerrold Brandell (Ed.), *Theory and practice in clinical social work* (3rd ed.). Cognella Academic Press.

Gebremariam, T., Mohamed, J., Bulhan, H., & Mekonnen, Z. (n.d.). Low levels of knowledge and attitudes towards plagiarism among university instructors and graduate students in Somaliland: Analysis from an online survey, Pre-print. https://doi.org/10.21203/rs.3.rs-3004077/v1

Gross, C. (2016). Scientific misconduct. *Annual Review of Psychology, 67*, 693–711.

Hayward, F. M. (2010). Graduate Education in Sub-Saharan Africa. In D. Teferra & H. Greijn (Eds.), *Higher education and globalization: Challenges, threats and opportunities for Africa* (pp. 33–49). Maastricht University.

Hayward, F. M., & Ncayiyana, D. J. (2015). Confronting the challenges of graduate education in sub-Saharan Africa. *International Higher Education, 79*(Winter), 16–18.

Ibegbulam, I. J., & Eze, J. U. (2015). Knowledge, perception and attitude of Nigerian students to plagiarism: A case study University of Nigeria. *International Federation of Library Associations and Institutions, 41*(2), 120–128.

Jowi, J. O. (2021). Doctoral training in African universities: Recent trends, developments and issues. *Journal of the British Academy, 9*(s1), 159–181. https://doi.org/10.5871/jba/009s1.159

Kahn, M. J. (2022). The status of science, technology and innovation in Africa. *Science, Technology and Society, 27*(3), 327–350. https://doi.org/10.1177/09717218221078540

Kibret, B. T., & Kebede, Y. D. (2016). Researching into Postgraduate Research in Addis Ababa University: Threats to the future generation of social, educational and behavioural researchers. *Bahir Dar Journal of Education, 16*(2), 116–142.

Lubinga, S., Ramnarain, J., & Tonkin, L. (2023). Quandaries of contract cheating in South African Higher Education Institutions: The way forward. *South African Journal of Higher Education, 37*(6), 239–254.

Mahabeer, P., & Pirtheepal, T. (2019). Assessment, plagiarism and its effect on academic integrity: Experiences of academics at a university in South Africa. *South African Journal of Science, 115*(11–12), 1–8. https://doi.org/10.17159/sajs.2019/6323

Mireku, D. O., Dzamesi, P. D., & Bervell, B. (2023). Plagiarism in Higher Education (PLAGiHE) within Sub-Saharan Africa: A systematic review of a decade (2012–2022) literature. *Research Ethics, 1–31.* https://doi.org/10.1177/17470161231189646

Mohamedbhai, G. (2013).Towards an African Higher Education and Research Space (AHERS). *A Summary Report. Association for Development of Education in Africa (January 2013).*

Mushawatu, Z. (2022, September 29). What can be done about the growth in dissertation mills? World University News – Africa Edition. https://www.universityworldnews.com/post.php?story=20220928203642416. Accessed on December 10, 2023.

Mwaka, E. S. (2017). Responsible conduct of research: Enhancing local opportunities. *African Health Sciences, 17*(2), 584–590. https://doi.org/10.4314/ahs.v17i2.36

Ndebele, P., Mwaluko,G., Kruger, M.,Ouwe, O. Oukem-Boyer, M., & Zimba, M. (2014). History of Research Ethics Review in Africa. In M. Kruger, P. Ndebele & L. Horn (Eds.), *Research Ethics in Africa: A Resource for Research Ethics Committees* (pp. 3–10).

Ndebele, H. (2020). Demystifying student plagiarism in academic writing: Towards an 'educational' solution. *Critical Studies in Teaching and Learning, 8*(2). https://doi.org/10.14426/cristal.v8i2.284

Njeri, S. W. (2016). Unethical practices in higher institutions of Learning: A Case of Kenyan universities. *Pyrex Journal of Educational Research and Reviews, 2*(3), 15–27.

Nolan, A. (2023). Artificial Intelligence in Science: Overview and Policy Proposal. In *OECD Artificial Intelligence in Science: Challenges, Opportunities and the Future of Research* (pp. 43–45). OECD Publishing. https://doi.org/10.1787/a8d820bd-en

Okonta, P., & Rossouw, T. (2012). Prevalence of scientific misconduct among a group of researchers in Nigeria. *Developing Bioethics*. https://doi.org/10.1111/j.1471-8847.2012.00339.x

Ormond, E. (2020). The Ghost in the Machine: The Ethical Risks of AI. *The Thinker, 83*(1), 4–11. https://journals.uj.ac.za/index.php/The_Thinker/article/view/220. Available at SSRN: https://ssrn.com/abstract=3719745 or https://doi.org/10.2139/ssrn.3719745

Owunsu, et al. (2022). Assessment of the Operational Characteristics of Research Ethics Committees in Ghana. *Journal of Empirical Research on Human Research Ethics, 17*(1–2), 114–128.

Renn, K. A., & Smith, B. R. G. (2023). Ecological models in higher education research: Overview and synthesis. *New Directions for Higher Education, 11–22.* https://doi.org/10.1002/he.20491

Resnik, D. R. (2018). Scientific Misconduct and Research Integrity. *The International Encyclopedia of Ethics*. https://doi.org/10.1002/9781444367072.wbiee001.pub2

Rossouw, T. M., Van Zyl, C., & Pope, A. (2014). Responsible conduct of research: Global trends, local opportunities. *South African Journal of Science, 110*(1–2), 1–6.

Selemani, A., Chawinga, W. D., & Dube, G. (2018). Why do graduate students commit plagiarism? An empirical study. *International Journal for Educational Integrity, 14*, 7. https://doi.org/10.1007/s40979-018-0029-6

Sentleng, M. P. (2010). Plagiarism among Undergraduate Students in the Faculty of Applied Science at a South African Higher Education Institution, MSc Thesis, University of Western Cape, South Africa.

Stella-Maris, O. (2014). *An investigation of plagiarism by Nigerian students in Higher Education*. PhD dissertation, Coventry University, UK.

Stella-Maris, O., & Awale-Ale, A. (2017). Exploring students' perception and experience of ghostwriting and contract cheating in Nigeria Higher Education Institutions. *World Journal of Educational Research, 4*(4), 501–572. https://doi.org/10.22158/wjer.v4n4p551

Tarisayi, K. S. (2021). Luster and shadows: Unveiling the gaps in South African University plagiarism policies amidst the emergence of AI-generated content. *AI and Ethics*. https://doi.org/10.1007/s43681-023-00333-1

Teferra, D. (2003). Scientific communication and research in African Universities – Challenges and opportunities in the Twenty-First-Century. In D. Teferra & P. Altbach (Eds.), *African Higher Education: An International Reference Handbook* (pp. 128–142). Indiana University Press.

Tijssen, R., & Winnink, J. (2022). Global and local research excellence in Africa: New perspective in performance assessment. *Science, Technology and Society, 27*(3), 368–387.

Tong, P., & An, I. S. (2024). Review of studies applying Bronfenbrenner's bioecological theory in international and intercultural education research. *Frontiers in Psychology, 14*, 1233925. https://doi.org/10.3389/fpsyg.2023.1233925

Turner, J. H. (2010). *Theoretical Principles of Sociology, Vol. 1: Macrodynamics*. Springer Science + Business Media.

Turner, J. H. (2012). *Theoretical Principles of Sociology, Vol. 3: Mesodynamics*. Springer Science + Business Media.

UNESCO Institute for Statistics (UIS). Science, technology and innovation: Researchers (in full-time equivalent) per million inhabitants. http://data.uis.unesco.org/index.aspx?queryid=3685. Accessed on February 28, 2024.

UniRank. (2023). *Snapshot of Higher Education in Afric*a. Available at (https://www.4icu.org/Africa/), accessed on 24/12/2023

University World News. (2023, January 28). 'Contract cheating' in universities is a growing threat. https://www.universityworldnews.com/post.php?story=2023012813094930

Van dis, E. A. M., Bollen, J., Zuidema, W., Van Rooij, R., & Bockting, C. L. (2023). ChatGPT: Five priorities for research. *Nature, 614*(7947), 224–226. https://doi.org/10.1038/d41586-023-00288-7

United Nations. Economic Commission for Africa. (UN-ECA). (2018). Towards Achieving the African Union's recommendation of expenditure of 1% of GDP on research and development. Addis Ababa. https://hdl.handle.net/10855/24306"

Walker, C. (2023). Understanding the 'supply end' of contract cheating: A Kenyan youth (un)employment perspective. In S. E. Eaton (Ed.), *Handbook of Academic Integrity*. Springer. https://doi.org/10.1007/978-981-287-079-7_112-1

Walker, C. (2019). *The White-Collar Hustle: Academic Writing and the Kenyan Digital Labour Economy*. https://ora.ox.ac.uk/objects/uuid:35c57129 11cb-4fad-a91f-65b2f3849b7a. Accessed on January 21, 2024.

Were, E., et al. (2023). Institutional capacity to prevent and manage research misconduct: Perspectives from Kenyan research regulators. *Research Integrity and Peer Review, 8*, 8. https://doi.org/10.1186/s41073-023-00132-6

World Intellectual Property Organization (WIPO). (2023). *World Intellectual Property Indicators 2023*. WIPO. https://doi.org/10.34667/tind.48541

World Bank. (2023, November 27). *Research and Development Expenditure (% of GDP)*. https://data.worldbank.org/indicator/GB.XPD.RSDV.GD.ZS. Accessed on February 28, 2024.

World Bank. (2002). *Constructing Knowledge Societies: New Challenges for Tertiary Education. Directions in Development*. World Bank.

World Economic Forum. (WEF). (2023). *There are not enough scientists in Africa. How can we turn this around?* https://www.weforum.org/agenda/2017/05/scientists-are-the-key-to-africas-future/. Accessed on December 25, 2023.

CHAPTER 11

# Open Science in the African Context

*Angel Y. Ford, Daniel Gelaw Alemneh, and Abebe Rorissa*

## Introduction

Open science is a set of principles and practices that aim to make scientific research procedures and products accessible to everyone for the benefit of all, especially those in developing regions like Africa. Open science's nature and ultimate goal support the rights enshrined within The United Nations Universal Declaration of Human Rights, which addresses every aspect of individuals' social, political, economic, health, and cultural lives (UN, 1949). In 1966, the widespread adoption of the

A. Y. Ford (✉)
Department of Information Sciences and Technology, University at Albany, Albany, NY, USA
e-mail: ayford@albany.edu

D. G. Alemneh
Digital Libraries, University of North Texas, Denton, TX, USA
e-mail: Daniel.Alemneh@unt.edu

A. Rorissa
School of Information Sciences, College of Communication and Information, The University of Tennessee, Knoxville, TN, USA
e-mail: arorissa@utk.edu



D. Teferra (ed.), *Research and Innovation in African Higher Education*,
https://doi.org/10.1007/978-3-031-92909-0_11

legally binding International Covenant on Economic, Social and Cultural Rights (ICESCR), also more recently ratified by African countries, made the Universal Declaration of Human Rights more than just a declaration, but rather something governments must adhere to (Resolution, 1966). The crucial Article 15 of the ICESCR, specifically addresses the right to science, including scientific inquiry and the production of and access to scientific information. Universal Human Rights can only be realized if the right to science is protected and the benefits from scientific discovery are also realized. Part of that protection, through Article 15, emphasizes access to scientific and other information, requiring governments to protect the rights to the benefits of scientific inquiry and by encouraging them to promote scientific progress, with a particular emphasis on benefiting communities that are in greatest need. Open science supports the accomplishment of these goals.

A common misconception about open science is that making research outputs open to all is the primary objective. Whereas Open Access (OA), the movement to make research outputs accessible globally, is a large part of open science, it is only one aspect among several. Open Access may increase the number of scholars that can consume research, but it does not ensure those same scholars are able to disseminate their research outputs through OA publications. In fact, OA can be seen as moving the financial barriers from consumption, subscription fees, or paywalls, to dissemination, author processing charges or open access fees (Chakravorty et al., 2022). Since OA is an aspect of open science, these equity concerns are challenges that must be addressed. However, open science efforts also include open-source software and data, open educational resources (OER), open research processes and procedures, and open peer reviews. In addition to OA publications, open science encourages the open dissemination of methods, procedures, and datasets even before the final peer-reviewed article is published. This rapid release of even the earliest parts and processes of research speeds up access to the wider scholarly community.

With so many aspects of open science, efforts are needed by various stakeholders to focus on one or more processes or products. Some organizations or institutions focus on and promote one area of open science, such as OpenStax does with OER. OpenStax is run by Rice University and works to make free peer-reviewed textbooks openly accessible for secondary educators, students, and college and university students and faculty (OpenStax, n.d.). These efforts are highly beneficial for many educators and students globally, and as the focus of this chapter is on Africa, these types of resources could be used by those involved in research and graduate level education in that context. Whereas all aspects of open science work toward the human rights of accessible knowledge, this chapter focuses on open science related to the stages of basic and applied research, and graduate level education.

It is helpful to examine the definitions shared by various stakeholders and promoters to further examine open science and the benefits and challenges associated with the movement. Many definitions exist; however, UNESCO provides a comprehensive definition (2021).

> An inclusive construct that combines various movements and practices aiming to make multilingual scientific knowledge openly available, accessible, and reusable for everyone, to increase scientific collaborations and sharing of information for the benefits of science and society, and to open the processes of scientific knowledge creation, evaluation, and communication to societal actors beyond the traditional scientific community. It comprises all scientific disciplines and aspects of scholarly practices, including basic and applied sciences, natural and social sciences, and the humanities, and it builds on the following key pillars: open scientific knowledge, open science infrastructures, science communication, open engagement of societal actors and open dialogue with other knowledge systems. (p. 7)

Another definition is provided by Foster, an organization in Europe promoting open science.

> Open Science is the practice of science in such a way that others can collaborate and contribute, where research data, lab notes and other research processes are freely available, under terms that enable reuse, redistribution and reproduction of the research and its underlying data and methods. (Foster, n.d)

*Open Responsible Research and Innovation to further Outstanding Knowledge* (ORION), defines open science as "the movement to make scientific research, data and their dissemination available to any member of an inquiring society, from professionals to citizens" (ORION, n.d.). As can be seen from the definitions provided, ideally open science includes all stages of research studies being open and transparent. This increases the likelihood that the quality of research methods and data will be improved, increasing the replicable nature of individual studies. The open science movement aims to encourage more open and transparent communication between researchers (ASSAf, 2018). A fully open study informs readers about the entire research process, from forming research questions to the rationale for the chosen methodologies. Open science encourages clarity and details in how the data was collected and analyzed. In addition, peer reviews in an open science environment are open and transparent so that individuals not involved in the study can see the feedback the researchers and authors receive. Additionally, the publication and dissemination of the research outputs are open access.

Throughout this chapter, we will discuss the benefits and challenges of open science, what open science looks like in the digital age, and open science in the African context. We will also discuss the geopolitical challenges specific to Africa, the efforts being undertaken to overcome them, and why indigenous and local scholars could contribute to these efforts. To conclude this chapter, we suggest possible future research and initiatives that would benefit the open science movement and ultimately benefit researchers, graduate level education, African countries, and the entire world.

## Benefits of Open Science

Open science offers numerous benefits that impact individual scholars, research teams, institutional progress, and scientific fields, especially those in developing countries, such as those found on the African continent. These benefits include strengthened scientific collaborations, positive shifts in research culture, reduced barriers for scholars feeling disconnected from wider research communities, improved scholarly communication, and advancements across scientific domains. In addition to these benefits, open science establishes an environment for universal coding and storage of data that will enable researchers to use AI tools and to make collaborations easier and many aspects of research more efficient.

Firstly, open science fosters scientific collaborations by ensuring equitable and transparent sharing of the entire research process, including research outcomes. This inclusivity reduces invisible barriers that may otherwise exclude certain scholars, particularly those in African countries, or other underrepresented countries, from engaging in scientific endeavors. The open discourse surrounding decision-making, methods, procedures, data processing, and storage promotes inclusivity, encouraging collaboration across disciplinary and geographical boundaries. As a result, interdisciplinary and cross-national collaborations flourish, incorporating diverse methods and perspectives. The growing interdisciplinary field of studies facilitates amalgamations of diverse methods, theoretical frameworks, tools, and processes that originate from various disciplines and continue to be developed, adopted, and extended through further research, teaching, and practices (Heisig, 2022). The more open that science becomes, the more likely scholars from one research circle will be able and willing to cross into other research circles, causing the metaphorical silos to disintegrate.

Additionally, open science encourages the formation of larger research teams with specialized roles for team members, such as data collection, storage, and analysis. This specialization allows individuals to focus on their areas of expertise, enabling teams to tackle complex projects more effectively and creating the likelihood that teams can effectively engage in multiple projects simultaneously (Thibault et al., 2023). Unlike traditional models, where researchers are expected to fulfill multiple roles, open science allows individuals to concentrate on specific tasks, enhancing overall research efficiency and quality (Stracke, 2020; Thibault et al., 2023). Individuals can focus on what they are adept at and let others do the remaining tasks. Currently, many teams are relatively small, and researchers are expected to fill several roles throughout the process while maintaining mysterious methods.

Science would benefit from open science procedures that allow individuals to grow in one or a few areas of methodology rather than the slow process of having researchers engage at multiple points in the research process and with a variety of methodologies. Since each aspect of the scientific process would provide credit to individuals, there would be incentives for scholars to focus their energies on the tasks they are assigned and less emphasis on each scholar battling for the position of first or second author on a publication produced from the research (Chiware & Skelly, 2022).

Moreover, open science contributes to improving research cultures by fostering collaboration over competition, thereby advancing scientific progress for societal benefit. Open science could help researchers and other stakeholders "embrace a collaborative spirit to iteratively improve our research practices and infrastructures" (Thibault et al., 2023, p. 2).

This inclusive approach also opens opportunities for scholars from underrepresented regions to participate in global scientific discourse and access usable databases (Ford & Alemneh, 2022a).

By changing the culture and opening the discourse for more scholars, the efforts toward open science would also reduce injustices experienced by scholars in low- and middle-income countries (LMIC), particularly those in Africa, not only through open dissemination of research outputs but by the possibility of these researchers gaining access to data and engaging more readily in all stages of the research process, particularly in scholarly communication (Ford & Alemneh, 2024). Open science can help tear down barriers between low- and high-income scholars (Staunton et al., 2021). Open science promotes equitable participation in research and education by reducing technological and financial barriers and facilitating global scientific advancements.

Additionally, transparency in open science minimizes mystery and ambiguity and enhances reproducibility (Thibault et al., 2023). By openly sharing methods and procedures, researchers can accurately replicate studies, saving time and resources. Although simply making the research process open does not guarantee rigor, it enables easier evaluation and fosters comprehensive reporting of research findings (Thibault et al., 2023). Much published research does not contain thorough methods and procedures sections, causing difficulty in replication (Thibault et al., 2023). In other words, open science would promote access to more comprehensive and detailed information about research, rather than focusing almost entirely on published findings that do not adequately describe the processes for evaluating credibility. Interestingly, peer reviewers have yet to provide the pushback necessary for authors to include more detailed methods and procedures. Whether this opaque nature in methods sections is due to word limitations set forth by the journals or purposeful decisions made by authors, open science would promote the expectations that methods and procedures be more thorough and replicable. Ultimately, this would improve science.

Open Access (OA) to scientific knowledge, a cornerstone of open science, advocates for unrestricted access to publications and data. Open Access promotes innovation, knowledge dissemination, and societal welfare by facilitating access to research outputs and fostering their translation into practice. For instance, OA spurs new ideas and discoveries and makes their availability and accessibility possible (Ford & Alemneh, 2022b). OA also leads to increased use of research and development findings and their translation into practice, benefiting and improving education, the economy, and society's overall welfare (Fell, 2019). For scholars publishing in OA, there is a possible increase in citations and recognition of what they contribute to the field (Stracke, 2020).

Increased transparency and systematic labeling of data for usability, areas encouraged by open science, will also make it easier to employ artificial intelligence (AI) tools for analysis (Thibault et al., 2023). Together, open science and AI have the potential to accelerate and enhance several aspects of the research process (Beck & Poetz, 2024). Several ways this will occur include automating certain routine research tasks, efficient analysis of large datasets; enhancing and increasing efficiency in interdisciplinary research with the ability to rapidly combine knowledge across disciplines; and improving dissemination of scientific findings outside of research communities by rewriting results in simplified text for laypersons. With the increase of open-source AI tools, researchers with limited resources, such as those in LMICs, may be afforded the opportunity to engage meaningfully with open-source data and contribute to their chosen fields (Beck & Poetz, 2024). Open data also allows for graduate level educators and students to work with real data and engage in meaningful and real-world practice in their fields. A more thorough examination of how open science and AI can work together is outside of the scope of this chapter, however, the advancements are anticipated to expand rapidly.

While some benefits of open science have been widely recognized, others are still emerging. With increased promotion and engagement, particularly in regions with underrepresented scholars such as those found in Africa, the potential for broader benefits becomes more attainable. In the following section, we explore the challenges associated with open science.

## Challenges of Open Science

As with any innovation, open science must overcome challenges for comprehensive, effective, and successful adoption. It is helpful to keep in mind that with open science, some of the aspects of this framework that weigh in as benefits can also be considered challenges. For example, whereas transparency is a key component of open science and the replicability of studies, it is also a challenge in how data and all components of studies must be accessible to those not directly involved in the original data collection, data labeling, storage, analysis, etc. For instance, openly sharing datasets requires systematically labeled data across different disciplines in order for the datasets to be usable by anyone (Thibault et al., 2023). This entails systems of data labeling that are universal in a way datasets that remain siloed in one discipline need not be. For systems to be in place for labeling within and across disciplines, collaborations need to occur between fields of study with stakeholders that may not see the added investment as worthwhile (Allen & Mehler, 2019; Stracke, 2020). Creating and using cross-disciplinary and cross-national systems requires buy-in from several stakeholders willing to advance policy and practice to encourage researchers to invest the time and energy to provide details with their data and use these systems. This is a big challenge that organizations with frameworks for open science are attempting to address.

Another challenge is the current misalignment of the expectations of open science and the current measures for publications for scholars seeking promotion and tenure (Allen & Mehler, 2019). To overcome this lack of incentive structure, stakeholders must invest in and promote open science by making each step in the process count toward professional advancement (Stracke, 2020). For example, researchers and scholars who invest the extra time and energy to make their datasets and procedures available and accessible to other scholars through proper labeling of variables and detailed step-by-step instructions for the methods employed, would then be able to track those efforts and use them in a dossier for promotion and tenure. Such efforts would ensure faculty involved in any aspect of an open science study can receive credit toward promotion, not just those writing up the results in a manuscript found worthy of peer-reviewed publication. This could mean that fewer faculty will be forced to focus only on publishing results and findings. Instead, they could focus on tasks such as designing solid methods sections to be published before the full study is realized or collecting data in the most efficient and ethical manner to respect human subjects. This would allow for more emphasis to be placed on high-quality methods rather than solely on a high quantity of published manuscripts.

An additional challenge is shared in the UNESCO Recommendation on open science, one of the first international standard-setting instruments on open science. While it is stated that access to scientific knowledge should be as open as possible, sometimes access may need to be restricted to protect human rights, confidentiality, intellectual property rights, personal information, threatened or endangered species, and sacred and secret indigenous knowledge (UNESCO, 2021). The protection of some data will not be explored fully in this chapter, but it should be noted that this is a challenge that will need to be addressed as open science expectations expand.

The use of AI in conjunction with open science also introduces unique challenges. In addition to the need for researchers disseminating data to use universal labeling so that other researchers can use the data, appropriate labeling is necessary for using AI with data analysis. Unfortunately, AI is known to have biases, and universal labeling does not remedy this problem because it is based on the data training the AI. Freeing the data from biases will ensure that machine learning and analysis are ethical and do not reinforce or exacerbate biases in research tasks and collaborative projects (Beck & Poetz, 2024). This challenge directly requires data and research to be collected and compiled from not only dominant populations but also minoritized people groups. Currently, much of the data and research come from core research countries with research populations consisting mainly of individuals and groups from dominant cultures (Demeter, 2020). Until these biases in representation are remedied, AI tools may widen gaps. The next section will expand on how the digital age, including the use of AI, allows for and encourages open science, even with some of the current challenges.

## Open Science in the Digital Age

The accessibility of big data and open data has sparked significant transformations and innovations within our knowledge-based society. As detailed in the benefits section of this chapter, open science holds promise for advancing societal well-being. Leading international research and funding bodies, including the United States National Science Foundation (NSF), the National Endowment for the Humanities (NEH), the European Union, the African Open Science Platform (ASSAf), and various United Nations agencies, are envisioning a future where leveraging big data and open science enhances the knowledge society and reshapes its development within the burgeoning knowledge-based global economy. With increasing policies mandating free, immediate, and equitable access to funded research, national and international initiatives, practices, and compliance mechanisms play pivotal roles in forging a more open and equitable global scholarly communication ecosystem.

Establishing an interoperable and efficient network of repositories is a cornerstone of national research infrastructure. In November 2023, the U.S. Repository Network (USRN) initiated a pilot project to enhance the discoverability of articles within repositories. This project collaborates with CORE, a nonprofit aggregator based at the Open University in the UK, to assess and refine local repository practices (SPARC, 2023). Similarly, Horizon Europe represents the European counterpart to such research and innovation programs for 2021–2027, boasting a budget of €95.5 billion. Like its predecessor, Horizon 2020, Horizon Europe addresses a wide array of global societal challenges, from climate change to the attainment of the UN's Sustainable Development Goals. The program fosters collaboration and amplifies the impact of research and innovation in crafting, supporting, and implementing EU policies while tackling global challenges. It promotes the generation and equitable dissemination of cutting-edge knowledge and technologies (Horizon Europe, 2024). Efforts are also being seen across Africa through the initiation of the African Open Science Platform (ASSAf, 2018).

Digital technology empowers researchers and authors to swiftly and broadly disseminate their work by circumventing traditional print publishing processes. In the digital age, open science can unfold as soon as each research process step is determined, significantly accelerating the pace of distribution compared to traditional print-based mechanisms. Electronic dissemination via the Internet also enables researchers to reach a far broader audience than print publications. These open science practices facilitate cross-national and cross-disciplinary collaboration, potentially fostering larger research teams by recognizing the contributions of individuals involved in all steps of the research process, including proposal writing, methodological choices, data collection, analysis, and publication of study findings (Thibault et al., 2023).

Advancements in digital technologies profoundly influence the creation, access, utilization, and preservation of information resources. Gidlund and Sundberg's (2022) research systematically explored the evolution of the concept of digitalization in academic discourse, revealing a recent convergence toward associating digitalization with the idea of a digitally transformed society. Furthermore, Phillips et al. (2014) observed a significant increase in the inclusion of URL references in Electronic Theses and Dissertations (ETDs), indicating the growing importance of web content as a subject for research and scholarly communication.

The proliferation of digital content and retrospective digitization initiatives underscores the increasing significance of web-based resources in academic discourse.

The digital age also impacts open science through mechanisms such as version control, digital events, and broader participation and engagement. Online document versions can be easily updated without the constraints of print-based publishing. Digital events, such as conferences and webinars, transcend geographical barriers, enabling global participation and fostering connections among individuals and groups. These events can be recorded and shared, extending their reach and contributing to the formation of global networks. Additionally, the openness of science allows for increased AI integration. This can potentially automate various research processes, expediting scientific advancements and democratizing research opportunities, particularly in LMICs (Beck & Poetz, 2024). The digital age we are in and the move toward open science enhance a research landscape that will advance science, empower educators of research, as well as their students, and bring global benefits.

## Open Science in the African Context

In 2018 a concerted effort by stakeholders in Africa was undertaken to assess and inform scholars and researchers about the movement toward open science. A group of experts gathered in South Africa to discuss and establish the African Open Science Platform (ASSAf, 2018). The mission of The Platform "is to put African scientists at the cutting edge of contemporary, data-intensive science as a fundamental resource for modern society" (ASSAf, 2018, p. 4).

> Open Science is a vital enabler: in maintaining the rigour and reliability of science; in creatively integrating diverse data resources to address complex modern challenges; in open innovation and in engaging with other societal actors as knowledge partners in tackling shared problems. It is fundamental to realisation of the SDGs. (ASSAf, 2018, p. 4)

In addition to *The Platform* document, a *Landscape Study* (ASSAf, 2019) was produced, examining many aspects of the current status of open science throughout the African continent. These included the complex nature of ICT infrastructure; training; research and development investment by African countries (R&D); and other aspects of governmental and political commitment to open science. Chiware and Skelly (2022) suggest African policymakers continue to articulate and disseminate the benefits of open science, as well as the importance of implementation training on many aspects, including data governance and developing frameworks that align internationally. They also suggest the establishment of incentives throughout Africa for scholars to work in open science models.

In reviewing the literature of the past few decades, there is no shortage of views on the correlation between the emphasis on research and development (R&D) and national development. Nchake and Shuaibu (2022) and Alemneh and Hastings (2006), among others, noted that power and wealth are increasingly measured by the amount of access one has to information and by one's ability to obtain and use that information effectively. In other words, the distinction between highly developed and less developed countries has already become a distinction between countries with low versus extensive ICT infrastructure. In fact, as can be seen from Fig. 11.1, it is not an accident that developed countries allocated up to 5% of their already high GDPs. According to the United Nations (2024), Research and development (R&D) expenditure as a proportion of Gross Domestic Product (GDP) is defined as the total intramural expenditure on research and experimental development (R&D) performed in the national territory during a specific reference period expressed as a percentage of national GDP.

Similarly, Sustainable Development Goal 9 is to "build resilient infrastructure, promote inclusive and sustainable industrialization and foster innovation" (United Nations, 2024). This indicator measures expenditure on research and development (R&D) activities as a percentage of the total gross domestic product (GDP) of a given country. As can be seen from Fig. 11.1, the share of sub-Saharan African countries (0.3%) in terms of their GDP spent on research and development is way below the world average (1.9%). Recognizing the inclusive growth effect, the African Union suggests 1% R&D, but this is not yet being met in African countries, with only a couple of countries even coming close (ASSAf, 2019).

Despite efforts to inform and promote open science, several barriers exist, hindering the adoption of open science in Africa. As already discussed, major obstacles to open science adoption in Africa are related to finances and infrastructure. In reviewing barriers to harnessing the full power of the Internet and ICT, Alemneh and Hastings (2006), Nchake

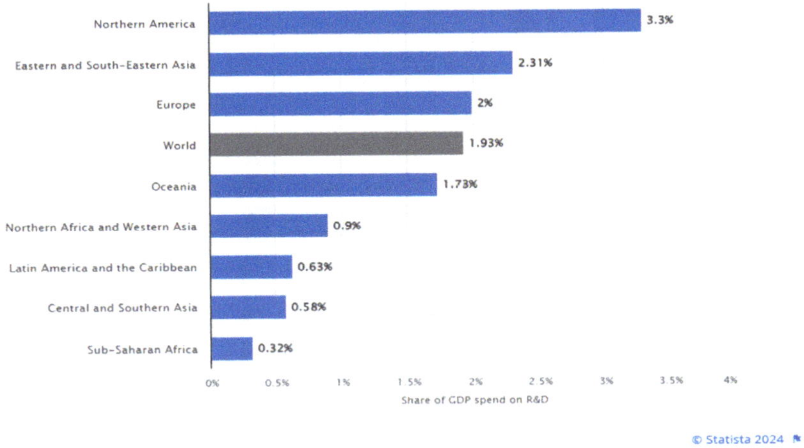


**Fig. 11.1** Share of gross domestic product (GDP) spent on research and development (R&D) worldwide in 2020, by region (*Source* UNESCO Institute for Statistics. Share of gross domestic product (GDP) spent on research and development (R&D) worldwide in 2020, by region. In Statista. Retrieved April 30, 2024, from https://tinyurl.com/mrtn35eu)

and Shuaibu (2022), among others, noted that although digital technologies provide scholars with access to more diverse and previously unavailable content that span myriad technologies across institutions and nations, these technologies have not been fully exploited in all parts of the world, Africa in particular. They identified the critical challenges for digital development in sub-Saharan Africa, including underdeveloped digital infrastructure, lack of accessible and affordable connectivity, limited skills for digitally enabled services, and inadequate and backward regulatory and policy frameworks. However, as Fig. 11.2 shows, the sub-Saharan African region has made substantial strides toward digital transformation in the last two decades. Hundreds of millions of people have gained access to the Internet and productively utilize a wide variety of digital services, such as mobile payments and online learning platforms (World Bank, 2023).

Various empirical studies highlight internet availability's direct and indirect impacts on jobs through entrepreneurship, innovation, and

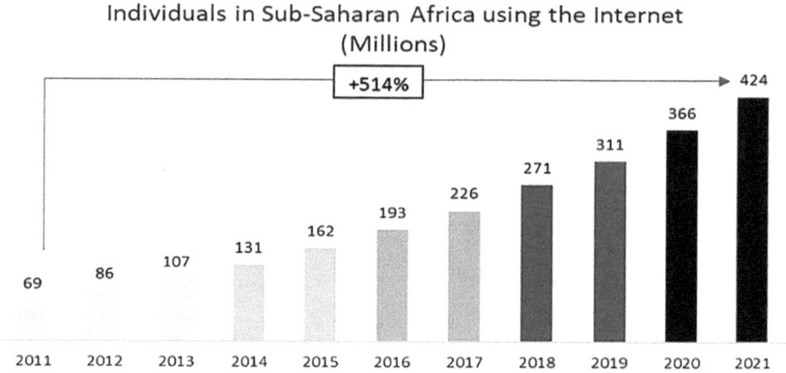


**Fig. 11.2** Sub-Saharan Africa internet users (World Bank, 2023)

foreign direct investment. The lack of infrastructure for science communication significantly hinders developing nations' ability from both actively participating in knowledge generation as well as from enhancing the visibility of their scholarly works (Beyene et al., 2022). The negative impact these infrastructure issues have on graduate level education are challenging to debate. Despite the good news, Nchake and Shuaibu (2022) noted that although Africa's infrastructure has been improving, albeit slowly, the continent still needs to address all infrastructural challenges and will require more and better investment to achieve the desired inclusive growth. Similarly, a World Bank (2023) report indicates that Africa's internet infrastructure coverage and quality still lag behind other regions. Roughly 84% of people across countries in sub-Saharan Africa live in areas where 3G service is available. Furthermore, sub-Saharan Africa has the widest gender gap (37%) in mobile internet use globally, with over 190 million women still not using mobile internet services (Shanahan, 2022). Open science is difficult, if not impossible, to use by those without internet access, keeping this a foundational concern to the right to science.

In addition to the infrastructure issues and national-level investments, other financial considerations, such as OA processing fees, continue to hinder research dissemination in Africa. Although OA can reduce costs for accessing research outputs, it creates a new obstacle for scholars who cannot pay the article processing fees to publish. The current representation of authors of OA is predominantly from higher-income countries as opposed to lower-income countries. In fact, not only are fewer OA publications coming from lower-income countries, but fewer of them have the DOAJ Seal, a measure of quality and credibility, in their OA peer-reviewed journals than do higher-income countries (Patra & Roy, 2023). These facts must be a significant consideration when implementing an open science policy that could have similar effects if not written and administered in an equitable manner.

The critical aspects of infrastructure, funding, resources, and technology are closely tied together and must be explored, as they profoundly impact the movement toward open science. Any institution or entity that exerts control over the infrastructure, funds, and other resources, including the necessary ingredients of open science, open access, and open data, is bound to wield significant power in terms of their social, political, economic, and other benefits (Fisher & Streinz, 2022). In this age of information, knowledge, and data, and given that access to data drives scientific inquiry and progress, any uneven access and control over data pose a challenge to equitable economic development (Fisher & Streinz, 2022).

## Indigenous and Local Knowledge Contributions

Within the context of open science and science in general, citizen science and indigenous knowledge should be considered as they both can contribute significantly to the redesign of scientific research and graduate education. These contributions are especially important in global priority areas like climate change adaptation and public health, which are often perceived as operating at national or international levels, but in reality, most decisions remain local. As de Sousa Santos (2018) argues, there is a need to incorporate non-Western voices in academia and science.

By creating synergies, scientific research can benefit from citizen science and Indigenous knowledge. Involving local people and indigenous communities in research creates more transparent processes and increases public understanding of scientific methods. It also allows communities to advocate for research that addresses their concerns (Tengö et al., 2021). Integrating Indigenous knowledge into scientific frameworks helps decolonize research and graduate programs, challenging traditional Western dominance in higher education and scientific inquiry (de Sousa Santos, 2018; Kovach & Forshaw, 2024; Meridith, 2024). Such localized understanding and indigenous approaches to research and education offer alternative approaches that are often more sustainable and community-focused than those being imposed from outside of the local and regional contexts.

## Open Science Platforms and Stakeholders

In this section, the discussion delves into platforms supporting open science and stakeholders who can promote its global adoption, particularly in Africa. Numerous organizations and institutions advocate for open science. For instance, the Center for Open Science champions transparency, sharing, and inclusivity in science. They provide guidance, frameworks, shared research, training, and translations of support materials into multiple languages to facilitate the transition (Center for Open Science, n.d.). The Scholarly Publishing and Academic Resources Coalition (SPARC) also advocates for Open Access (OA). SPARC boasts a membership of approximately 250 libraries and academic organizations, primarily in North America. Affiliated SPARC coalitions in Africa, Europe, and Japan complement this membership. As a driving force for change, SPARC focuses on policy advocacy, supporting member initiatives, and fostering communities to advance the vision of knowledge as a public good. SPARC addresses the exclusionary nature of knowledge systems resulting from racism, colonialism, and other historical injustices. One notable project is the Right to Research Coalition (R2RC), an international alliance of over 90 undergraduate and graduate student organizations in more than 100 countries worldwide, advocating for openness in research through advocacy and education (SPARC, 2024).

Regardless of the platforms used, open science should adhere to the FAIR principles: findable, accessible, interoperable, and reusable (Hey, 2022; Wilkinson et al., 2016). FAIR principles in the African context have additional concerns, including fewer repositories, the concerns of geoblocking, and purposeful restriction of access (Shanahan & Bezuidenhout, 2022). Science truly becomes open when it is accessible globally. Currently, isolated instances of open science can be found due to inequalities in scholarly communication and the dominance of Western scholars in research outputs (Canagarajah, 2002; Demeter, 2020).

Numerous platforms can be utilized to foster equitable and fully open science, benefiting scholars worldwide, especially those in lower-income countries. Google Scholar and other free online search engines could be adapted to host and share links to all stages of research. In the African context, initiatives like The Africa Open Science Platform (https://aosp.org.za/), African Journals Online (AJOL), and the International African Institute could be promoted and expanded to advance open science objectives. Stakeholders interested in embracing open science in Africa include African researchers, global researchers, academics globally, and policymakers. Evidence suggests that international collaborations thrive when contexts differ. Open science could facilitate increased cross-national collaborations within and among African countries. Collaborating on research across diverse contexts can yield significant benefits (Page, 2019). To effectively tackle global challenges, UNESCO (2021) recommends developing strategies to monitor open science's effectiveness and long-term efficiency. Multi-stakeholder participatory approaches could strengthen the connection between science, policy, and society, enhancing transparency and ensuring inclusive, equitable, and high-quality research.

## Moving Forward

All indications are that open science will expand and make all research stages increasingly open for society's benefit. Future research around open science practices could include the benefits for scholars and graduate education in different geopolitical locations and in a variety of disciplines. Questions about whether open science works toward equity in consumption and production in ways complicated by earlier stages of the more restrictive OA movement need answering. Research could also include implementing and evaluating initiatives incorporating open science metrics for promotion and tenure in colleges and universities. The increased employment of AI will also encourage and open doors for research on the best practices in labeling data for machine learning and the ethical considerations of the confluence of AI and open science.

Research about the benefits of open science could be studied quantitatively and qualitatively to produce evidence that can be used to promote the best practices in all steps of the research process. Studies in specific disciplines could further advance understanding of the benefits that may differ based on the fields of study. Studying open science in various disciplines could also reveal the unique challenges and best practices in specific fields to encourage embracing what is best for each discipline.

Discovering and promoting the most effective and universal way to label data will be important as open science expands. Therefore, any research supporting these methods will help to advance the promotion and ease of the transformation. As discussed in the section on challenges, systematic labeling of data would be a critical component of making data truly open and usable across disciplines, across national borders, and usable to forms of data analysis advancements witnessed with AI applications. In light of emerging AI technology and the rapid advancements in science, the roles of stakeholders in promoting actions and policies that advance openness and equity in research and education systems will become increasingly important.

## Conclusion

In this chapter, we have focused on open science's concepts and implementation as well as the benefits and challenges, particularly in the context of Africa. Within the African context it is critical to continue to expose and deal with the infrastructure issues that hinder fully embracing and participating in open science. Through the pandemic and now in the midst of the aftermath, open science has gained a spotlight, resulting in rapid and significant advancements in research, disease prevention, economic development, crisis management, and more. The pandemic also highlighted the need for OER for equity in education, especially research-intensive graduate level education. In particular, and in the context of Africa, open science continues to enhance the capabilities of scholars to participate actively in the knowledge economy; however, there remains ample room for improvement. The African governments should emphasize policy frameworks to support various local open science initiatives, and embrace the ideas and efforts of indigenous and local scholars in this process. Open science practices not only break down barriers between disciplines and between geopolitical dissemination of outputs, but these practices work to tear down silos that stifle scholarly communication and scientific advancement. Opening the processes of science, from the development of ideas to how studies are reviewed and evaluated for originality, credibility, and values, as well as sharing results openly, speeds up the rate at which research can be conducted and the benefits promulgated.

## References

Academy of Science of South Africa (ASSAf). (2018). *The African open science platform: The future of science and science for the future.*

Academy of Science of South Africa (ASSAf). (2019). *African open science platform part 1: Landscape study.*

Alemneh, D. (Ed.). (2022). *The Handbook of Research on the Global View of Open Access and Scholarly Communications.* IGI Global.

Alemneh, D. G., & Hastings, S. K. (2006). Developing the ICT infrastructure for Africa: Overview of barriers to harnessing the full power of the internet. *Journal of Education for Library and Information Science, 47*(1), 4–16. https://doi.org/10.2307/40324333

Allen, C., & Mehler, D. M. (2019). Open science challenges, benefits and tips in early career and beyond. *PLoS Biology, 17*(5), Article e3000246. https://doi.org/10.1371/journal.pbio.3000246

Beck, S., & Poetz, M. (2024). Artificial intelligence and the changing costs and benefits of engaging in open and collaborative science. *The Journal of Open Commons & Organizing (JOCO), 2*(2), 28–31. https://tinyurl.com/bexr4p5h

Beyene, M., Tekle, S. M., & Alemneh, D. G. (2022). Open access initiatives in Ethiopia's higher learning institutions. In D. Alemneh (Ed.), *Handbook of Research on the Global View of Open Access and Scholarly Communications* (pp. 23–43). IGI Global Scientific Publishing. https://doi.org/10.4018/978-1-7998-9805-4.ch002

Canagarajah, A. S. (2002). *A geopolitics of academic writing.* University of Pittsburgh Press.

Center for Open Science. (n.d). *Open science framework.* https://osf.io/

Chakravorty, N., Sharma, C. S., Molla, K. A., et al. (2022). (2022) Open science: Challenges, possible solutions and the way forward. *Proceedings of the Indian National Science Academy, 88*, 456–471. https://doi.org/10.1007/s43538-022-00104-2

Chiware, E. R. T., & Skelly, L. (2022). Open Science in Africa: What policy-makers should consider. *Frontiers in Research Metrics and Analtics, 7*, Article 950139. https://doi.org/10.3389/frma.2022.950139

Demeter, M. (2020). *Academic knowledge production and the global south: Questioning inequality and under-representation.* Palgrave Macmillan.

Fell, M. J. (2019). The economic impacts of open science: A rapid evidence assessment. *Publications, 7*, 46. https://doi.org/10.3390/publications7030046

Fisher, A., & Streinz, T. (2022). Confronting data inequality. *Columbia Journal of Transnational Law, 60*(3), 829–956.

Ford, A. Y., & Alemneh, D. G. (2022b). The role of open access in equitable research curriculum and research outputs. In D.G. Alemneh (Ed.),

*Global View of Open Access and Scholarly Communications* (pp. 126–147). IGI Global. https://doi.org/10.4018/978-1-7998-9805-4

Ford, A., & Alemneh, D. (2022a). Scholars experiencing epistemic injustice due to management of scholarly outputs. *Proceedings of the Association for Information Science and Technology, 59*(1), 67–75. https://doi.org/10.1002/pra2.605

Ford, A. Y., & Alemneh, D. G. (2024). Inclusive global scholarly communication: Toward a just and healthier information ecosystem. *Journal of the Association for Information Science and Technology,* 75(10*),1058–1069.* https://doi.org/10.1002/asi.24899

Foster. (n.d). *The future of science is open.* https://www.fosteropenscience.eu/

Gidlund, K. L., & Sundberg, L. (2022). Unveiling 100 years of digitalization as a scholarly object. *First Monday, 27*(8). https://doi.org/10.5210/fm.v27i8.12319

Heisig, P. (2022, June). *Proceedings of the 17th International Conference on Knowledge Management.* https://tinyurl.com/43trmtzc

Hey, T. J. (2022). Open science and Big Data in South Africa. *Frontiers in Research Metrics and Analytics, 7.* https://doi.org/10.3389/frma.2022.982435

Horizon Europe. (2024). European Union's Research and Innovation Funding Programme until 2027. https://tinyurl.com/2nammen2

Kovach, M., & Forshaw, L. (2024). Wâhkôhtowin (a Kinship) of the Indigenous Episteme, Circlework and Epistemic Justice in Indigenous Research. In *Universities and Epistemic Justice in a Plural World: Knowing Better* (pp. 139–153). Springer Nature Singapore.

Meredith, M. (Ed.). (2024). *Universities and epistemic justice in a plural world: knowing better* (Vol. 12). Springer Nature.

Nchake, M., & Shuaibu, M. (2022). Investment in ICT infrastructure and inclusive growth in Africa. *Scientific African, 17.* https://doi.org/10.1016/j.sciaf.2022.e01293

OpenStax. (n.d). *OpenStax about us.* https://openstax.org/about

ORION. (n.d.). *About ORION.* https://www.orion-openscience.eu/about

Page, S. E. (2019). *The diversity bonus: How great teams pay off in the knowledge economy.* Princeton University Press.

Patra, S. K., & Roy, U. (2023). Is open science a developed countries' phenomenon? A case study of journals registered in the DOAJ. *Journal of Data Science, Informetrics, and Citation Studies, 2*(3), 233–242. https://doi.org/10.5530/jcitation.2.3.31

Phillips, M., Alemneh, D., & Reyes Ayala, B. (2014). Analysis of URL references in ETDs: A case study at the University of North Texas. *Library Management, 35*(4/5), 293–307. https://doi.org/10.1108/LM-08-2013-0073

Resolution, G. A. (1966). International covenant on economic, social and cultural rights. *General Assembly resolution A, 2200.*

Shanahan, M. (2022). *The Mobile Gender Gap Report 2022.* https://tinyurl.com/3r3pya9c

Shanahan, H., & Bezuidenhout, L. (2022). Rethinking the a in FAIR Data: Issues of data access and accessibility in research. *Frontiers in Research Metrics and Analytics, 7*, Article 912456.

de Sousa Santos, B. (2018). *The end of the cognitive empire: The coming of age of epistemologies of the South.* Duke University Press.

SPARC. (2023). *US Repository Network Pilot Project.* https://tinyurl.com/3yezvcdn

SPARC. (2024). *About SPARC.* https://sparcopen.org/

Staunton, C., Barragán, C. A., Canali, S., Ho, C., Leonelli, S., Mayernik, M., Prainsack, B., & Wonkham, A. (2021). Open science, data sharing and solidarity: Who benefits? *History and Philosophy of the Life Sciences, 43*(4), 1–8.

Stracke, C. M. (2020). Open science and radical solutions for diversity, equity and quality in research: A literature review of different research schools, philosophies and frameworks and their potential impact on science and education. *Radical solutions and open science: An open approach to boost higher education*, 17–37.

Tengö, M., Austin, B. J., Danielsen, F., & Fernández-Llamazares, Á. (2021). Creating synergies between citizen science and Indigenous and local knowledge. *BioScience, 71*(5), 503–518.

Thibault, R. T., Amaral, O. B., Argolo, F., Bandrowski, A. E., Davidson, A. R., & Drude, N. I. (2023). Open Science 2.0: Towards a truly collaborative research ecosystem. *PLoS Biology, 21*(10), e3002362. https://doi.org/10.1371/journal.pbio.3002362

UNESCO. (2021). *UNESCO Recommendation on Open Science.* UNESCO. https://doi.org/10.54677/MNMH8546

United Nations. General Assembly. (1949). *Universal declaration of human rights* (Vol. 3381). Department of State, United States of America. https://tinyurl.com/2chv95ss

Wilkinson, M. D., Dumontier, M., Aalbersberg, I. J., Appleton, G., Axton, M., Baak, A., Blomberg, N., Boiten, J. W., da Silva Santos, L. B., Bourne, P. E., Bouwman, J., & Mons, B. (2016). The FAIR Guiding Principles for scientific data management and stewardship. *Scientific Data, 3*(1), 1–9. https://doi.org/10.1038/sdata.2016.18

World Bank. (2023). *Digital Africa: Technological Transformation for Jobs.* https://tinyurl.com/6a9d6nx2

World Bank. (2024). *Digital Transformation Drives Development in Africa.* https://tinyurl.com/59m2wnn2

CHAPTER 12

# Research and Innovation in Advancing Knowledge for African Development

*Damtew Teferra*

## Introduction

Research and innovation are a powerhouse of knowledge production. The importance of research, as a central hub for knowledge production has received huge recognition as the world ushered the twenty-first century dubbed as the knowledge era where society massively depends on knowledge—unlike any other times in human civilization. The new information and communication technologies have created new conditions for the emergence of knowledge societies. This emerging global information society only finds its *raison d'être* if it serves to bring about a higher and more desirable goal, namely the building, on a global scale, of *knowledge societies* that are a source of development for all, first and foremost for the least developed countries (UNESCO, 2005).

It is important to note from the outset that, the underlying issues that affect the state of research in the continent—each issue that begs massive coverage on its own right—are too numerous, as they are

D. Teferra (✉)
School of Education, University of Kwazulu-Natal, Durban, South Africa
e-mail: teferra@ukzn.ac.za



D. Teferra (ed.), *Research and Innovation in African Higher Education*,
https://doi.org/10.1007/978-3-031-92909-0_12

complex. In analysing the state of research and innovation in the continent, the chapter here attempts to capture the key highlights that typically confronts the sector.

The issue of African higher education roared into play again (since the independence days) in the early 2000 following the official acknowledgement and recognition of the importance of the sector to national development, as expressed in series of policy documents by the World Bank—key player in African higher education development and others. *Peril and Promise* (World Bank & UNESCO, 2000) noted:

> The world economy is changing as knowledge supplants physical capital as the source of present (and future) wealth. Technology is driving much of this process, with information technology, biotechnology, and other innovations leading to remarkable changes in the way we live and work. As knowledge becomes more important, so does higher education.

It went on to state that:

> This poses a serious challenge to the developing world. Since the 1980s, many national governments and international donors have assigned higher education a relatively low priority. Narrow—and, in our view, misleading—economic analysis has contributed to the view that public investment in universities and colleges brings meager returns compared to investment in primary and secondary schools, and that higher education magnifies income inequality.

This marked a remarkable recognition and turnabout of the Bank and an implicit admission of its fault that its economic analysis studies that narrowly focused on a rate of return on education investment in the past—that had been assailed by many hitherto—were flawed.

It concluded:

> As a result, higher education systems in developing countries are under great strain. They are chronically underfunded, but face escalating demand—approximately half of today's higher education students live in the developing world. Faculty are often underqualified, lack motivation, and are poorly rewarded. Students are poorly taught and curricula underdeveloped. Developed countries, meanwhile, are constantly raising the stakes. Quite simply, many developing countries will need to work much harder just to maintain their position, let alone catch up.

In *Constructing Knowledge Societies* the World Bank (2002) reaffirmed that:

> Tertiary education is more than the capstone of the traditional education pyramid; it is a critical pillar of human development worldwide....Universities are clearly a key part of all tertiary systems, but the diverse and growing set of public and private tertiary institutions in every country... forms a network of institutions that support the production of the higher-order capacity necessary for development.

In *Accelerating Catch up*, the World Bank (2009) further pronounced more intensive knowledge growth that emphasized human capital development by stating:

> The key to economic success in a globalized world lies increasingly in how effectively a country can assimilate the available knowledge and build comparative advantage.... Capital is a necessary handmaiden, but the arbiter of economic success—even survival—in the world today is the capacity to mobilize knowledge and to use it to the fullest.

Multiple such policy documents from multilateral and bilateral agencies as well as massive economic, political, and demographic shifts have created immense opportunities for advancing higher education in Africa. Currently, the sector is undergoing a transformation wrought by massive expansion, and what makes Africa's growth unique is that it has seen a 'flash flood' of growth with consequent implications that range from quality to funding, from governance to employment. Ironically, despite this massive growth, the system still remains the world's least developed which means that it must do more in facing the dual and contradictory challenges of increased expansion and improved quality (Teferra, 2014).

Furthermore, driven by the desire for national development and global competitiveness, a growing recognition on the significance of a robust research and graduate programmes as key structures for knowledge production and their support has taken place. According to World Bank (2014) Sub-Saharan Africa's (SSA) share of the global output in research papers is minor but growing. It increased from 0.44 per cent in 2003 to 0.72 per cent in 2012. In terms of citation impact, the region's share of global citations also grew, doubling from 0.06 per cent in 2003 to 0.12 per cent in 2012. Globally, research output is dominated by natural science subjects, and the same is the case for Sub-Saharan Africa (SSA).

Health sciences form the largest share in almost all subregions, with only South Africa as the exception. Social sciences (including arts and humanities) and life sciences occupied the smallest share of SSA's research output, although social science is the fastest growing group. A study sponsored by British Council and DAAD (2018) indicates similar patterns in that science, technology, engineering, and mathematics (STEM) subjects feature strongly in both the current research output and national policy documents dictating PhD capacity building. Despite difficulties in cross-country comparisons of disciplinary focus, this focus on STEM is also evident in PhD provision, with a variety of core and applied sciences provided by institutions.

This chapter offers a deeper analysis and synthesis of the most outstanding issues affecting research and innovation, many also covered in this book extensively. As it enriches the individual chapters and the book as a whole, the chapter also draws on global and comparative perspectives on the respective themes.

## Human Capital: The Global Currency

Human Capital Theory posits that individuals and society derive economic benefits from investing in education, skills, and training, which increases workers' productivity and earnings potential. Originating from economists such as Gary Becker (1962) and Theodore Schultz (1961), this theory emphasizes that education and skills training as essential investments to increase an individual's economic value and contribute to broader economic growth.

Human Capital Theory advances that workers with higher education and skills are more competitive and likely to command higher wages. For societies, investing in human capital is seen as crucial for fostering innovation, productivity, and long-term prosperity. Notwithstanding some critiques of the theory, the growth accounting literature posits that education, through increasing the human capital stock of individuals, improves their productivity and contributes to economic growth (Petchko, 2018) as it also advances critical humanistic and social capital building dimensions and its role as an important global public good (World Bank & Unesco, 2000).

OECD countries have the most robust human capital development in the world. Most of the indicators of human capital development—including health and education indicators—suggest that OECD members have better human capital development than other economic blocs (World Bank, 2022 in Solarin et al., 2024). By comparison, Africa lags behind this critical aspect of human capital development, with a lowest participation rate in higher education—subsequently research and graduate education. Citing comparative analyses of developing regions on World Bank data in 2020 Ouedraogo et al. (2022) observe that Africa faces the deepest human capital deficit in the world.

It is in recognition of this deficit that Agenda 2063 of the African Union (2015) calls for 'well-trained and adequately skilled citizens supported by science, technology and innovation for a knowledge society'. This is expressed in the Union's strategies in Continental Education Strategy for Africa (CESA 2016–25) and Science, Technology & Innovation Strategy for Africa (STISA-2024) which align with many multilateral development discourses on this matter.

## Academics and Researchers

In advancing research and innovation, competent academics and researchers in sufficient numbers remain paramount. Academic staff is at the heart of a higher education institution, and its abundance and quality have thus great implications for students, institutions, and nations alike (Teferra, 2015a). Altbach (2006) stresses that without a strong, committed academic profession, higher education cannot provide effective teaching or top-quality research. In knowledge-based economies, universities must have academic staff who are well qualified, well trained, and committed to academic work (p. 25) if they are to meaningfully and effectively contribute to development.

The huge expansion of the higher education sector in Africa in a short period of time took place without comparable efforts to supply the requisite number of academics—the human capital. The phenomenal growth meant that academics have been overstretched in an increasingly non-conducive academic and research environment where their major roles have increasingly dwindled to teaching and instruction, leaving very little room for research undertakings. The expansion of private institutions which are often dependent on academics in public institutions has made matters worse as this created a 'moon-lighting' opportunity for them to disproportionately engage in these institutions whose primary, if not exclusive, mission has been teaching. The interest of academics in moonlighting has escalated with increasingly divided loyalty—and role—of academics towards research.

In comparison, countries in the North American region have the highest researcher density per million population standing at 4,432 followed by those in the South Asian region at 263 and the lowest in the African region at 124 (UNESCO, 2021). It is important to note that ultimately these densities typically determine the extent of collaboration, with implications for research productivity, outcome, impact, citation, and networking, among others.

A doctoral degree has become a common requirement for academic positions at four-year universities and, increasingly, at junior colleges (Altbach, 2007). A PhD is often assumed as an entry point to a robust research undertaking and a yardstick to research competence. Yet, the African higher education landscape has a meagre number of academics with PhDs—and even more meagre academics with professorship. This has direct implications for graduate supervision, intellectual leadership, and international networking—with immediate implications on research and knowledge production.

As a consequence, a number of countries are enacting laws and advancing directives that demand a doctorate qualification for academic positions in a university. In South Africa, the government has set a target of 75 per cent of academic staff, by producing a total of 5,000 PhDs per annum, by 2030. In Senegal, a PhD qualification became mandatory for all academics in public universities as part of the 2012 licence-maîtrise-doctorat (LMD) reform. The Kenya Commission for University Education has passed a regulation mandating PhD qualification for university teaching staff by 2018. A similar directive was issued by the Nigerian University Commission in 2015 for lecturers wanting to rise to the rank of senior lecturer and above. Also, in Ghana, the key higher education regulatory bodies—the National Council for Tertiary Education (NCTE) and the National Accreditation Board (NAB)—set the doctoral degree as the minimum qualification for university teaching. However, due to circumstances peculiar to the country's higher education sector, this policy has not been fully endorsed, as among others, shortages of academics with doctoral degrees in some specialized fields, which compel the universities to recruit staff with lower credentials (Ansah et al., 2019). The pressing need to fill academic positions for the massifying high education sector has been instrumental in advancing graduate programmes and research.

As indicated in this chapter elsewhere, Sub-Saharan Africa's modest growth in research output and improvement in citation impact has occurred against a backdrop of human and material resource challenges. For instance, the world average of researchers per million inhabitants in 2014 stood at 1,098.4. In SSA, the figure was only 87.8, compared to 166.5 in South and West Asia, and 434.9 in Latin America and the Caribbean (UNESCO, 2015). Between 2010 and 2013, 294,339 (9.3 per cent) of total enrolment were postgraduate students; of this, approximately 20 per cent were studying at the PhD level, which is far smaller compared to the master's level enrolments (Hayman & Ncayiyana, 2015 in PASGR).

In a number of African countries, the academics are ageing—and universities are not sufficiently attracting and maintaining competent staff who are increasingly opting for more attractive and conducive work and employment opportunities elsewhere. As the situation to attract new crop of academics has become dire, some countries also face ageing academics. South Africa, for instance, is concerned about ageing professors as a crisis is looming in all the universities as more than 1,430 professors and associate professors from 13 institutions would reach retirement age in the next 10 years (Govendar, 2014). Louw and Godsell (2011) maintain that there is an expected shrinking of the workforce through retirement and their mass exit may have significant implications for the sector.

Hayward and Ncayiyana (2014) hold that the challenge in recruiting and retaining faculty with senior academic qualifications and research experience—a prerequisite for quality research and innovation—represents an existential threat to the region's academic enterprise. Quoting a 2008 report Hayward and Ncayiyana (2014) note:

> Across Africa and disciplines, on average, only 70% of the required faculty positions are filled, and in some departments this is only about 30-40%. Not less than 40% of the faculty members in many universities in Africa are near retirement age, and over 30% of faculty sent overseas for training fail to return.

On the whole, according to Hayward (2010), fewer than 50 per cent of academic staff at African universities held doctoral degrees in 2009. It now appears that the total is even lower according to a data for 10 universities which shows an average of 38 per cent (Hayward & Ncayiyana, 2014) which the World Bank estimated it to 20 per cent (World Bank, 2012). Given the massive expansion over the years and the unconducive environments internally and externally, the figure may have diminished even further for many countries. For instance, a six-country commissioned study on PhD holders puts this figure from the high of 43 per cent in South Africa and Nigeria to 31 per cent in Ghana and 8 per cent in Ethiopia (British Council & DAAD, 2018).

The Commission for University Education of Kenya Report (2017/2018) showed that of 74 per cent of the faculty in public universities and 26 per cent in private universities, the majority are at the lecturer rank (40 per cent) followed by 33 per cent tutorial fellows, 12 per cent senior lecturers, 6 per cent graduate assistants, 5 per cent assistant professors and least of them all, 3 per cent professors. For instance, Rwanda, for the year 2020/2021, recorded 976 PhD, 2,113 Masters, and 871 Bachelors holders; in terms of growth, the PhD holders grew from 16.9 per cent (2016/17) to 19.0 per cent (2017/18) and from 20.3 per cent (in 2018/2019) to 22.7 per cent in 2020/21. A study on Demographics of African Academics (IUCEA, 2022) attributes this grim realities to the absence of programmes or appropriate facilities or qualified faculty; universities' practice of sending many of its faculty needing advanced studies, overseas, mostly to the USA and Europe where many opt to stay and others who return soon leave to go back.

The professoriate constitutes a very small minority of the academic staff in the flagship universities in Africa—and much less so in other 'non-flagship' institutions. With the expansion of the system and the recruitment of often newly minted PhDs, the number of the professoriate across national institutions may be spreading thin. This trend may deprive institutions seasoned academic drivers to enhance quality, increase research productivity, and build capability of graduate supervision, among others (Teferra, 2015a). For instance, of the total of 1,456 academic staff at the flagship university in Uganda, Makerere University, only 85—5.8 per cent—in 2019–20 were full professors. The figures for Tanzanian flagship, University of Dar es Salaam, stood at 3 per cent, where the number of full professors has over the years declined in proportion to the other academic ranks from 8.6 per cent in 2005/06 to 4.7 per cent (Ishengoma, 2017a). The flagship university in South Sudan, the University of Juba, had only 9 professors for the total of 360 academic staff which stands at

2.5 per cent. One of the highest in the continent, in this study, Nigeria's Ibadan University stood at 27 per cent (Teferra, 2015a).

## Centers of Excellence: Emerging Trends

Initiatives in developing research capacity and human capital development in the continent through Centers of Excellence (CoE) are growing. While there are a number of bilateral initiatives as advanced through, for example, DAAD, NORAD (NORHED), other major multilateral-supported ones include the African Union's Pan African University and the World Bank's Centers of Excellence.

Centers of Excellence (CoEs) have been promoted since the 1980s and 1990s in the USA and Canada, followed by developed other countries such as Australia (1990s), Finland (2007), the United Kingdom (2010), and Germany (2011). On the developing side, some Latin American countries have recently been experimenting and launching CoE programmes; and yet some suggest that existing analytical frameworks, coming from developed countries, may not be appropriate for developing countries and the need to explore for unique particularities (Gabriel & Terbullino, 2023) probably more akin to the African context.

Africa's Science and Technology Consolidated Plan of Action (2005–2014), a predecessor to Science, Technology and Innovation Strategy for Africa (STISA-2024) called for the establishment of regional networks of CoEs and a greater mobility of scientists across the continent. While a number of such centres and networks have been established in the continent, the African Science and Technology Fund is yet to materialize (UNESCO, 2021).

A brief discussion in the opening chapter and an extensive one in a dedicated chapter thoroughly discuss this topic in this book.

## Depriving Research: Stunting Growth

Probably, one of the most, if not the most, undisputed challenges of advancing research and innovation in Africa—and anywhere else for that matter—is funding. Even in the most industrialized and wealthy nations, institutions often grapple with inadequate funds, typically for research. According to UNESCO (2021), the G20 still accounts for nine-tenths of research expenditure, researchers, publications, and patents. Although research expenditure rose in most regions between 2014 and 2018, 80 per cent of the countries still invest less than 1 per cent of GDP in R&D. The challenge of research funding is pretty rampant in the so-called developing and emerging countries of the Global South, most typically, Africa, especially sub-Saharan Africa (Johnstone, 2004; Teferra, 2013).

African higher education faces considerable, and complex, challenges as it is striving to expand access while concurrently struggling to maintain quality—both objectives with considerable financial and logistical significance. Improving academic quality and expanding access do not lie on the same (if not necessarily opposite) trajectories, owing largely to the dynamics of resources (Teferra, 2013; Tamrat & Teferra, 2024).

According to the World Bank (2010), the investment required over the 2006 to 2015 period—to increase the capacity of current institutions (classrooms, libraries, laboratories, workshops, and lecture halls), establish new institutions for better distribution across the region, and improve administrative and teaching materials—is estimated at approximately US$45 billion (value in 2006) for public higher education as a whole, of which US$20 billion is for low-income countries. However, very few countries in Africa have the wherewithal to increase the public financing of higher education considerably. The tax base is generally low, and the share of the budget that could be earmarked for higher education is hard to increase when most of these countries must also meet a high demand for other sub-sectors in education and other sectors (Teferra, 2013).

In 2007, the African Union's Executive Council strongly urged all its member states to promote Africa's research and development and develop innovation strategies for wealth creation and economic development by allocating at least 1 per cent of GDP by 2010 (African Union, 2007). Similar calls have been made by UNESCO in a number of its deliberations and policy documents. And yet, virtually none has met that goal, where even South Africa, the leader in the continent, only made it to about 0.8 per cent in 2017 and the figure for the rest of Africa remains a fraction of the 1 per cent threshold, so declared. So, money stands out as probably the major challenge for the development of Africa's research, innovatioin and knowledge production.

A few countries however are making some visible strides to address this chronic challenge. For instance, Ghana and Nigeria have established Trust Funds—a Fund collected from a special value-added tax on goods and services—and Kenya established National Research Fund, as in the case in South Africa.

Compounded by these shortcomings, African research is heavily, and perilously, dependent on foreign-generated funds. The contribution of foreign resources to higher education development, especially research, is considerable. International 'aid' in support of higher education is on average US$600 million annually, one-quarter of all such resources to the education sector in Sub-Saharan Africa. In addition to the small amounts of foreign aid, two main factors limit the impact of this funding source. First, only 26 per cent of the aid to higher education goes directly to African universities and research centres while the rest goes to providing scholarships abroad or is accounted for by directly imputing student costs in the 'donors' universities. Second, such resource is highly fragmented, owing partly to the lack of coordination among donors (Varghese, 2021). Moreover, aid is increasingly supporting the education sector as a whole and is being provided in the form of overall or sector-wide budget support. While the World Bank (2010) declares considerable flexibility in how governments allocate their own budget to education, the practice in terms of flexibility however has not been that robust.

The funding that is generated externally does not only sink into scholarships for the donor's universities. Equally, a host of enterprising 'mid-wife' agencies—based in the donors' capitals—are also systematically siphoning off these resources as coordinating agencies, technical agencies, and so forth. Furthermore, while increasingly a few 'progressive donor' countries and organizations are countering it, much of the research grants in collaboration schemes still often tend to be marshalled at the donor's universities—with considerable size of the pie remaining at the donor's institutions.

This practice is frequently justified through arguments that African countries and institutions lack the requisite skills, capacity, or procedural rigour to effectively manage these resources. Concerns regarding transparency and accountability are often cited as additional barriers. However, these justifications are increasingly being scrutinized, particularly in cases where projects are extended or renewed, sometimes multiple times, with no corresponding transfer of leadership or capacity-building efforts.

Even when sufficient time and resources are available during the project cycle to cultivate local expertise and institutional capability, the transition of leadership in resource management often remains the exception rather than the norm. This persistent pattern underscores a reluctance or systemic oversight in recognizing and utilizing the growing capabilities of African institutions. It perpetuates dependency, undermines ownership, and hampers the development of robust local governance structures essential for sustainable growth and self-reliance. The need to challenge and reform this entrenched practice is vital for fostering genuine partnerships that prioritize mutual respect, capacity building, and the empowerment of African institutions. Such an approach would ensure not only better alignment with local contexts and priorities but also more equitable and effective management of resources in the long term.

A brief discussion in the opening chapter and an extensive one in a dedicated chapter thoroughly discuss financing research in higher education in this book.

## Sound Infrastructure: Enviable Amenity

The manifestation of poor funding, the institutional infrastructure in the continent typically lacks the requisite resources for advancing quality research and graduate programmes. And yet, robust infrastructure is critical for strong research and graduate programmes. Well-equipped and supplied labs, libraries, and facilities; strong and reliable internet access—with the requisite human capital—are paramount for sustained quality research and innovation. And yet, African institutions typically lack these enabling and conducive environments that are key for undertaking meaningful research; and when they exist they are far from adequate.

Since the outbreak of the COVID-19 pandemic, institutions have been urging their respective governments to adequately equip them with the necessary digital infrastructure, as it has now become more evident on its critical role such resources play in advancing teaching, learning, and research. There is now a better sense and understanding of the significance of digital infrastructure in expanding access and enriching the teaching and learning process, though not so much in promoting research.

As research agenda has become increasingly larger and broader so is the need for comparable infrastructure to accommodate those needs. This means that advancing major research agenda requires building major research infrastructure—and sustaining it as well. In order to attract major research initiatives into institutions, for that matter countries, the capacity of building such infrastructure has become more paramount. The massive Square Kilometre Array (SKA) project, an international effort to build the world's largest radio telescope, based in South Africa is one excellent example.

In Kenya, big information technology companies—such as Microsoft, Alphabet Google, Cisco, Nokia, Siemens—have been attracted to establish their offices in the country. For instance, IBM agreed to collaborate with the Government of Kenya in research and human resource development to develop at least four PhD research scientists annually and share proceeds from any innovations (Brooks, 2020; Ndemo, 2022). Similarly, in Rwanda the establishment of Kigali Innovation City is anticipated to earn it a major boost as a tech hub. The project is designed to accommodate world-class universities, research and development centres, technology companies, and innovative start-ups (Karanga, 2021). Favourable government policies including the allocation and provision of land and facilities, among others have been instrumental in attracting and advancing research and innovation in countries where such measures have been systematically taken.

An extensive study on African research infrastructure in this book emphasizes that existing physical and digital infrastructure and resources in Africa, that are typically lacking, must be leveraged and networked to increase utilization efficiency at a national and regional level and reduction in maintenance and operating costs through shared services. The study posits that, at high policy levels, the importance of research infrastructure in achieving Africa's socio-economic development objectives has now received increased recognition. It concludes that this improved awareness and recognition are essential to strengthening and prioritizing the development of research and innovation infrastructure across the continent; but states that this remains far from clear how best to formulate, implement, evaluate, and govern policies, strategies, and frameworks on research infrastructures at regional and continental levels to ensure mutually reinforcing and complementary benefits for countries in Africa. A brief account on the topic is also provided in the opening chapter.

## Misplaced Egalitarianism: Undercutting Differentiation

Africa currently boasts some 2,000 universities enrolling an estimated 20 million students. African higher education has seen massive expansion in a rather short span of time with implications for quality education—and research. Much of the expansion, including in graduate programmes, often has taken place without commensurate resources—human, material, logistical, administrative, and management capacity—aggravated by the massive enrolment pressure.

One of the challenges of advancing research in African institutions emanates from a sense of egalitarianism that unduly pervades in a nation's universities—regardless of their age, profile, and status, largely because of the sensitivities of establishing hierarchies in the national institutional and knowledge grid. In some countries, this tendency is so pervasive that it tends to disregard even the oldest and well-established post-independence institutions which already enjoy national prominence. Increasingly, but troublingly so, many new public institutions are being established in Africa in which crass politics are interlaced with narrow ethnic, religious, and other sectarian lines, which thwart the emergence of a robust academic and research practice and culture. Such practices and phenomena put an immense hurdle in the path of 'Africa's knowledge project' and needed to be pursued with considerable sensitivity and firm persuasion. In the end, an unadulterated egalitarian predisposition that dangerously ignores a country's existing and potential competitive knowledge advantage comes with serious consequences (Teferra, 2015b).

According to Altbach (2007) allowing such 'flagship' or 'research' universities to flourish requires a way to differentiate them from other types of postsecondary institutions, provide funding at a higher level, and legitimize the idea that these institutions are indeed special and serve a crucial role in society. To be sure the imperative of differentiation is evident as even the most advanced and richest countries could afford—or plan to have—only a few them. Institutions designated as research universities are few and far between. In many countries, there may just be one or two research universities because of their cost and resources available. Even in fairly large countries, the number of such institutions is often small—in the United Kingdom, perhaps 20 as in Japan and China (Altbach, 2007), though these numbers have soared over the last 15 years as in China where a more nuanced differentiation approach, of not just institutions but programmes, identifies some 140 institutions and over 300 subject disciplines (Sharma, 2022).

In reaction to an affirmation of an outstanding role of human capital development, the Japanese government has announced the creation of the 10-trillion-yen (approximately 70 billion dollars) University Endowment Fund to support the building of world-class research universities. Those universities deemed capable of achieving research of the highest international standards were to be designated as universities for research excellence and allocated a share of the fund's profits with intention to dramatically strengthen their research power by providing long-term and stable financial support (Japan.gov, 2022).

In India, the National Education Policy 2020 suggests that about 100 universities be identified as research universities in the near future. These universities will focus strongly on research and doctoral programmes, in addition to having high quality education at bachelor and masters' degree levels. The rest of the more than 900 universities will be teaching universities, which will mainly deliver high quality education. These universities are also expected to do a modest amount of research and have small doctoral programmes. This differentiation is considered extremely important, or else, all universities trying to do both research and education without adequate resources or the quality of faculty that is needed for high quality research, means that they will end up being mediocre at both (Altbach & Jalote, 2020).

For Africa's higher education to truly thrive, institutional differentiation and diversity must be prioritized over blanket egalitarianism and isomorphic tendencies. Striving for a uniform higher education system that mirrors ideals of populist egalitarianism may undermine efforts to meet complex developmental goals, stifle innovation, and limit global competitiveness. Effective nation-building and economic advancement are fostered by advancing a diverse range of institutions—each with unique strengths, specializations, and missions aligned with national needs and regional contexts. Egalitarianism in higher education, while rooted in noble intentions, could lead to homogeneity that impedes creativity, limits specialization, reduces the system's adaptability to changing needs, and inhibits selective and systematic approaches. A one-size-fits-all approach can inadvertently create 'isomorphic clones' rather than fostering a dynamic and resilient educational landscape. When all institutions are expected to operate at a uniform level, they may lose the ability to innovate or address specific local and regional needs effectively. The world's leading education systems, have achieved strength by embracing both the diversity and specialization of institutions, which collectively contribute to a vibrant educational ecosystem. In short, differentiation—rather than uniformity—provides the flexibility necessary for addressing diverse social and economic challenges (Teferra, 2012)—and global competitiveness.

In an article 'African universities should differentiate their missions clearly' Paterson and Luescher (2022), quoting Tade Aina, a senior program officer earlier at Mastercard Foundation and now at Carnegie Corporation of New York, note that 'The notion that there is a single ideal university must be resisted in favour of one that values a plurality of institutional types and promotes intentional differentiation in national higher education systems'. This affirms further that the culture of isomorphism that pervades academic institutions needs to be systematically resisted.

Differentiation allows institutions to focus on areas of strength, such as research-intensive universities, vocational and technical training institutes, community colleges, and specialized research centres. This focus enhances quality, fosters innovation, and meets a range of needs that are central to both national development and Africa's position in the global knowledge economy. By fostering distinct institutional profiles, Africa can create a higher education system that maximizes access and equity while promoting excellence across the board.

Isomorphic pressures, however, are still strong, as international ranking systems, funding frameworks, and accreditation models often reward homogenization, pushing institutions to resemble those in advanced countries. For African universities to assert global competitiveness, they must resist such pressures and instead establish models that align with their unique challenges, resources, and aspirations. Universities across Africa would thus benefit from an intentional pursuit of diversity and specialization to serve as agents of national development. Differentiated roles and missions should be backed by policies that incentivize specialization, foster innovative funding models, and prioritize sustainable growth. Achieving this balance calls for policy frameworks that promote institutional autonomy and flexibility while addressing core areas such as access, equity, and quality.

Despite considerable reluctance, some signs of a differentiated higher education system—in response to the growing narratives, imperatives, and needs—are evident in the continent. For instance, Ethiopia, a country which has registered phenomenal growth in higher education has made efforts in differentiating its higher education sector, whose implications are yet to be discerned. In South Africa, a differentiated higher education system is evident, as is also a rising interest in 'growing our own timber' in respective institutions—meaning producing own academic staff and doctorates at same institution (Teferra, 2015c).

In conclusion, Africa's higher education systems will thrive by promoting institutional diversity and specialization, laying the groundwork for a sustainable and resilient educational ecosystem. Embracing differentiated missions and specialized roles, rather than prioritizing equality across institutions, is crucial for fostering research and graduate education in Africa, key both for national growth and competitive global engagement.

## International Dimension: Double-Sided Sword?

The importance of internationalization of higher education, in the era of the knowledge economy, has been growing in leaps and bounds for its anticipated contribution to quality higher education, advancing research, regional/global integration, and fostering human resource capacity. The elements of internationalization—i.e., mobility of scholars and students, regional and international networks, quality regimes (accreditation and ranking bodies), curricular reform, research initiatives, publication and communication (journals and databases), and new forms of educational delivery—pose new challenges, opportunities, and risks to the higher education system around the world. This situation especially prevails in Africa, as the weakest player in the internationalization of higher education (Teferra, 2014).

The manifestation of internationalization in African higher education research and graduate education is paramount. As noted above, quite a substantial amount of resources for research in Africa is generated from external (international) resources rendering it heavily dependent on them—with consequences for the trajectory of research, sustainability, and equity. Until such time that African countries commit dedicated, sustained, and meaningful resources for advancing research, the impact of the dependency may remain undiminished. It remains intriguing why countries which commit their sizeable resources to education and higher education, fail to commit (sizeable) resources to advancing research—when this has proven to be critical to development and advance global competitiveness.

Academic mobility lies at the epicentre of internationalization and the internationalization discourse (Teferra, 2020). The mobility of scholars and students in advancing research, innovation and graduate education plays a key role in the realization of the internationalization phenomenon.

The IAU (2015) affirms that, student mobility remains the most important internationalization activity though it benefits less than 5 per cent of students; and governments, institutions and individuals participate in this exercise for different reasons. That noted, the mobility however has been typically unidirectional in nature where only African students travelling overseas, with only limited academics doing the same.

Massive brain drain, the manifestation of academic mobility, has been widely criticized as an artefact of the phenomenon of internationalization. A lot has been written on the impact of a disproportionate number of African students not returning to the continent, though the manifestation of the phenomenon has seen considerable changes, among others, with the advent of enabling technologies. This has been particularly so following the outbreak of COVID-19 which has seen a very active involvement of the African intellectual diaspora in research and development, albeit largely focused on the pandemic.

While acknowledging that internationalization is 'an important policy and strategy for most universities worldwide', even the IAU (2015) has expressed caution about its unintended consequences and tried to alert institutions (particularly in the South) of the need to ensure that its outcomes are positive and bring reciprocal benefits to all concerned. Possible unintended outcomes of internationalization mentioned by the IAU include uneven benefits arising from differential access to resources and the entrenching of asymmetrical power relations between institutions based (again) on unequal access to the resources and capacities needed to successfully implement internationalization strategies (Ishengoma, 2017b).

A brief discussion in the opening chapter and an extensive one in a dedicated chapter thoroughly discuss internationalization in this book.

## Intellectual Diaspora: Untapped Treasure

A literature on the mobility of African academics and scholars often on the account of deficit, described as brain drain, abound. Africa has seen a massive exodus of its intelligentsia over the years due to social, economic, and political upheavals that chronically engulfed the continent. Universities have lost some of their brightest and smartest academics and researchers driven not only by internal factors but greener pastures elsewhere. This has had a massive impact on the socio-economic development of the continent and remains a major challenge to research and development in Africa as studies reveal that as many as 20,000 professionals exit the African continent each year to Western countries (WHO, 2017).

The effort to return African immigrant intellectuals to their homelands permanently has been an uphill struggle—and had been ill-advised. As a consequence, a new discourse and approach to mobilize intellectual diaspora communities to enhance the continent's social, economic, and intellectual progress without necessarily relocating them physically has been gathering momentum (Teferra, 2004; Woldegiyorgis in this book). That momentum has gathered more steam as efforts to deploy the intellectual diaspora has intensified riding on the back of technological advancements that propelled it further—creating a unique opportunity and environment.

The dominant discourse around the African academic diaspora follows a distinct pattern of deficit: the wide-ranging costs of losing some of the continent's best and brightest intellectuals. However, this clouds the expansive and often innovative relationships that African academic diasporans have forged with scholars and institutions across the continent—relationships that build and reinforce both scholarly and personal engagements (Foulds and Zeleza, 2014).

Increasingly, there is a growing interest to draw the intellectual diaspora to support research, graduate supervision, teaching and learning, and networking in African universities. A flurry of activities including dedicated programmes such as the Carnegie Corporation of New York's African Diaspora initiative are cases in point. Oanda (2015) notes that.

> While academic discussions on the negative effects of intellectual brain drain have been widely documented in the literature, the recourse to the academic diaspora as a resource to revitalise higher education institutions in Africa is recent. This recent positive consideration of the academic diaspora has largely been driven by academics in the African Diaspora, a reaction to the increased visibility of the African Diaspora generally as an economic resource to develop Africa, as attested by the African Union's recognition of the Diaspora as its 6th region.

The potential of scholastic capital of the diaspora community can be gauged by the staggering statistics of the volume and quality of this community abroad, many of whose members pursue academic and scholarly professions as university professors, researchers, engineers, medical doctors, and high-level technicians. For instance, in the USA alone, one in two African diaspora has a university degree. The need to mobilize this potentially powerful force goes beyond the oft-cited economic benefits as it plays a considerable role in stimulating and catalysing home-based academic and scholarly institutions (Teferra, 2003, 2018, 2021a, 2021b).

An increasing number of African countries have developed national diaspora policies and strategies that see beyond the traditional contribution of their diasporas in financial remittance and foreign direct investment. Intellectual remittance, public diplomacy and political leverage, transfer and adoption of technology, and innovation and entrepreneurship are some of the new areas gaining emphasis. While the extent to which such policies and strategies have been furnished with the appropriate institutional infrastructure and required resources deserves a critical investigation on a country-by-country basis, it is widely observed that the practice of engaging with the diaspora cascades down to local and institutional levels. One of the areas where such a pattern is observed is higher education—research and graduate education in particular (Woldegiyorgis, in this book). As diaspora engagements typically occur in informal and ad hoc basis commonly relying on personal connections and experiences, professional networks, and relations with alma maters, starting as informal communication and taking shape in due course, this reality makes it difficult to account for the role of the academic diaspora in the advancement of graduate education and research in Africa (Teferra, 2005; Woldegiyorgis, 2021).

The role and contribution of the intellectual diaspora in advancing higher education in Africa are now well established. Countries are actively seeking to tap them in a more enhanced way through duly established offices at ministries, typically foreign/home affairs, and international offices at institutional level. It appears that the world has now been conditioned to transition from the deficit laden and emotive ridden discourse in the form of 'brain drain' that dominated the dialogue on human mobility for a long time, to a trendy, rewarding and pragmatic form in 'brain circulation'. This growing trend is robustly manifesting itself at the centre of the interchange between the intellectual diaspora and higher education in developing and emerging countries (Teferra, 2021a).

As the diaspora is widely acknowledged as a critical resource for the development and revitalization of higher education in Africa, these developments are vital in advancing research, innovation, and graduate studies in Africa. However, tapping that resource, and forging mutually beneficial academic relationships with diasporans and Africa-based scholars and institutions, remains tricky (Dell, 2020) and fraught with challenges (Teferra, 2003). A brief discussion in the opening chapter and an extensive one in a dedicated chapter discuss intellectual diaspora in this book.

## Research Leadership: Quest for Key Captains

Leadership plays a critical role in advancing research by fostering a conducive environment for innovation, collaboration, and growth. Effective leaders set strategic priorities, secure funding, and build networks that enable researchers to thrive. Good and able leadership in research enhances team performance by promoting interaction and advance collaboration which are vital for addressing complex research challenges (Musiige & Maassen, 2015, pp. 112–113) and advance innovation; and its lack could also be a hurdle (Sodedji, Assogbadjo, and Osiru in this book).

The unique nature of governance and leadership in higher education institutions has been well established. Even under less straining financial and resource states, leading institutions successfully, however success is defined, is not an easy fate owing to the fact that typically, university leadership is more collegial than hierarchical. Furthermore, the quality of products, such as graduates and research outputs as well as organizational processes, are difficult to (readily) establish their worth (Cohen et al., 1972). The changes in external and global environments and institutional governance, in terms of accountability and autonomy, over the years have made the leadership terrain more strenuous.

There is a consensus that research leaders are at the forefront of their field in terms of publication quality and numbers, attract large research grants, supervise and mentor graduate students, successfully implement large-scale research programmes and leading and running large research groups and large research facilities. Furthermore, research leadership involves a continuous learning journey with pre-defined stages and transition points: early career (doctoral candidates, doctoral graduates, and postdoctoral fellows) and mid-career (managing small research teams). In Africa, little evidence exists on the styles and perspectives of leadership within research contexts. That noted, African research leadership can be considered a combination of leading self, leading others, and leading research excellence (Vitae, 2020: 11)—a tall order.

Successful leadership of institutions often depends on, among others, seasoned personnel that are endowed with sound academic exposure and extensive experience. Developing and leading a robust research programme thus particularly requires eminent and well-established researchers and academics supported with a host of resources—often lacking in the continent.

Strong leadership helps navigate these limitations by building partnerships, both at home and globally. Leadership is pivotal in advancing research in Africa, as it drives innovation, resource mobilization, international collaboration, ethical standards, and institutional development, all of which are crucial for overcoming the continent's unique challenges. Effective research leadership ensures that strategic priorities align with local and global needs. African leaders in research institutions and universities thus play a key role in setting research agendas, fostering collaboration, and securing funding, all of which are essential for building robust research ecosystems.

The proliferation of academic institutions in Africa in a short span of time is such that only a small number of high-calibre expertise commensurate with the underlying roles and tasks exist in these institutions. As also noted elsewhere, a large number of prominent African academics are ageing and are also migrating in effect depriving the leadership landscape. Furthermore, the quality of doctoral training in the continent is such that, it is not sufficiently geared towards building the requisite tenets of research leadership.

The massive growth of enrolment across Africa in a short span of time has put increased strain on its heavily burdened higher education sector, which struggles with limited financial, physical, and human resources. There are insufficient numbers of experienced staff to meet the growing demand, putting academics early in their careers under increased pressure, often with very heavy teaching and administrative workloads. This, in turn, potentially undermines the quality of instruction and research output, and the ability of institutions to recruit and retain talented staff (Association of Commonwealth Universities, 2016) with implications to the development of research leadership in the continent.

It should be noted that even when individuals with such calibre exist in the continent, they are often preoccupied with tedious administrative and management roles and/or self-serving private activities such as moonlighting or consultancy services. Furthermore, even when the requisite leadership calibre exists, it is often an onerous task to lead financially strained institutions however committed they may be.

## International Regimes: The Realm of Academic Collaboration

The world is actively engaging with Africa as expressed in multiple high-profile country-to-continent summits such as China-Africa, India-Africa, Japan-Africa, Russia-Africa, and USA-Africa and continent-to-continent summits such as the Europe-Africa summit. Components of such summits and communiques speak of strengthening and supporting research within the higher education sector and beyond.

At continental and international platforms, numerous dialogues, policies, and strategies to advance research in the continent have been meted over the years. Some of these major recent efforts include the African Higher Education Summit in Dakar 2015, the Continental Education Strategy for Africa (CESA 2016–2025), Science, Technology and Innovation Strategy for Africa (STISA) of the African Union, and the establishment of the African Research Universities Alliance (ARUA). Of course, virtually all relevant African higher education conferences and seminars underscore the significance of advancing research and the need to realize it. There is no apparent lack of 'political' support for advancing research.

Some countries have had a robust research and graduate education development schemes in the continent for a long time. For instance, Norway has dedicated schemes through programmes such as NUFU, NORHED, NORPART (NORAD, 2023) and so is Germany, through DAAD. The extensive and massive contribution of Norwegian and Swedish support to the development of Tanzanian and Ethiopian research and graduate education through partnerships with their respective institutions is a case in point. The strengthening of science granting councils in Africa to support research through the consortium of numerous development partners is another notable example of international interventions in African research.

US-based foundations are also known to have played a pivotal role in the development of contemporary higher education and research in Africa over the years. However, while a few such institutions such as Mastercard and Carnegie continue to support the sector, the enthusiasm for supporting the sector since the Partnership for Higher Education in Africa, a consortium of first four and then later seven US-based foundations in 2000s, is yet to re-emerge.

Development partners declare their global engagements typically guided by major development regimes as SDGs. And yet the SDGs—with 17 goals and 169 targets—are so broad and so comprehensive that one could capture virtually all development challenges in the SDGs with effect of fragmentation in their interventions, as well as incoherence in terms of focus. Even when a common topical theme is identified for intervention, the manner, scope, and modalities would matter in delivering a meaningful and sustained outcome, diminishing the impact and effect of the interventions.

The Global North remains the epicentre of the world academic collaborations. Countries in the Global South, typically the so-called developing countries, have mainly collaborated vertically rather than (and including) horizontally. The Global South remains at the margins of this phenomenon of research and knowledge brokerage (Teferra, 2022). There is near unanimity—and a renewed call—for South-South collaboration which is often astoundingly sustained through the intervention of sources—and forces—in the North. Much has been said about the need to change the paradigm—and this external dependency, often without commensurate follow up action calling for a more progressive discourses on academic collaboration. The 'polygamous' nature of collaborations, and the unequal and inequitable nature, particularly in the context of Africa may, however, require a deeper and more extensive analysis of this mode and pattern of research and academic collaboration (Teferra, 2022a, 2022b).

A multitude of intentions drives institutions to engage in academic collaborations, mainly dictated by necessity. The imperatives of academic collaboration are many and varied and include generating resources, developing academic capacity, exchanging experiences, and enhancing the institutional profile. Institutions also engage in collaboration to pursue mega initiatives (such as human genome projects) and tackle major global challenges (like climate change and diseases such as COVID-19). Such endeavours mainly take place within the framework of North–North and, to certain extent, North–South collaboration. South-South collaboration has been less evident, although this trend appears to be changing steadily with growing interest, focus and drive in these regions (Teferra et al., 2022). This noted, the intentions to academic collaboration varies from region to region and country to country, though considerable similarities are apparent.

For that matter, to participate in major regional and international research collaborations—for instance in human genomics, space, pandemic, environment, climate—national institutions should be able to afford decent resources and infrastructure which are important—and may be mandatory—for research collaboration and cooperation. A basic minimum capacity threshold needs to be fulfilled for advancing and sustaining meaningful cooperation (Teferra et al., 2022) compounding the nature and praxis of collaboration.

A far-reaching new Charter seeks to rebalance the academic collaboration ecosystem in an equitable manner and give African research its rightful position as an equal player in global scientific production. The Charter has been facilitated by two universities in Africa, i.e., the University of Cape Town and the University of South Africa, and the University of Bristol in the United Kingdom. The Charter has garnered considerable endorsements primarily from the Association of African Universities and key regional university associations, higher education institutions, and academic organizations and networks in Africa and beyond including the African Academy of Sciences, the Council for the Development of Social Science Research in Africa (CODESRIA), and the International Network for Higher Education in Africa (INHEA).

## Conclusion

The creation of new knowledge has become a global project, but Africa's voice is often missing. If it is to take control of its own future, Africa must advance knowledge production systematically—and vigorously. Research is therefore very critical for the development of the continent which faces a plethora of social, economic, ecological, climatic, and health challenges.

The African higher education landscape has witnessed massive growth in the last decades with huge implications for research and innovation. While the unprecedented growth has spurred expansion of graduate programmes in numerous countries—in a number of cases mounted to advance research and also capacity building—it has had mixed results. It is true that the graduate programmes promptly provided the requisite academics for the sprouting institutions and programmes, but the overstretched systems did not often sufficiently focus on or guarantee the quality of the outputs in terms of research and graduate studies. It is often stated that whatever research capacity and research calibre that may have existed pre-expansion, that situation has not advanced in accordance with the trajectory of the growth. In fact, the expansion has meant that academics turned all their time and commitment to lectures as universities grapple with overcrowded classes and schedules, relegating research, as one of the principal tasks of academics.

Whatever research undertaking that takes place in Africa, it typically happens within the realm of the university environment except in few countries in French speaking Africa and South Africa—Africa's research powerhouse, with a robust research engagement outside of universities. Middle-income aspirant countries such as Kenya, which tend to attract a fair share of multinational corporations, has also shown growth in research capabilities. This as it may, the primary focus of this book lies on research in African universities whose typical staple comes from their graduate studies.

African countries are striving to build the capacity of research, innovation as well as promote graduate education spurred by multiple concurrent imperatives. That as it may, the challenges facing their advancement in the continent abound. The issues that African research grapples with are not simply those discussed here in this book. Numerous other challenges besetting the advancement of the knowledge domain remain and some of these include poor academic freedom and institutional autonomy, language barriers, lacking research policies, and academic/research culture, perceptions of the global academic community towards African research, and impact of rankings, among others. For instance, most African countries lack a coherent research policy, if at all. According to a sub-Saharan Africa study on research and PhD capacities, the majority of Nigerian deputy vice chancellors and registrars interviewed were unaware of any national research agenda to serve as a guide for various universities' research focus. Data from the sampled institutions indicated that the decision to initiate or establish PhD programmes lay with the respective departments and faculties informed by a number of institutional factors such as availability of qualified and experienced lecturers or supervisors in the faculty or departments. The research priorities of the PhD students in turn were usually guided by their interests and career choices and not for the fulfilment of any national development or research agenda. In terms of external parties using research produced at tertiary institutions, it was observed that multinational donor agencies did turn to practical research reports that addressed specific policy problems (British Council & DAAD, 2018).

It is well established that academic freedom plays a vital role in promoting research and innovation. And yet, in many African countries, the traditional threats to the exercise of academic freedom inherent in any scientific research activity still remain, even as new local and international ones emerge. Unwittingly or not, scientists can necessarily, challenge dominant socio-political discourses, or even holders of knowledge or obsolescent technology with their discoveries, inventions, or innovations, thus needing that privilege to effectively fulfill their functions (Khelfaoui & Ogachi, 2011). An extensive study by Appiagyei-Atua et al. (2016) indicates that while Africa has come a long way in restructuring its laws to accommodate African academic freedom, most countries are lagging behind. Further, it would appear that the previous impetus to protect academic freedom provided by the Kampala and Dar es Salaam Declarations on academic freedom has dissipated. That said, the conditions for the exercise of institutional autonomy and academic freedom have improved in many African universities over the last two decades, since the eve of the twenty-first century due to the fizzling of one party-governments that in the past undermined institutional autonomy and academic freedom. However, recent surveys on the quality of academic freedom in the continent show mixed results, but that tends towards an increasing abrogation of academic freedom, both directly and indirectly in most of the countries (Oanda, 2023).

Rankings also have direct implications on advancing research and innovation in the continent. Invariably, rankings place most African institutions at the bottom end of the ranking tables while an exceptionally handful listed in the 'enviable' zones. This controversial phenomenon (Teferra, 2021b) has considerable implications for those at the lowest rung of the ladder, for instance in institutional collaboration where the tendencies of partnership interests remain strong among 'equals'. Similarly, funding organizations are also known to be gravitated towards highly ranked institutions in the global knowledge market place where vigorous competition is rampant and African institutions are not sufficiently geared up to it.

Research and innovation are critical for the development of the continent which faces a plethora of social, academic, economic, political, ecological, climatic, and health upheavals. In the knowledge and information era where they are considered a panacea to these challenges, advocating for their advancement may appear unwarranted, if not redundant. However, decades-old experience and trajectory of the continent on research development dictates that a strong emphasis needs to be constantly placed in advancing research and its mechanisms of delivery.

The knowledge spill over theory of entrepreneurship underscores that for knowledge, in this case, research output, to contribute to innovation and hence economic development, it must move from universities and other knowledge producers to knowledge users, particularly entrepreneurial incubators or else the economy will not significantly benefit from knowledge production (Acs et al., 2009). This is to note that producing knowledge, through either solo or collaborative research, on its own is inadequate as the phenomenon of what is called Swedish Paradox—high R&D performance but low aggregate economic performance—points.

Finally, the drive for the advancement of knowledge has become a global project; and Africa has to make considerable catch up by marshalling sustained resources and favourable policies. If Africa is to take control of its own future, it must advance research and knowledge production more systematically, more deliberately—and more robustly.

## References

Acs, Z. J., Braunerhjelm, P., Audretsch, B. D., & Carlsson, B. (2009). The knowledge spillover theory of entrepreneurship. *Small Business Economics, 32*, 15–30.

African Union. (2007). Decisions and declarations. Assembly of the African Union Eighth Ordinary Session, 29–30 January 2007, Addis Ababa, ETHIOPIA, Assembly/AU/Dec.134–164 (VIII); Assembly/AU/Decl.1–6 (VIII).

African Union (2015). Agenda 2063: The Africa we want. https://au.int/en/agenda2063/overview

Altbach, P. G. (2006). The tyranny of citations. In P. G. Altbach (Ed.), International higher education: Reflections on policy and practice (pp. 87–90). Boston College.

Altbach, P. G. (2007). Doctoral education: Present realities and future trends. In J. J. F. Forest & P. G. Altbach (Eds.), *International handbook of higher education* (pp. 65–81). Springer.

Altbach, P. G., & Jalote, P. (2020, September 26). *When will India build world-class research universities?* https://tinyurl.com/9cpah7xf

Ansah, F., Swanzy, P., & Obeng, R. A. (2019, Jan 11). *No PhD, no tenure policy—Is it the best way forward?* https://tinyurl.com/528bupf4

Appiagyei-Atua, K., Beiter, K. D., & Karran, T. (2016). A review of academic freedom in African universities through the prism of the 1997 ILO/UNESCO recommendation. *AAUP Journal of Academic Freedom, 7*, 1–23. https://tinyurl.com/hufhtsdy

Association of Commonwealth Universities. (2016). *The next generation: Ideas and experience in African researcher support*. https://tinyurl.com/3jxma8e5

AUC: https://tinyurl.com/kukcaewr

Becker, G. S. (1962). Investment in human capital: A theoretical analysis. *Journal of Political Economy*, (70) 5, 9–49.

British Council and DAAD. (2018). *Research and PhD capacities in Sub-Saharan Africa—Nigeria report*. British Council.

Brooks. (2020). *Top 5 reasons why Kenya is a leading tech hub*. https://tinyurl.com/4f5ekf7x

Cohen, M. D., March, J. G., & Olsen, J. P. (1972). A garbage can model of organisational choice. *Administrative Science Quarterly, 17*(1), 1–25.

Commission for University Education. (2017/2018). Kenya. https://tinyurl.com/y4yzvnt3

DAAD. https://tinyurl.com/4d9c3k3s

Dell, S. (2020, February 22). Tapping into the diaspora—The search for sustainability. *University World News*. https://tinyurl.com/bde7fmsb

Foulds, K., & Zeleza, P. T. (2014). The African academic diaspora and African higher education. *International Higher Education*, (76), 16–17.

Gabriel, P., & Terbullino, C. (2023). Centres of excellence in Latin America: How do these differ from other experiences? *Science and Public Policy, 50*, 591–602. https://doi.org/10.1093/scipol/scad003

Govendar, P. (2014, April 6). Fear of brain drain as profs retire en masse. *Sunday Times*. Retirement. https://tinyurl.com/33vhp4z9

Hayward, F. M. (2010). Graduate education in Sub-Saharan Africa. In D. Teferra & H. Greijn (Eds.), *Higher education and globalisation: Challenges, threats, and opportunities for Africa* (pp. 33–49). Maastricht University/ Boston College.

Hayward, F. M., & Ncayiyana, D. J. (2014). Confronting the challenges of graduate education in Sub-Saharan Africa and prospects for the future. *IJAHE, 2014*, 173–216.

Hayward, F. & Ncayiyana, D. J. (2015) Confronting the challenges of graduate education in SubSaharan Africa. *International Higher Education, 79*, 16–18. Winter 2015

IAU. (2015). *Internationalization of higher education: An evolving landscape, locally and globally*. IAU.

Ishengoma, M. J. (2017a). The role of African Flagship Universities: The case of the university of Dar es Salaam. In D. Teferra (Ed.), *Flagship universities in Africa* (pp. 373–423). Palgrave MacMillan.

Ishengoma, J. M. (2017b). North–South research collaborations and their impact on capacity building: A Southern perspective. In T. Halvorsen & J. Nossum (Eds.), *North–South knowledge networks towards equitable collaboration between academics, donors and universities*. African Minds. 149–186.

IUCEA. (2022). Demographics of African faculty in the East African Community. Interim Report December 2022.

Japangov. (2022, September 30). *Research universities seek to be competitive and collaborative*. https://tinyurl.com/mrzpwpcv

Johnstone, D. B. (2004). Higher education finance and accessibility: Tuition fees ans student loans in sub-saharan Africa. *Journal of Higher Education in Africa, 2*(2), 11-36.

Karanga, M. (2021). *Leveraging Rwanda's position as a tech hub*. https://tinyurl.com/3eesu2hm

Khelfaoui, H., & Ogachi, I. O. (2011). Introduction—Academic freedom in Africa: Between local powers and international Donors. *Journal of Higher Education in Africa, 9*(1&2), v–xiii.

Louw, J., & Godsell, G. (2011). Multiple paths to success. In N. Cloete, J. Mouton, & C. Sheppard (Ed.), *Doctoral education in South Africa* (pp. 125–172). African Minds.

Musiige, G., & Maassen, P. (2015) Faculty perceptions of the factors that influence research productivity at Makerere University. In N. Cloete, P. Maassen, & T. Bailey (Eds.), *Knowledge production and contradictory functions in African higher education*. African Minds.

National Research Fund-Kenya https://tinyurl.com/bdewuk5u

Ndemo, B. (2022). *Kenya becoming a global ICT hub*. https://tinyurl.com/n3e9uewp

Norad. https://tinyurl.com/3x4f6e86. Accessed on August 8, 2023.

Oanda, I. (2023). The hollowing out of academic freedom from African universities; from external capture to internal implosion. In R. J Tierney, F. Rizvi, & K. Ercikan (Eds.), *International encyclopaedia of education* (4th ed., pp. 114–123). Elsevier. https://tinyurl.com/ty6c6bxy

Oanda, I. O. (2015). Engaging the African academic diaspora: How ready are universities in Africa?. *IJAHE*, 25–53.

Ouedraogo, I., Tabi, H. N., Ondoa, H. A., & Jiya, A. N. (2022). Institutional quality and human capital development in Africa. *Economic Systems, 46*(1), 100937. https://tinyurl.com/3n3fdwap

Paterson, M., & Luescher, T. M. (2022, April 28). *African universities should differentiate their missions clearly*. https://tinyurl.com/2s3ezcwf

Petchko, K. (2018). Theory and theoretical frameworks. In K. Petchko (Ed.), *How to write about economics and public policy* (pp. 181–206). Academic Press. https://tinyurl.com/2h9vjzmu

Science Granting Councils Initiative. (SGCI). https://sgciafrica.org/

Schultz, T. W. (1961). Investment in human capital. *American Economic Review, 51*(1), 1–17.

Sharma, J. (2022, February 17). *More universities become 'world class' to meet China ambitions.* https://tinyurl.com/35xkuy4w

SOFRECO. (2007). *Study on the contribution of the alumni and diaspora to the joint Africa-EU strategy: Final report.* https://tinyurl.com/bdz697df

Solarin, S. A., Gil-Alana, L. A., Hernández-Herrera, M. (2024). Persistence of human capital development in OECD countries over 150 years: Evidence from linear and nonlinear fractional integration methods, *Economic Systems, 48*(3), 101215. https://tinyurl.com/3xtxczjp

Tamrat, W., & Teferra, D. (2024). Africa's position in the global private higher education sphere: Progress and trajectories. In W. Tamrat & D. Teferra (Eds.), *Emerging dynamics in the provision of private higher education in Africa* (pp. 247–268). Palgrave MacMillan.

Teferra, D. (2003). *Unleashing the forces of the Diaspora: Capitalizing on brain drain in the era of information and communication technologies.* https://tinyurl.com/396er88d

Teferra, D. (2004). Mobilizing Africa's intellectual diaspora. *International Higher Education,* 20–22.

Teferra, D. (2005). Brain circulation: Unparalleled opportunities, underlying challenges, and outmoded presumptions. *Journal of Studies in International Education, 9*(3), 229–250. https://tinyurl.com/29cw2nyc

Teferra, D. (2012, October 22). Construct, re-construct or self-destruct: Strategies for Africa. *Inside Higher Education.* https://tinyurl.com/ysyxk7fe

Teferra, D. (2013). Introduction. Palgrave Macmillan. In D. Teferra (Ed.), *Funding higher education in Sub-Saharan Africa* (pp. 1–12). Palgrave MacMillan.

Teferra, D. (2014). Charting African higher education: Perspectives at a glance. *International Journal of African Higher Education, 1*(1), 9–21.

Teferra, D. (2018). *Unleashing the forces of the Ethiopian Intellectual Diaspora.* https://tinyurl.com/28n238hf

Teferra, D. (2015a). African flagship universities: Their neglected contributions. *Higher Education, 2016*(72), 79–99.

Teferra, D. (2015b, March 20). Lobbying for higher education on parallel agendas. *University World News.* https://tinyurl.com/3tyr2xmk.

Teferra, D. (2015c). Manufacturing—and exporting—Excellence and "Mediocrity": Doctoral education in South Africa. *South African Journal of Higher Education, 29*(5), 8–19.

Teferra, D. (2020). The irrelevance of the re-configured definition of internationalisation to the global south: Intention versus coercion. *International Journal of African Higher Education, 7*(2), 157–172.
Teferra, D. (2021a). Editorial: The role of the African Intellectual Diaspora in advancing higher education. *IJAHE, 8*(2), 1–9.
Teferra, D. (2021b). The treacherous adventure of ranking African Universities. In E. Hazelkorn & G. Mihut (Eds.), *Research handbook on university rankings: Theory methodology, influence and impact* (pp. 399–412). Edward Elgar Publishing.
Teferra, D., & Tamrat, W. (2021). Box 1.1. Higher educaiton in Africa. *In the handbook of international higher education*....(p. 5).
TETFund https://tinyurl.com/fu2x7bkt
UNESCO Institute for Statistics. (2015). Researchers per million inhabitants (FTE), 2014.
UNESCO. (2005). Towards knowledge societies.
UNESCO. (2021). *Unesco science report.* https://tinyurl.com/4xb3ksuy
Varghese, N. V. (2021). Changing strategies for financing higher education in India. *Aarthika Charche, 6*(1).
Vitae. (2020). *What do researchers do?* https://tinyurl.com/mr45b7kb
Woldegiyorgis, A. A. (2021). Transnational diaspora engagements in higher education: A case of Ethiopian-born academics in the US. *International Journal of African Higher Education, 8*(2), 43–64.
World Bank. (2002). *Constructing knowledge societies: New challenges for tertiary education.* World Bank.
World Bank (2009). *Accelerating catch-up: Tertiary education for growth in sub-saharan Africa.* World Bank.
World Bank. (2010). *Financing higher education in Africa.* World Bank.
World Bank. (2012). *Strengthening tertiary education in Africa through Africa centers of excellence.* World Bank.
World Bank. (2014). *A decade of development in Sub-Saharan African science, technology, engineering and mathematics research* (Working Paper No 91016). https://tinyurl.com/4ynm8tbm
World Bank. (2022). *World Development Indicators.* https://tinyurl.com/3u5ymvxh (Accessed June 28, 2022).
World Bank and UNESCO. (2000). *Higher education in developing countries: Peril and promise (English).* World Bank Group.

# Index







D. Teferra (ed.), *Research and Innovation in African Higher Education*, https://doi.org/10.1007/978-3-031-92909-0

**D**

Kolibri 360 GmbH
Ferdinand-Jühlke-Straße 7
99095 Erfurt, Deutschland
produktsicherheit@kolibri360.de